The

United States
Pony Club
Manual of
Horsemanship

······················

Also by Susan E. Harris

Horsemanship in Pictures

Grooming to Win, Second Edition

Horse Gaits, Balance and Movement

The United States Pony Club Manual of Horsemanship:
Basics for Beginners/D Level

The United States Pony Club Manual of Horsemanship:
Intermediate Horsemanship/C Level

The
United States Pony Club Manual of Horsemanship

· ·

Advanced Horsemanship
B/HA/A Levels

written and illustrated by

Susan E. Harris

Ruth Ring Harvie, USPC Editor

HOWELL
BOOK
HOUSE

Howell Book House
A Simon & Schuster Macmillan Company
1633 Broadway
New York, NY 10019

MACMILLAN is a registered trademark of Macmillan, Inc.

Library of Congress Cataloging-in-Publication Data

Harris, Susan E.
    The United States Pony Club manual of horsemanship: advanced horsemanship, B/HA/A levels / written and illustrated by Susan E. Harris; Ruth Ring Harvie, USPC editor.
        p.   cm.
    Includes index.
    ISBN 0-87605-981-7
    1. Horsemanship.   2. Ponies.   3. United States Pony Clubs.
I. Harvie, Ruth Ring.   II. United States Pony Clubs.   III. Title.
SF309.H365   1996
798.2—dc20   96-7233
                                                           CIP

Manufactured in the United States of America
10 9 8 7 6 5 4 3 2 1
Book design by Kris Tobiassen

Contents

Foreword

For many years I have watched Pony Clubs provide grass-roots instruction and activities essential to the development and nurture of future participants in the international equestrian disciplines. Although some young people aspire to representing their country in competition, others choose a path of teaching, training, or simply a lifetime of dedication to a sport in which they take continuing pleasure.

These books speak to a variety of goals and interests. The subject matter is designed to accommodate young people's attraction to, fascination with, and affection for horses as it introduces them to ever-increasing depths of knowledge. The emphasis on responsible use and care of horses at all times and in all phases of horsemanship should instill in young people a sense of pride and accomplishment based on high yet attainable standards.

Author Susan E. Harris writes with charm and a style that speaks to different ages directly and honestly. Her background as a teacher, trainer, author, and clinician make this book attractive and useful to all those who teach children and horses. Her continued interest in and respect for the basics of good horsemanship worldwide should keep professionals, amateurs, and volunteers of both categories fresh, inspired, and informed. More important, her style promises to make these books the "best friends" of young people who love horses.

Donald W. Thackeray

A Note from the United States Pony Clubs, Inc.

The first requests from U.S. Pony Club members for a manual of their own were received when U.S. Clubs were founded in 1958. By 1979, it was determined that there was a need for a text that matched our standards, used terms specific to North America, and was written at a reading level comfortable for the majority of our members.

Author and illustrator Susan E. Harris, an experience and successful riding instructor, has received guidence from an advisory panel that represents years of teaching, coaching, and examining riding and horse management skills within the USPC and the Canadian Pony Clubs. We wish to express our thanks to consulting editors Laurie Chapman-Bosco, H. Benjamin Duke III, Dru Malavase, and Jessica Jahiel; vice presidents of instruction Melanie Heacock and Marilyn Yike; also Diane Hunter, Sally Graburn, Shelly Kinkaid, Cathy Frederickson, Maureen Pach, and national examiners of the United States and Canadian clubs. Ruth Ring Harvie has coordinated input from consultants and committees.

Although we do not claim to cover all special interest areas, we have carefully listened to and considered all suggestions. The late Colonel Donald W. Thackery, who wrote the forward, was a longtime friend, advisor, and committee member of the USPC. Despite his duties as United States representative to the Federation Equestre Internationale and his duties as an I-Level dressage judge, he took time to make in-depth suggestions that have been incorporated into this volume. For his tutelage, interest, and lifelong support, we are extremely grateful.

Plainly, this manual represents several years of research. We hope young riders everywhere will enjoy Susan Harris's exceptional work as much as we do.

About the U.S. Pony Clubs, Inc.

Pony Club started in Great Britain in 1928 with 700 original members. By 1992 there were more than 125,000 members in 27 countries, making it the largest junior equestrian group in the world. Each club is run by a volunteer District Commissioner and other elected officers. At this writing, the United States Pony Clubs have approximately 11,000 members in more than 500 clubs.

The three volumes of the USPC Manual of Horsemanship are written especially for Pony Club members and for the volunteers who lead and teach them, but they will also be helpful to anyone who wants to learn or teach good horsemanship. In these manuals, the emphasis is on how children learn, rather than on subject matter alone. Progress along a continuum of learning is stressed, instead of mere acquisition of facts.

The manuals provide an introduction to the curriculum of the U.S. Pony Clubs, and are written to help young people meet the current U.S. Pony Club Standards of Proficiency. However, the levels of proficiency required by the standards cannot be achieved by book work alone. Practical hands-on learning is essential, as is good mounted instruction at all levels. As in any course of study, effective teaching and learning require outside reading and supplemental material. Content from the U.S. Pony Club's most recently published standards and reading lists, and individual teachers' resources will be necessary to augment this textbook.

Pony Club supports the ideal of a thoroughly happy, comfortable horseperson, riding across a natural country, with complete confidence and perfect balance on a horse or pony equally happy and confident and free from pain or bewilderment.

U.S. PONY CLUBS MISSION STATEMENT

The United States Pony Clubs, Inc., an educational organization, teaches riding, mounted sports, and the care of horses and ponies, and develops in youth the characteristics of responsibility, sportsmanship, moral judgment, leadership, and self-confidence.

USPC's Guiding Beliefs

- USPC is an educational organization.
- The local club is the core of the USPC.
- USPC provides an opportunity for shared fun and cooperative work with others.
- Fair and friendly competitions develop teamwork and sportsmanship.
- USPC is beneficial for both horse and rider.
- USPC is committed to safety.
- USPC requires parental involvement and support.

For more information about the U.S. Pony Clubs, or if you would like to join a Pony Club or start a Pony Club in your area, please contact:

U.S. Pony Clubs, Inc.
The Kentucky Horse Park
4071 Iron Works Pike
Lexington, KY 40511
(606) 254-PONY (7669)

The following trademarks are owned by the United States Pony Clubs, Inc., and are protected by Registered Trademark®: USPC, United States Pony Clubs, and design (official seal).

Notes about the USPC B, HA, and A Levels

Everyone joins Pony Club as an unrated member and progresses through the lower level ratings (D-1 through C-2) at their own pace. These are tested by a local Pony Club Examiner. The C-3 rating is taken at a Regional Testing, and the B, HA, and A are national ratings, administered by the National Testing Committee. The requirements for each rating are called the Standards of Proficiency.

The D Rating is an introduction to riding, establishing a foundation of safety habits and knowledge of the daily care of pony and tack. The C Pony Club member is learning to become an active horseperson, to understand the reasons for what he or she is doing, and to care for a pony and equipment. The C-3 is a regional rating that reflects a basis of competence in horse care and riding that will enable a lifetime of pleasure in a variety of equestrian sports.

The B, HA, and A Levels are national ratings, requiring a much greater depth of knowledge and proficiency than the earlier ratings. Successful candidates are competent, all around horsepersons, active and participating members of USPC, who participate in a variety of Pony Club activities. They are also thoughtful leaders who set an example for all levels.

In addition to its instructional programs, the USPC offers a variety of activities at Club, Regional, Inter-Regional, and National Levels for team and individual participation. These activities include Combined Training, Dressage, Foxhunting, Know-Down, Mounted Games, Show Jumping, Tetrathlon, and Vaulting.

Note: Achieving a rating does not necessarily qualify a Pony Clubber for participation in any horse sport. To compete safely or qualify as a team member for a particular activity, further study, preparation, and specialized coaching may be necessary.

General requirements for the B, A, and HA ratings are discussed below. For specific requirements in each area of testing, please see the USPC Standards of Proficiency (in the Appendix).

The B Rating

The B Rating is a medium level of horsemanship, built on the fundamentals taught at the D (basic) and C (intermediate) levels, and leading to the A (advanced) Level. To qualify at B Level, you must be an active horseperson and Pony Club member who is interested in acquiring further knowledge and proficiency in all phases of riding, horsemanship, and horse care. You must also be able to contribute to the education of younger Pony Club members.

B-Level Horse Management and Knowledge

To achieve the B rating, you must be a competent and thoughtful horseperson, able to care for your own or another person's horse while maintaining its proper physical and mental condition. You must understand the reasons for what you do, based on the physiology and needs of the horse, and through discussion and demonstration, show a knowledge of horse management, veterinary care, longeing, and teaching principles. You must also be able to explain and demonstrate these skills to younger Pony Clubbers, and teach safe mounted and dismounted lessons, on the flat and over fences.

A B-Level horseperson is expected to demonstrate maturity and sound judgment in the care of horses and equipment, and understand the reasons for what he or she does. He or she must present him- or herself, horse, and equipment properly turned out, and must be able to care for another person's experienced horse, maintaining its condition. He or she must be able to discuss and demonstrate knowledge and practical experience in the following subjects:

- Horse care and management
- Feeding and nutrition
- Health care and veterinary knowledge
- Hoof care and shoeing
- Bandaging

- Conformation and lameness
- Travel safety
- Longeing
- Teaching principles (mounted and dismounted instruction)

B Level Riding

The goals of the B Level are:

- Correct, balanced, supple, and independent seat at all gaits, on the flat, over fences, and in the open.
- Effective, tactful use of aids, with knowledge and ability to explain reasons for their use.
- Understanding and application of basic principles of dressage, including movements and school figures appropriate to First Level.
- Ability to:
  - Ride horse forward, establishing and maintaining a regular pace, with horse balanced, supple, moving with rhythm and impulsion, and accepting the aids.
  - Jump gymnastics, stadium obstacles and courses, and cross-country obstacles and courses up to 3'7", with security, control, and correct and functional style.
  - Ride without stirrups at all gaits, over fences and gymnastics.
  - Handle disobediences competently and confidently.
  - Analyze obstacles, gymnastics, and courses, formulate a riding plan, and discuss performance of horse and rider.
  - Ride an experienced, unfamiliar horse on the flat, over fences, and in the open, demonstrating tactful and effective riding and ability to ride the horse at its level of training without confusing it or impairing its training. Ability to analyze and discuss performance of horse and rider, including reasons for any disobediences.
- Knowledge of pace and galloping position (240, 350, and 400 meters per minute), ability to ride in control when cantering and jumping in a group in the open.

The A and HA Ratings

The A, which is the highest Pony Club rating, is divided into two parts: the HA, which covers horse management, teaching, and training, and the A, which tests the riding phase. The HA has the knowledge, experience, and maturity to evaluate and care for a horse's needs efficiently and in a variety of circumstances, and to teach riding and horse care to others. The A is able to ride horses at various levels of schooling with judgment, tact, and effectiveness, to train young horses, and to retrain spoiled horses.

HA Requirements

HA candidates must demonstrate a sound knowledge of horses, their care, equipment, and training requirements. They must be able to teach stable management and conduct mounted lessons, showing an understanding of safety practices and using teaching techniques appropriate to different age levels. They must demonstrate the ability to make informed decisions about all aspects of running a barn, including daily routine and emergency procedures.

HA candidates are expected to show a knowledge of all the topics listed under B-Level horse management requirements, but in greater depth. In addition, they must demonstrate knowledge of the following subjects:

- Stable management and record keeping
- Stable construction and pasture management
- Equine anatomy, physiology, and diseases
- Special care, including restraint and common medications
- Presentation and evaluation of horse for sale
- Training and longeing techniques for various stages of training
- Teaching techniques for various ages and levels of students

The A Rating

The USPC A Rating is for accomplished, advanced horsemen and horsewomen who are qualified to ride, teach, and train according to sound, classically correct principles. (The HA rating, which includes horse knowledge, stable management, longeing, and teaching, must be completed before taking the A-Level riding test.)

A-Level Riding

The goals of A-Level riding (in addition to B-Level goals) are:

- A secure, balanced, independent, and classically correct seat on the flat, over fences, and in the open.

- Correct, independent, and effective use of aids, with tact, empathy, and good judgment, considering the level of the horse's training, his needs, and his nature. Understand proper use and effect of the natural and artificial aids.
- Ability to:
  - Ride different horses at various stages of training, including schooled, green, and spoiled horses, displaying a confident, consistent, and effective performance on each.
  - Assess each horse's level of schooling; ride with tact and empathy for its capabilities; and demonstrate schooling techniques appropriate for its stage of training. Recognize problems, and be able to formulate a long-term plan to improve the horse's training.
  - Perform exercises to improve each horse's relaxation, rhythm, free forward movement, impulsion, engagement, lightness, and contact, and ride the horse "on the bit" (to the horse's ability).
  - Ride school figures and movements appropriate to Second Level dressage, maintaining rhythm, impulsion, correct bend, carriage, and balance (to horse's ability).
  - Set up and ride effectively over cavaletti, gymnastics, and stadium fences, at heights and distances appropriate for horse (up to 3'9"). Know and be able to demonstrate the effectiveness of various cavaletti and gymnastic exercises, type and shape of fences, and distances as training aids.
  - Handle a difficult or refusing horse effectively, with tact and understanding.
  - Ride at the gallop up to 520 meters per minute, demonstrating effective galloping position, pace, and adaptation to varied terrain, over fences up to 3'7", including ditches, banks, drops, water, and combinations.

Before You Begin

ABOUT THIS BOOK

This book is written for Pony Club members, instructors, and others who want to develop their horsemanship and horse management skills and knowledge to advanced levels. It follows the standards and system of instruction of the U.S. Pony Clubs, Inc., and is based on the fundamentals taught in the USPC D and C Levels and covered in the previous *USPC Manuals of Horsemanship: Basics for Beginners/D Level* and *Intermediate Horsemanship/C Level*. The first part of this book covers the principles of dressage, riding, and training on the flat, over fences, and in the open, longeing, and teaching horsemanship. Part Two includes horse anatomy, physiology, conformation and movement, and Part Three covers horse management, including stable management, nutrition, diseases and health care, bandaging, travel safety, tack, and equipment.

To get the most out of this book, you need to know the material covered in the first two manuals. Certain topics covered there are not repeated here, and the riding skills taught at this level are based on a foundation of proficiency in the basic and intermediate skills and knowledge. Even if you are already an experienced horseperson, reviewing the first two manuals will help you check your basics and be consistent in the progression of your riding, training, knowledge, and teaching. To prepare for the USPC B, HA, or A ratings, you must also be familiar with the USPC Standards of Proficiency and must study additional sources. (See Appendix and the current USPC reading list.)

WHAT YOU WILL NEED

The USPC B and A Levels are advanced levels of horsemanship, based on the fundamentals taught at the D (basic) and C (intermediate) Levels. To work safely at this level, you must have:

- Completed all C-3 Level work satisfactorily; understand and be able to perform all skills in lower levels. (Even if you are not a Pony Clubber, you still must have mastered all skills through USPC C-3 Level to work safely at this level.)
- Safe and suitable attire and equipment, including ASTM/SEI certified helmet. (See the USPC D Manual, Chapters 12 and 13, or current *USPC Horse Management Handbook* for details.)
- A suitable horse: sound, mature and experienced; able to work on the bit in First Level dressage; capable of jumping gymnastics, stadium courses, and cross-country obstacles up to 3'7". You must ride different horses, not just your own.

   For A-Level work, you will need to ride horses trained to Second Level or above, capable of jumping 3'9" to 4', and school green horses and problem horses at various levels of training.
- A correct and secure seat with good balance and position; correct use of aids, knowledge of theory and reasons for their use.
- Experience and instruction in jumping with correct and secure position, balance, and good control over gymnastics, stadium obstacles, combinations, and courses up to 3'3".
- Experience and instruction in riding in the open with security and control, jumping a variety of cross-country obstacles up to 3'3", plus knowledge of pace and ability to ride at a controlled gallop over natural terrain.
- **(Most important!) An experienced instructor who is familiar with the work covered in this book, and able to teach to the standard required.**

Your instructor should review the USPC C-3 Standard with you, and evaluate your skill level, knowledge, strong points, and areas which need work. If any of the C-3 basics are weak, you need further instruction and practice to bring them up to standard before you can work safely at this level. Both you and your horse must be fit, confident, and capable of handling the work.

*This book is not intended as a substitute for professional advice
and guidance in the field of horseback riding. A person should take
part in the activities discussed in this book only under the supervision
of a knowledgeable adult.*

All USPC tests in this book are current as of 1995.

PART ONE

·······················

Riding, Training, and Teaching

CHAPTER 1

Dressage and Training Principles

In its simplest sense, dressage means "training."

Dressage is a basis for training horses of all types. When basic dressage training is completed, a horse should be not only a pleasure to ride but also prepared for specialized training in any discipline. In addition, dressage can be used to improve movement and to rehabilitate horses with poor muscle development, stiffness, or movement problems due to incorrect riding or training. Dressage is important in a rider's education, as it develops a supple, balanced seat, correct and subtle application of the aids, and understanding of movement and training.

Dressage can also be a competitive sport (to Olympic level) or an exhibition of equestrian art.

PRINCIPLES OF DRESSAGE

Dressage is based on classical principles and methods that have been proven over several centuries. These principles, in brief, are as follows:

- Dressage employs natural gaits and movements of the horse (instead of artificial "tricks"). One goal of dressage is to produce

Upper-level competition gives Pony Club members an opportunity to apply what they have learned and to polish their skills. *Photo: U.S. Pony Clubs, Inc.*

under saddle the most beautiful movements the horse is capable of when free.

- Dressage training is progressive; each stage is based on the foundation of previous work. Dressage emphasizes the development of qualities such as balance and suppleness, rather than performing movements.
- The purpose of dressage training is the gymnastic development of the horse: developing strength, suppleness, balance, and good movement, based on an understanding of horse anatomy, movement, and biomechanics. Good dressage makes a horse's gaits more beautiful and pleasant to ride, and makes him stronger, sounder, and prolongs his useful life.
- The goals of dressage are harmony, unity, and cooperation between horse and rider, without the use of force. The rider's aids should be so subtle as to be nearly invisible; the horse gives the impression of doing of his own accord what the rider asks.

• A balanced, supple, and independent seat, which permits correct and subtle application of the aids, is essential for dressage training at any level.

GAITS AND MOVEMENT

In order to ride and train well, you must know about the horse's body mechanism, and how he moves in each gait. Good movement is beautiful, easy to ride, and develops the horse's muscles and makes him stronger and more capable. Poor movement is ugly, hard to ride, and damaging to the horse. It is important to recognize the elements of good and poor movement, and to be able to help each horse move as well as he is able.

No horse moves under a rider exactly as he does when free. Horses must learn how to balance and carry themselves under a rider's weight. Strengthening the back muscles, developing engagement of the hind legs, and learning to move with relaxation, regularity, and freedom are most important.

The Circle of Muscles

The major muscle groups used in movement (locomotion) make up the "circle of muscles." When a horse moves well, his muscles and major muscle groups work in harmony, without overstressing or underusing any single muscle or muscle group. Poor movement (often related to tension, crookedness, poor balance, and the effects of bad riding) puts excessive stress and strain on some muscles, leading to uneven muscle development, stiffness, and often injury.

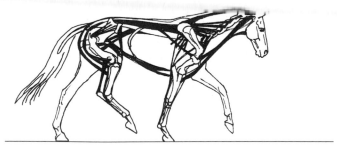

In good movement, the circle of muscles works in harmony

Engagement

"Engagement" is the degree to which the horse reaches forward under his body with his hind legs. Greater engagement means more thrust, power, and balance. Lazy, short, or restricted hind legs, or those that swing out behind more than they reach forward under the horse, show a lack of engagement.

Engagement is essential to balance. In turning and bending, the engagement of the inside hind leg is especially important for balance, security, and power.

There are two types of engagement:

Swinging Engagement   The hind legs swing forward with long strides and little flexion, resulting in "pushing power." This is expressed in long, low, forward-moving gaits.

Tucking Engagement   The hindquarters are tucked under the horse, flexing the lumbosacral joint, bending the joints of the hind legs and resulting in "carrying power." This is expressed in collected gaits, downward transitions, and rebalancing.

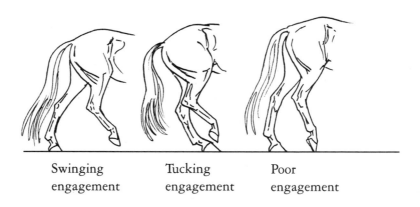

Swinging   Tucking   Poor
engagement   engagement   engagement

THE GAITS

Regular or "pure" gaits are those in which the horse moves with a correct pattern of footfalls, with clear, regular, and evenly spaced beats. Irregularities, unevenness, or unlevel steps may indicate a momentary error, a chronic problem, or unsoundness. If a horse moves with pure gaits when free and shows irregularity when ridden, the cause is usually tension created by incorrect riding.

Walk

- A four-beat gait without suspension.
- Pattern of footfalls: left hind, left fore, right hind, right fore.
- Regular and unconstrained, moving forward with good engagement, evenly spaced beats (1—2—3—4), without any tendency to pace (1-2, 3-4), hurry, or break into a jog.
- In training, good for developing relaxation, engagement, and stretching, and for introducing lateral work.
- Reflects the quality of the other gaits and of overall training. Improper training methods or collecting the walk too much or too early in training shows up in a short, restricted, or irregular walk. The walk is the easiest gait to ruin and the most difficult to fix once spoiled.

Types of Walk

Working Walk Regular, unconstrained walk used in early stages of training. The horse walks energetically but calmly, with even steps, maintaining light, steady contact.

Free Walk Relaxed walk in which the horse has complete freedom to stretch his head and neck down and out. He should overstep as in the medium walk, but with maximum reach, so his strides are longer and more ground-covering. It may be ridden on a "loose rein" (on the buckle), or "long rein" (allowing the horse freedom to lower and stretch out his head and neck while still maintaining contact).

Medium Walk Free, regular, unconstrained walk with moderate extension, on the bit, with light but steady contact. The hind feet touch down in front of the prints of the front feet (overstep).

Extended Walk The horse covers as much ground as possible without hurrying or losing the regularity of his steps. His hind feet overstep, touching the ground well in front of the prints of the front feet. The rider allows his head and neck to stretch out, without losing contact or balance.

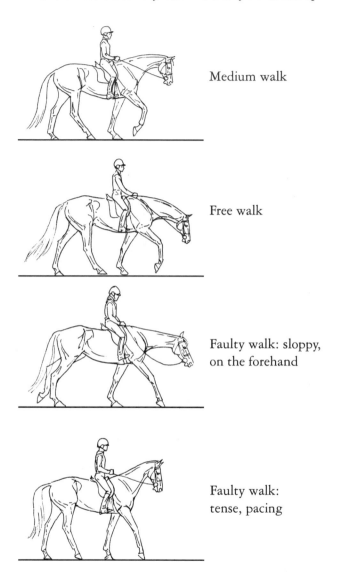

Medium walk

Free walk

Faulty walk: sloppy,
on the forehand

Faulty walk:
tense, pacing

Collected Walk   Active, balanced walk with shorter, higher, but regular steps. The horse should "march" forward, on the bit, with his neck arched and raised, maintaining a light, steady contact. His hind legs are engaged, with good balance and elastic hock action. Each step covers less ground than in other walks, because the joints of the hind legs bend more, making the steps shorter and higher; the hind feet touch down in or behind the prints of the front feet.

Faulty Walks   Lazy, dragging walk; short strides; failure to stretch out and down when allowed; breaking into a trot; and pacing, which is an expression of tension in the back. Most serious faults are usually caused by restricting the walk or practicing collected walk too much or too early in the horse's training.

Trot

- A two-beat gait in which the horse springs from one diagonal pair of legs to the other, with a moment of suspension in between.
- Regular, free, and elastic, with a steady rhythm, with hind legs well engaged and a round, swinging back.
- An excellent gait in which to develop the horse's rhythm, straightness, impulsion, roundness and suppleness.

Types of Trot

Collected Trot   Horse moves forward with shorter, lighter, and higher steps, remaining on the bit with neck raised and arched. His hindquarters are well engaged, with energetic impulsion; this lightens his forehand, makes him more mobile, and enables his shoulders to move with greater ease in any direction.

Working Trot   Pace between collected and medium trot, in which a horse not yet trained and ready for collected movements shows that he is properly balanced and goes forward with even, elastic steps, active hocks, and impulsion from the hindquarters, remaining on the bit.

Medium Trot   Pace between working and extended trot, but more round than extended trot. The horse goes forward with free, moderately extended steps and obvious impulsion from the hindquarters. The steps should be even, and the movement balanced and unconstrained. The horse remains on the bit; the rider allows him to carry his head and neck a little more in front of the vertical than in collected or working trots, and to lower his head and neck slightly.

Extended Trot   Horse covers as much ground as possible, lengthening his steps to the utmost as a result of great impulsion from the hindquarters, while maintaining the same rhythm. He remains on the bit as he lengthens his frame, but maintains balance without leaning

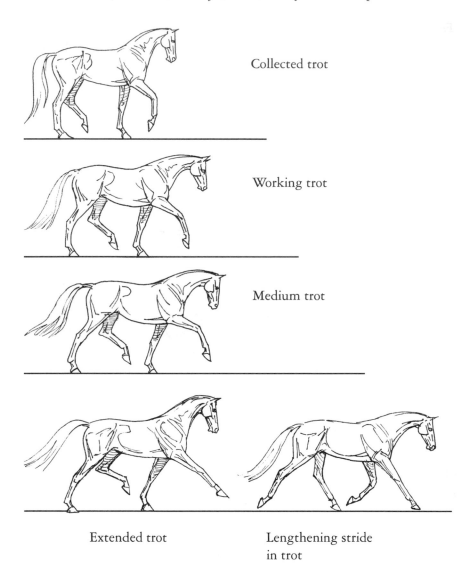

Collected trot

Working trot

Medium trot

Extended trot

Lengthening stride
in trot

on the bit. The forefeet should touch the ground at the spot toward which they are pointing.

Faulty Trots   Common faults in the trot include moving with a stiff or hollow back, irregular trot (diagonal pair separates, with front or hind foot striking the ground first), incorrect lengthening ("running"

FAULTY TROTS

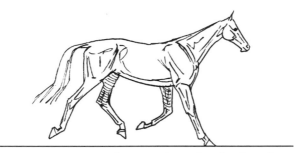

Irregular trot: front foot landing first

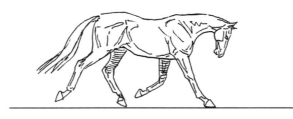

Incorrect trot: running on the forehand

or quickening the steps; leaning on the bit and "running into the ground"); short strides; uneven steps.

Canter

- A three-beat gait with a moment of suspension, in right or left lead.
- Pattern of footfalls: outside hind leg, diagonal pair (inside hind and outside foreleg together), inside foreleg, suspension.
- Light, regular, and cadenced; balanced, with hindquarters well engaged; supple; straight. It has activity (especially in hindquarters), roundness, and suspension or "jump."
- Should be executed on the correct lead.
- The canter can develop impulsion, balance, roundness, and free forward movement.

Good canter: round, with suspension

Poor canter: flat, hollow, four beat, insufficient suspension

Types of Canters

Collected Canter   Light, cadenced canter in which the horse moves forward with neck raised and arched, on the bit. Hindquarters are well engaged and active; the forehand is light, with shoulders free, supple, and mobile. Strides are shorter and higher than in other canters, but the horse is more active and mobile.

Working Canter   Pace between collected and medium canter, in which a horse not yet trained and ready for collected movements shows himself properly balanced and goes forward on the bit, with even, light, and cadenced strides, active hocks, and lively impulsion from the hindquarters.

Medium Canter   Pace between collected and extended canter. The horse goes forward with free, balanced, and moderately extended strides, and obvious impulsion from the hindquarters, on the bit. The rider allows him to carry his head a little more in front of vertical than in collected or working canter, and to lower his head and neck slightly. The strides should be long, even, and unconstrained.

Extended Canter   Horse covers as much ground as possible, lengthening his strides to the utmost as a result of great impulsion from the hindquarters, without losing calmness, balance, or lightness. He remains on the bit without leaning on it but is allowed to lower and extend his head and neck, with his nose pointing more forward.

Faulty Canters   Disunited canter (one lead in front and the other behind); wrong lead; irregular four-beat canter (diagonal pair separates, with foreleg or hind leg striking ground first); "flat," with loss of suspension or "jump"; crooked (especially hind leg carried to inside); lacking balance (leaning or "running" on the forehand); short; stiff.

MOVEMENT PROBLEMS

There are several syndromes (sets of symptoms) of faulty movement that result in inefficient gaits that are hard to ride and cause discomfort and even unsoundness. These may be caused by physical weakness, poor use of the body, conformation problems (see Chapter 8), and especially by incorrect riding and training, and overstressing immature horses. Good riding and training can do much to improve the horse's strength, muscle development, and athletic use of his body.

On the Forehand

Problems on the forehand occur when the horse moves with poor engagement, therefore carrying too much weight on the forehand. This overloads his front legs and makes him clumsy and unbalanced, and he may lean on the bit and pull. This problem is often seen in green and underdeveloped horses that have not yet learned to balance themselves under a rider, "overbuilt" horses (high in the hips and low in the forehand), weak, tired, or lazy horses, and poorly ridden horses. There are two common variations:

Slowness   The horse moves slowly, with a low head carriage; he acts sleepy, bored, and inattentive. He takes short, dragging steps with little energy, and may shuffle, stumble or have a four-beat canter. He is apt to break to a slower gait when asked to turn. This problem is common in tired or lazy horses, young horses not yet strong enough to carry themselves under a rider, and poorly ridden horses.

To Improve: Ride in balance without leaning forward; use leg aids and half-halts to call for attention and energy; engage the hind legs; and rebalance the horse. Pulling the head up with the reins will not work; it must be "sent" upward by engaging the hindquarters.

Running   The horse moves too fast, with too much weight on his forehand, causing him to "run" or quicken his strides in an effort to keep up with his balance. His gaits become irregular, and he rushes or scrambles on turns, especially at the canter. He may lean heavily on the bit or overflex, curling his head into his chest. This problem is typical of green, unbalanced, or poorly ridden horses, especially at faster paces. The speed and lack of balance disturb and distress the horse as much as the rider; he needs help!

To Improve: Slow the pace and re-establish calmness; working in a large circle may help. Use half-halts and transitions to help the horse rebalance himself. When the pace is slower and steadier, use tactful leg aids to encourage better engagement of the hind legs instead of quick, short strides.

Inverted (Hollow, Above the Bit)

The horse moves with a stiff, hollow back; a high head; and short, quick, and irregular steps, with poor engagement. He throws his head up and pokes his nose out, making correct contact impossible. His movement is stiff, irregular, and difficult to ride, and instead of walking he may jig or pace. His stiff, hollow back causes soreness in his back and hind legs, which adds to his tension and makes him more difficult to control. This is common in hot, nervous horses that are overexcited, but the problem can also be caused by pain or fear, an ill-fitting saddle, rider stiffness, poor seat and/or hands, or in young, undeveloped horses that are uncomfortable under the rider's weight.

To Improve: Calmness, comfort, and better rhythm must be restored so the horse can unlock his tense muscles, engage his hind legs, and use his circle of muscles better. This will bring his back up and allow him to reach forward to the bit. You must ride in balance and use tactful aids to slow and steady his tempo, then ask for longer strides; your

FAULTY MOVEMENT SYNDROMES

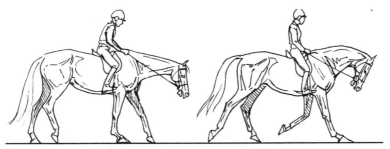

On the forehand; lazy   On the forehand; running

Inverted; hollow   False collection; hollow

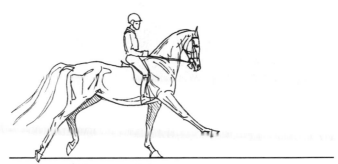

False extension

hands must be gentle and sympathetic, especially when the horse begins to take contact with the bit. Check the saddle fit and be sure that the bit is mild and comfortable. Cavaletti work (only if done calmly and in rhythm) can help the horse learn to engage his hind legs, round his back, and stretch his neck out and down.

False Collection (Hollow, Behind the Bit)

The horse moves with short, irregular strides and poor engagement. His back is tense and hollow, and he draws back from the bit, retracting his neck and evading contact. Like the inverted horse, he may pace instead of walking and is stiff, uncomfortable, and difficult to ride; his trot becomes irregular and his canter may have four beats. At faster gaits, he may overflex his neck and drop his chin against his chest, making control very difficult. This problem is often caused by misguided efforts to force a horse into collection by working from front to back or through the misuse of severe bits, draw reins, or pulling hands.

To Improve: This problem is similar to that of the inverted horse, in that the horse needs to relax, find his rhythm, and restore his engagement and use of his circle of muscles. However, it is harder to cure because he has learned an incorrect response: to retract his neck, overflex, and withdraw from the bit. The methods are the same: re-establish relaxation, ride in balance, slow the tempo, and encourage longer strides and better engagement of the hind legs to bring the back up and encourage the horse to reach out and take contact with the bit. It usually takes more skill, work, and patience to solve this problem than that of the inverted horse.

False Extension (Hollow, Stiff, and Irregular)

The horse moves with energetic but stiff, irregular steps. His back is hollow, and his hind legs swing farther out behind than they reach forward. In the trot, his front legs extend stiffly forward with toes pointing up (toe flipping or "goose-stepping"), and the diagonals begin to separate (cannon bones of the diagonal legs are not parallel). His canter is irregular, usually with four beats. His neck is stiffly retracted, and he does not use his circle of muscles in harmony. This type of movement is often seen when a horse is driven forcibly against a harshly restraining hand. Because it is done with energy and force, it is very damaging and causes soreness and damage to the back, stifles, and hocks.

To Improve: The horse must go back to a longer, more natural frame and regain rhythm, relaxation, engagement, and use of his circle of muscles. Cavaletti work may help if done calmly and in rhythm.

Rehabilitating a horse with this problem requires a very good and perceptive rider, who can recognize the warning signs of tension and incorrect movement, especially when asking for more advanced work.

Crookedness (One-Sidedness)

The horse moves slightly sideways, with his head, shoulder, or hip carried to one side. This restricts his freedom of movement, interferes with impulsion, and causes stiffness, especially in turning. He takes a stronger contact with the bit on one side (stiff side), and tends to avoid contact on the other (hollow side). He may tilt his head, instead of flexing correctly at the poll. This problem often occurs when a horse is weak in one hind leg; he protects the weaker leg by moving slightly sideways instead of engaging it strongly, and avoids carrying as much weight on it as he should in collected movements. This makes it more difficult for him to turn or bend in one direction, and he may have difficulty taking one lead at the canter.

All horses are asymmetrical, or one-sided, to some degree; one of the goals of training is to develop the horse more evenly. However, a horse that habitually moves crookedly should be checked by a veterinarian to see whether unsoundness may be a factor.

To Improve: The crooked horse needs to strengthen the muscles of his weaker side and become more supple on his stiff side. He must learn to engage both hind legs equally, and to be able to carry more weight on his weaker hind leg (especially in turns, cantering, and lateral work). He must also learn to carry his weight more equally on both shoulders, remaining upright and bending instead of leaning in a turn, and to take equal contact on both reins.

Correct turning, bending, and lateral work can improve a horse's straightness and lateral balance. Use half-halts to balance the horse before, during, and after each turn or corner, and use both inside and outside aids to help him track straight through the turn. Be careful to ride in good balance, without collapsing in the hip or rib cage, leaning, or sitting unevenly. Lateral work such as leg-yielding, shoulder-in, and haunches-in can help to strengthen and supple the horse and help his ability to use his hind legs more equally, but this work must be done correctly. Cavaletti on a curve (properly spaced and ridden) may help. It takes an experienced and perceptive trainer, assisted by an observer on the ground, to know whether an exercise is helping, and when it is time to quit.

Incorrect movement. Horse moves stiffly, with disengaged hind legs and a hollow back. Rider is out of balance, behind the motion, and driving the horse against stiff, pulling hands. *Photo: C. H. Hamilton III.*

QUALITIES DEVELOPED THROUGH DRESSAGE

The purpose of dressage is to develop the qualities necessary in a good riding horse, not performing tests or movements. These basic qualities are important for all horses, not just dressage horses! If they are neglected, or if they are not developed in the proper order, the horse is missing a basic block in his foundation, and his training will fall apart, especially when he is asked to do more advanced work in any specialty.

The basic qualities of dressage, in order, are:

1. Calmness, relaxation, and confidence.
2. Regular gaits with true rhythm and steady working tempo.
3. Free forward movement.
4. Contact and "connection" from hind legs to the bit.

5. "On the aids" (including "on the bit").
6. Straightness.
7. Improvement of balance and suppleness (lateral and longitudinal).
8. Impulsion (increased thrust from hindquarters through elastic, swinging back).
9. Collection, self-carriage, and lightness.

Obedience, submission, attention, confidence, and harmony between horse and rider develop and increase throughout the training process. These depend greatly on the tact, skill, and understanding of the trainer.

These qualities must be developed in the proper order, as each forms the foundation for the next. (For instance, straightness cannot be achieved until the horse is "on the aids," which in turn depends on the preceding qualities.) This is true in the training of young horses, the retraining of spoiled horses, and even in the warmup of a trained horse.

Definitions of Basic Qualities Developed through Dressage

Calmness and Relaxation   Mental calmness and athletic or working relaxation (absence of excess mental or physical tension). Relaxation does not mean laziness or inattentiveness.

Signs of relaxation include:

- Soft expression of eye and face; ears not stiffly fixed.
- Deep breath (like a sigh) and/or "blowing the nose" (a long, gentle snort); usually observed during warmup.
- Mouth closed, with lips relaxed; tongue in place under the bit; horse chews the bit softly.
- Relaxation of poll, throat, and jaw results in opening of salivary glands, creating a wet, relaxed mouth and a small amount of foam.
- Tail swings softly in rhythm with the gait, indicating a relaxed, swinging back.
- Muscles contract and relax freely and easily in the rhythm of the gait.
- Horse is willing to stretch his head and neck forward and downward, moving with a round topline and an elastic, swinging back.

Rhythm, Tempo, and Regularity of Gaits

Rhythm   The pattern of footfalls or beats of a gait. Rhythm must be correct, clear, and steady, without shuffling or faulty gait patterns.

Tempo   The rate of repetition of the rhythm (quick or slow). It is not the same as speed (miles per hour) or rhythm (pattern of footfalls). Every horse has his own best working tempo in each gait, in which he can move most efficiently. Tempo should remain the same within a gait, even when lengthening or shortening stride.

Regularity   Refers to the rhythm, evenness, levelness, and purity (correctness) of the gait. Irregular gaits are faulty gaits.

Free Forward Movement

Forward Movement   Moving forward with powerful strides from the hindquarters. (Not to be confused with speed or quickening the tempo!)

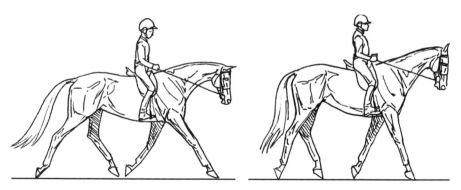

Free forward movement   Stiff, constrained movement

Freedom of Movement   The horse's muscles are free and supple, his legs swing freely from the hips and shoulders, and he moves with a swinging back and relaxed neck.

Contact, Connection, Accepting the Bit

Accepting the Bit   The horse accepts the bit and the rider's rein aids calmly with a closed, relaxed mouth, neither pulling nor seeking to evade the bit.

"Making the Connection"   The horse, in response to the rider's leg aids, reaches forward from the hind legs, through his back, and extends his head and neck, creating contact with the bit.

Contact   The horse reaches out and takes a steady contact with the rider's hands, with reins lightly stretched, accepting the bit. He will stretch forward and down, seeking to maintain contact with the bit, when the rider lengthens the reins. Contact comes from the forward movement of the hind legs, stretching through the back and neck, not from pulling the hands backward.

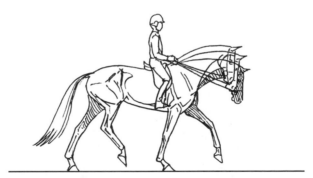

Contact: Stretching down into the bit

"On the Aids"

"On the Aids"   The horse accepts and responds to the rider's leg, seat, and rein aids, causing him to engage his hind legs, round his back, slightly arch his neck, and relax his poll, jaw, and mouth. This increases his attention and responsiveness to his rider. Being "on the aids" includes being "on the legs" and "on the seat" along with being "on the bit."

Straightness and Bending

Straightness   Straightness refers to a horse's alignment in motion. A horse is said to be straight when he delivers equal thrust from both hind legs, taking an equal contact on both reins, and his movement is as symmetrical as possible.

- A straight horse moves forward "on one track"—his hind legs follow directly behind his front legs. He moves straight on straight lines, and bends so that his hind legs "track" behind his front legs through curves and circles. As far as possible, he is equally balanced, supple, and powerful on both sides and when moving or bending in either direction.
- Straight movement is more efficient and allows the thrust from each hind leg to go forward through the body, instead of being dissipated by deviating to one side. It results in better lateral balance, greater suppleness, and pure gaits with greater impulsion.
- One of the goals of training is to develop the horse as evenly as possible on both sides, and to make him straight.

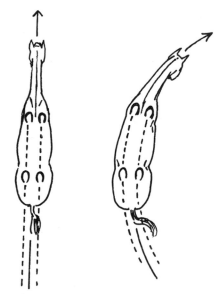

Straightness: The hind feet follow (track) the front feet, on straight and curved lines

Bending

- When moving on a curved track, the horse's inside hind leg must engage and bend its joints more, and his outside hind leg must swing farther. The muscles on the outside stretch farther, while those on the inside of the bend soften.
- When bending correctly, the horse's hind legs follow in the tracks of his forelegs, he looks in the direction of the bend, and appears to bend evenly from his poll to his tail. He engages his hind legs (especially the inside hind leg), which rounds his back, and keeps his weight in the center, "standing up" instead of leaning through the turn, which improves his balance.

Crookedness

Factors which contribute to crookedness include the following:

- Horses (like people) are naturally asymmetrical; most horses are asymmetrical to the right (the right hind leg is stronger and tends to be carried forward, throwing the weight onto the left shoulder; the horse tends to resist the left rein, and to avoid contact on the right rein). This tendency may be present from birth, but is certainly aggravated by handling a horse mainly from one side and by longeing or riding more in his preferred direction.
- The rider's asymmetry (unconsciously giving stronger aids with one seat bone, leg, and rein, or sitting crookedly).
- Weakness or unsoundness, especially in one hind leg.
- The horse is wider at his hips than at his shoulders, like a long triangle. When ridden in a ring, he tends to move with his outside hip and shoulder parallel to the rail, which makes him move crookedly, with his inside hind leg tracking to the inside of his inside foreleg.

Improving Straightness

Exercises to improve straightness and lateral balance include:

- Working in both directions, changing the rein frequently, posting on both diagonals, and changing diagonals every few strides, to develop both sides of the horse and both hind legs more equally.
- Bending, first on large, easy curves and circles; later on smaller, more difficult ones.

- Riding "in position" (see page 60).
- For more advanced horses: shoulder-fore, shoulder-in, and counter-canter.

Balance

There are two types of balance: lateral (sideways) balance and longitudinal (back to front) balance. A rider should be in balance with his horse at all gaits, making it easier for the horse to carry him.

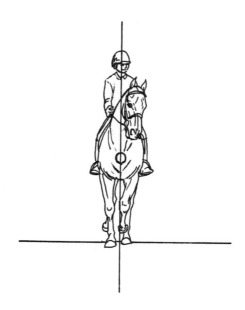

Lateral balance

Lateral Balance   The horse keeps his balance in the center and "stands up" through turns and circles, instead of leaning or falling in or out; he can maintain his balance during lateral movements.

Longitudinal Balance   The horse can shift his balance backward or forward as required. Keeping his balance slightly back lightens his forehand and makes him more maneuverable.

Longitudinal balance

Self-Carriage The horse "carries himself" in a state of balance without needing prompting from the rider.

Suppleness

Suppleness is the horse's ability to shift his balance smoothly forward and back as well as laterally, especially in transitions. A supple horse is pliable and bends easily, but suppleness must *not* be confused with flexibility (especially flexibility of the neck). A supple horse is said to be "through": he allows the aids (especially rein aids and half halts) to go through his body and influence the hind legs without being blocked by tension or resistance.

Impulsion

Impulsion is thrust from the hindquarters, which sends the horse forward and gives life and energy to the gaits, passing through his elastic, swinging back. Impulsion comes from the desire to go forward, but cannot be expressed as true impulsion until straightness and balance are developed. It must *not* be confused with speed, quickening the tempo, nervousness, or wild, uncontrolled energy.

Collection and Lightness

Collection   This is a state in which the horse is gathered together. As he engages his hindquarters, his hind legs bend more in every joint and carry more weight. His balance shifts to the rear, and his back and neck rise, making his forehand lighter. His steps become shorter, more elevated, and elastic, and he moves with lightness and energy.

COLLECTION

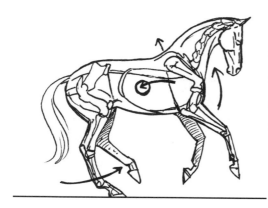

- Hindquarters engaged
- Balance shifts to rear
- Forehand light
- Steps shortened and higher

Collection can only be achieved by a horse that has developed all the other qualities that come before. Trying to force collection before a horse is ready for it creates discomfort, resistance, and poor movement, and can ruin a horse's training.

Lightness   When a horse moves with impulsion, suppleness, and the right degree of self-carriage, he is light: athletic, and able to move in any gait or direction at the slightest indication. Lightness is highly dependent on good riding and on harmony between horse and rider.

Obedience, Submission, Harmony, and "Throughness"

The goal of dressage is willing cooperation, not domination of the horse by force. The process starts with attention, confidence, and simple obedience, and is further developed and refined throughout the training process. The end result should be a horse and rider who work together in harmony; the horse appears to perform of his own free will what the rider asks of him, and expresses his beauty and spirit in his movements.

Obedience   An obedient horse is attentive to his rider, and complies promptly with his rider's requests (to the best of his ability) without evasion or disobedience. In order for the horse to understand and obey, the rider must give clear, correct, and properly timed aids.

Submission   Submission means "yielding." The horse yields to the rider's aids willingly, without resistance, evasion, or physical stiffness. Submission is expressed especially in relaxation of the jaw and flexion of the poll, in response to the rider's correct aids. (Submission is not a "head set" or fixed position of the head and neck!)

"Throughness"   The horse allows the effect of the aids (especially rein aids and half halts) to go through his body and influence his hind legs, without being blocked by stiffness or resistance. A horse can only be "through" when he is balanced, supple, and in harmony with his rider.

Frame (Outline)

A horse's *frame or outline* depends on his level of training and what he is doing at the moment. The frame is determined by the horse's ability to engage his hind legs and round his back, and by the resulting carriage of his head and neck. It is *not* achieved by pulling the horse's nose in, or forcing him to adopt a vertical head carriage!

A green horse should work in a natural, fairly long frame, which is appropriate for long strides, free forward movement, and establishing basic balance. As the horse becomes stronger and better balanced, he is able to engage his hind legs under his body, raise his back, and shift his balance to the rear; his head and neck carriage become higher, and his base of support and his frame become shorter. Because working in a short frame requires balance, suppleness, and strength, only a strong, supple, advanced horse can work in a short frame for a sustained period.

Even in a short frame, the horse should be round, free, and active, and willing to lengthen his frame and stretch "down and round" whenever the rider asks.

FRAMES AT VARIOUS STAGES OF TRAINING

Green horse (Pre-training through Training Level)

First Level frame

Second Level frame

Advanced frame
(F.E.I. dressage levels)

Forcing a horse into a frame with restricting hands or control devices causes tension, stiffness, and discomfort. This can ruin a horse's gaits, movement, and training, as well as creating resistance, and it can result in physical damage.

THE TRAINING PROCESS

The basic training of a horse normally takes about two years, from starting the young horse under saddle through developing and confirming the basic qualities of a good riding horse. A horse should receive a thorough, systematic basic training, adapted to his particular needs and abilities, and should be gradually trained to strengthen and supple his body and develop his ability to move well. He will need time and practice under an experienced rider to confirm his training and to avoid confusing him and developing bad habits. A young horse, no matter how gentle, should *not* be ridden by inexperienced riders until his training is confirmed.

At the end of his basic training, the horse should be well developed physically and should move with good balance and comfortable gaits. He will be well educated to the rider's aids and control, capable of First- to Second-Level dressage work, experienced at hacking quietly across country, and capable of jumping simple gymnastics, small courses, and a variety of natural fences. He should be well mannered and a pleasure to ride, and is ready to go on into specialized training for advanced work in dressage, jumping, or eventing.

Stages of Training

Basic training is broken down into progressive stages. There is no absolute timetable for completing these stages; instead, it depends on the maturity of the horse, the skill and experience of the trainer, and circumstances like the horse's health, soundness, and mental attitude. Training must progress gradually at a pace appropriate for the individual horse, starting with a foundation of correct work and moving on only when the horse is fluent, confident, and physically ready for the next step. Rushing the early training or skipping ahead to advanced movements without proper preparation will handicap the most talented horse, and can result in a horse with mental, physical, and/or performance problems.

While even very young horses can benefit from daily handling and ground training to develop confidence, obedience, and manners, *they are not physically or mentally mature enough to be ridden regularly before the age of three;* even later for slow developers. Training horses too young and too hard jeopardizes their future soundness and careers.

Basic training (on the flat) is broken down into progressive stages:

Manners and Basic Ground Handling   The young horse is taught to lead, tie, to have good manners during grooming, foot care and other handling, and to load in a trailer. The object is to develop confidence, obedience, and manners. This type of handling is best carried on from a very early age.

Ground Training   Includes work in hand, parallel leading, longeing, ground driving (long lining), and sometimes driving (to cart). The object is to establish obedience to voice commands and whip and rein signals; to introduce the bit, bridle, surcingle, saddle and other equipment; and to develop confidence, obedience, and free forward movement.

Starting Under Saddle (Backing)   The young horse learns to accept a rider on his back, at a walk and later a trot, making simple transitions, and turning. The object is to establish confidence, calmness, obedience, and basic control, and to familiarize the horse with carrying a rider. Sometimes this is carried out on a longe line; some trainers use a quiet, experienced horse to accompany the colt and give him confidence.

Basic Training Under Saddle   Introduces the young horse to being ridden at walk, trot, and canter, with simple aids and basic control. Object is to establish calmness, relaxation, and teach the horse to carry the rider's weight while moving comfortably and calmly in a long frame, to establish free forward movement, and to have the horse accept the rider's weight and simple aids. Exercises include: working walk, trot and canter, simple turns, and large circles.

Pre-Training/Training Level   Object is to establish relaxation, confidence, and free forward movement with a clear and steady rhythm in working gaits, accepting the bit. The horse is taught to reach forward in response to the rider's aids and begins to work on contact. Exercises include: working walk, trot, canter; free walk; 20 and 15 meter circles. Basic bending and changes of rein. Halts through the walk; canter from trot. Work on contact, accepting the bit; introduce stretching the top line.

First Level   Object is to improve contact and connection, developing ability to go "on the aids" and "on the bit." Develop the "pushing power" of the hindquarters; improve balance (lateral and longitudinal) and develop straightness and increased bending. Exercises: working gaits; 10 meter circles and half circles; halt-trot and trot-halt transitions; lengthening stride in trot and canter; leg yielding; shoulder-fore; change of leads through the trot; shallow loop at canter, maintaining same lead.

Second Level   Object is to improve previous work, especially straightness and bending, to develop suppleness, balance, and a degree of self-carriage, and to develop impulsion and the beginnings of collection. The horse becomes through: hc allows the aids (especially rein aids and half-halts) to go through his body to influence the hind legs, without being blocked by tension or resistance. Work includes: working and medium gaits; collected and extended trot and canter (no collected walk); canter-walk and walk-canter transitions; simple change of leads (through the walk); counter canter; 10 and 8 meter circles (voltes). Shoulder-in, haunches-in, turns on the haunches, rein-back; demonstrate ability to remain in self-carriage while rider "gives the reins" briefly.

WORK IN THE OPEN

Work in the open should be included in the basic training, as soon as the horse is calm and obedient to simple aids. The young horse should be ridden out in company with a quiet, older horse, who will give the youngster confidence and set a good example. For nervous horses or those that are overwhelmed by new sights and sounds, begin with short, quiet walks, accompanied by a "baby-sitter" (an older, quiet horse) while cooling out at the end of training sessions, or even leading the horse out to "see the sights" on foot. For safety's sake, ride in a safe area (preferably an enclosed field), and never alone.

As the horse becomes accustomed to riding outside and his training progresses, his training should be carried on outside as well as in the ring. Riding over natural, rolling terrain in all gaits will improve his balance and fitness, and teach him to handle footing, terrain, and simple natural obstacles. The more time he spends moving freely forward in natural conditions, the better for his later training, especially if he is to become a hunter, jumper, or event horse, or simply an all-around pleasure horse.

RESCHOOLING

Reschooling a horse that has been badly trained often takes longer and can be more difficult than training an unspoiled young horse. A poorly schooled horse's muscles are not developed so that he can move easily and correctly under the rider. He is very likely in discomfort when he is ridden, and may have developed defenses to protect himself from pain. In addition, he has learned incorrect responses to the aids, and he may be confused, frustrated, and resistant. Reschooling should start with the basics (in ground training and longeing first) to re-establish relaxation, free, regular movement, and the essential foundation qualities. It will take patient work, choosing the right exercises, to develop his physical ability to work correctly, and mental attributes such as relaxation, confidence, obedience, and willingness. You will make more progress if you reward the slightest effort in the right direction promptly and generously, rather than punishing his mistakes.

STARTING THE YOUNG HORSE OVER FENCES

Jumping should not be considered until a horse is at least four years old; later if he is a slow developer. At three years, a young horse has nearly reached his mature height and weight, but his muscles, tendons, and joints are immature, and his skeletal system will not be fully mature until age six. Jumping puts extra stress and concussion on developing bones; too strenuous jumping at too early an age can lead to early unsoundness and cut short a promising career. Don't let yourself be tempted to jeopardize your horse's future, even though this practice is far too common!

On the other hand, it is not necessary or even advisable to wait until the dressage work is perfect before starting basic jumping training. Easy work over ground poles can be incorporated into your flat work as soon as the horse is calm, obedient, and reasonably well balanced. When done correctly, this can improve his engagement, rhythm, and balance, and help him strengthen his back and hindquarters.

As your horse develops a greater degree of balance and fitness, you can introduce trotting over cavaletti, low cross-rails, and small logs on the trail. The object is to teach him to go calmly, straight, and freely forward in rhythm over low and easy obstacles, and develop his confidence, obedience, and a matter-of-fact attitude about jumping.

PROGRESSIVE GYMNASTIC FOR GREEN HORSE

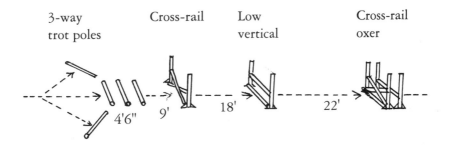

The next step is simple gymnastics: ground poles and cross-rails at easy distances, gradually progressing to simple one and two-stride gymnastics, low bounces, and progressive gymnastics. The purpose is to teach the horse to jump with good style and to take off at the right point. As the horse becomes more confident and consistent, the fences can be gradually raised to about 2 feet to 2 feet 6 inches.

Young horses must not be overjumped—this can lead to injuries and concussion-related ailments such as splints, and can sour a horse on jumping. As you begin to use gymnastic exercises with multiple jumping efforts, limit your jumping work to three times a week. If a green horse begins to act sullen, tired, or uninterested, or if jumping causes tension or has a negative effect on his flat work, stop jumping for a while and give him more time off.

At this stage, the horse should trot to most fences, including the first fence in a gymnastic line. He will soon learn to canter away from fences, and to take canter strides in gymnastics where it is easy to do so. If you canter him to fences before he has learned to balance himself and to adjust his strides, he is more likely to arrive at a bad takeoff distance and have a bad jump, a scare, or a refusal. Don't be tempted to override him to "put him right" at his fences; if you do this, you will make him dependent on you (when he should be learning to judge fences for himself), and you can spoil the qualities you are working to develop in his flat work.

When you do begin to canter fences, use a placing pole at first to help him find the correct takeoff distance. If he has trouble maintaining a balanced, steady canter to a fence, go back to flat work and gymnastic jumping. If he begins to get "strong," halt on a straight line after the fence, and spend more time trotting into fences.

As the horse's jumping style becomes more consistent, he should be introduced to a variety of very low fences of all types. Try to jump each fence the first time without a refusal—circle in front of the fence until he is reliably in front of your leg and feels willing to go forward over it, or have him follow an experienced horse over (at a safe distance). This develops his obedience and confidence. At first, jump only fences that can be lowered if his confidence is not up to the task. Later, as he becomes more reliable, you can jump small solid fences and simple natural fences while hacking out.

You can gradually incorporate different types of fences into your gymnastic work, and proceed to easy jumping lines. When your horse can maintain a steady pace and good balance through turns, you can begin to put two or more lines together, culminating in a simple course.

A good exercise at this stage (especially for horses that tend to get excited) is to warm up and do your flat work (in a light seat) between and around jumps and cavaletti. When your horse is going well (straight, balanced, and rhythmic, and listening to your aids), quietly trot or canter a fence, then go on with your flat work. This helps to relate your flat work to jumping, and keeps jumping from becoming too exciting.

By the end of the first year of training, most horses should be calm and confident when jumping a variety of low obstacles in and out of the ring, gymnastics, and a simple course. The actual training time depends on the individual horse, his maturity, and how he reacts to training. Remember, at this stage, attitude, confidence, and a good foundation are much more important than jumping height!

CHAPTER 2

Riding on the Flat

To ride safely and well, you must be fit, strong, and supple. You also must be aware of how your body works and what you are doing when you ride. Your mental attitude affects your riding, motivation, progress, and your relationship with your horse.

PHYSICAL AND MENTAL PREPARATION
FOR ADVANCED RIDING

Fitness and Health

Advanced riding is physically demanding. You must be strong enough to maintain position in motion, and your muscles and joints must be supple to absorb shock and follow the horse's movements. You must be able to ride actively for longer periods without tiring, and your muscles must be fit and accustomed to doing their job. Being fit also decreases your chances of injury. Fitness does *not* mean riding by force, or "muscling" your horse into obedience. No rider, however strong or fit, can succeed by pitting his strength against the horse!

Many riders are not fit enough for the demands of riding well, especially for cross-country riding. Riding and stable work may keep you fit enough for ordinary riding, but you may need additional fitness work for strength, endurance, weight control, or specific skills, especially if you spend much of each day sitting down.

Some fitness tips for riders:

- Maintain a healthy and balanced diet; avoid skipping meals and fad diets.
- To maintain fitness, you must exercise regularly—at least twenty minutes, three times a week; more often to improve fitness.
- Warm up your muscles and stretch before you ride or exercise.
- Walking, jogging, running, cross-country skiing, cycling, and swimming are good aerobic exercises to improve fitness.
- Flexibility and balance are as important as fitness and strength. Your coach or a fitness expert may suggest exercises for specific areas that need improvement.
- Being seriously overweight makes it more difficult to get fit and puts you at greater risk for injuries and health problems. However, size and weight are less important than fitness. Large people can ride well if they are fit and balanced.
- If you need to improve your fitness and/or lose weight, consult your doctor before starting any program or diet. A fitness program must be gradual, safe, and tailored to your needs.

Body Awareness

Most of the time, people are unaware of how their bodies are working. We all have unconscious habit patterns of how we use our bodies that feel right and normal to us, even if they hinder good riding. No one's kinesthetic sense (sense of what the body is doing) is perfect, so you may not realize when you are riding in a familiar but incorrect habit pattern, such as tilting forward or rounding your back.

In addition, no one is perfectly symmetrical; we all have a stronger side (and arm and leg). This can cause you to ride unevenly, or to use your aids more strongly on one side.

Even if you are not aware of how you use your body, your horse is. If you are stiff, crooked, or slightly out of balance, it interferes with his ability to move and carry you well. Many horses are blamed for clumsiness, unwillingness, or a bad attitude when they are really reacting to the rider's problems. When a rider becomes aware of his body and improves, his horse often improves dramatically.

Body awareness helps you to feel what you are doing, and release excess muscle tension that keeps you stuck in incorrect habit patterns. This makes it easier to feel your horse's movement and reactions, and to ride with sensitivity, tact, and "feel."

Some ways to improve your body awareness:

- Breathe deeply and naturally. Shallow breathing and holding your breath cause tension and block your ability to feel.
- When muscles are strongly contracted, they are unable to feel subtle changes. If you ride with force, grip, or unnecessary tension, you cannot feel what your body is doing, or your horse's reactions.
- Let your joints be free to absorb the horse's motion. Stiffening your joints or holding yourself tightly in a "perfect" position inhibits correct movement in your horse, and blocks your ability to feel and follow his motion.
- Check your position in a mirror. Is one shoulder lower than the other, one hip collapsed, or one hip or shoulder farther forward than the other? To release the tight muscles that cause crookedness, try riding for a few minutes with the arm on the "shorter" side extended up over your head.

CROOKED RIDER

- Head tilts
- Shoulder low
- One arm and hand stronger
- Collapsed hip
- Uneven weight on seat bones
- Elbow, knee, and toe stick out
- Stirrup shorter

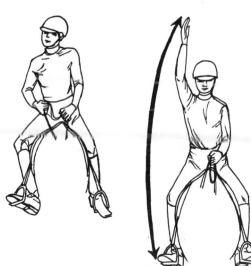

Correcting crookedness: Extend arm upward (palm in) to help lengthen muscles on short side

- Certain teaching methods, such as Sally Swift's Centered Riding®, can improve body awareness, freedom, and balance.

Mental Attitude

Your mental state affects your body, and the way you feel to your horse. Tension, fear, and anger create tension in your muscles; confusion or indecision cause jerky, random movements and aids. When you are calm, confident, and clearly focused, this is reflected in your muscles and movements. Excitement can be good (when it gives you energy and enthusiasm), or can work against you (if it makes you too tense or disorganized). Your horse may not be able to read your mind, but he feels and reacts to your unconscious physical responses to emotions and mood.

Mental preparation can greatly improve your riding and your ability to get the most out of instruction and competition. It helps you avoid confusion and ride as you plan to do, and even helps to coordinate your muscle movements.

Important aspects of mental preparation include the following.

- Focus: when you ride, clear your mind of other things (past and future), so you can concentrate on what you are doing *now,* in the present.
- Mental rehearsal (as if watching a mental videotape of how a perfect ride would look and feel) prepares your body and mind to repeat the movements as you visualized them. (On the other hand, concentrating on an error makes you more likely to commit it!)
- Before any movement, make a clear decision about what you and your horse are going to do. Riding positively with clear intent avoids confusion and indecision, which sap your confidence and that of your horse.
- Think in positive, not negative, terms. Your body cannot process negative commands well (such as "Don't look down"). Instead, remind yourself of what you *should* do (such as "Look up and ahead").

Progress in riding takes goals, organized effort, and self-discipline. Your attitude can influence your moods and motivation, which in turn affect how well you ride and achieve your goals.

Here are some ways to help your mental attitude work for you instead of against you:

- Set long-range goals, but break them down into smaller, manageable steps or subgoals. Achieving these smaller goals brings you closer to your larger goal and keeps you motivated.
- Mistakes are an essential part of the learning (and training) process. When you (or your horse) make a mistake, consider what you can learn from it, instead of blaming yourself or your horse.
- When you are tense, angry, or under stress, try taking several slow breaths as you count to ten or repeat a phrase like "It's okay, I can handle this." If this doesn't help, dismount and settle down before you continue to ride. You cannot ride well or safely while you are emotionally upset.
- Take time to notice what you and your horse do well, and enjoy the process of riding and working toward your goals. Constant self-criticism and focusing only on faults can make you tense and hard on your horse as well as on yourself, and it may prevent you from recognizing improvement.

THE RIDER: WORKING ON THE FLAT

Seat and Position

At this level, you must be able to ride with a secure, supple, and independent seat, in balance, with good position at all gaits. Your seat must follow the motion of the horse smoothly, without stiffness, tension, or loss of balance, which interfere with the horse's movement and your ability to apply the aids.

A rider is in balance with his horse when their balance or centers of gravity are united; they work together as one. Riding in balance requires a correct and balanced position, and a supple seat that adapts easily to the horse's changing balance.

Position Check

Correct position is important because its purpose is functional, not to look perfect. A good position is flexible and able to adapt to the needs of the horse or the situation, never artificial or posed. Good position and balance become even more important in more advanced work. Position and balance faults prevent you from smoothly following the free, swinging movement of the horse, which inhibits his movement and irritates and confuses sensitive and well-trained horses.

Each point of position has a functional reason (see the following chart for details).

POSITION ON THE FLAT

Position point	*Reason*
Seat bones in center of saddle seat. (Saddle must be correctly sized and balanced.)	Places rider in balance relative to saddle and horse.
Pelvis balanced on seat bones; not tipped forward or backward.	For balance and alignment of legs and upper body, especially the spine.
Weight equally balanced on both seat bones. Back straight; head balanced. Hips and shoulders even. Stirrups even.	For balance and alignment of legs, seat, upper body, and head. Uneven seat, incorrectly aligned spine, or unbalanced head cause imbalance, stress, and crookedness, and uneven aids.
Vertical line from ear through shoulder, hip, and heel; legs and feet under center of balance.	Rider in balance over feet; correct balance frees joints, allowing rider to stay in balance with horse in motion.
Eyes looking ahead, neither too high nor looking down.	Eyes control direction and balance of head and affect balance of entire body.
Head balanced over center; not tipped forward, backward, or to the side; neck long and free.	Head weighs 11 to 13 pounds and affects balance of body. Tension in neck and/or jaw is transmitted to shoulders, back, and other parts of body.
Shoulders hang wide and free, without excess tension.	Tense or misplaced shoulders affect breathing, arm position, and hands.
Upper arms hang down under end of shoulders, along middle of rib cage, with elbows bent.	Shoulder and elbow joints act as "shock absorbers" for hands and rein contact. Misplaced or

Position point	Reason
	rigid upper arms and elbows cause stiff, rough hands.
Straight line from elbow through forearm, wrist, hand, and rein to the bit. Height of hands depends on carriage of horse's head.	Allows bit to work without pulling up or down on mouth; places hands in best position for good contact and rein aids.
Wrists straight, knuckles between vertical and 30 degrees inside vertical.	Bent wrists cause tension, pulling. Horizontal knuckles cause elbows out, contract upper chest, pulling hands.
Hands in soft, natural fist; fingers closed, thumbs on top.	All joints of wrist, hand, fingers can function with flexibility, sensitivity, and secure hold on rein.
Chest and rib cage lifted, free from tension, able to breathe deeply and naturally.	Tension, slumping, or contraction in chest and ribs inhibit breathing and interfere with posture and balance.
Back long, tall, and elastic, without slumping or excessive arch or tension.	Slumping or overarching back causes balance problems, stiffness, and can lead to back injury.
Legs (especially hip, knee, and ankle joints) supple and free of excess tension.	Important in absorbing shock, maintaining position, and following horse's movement smoothly.
Thighs slightly rotated inward at hip joint; inner thigh and knee flat against saddle, without gripping. Knees flexible.	Places flat inner thigh against saddle for security without excessive muscle tension, which pushes rider up out of the saddle. Tight, pinching knees cause a pivoting, unsteady lower leg.
Calf softly stretched, with inner calf in contact with horse's side. Legs "embrace" the horse with steady, gentle contact.	Stabilizes lower leg; leg aids can be applied with small muscle movements. Consistent, quiet leg contact is reassuring to the horse.

Position point	Reason
Ankles flexible, not broken inward or rolled out.	To absorb shock and stabilize lower leg and foot position. Position faults lock and stiffen the ankles.
Foot placed directly under center of balance, with stirrup leathers vertical.	For balance, stability, freedom of joints to absorb shock. Vertical stirrup leathers indicate leg placed correctly under seat.
Foot rests securely in stirrup, at balance point of the foot (on or close to ball of foot). Heels lower than toes, flexing ankle down and back. (Degree of flexion determined by stirrup length.)	Proper foot placement stabilizes foot and lower leg position; important for overall balance, and assists in applying leg aids. Ankles flex under rider's weight, with motion of horse. Excessive pressure on stirrup locks ankle, causes tension.
Foot angle determined by rider's conformation: neither excessive toe-out nor toe-in. Foot flat on stirrup, not rolled onto outside.	Excessive toe-in or toe-out, or rolling foot onto the outside edge, robs ankle of flexibility and interferes with foot and leg position and leg aids.

Riding without Stirrups at All Gaits

Riding without stirrups at all gaits is a test of your seat and a good exercise to develop and refine riding skills, which should be included in your daily riding. Work without stirrups must be done correctly to be safe and beneficial. (For details on work without stirrups, review the USPC C Manual, pp. 49–52.)

Always warm up and make sure the horse's back is round and swinging before riding without stirrups, especially in a sitting trot.

Work without stirrups should include:

- **Longe lessons,** including exercises without reins and stirrups (all gaits): for balance, security, suppleness, and independent seat. Specific exercises for individual faults or weak areas.

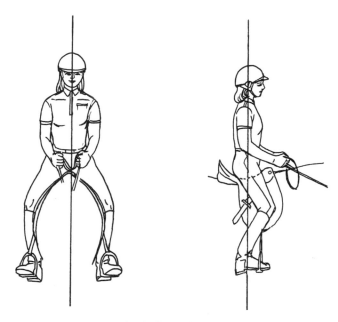

The balanced seat

- **Sitting (all gaits):** for deep, supple seat and to follow the motion of gaits more accurately.
- **Posting trot:** improves leg position, security, balance, and posting with the motion; develops strength and fitness, especially in leg muscles; good for jumping.
- **Half-seat:** same as posting trot; especially demanding of strength and fitness in leg muscles.

The Horse's Back

You can sit the trot only when your horse moves correctly, with a round, swinging back, and without excess tension in his back, neck, and hind legs. A stiff, hollow back causes a high head and a stiff gait, which is extremely uncomfortable. This prevents the horse from engaging his hind legs well, responding correctly to seat aids, and working "on the bit." Sitting the trot on a stiff, hollow horse hurts his back and makes the problem worse. Instead, work in rising trot to develop relaxation, better rhythm and tempo, and encourage the horse to engage his hind legs.

A tense, hollow back and high head may be caused by:

- Mental tension, nervousness, or frustration.
- Ill-fitting saddle (especially one that pinches the shoulders).
- Rider out of balance, stiff, bouncing, or hanging on the reins.
- Tempo too quick or inconsistent; rushing; irregular gaits.
- Horse has not yet developed strength or balance to carry rider in sitting trot. Don't ride sitting trot on young, green, or weak horses.
- Discomfort in mouth; not accepting bit; poor contact or rough hands.
- Soreness in back, hind legs, or elsewhere.

Horse moves "round," with back raised

Horse moves "hollow," with back dropped

Advanced Use of the Aids

By now, you should know the aids and their effects; you should coordinate your aids and use half-halts to rebalance your horse and call for his attention. (See USPC C Manual, Chapters 1, 2, and 3.) To ride with tact and harmony, your use of the aids must be developed further and become "educated."

To ride with educated aids, timing, and tact, you must have a balanced, supple, and secure seat. An incorrect or unbalanced position causes insecurity, muscle tension, and inadvertent movements that interfere with your aids and confuse your horse.

Aids: Good, Light, Crude, Educated

A rider's aids may be good, light, crude, or educated. "Good" aids are correct, clear, and effective but non-abusive. "Light" aids are non-interfering but tentative and passive; they tend to pacify a horse instead of insisting on obedience or improving his training. (Examples are riding with a loose rein, or keeping the legs off the horse's sides.) "Crude" aids are rough and often abusive; they confuse and upset horses and spoil their training. "Educated" aids are not only correct, but sense exactly how much pressure a horse needs, when to apply it, and when to release. The ability to sense what each horse needs and to ride with educated aids, in harmony with the horse, is called "equestrian tact."

To ride with educated aids and equestrian tact, you must develop feel and timing. Communication works both ways: from horse to rider, and from rider to horse. Your seat, legs, and hands must receive as well as send messages. To improve your feel, you must ride with good muscle tone, which maintains your position and keeps you from becoming loose and sloppy, but without excessive tension in your muscles. When muscles are tightly contracted, they are insensitive to subtle changes and cannot make fine, precise movements. Trying to "muscle" a horse into obedience with force causes him to resist with more strength and tension, creating a fight you cannot win.

The success of your aids depends not on strength but on timing. If you give an aid at the right point in the stride, your horse can respond easily. If you give the aid at the wrong time, he cannot respond even if he wants to. This leads to confusion, resistance, and training setbacks. It is even worse if you punish him unfairly for "disobedience" when you have not made it possible for him to obey. In order to time your aids correctly, you must understand the gaits, movement, and the order in which the horse moves his legs, and be able to feel the moment when he can respond as you ask.

As your aids, timing, and equestrian tact improve, your horse will give you more for less, responding promptly and generously to lighter and more subtle aids, which are nearly invisible.

Seat Aids

Seat aids can only be given from a correct, supple, and balanced seat. The seat can passively follow the motion of the horse's back or can be actively engaged, to influence the hindquarters. The seat can soften or "give," as a reward, or act strongly, as a correction. Active seat aids must be given in time with the movement of the horse's back, never as a long, hard muscle contraction; and only when the horse's back is round and swinging. A horse cannot respond to active seat aids when his back is "down," stiff, and hollow.

SEAT AIDS

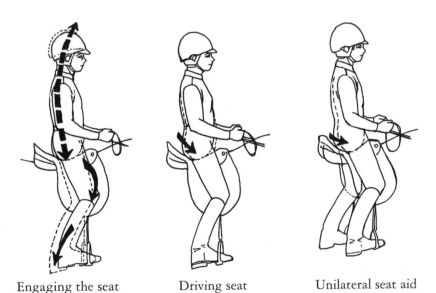

Engaging the seat   Driving seat   Unilateral seat aid

Engaging the Seat   Engaging the seat asks the horse to rebalance; it is done mostly with the deep, internal muscles at the center of your body. Taking a deep, powerful breath or briefly lengthening your spine engages these muscles, producing a subtle but clear aid. Your spine lengthens briefly: the lower back becomes flatter, the sacrum and tailbone move down and forward, and the upper body becomes taller. The knees release and sink downward, sending the lower legs down and back around the horse's barrel. This should be done in short pulsations, not long, hard muscular contractions, which stiffen you and throw you out of balance. To engage your seat correctly, your legs must come back under your seat.

Driving Seat   For a more active driving aid, used to send the horse forward, the seat "tucks" slightly forward and downward, lengthening the spine and sending the knees down and lower legs down and back against the horse's barrel.

Unilateral (One-Sided) Seat Aid   A unilateral seat aid engages or moves one seat bone (usually the inside seat bone) more strongly than the other, asking the horse to respond more strongly with one hind leg. It is used in bending and straightening the horse, canter departs, and lateral work.

To give a unilateral seat aid with the inside seat bone, place your outside leg about 4 inches behind the girth, and your inside leg in the normal position near the girth. Sit deep and tall, breathe, and feel for the moment when the horse slides your inside seat bone forward. As he does so, engage or tuck your seat, letting your inside seat bone move a little farther than usual. You may feel your horse respond with a longer step of his inside hind leg.

For a lateral (sideways) step, give the unilateral seat aid by "aiming" the inside seat bone diagonally forward and inward, toward the horse's spine. This asks him to engage his inside hind leg in a forward and sideways direction. (Never try to push a horse sideways by leaning, twisting, or collapsing your hip; this throws you off balance and confuses the horse.)

Leg Aids

Correct leg aids can only be given from a correct seat and leg position. Your inner legs gently "embrace" the horse with a continuous soft, passive contact; the horse must learn to accept this gentle contact. If your legs are stiff, gripping, unsteady, or held away from the horse's side, he cannot feel clear, precise leg aids.

Leg aids should be given with the inner calf, not with the heel, ankle, or back of the calf. A brief twitch of the calf muscle against the barrel is an active leg aid. Briefly pressing your foot down and backward into the stirrup stretches the calf muscle around the horse's barrel, creating a subtle and almost invisible aid. A tiny, almost invisible "rub" of the calf muscle, as if ruffling the horse's hair from back to front, is a subtle aid to go forward, bend, or engage the hind leg. If the horse does not respond to light leg aids, reinforce with a tap of the whip, instead of using harder leg aids.

Leg aids can be given in three positions:

- **Normal position (close to the girth):** for forward movement, more engagement, or bending.
- **Inside leg slightly behind the girth (about 1 inch back):** for yielding or lateral movement from the inside, as in turns on the forehand or leg-yielding.
- **Outside leg about 4 inches behind the girth:** passively or actively controls the hindquarters, preventing them from swinging out.

LEG AID POSITIONS

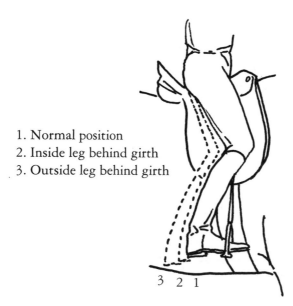

1. Normal position
2. Inside leg behind girth
3. Outside leg behind girth

Rein Aids

Good rein aids can only be given from a correct and balanced seat, with back, shoulders, arms, and hands used correctly. Rein aids are changes of pressure, *not pulling*, and must *always* be supported by leg aids. The forearms and reins should form a straight line from elbow to the bit. Correct contact and rein aids go through the rider's hands, wrists, and forearms to the elbows, the back of the upper arms, and the back and shoulder blades. "Busy" hands that pull, nag, and fiddle, or overuse of hands without supporting leg aids ("riding the horse from front to back") will quickly spoil the horse's response to rein aids.

Good rein aids cannot be given unless the horse is ridden from "back to front": the legs ask for energy from the hindquarters, the seat regulates it as it goes through the horse's back, and the hands receive and regulate it.

The reins can be used in the following ways:

- **Passive or soft contact:** reins lightly stretched (straight, not sagging); elastic shoulders, elbows, wrists, and fingers keep the contact steady while following the motion of the horse's head.
- **Active rein aid ("taking"):** hand squeezes briefly, as if squeezing water out of a sponge—*not* pulling. Asks for a response from the mouth, through the body, to influence the hind leg on the same side. Small changes in the direction of the pressure (backward, outward, or inward) can create different rein effects (direct rein, opening rein, indirect rein, etc.).
- **Releasing ("giving"):** easing the contact by briefly relaxing the pressure of the fingers (but *don't* let the rein slip through the fingers).
- **Supportive rein:** used on either side (on straight lines), and especially on the outside rein (on circles or curved lines) to keep the horse tracking correctly instead of falling in or out. May be passive contact, slightly stronger (holding), or active, as needed.
- **Holding (non-allowing) rein:** contains the energy; resists the horse's efforts to push his head forward, or pull the rider's hands forward. The rider must resist, *not pull*, primarily with back of the upper arms, shoulder blades, back, and seat; must be elastic, not stiff, even when strong. Used when asking the horse to flex at the poll and "round up" in his back and neck.

Developing Better Half-Halts

A half-halt is a momentary rebalancing that engages the rider's seat, legs, and deep inner muscles of the torso, in a brief pulsation timed with the rhythm of the gait. It asks the horse to rebalance by engaging his hind legs more deeply, and it calls for more energy and attention. Half-halts are used to improve the horse's movement, balance, and impulsion, and to prepare for transitions and movements.

Good half-halts are executed with precision rather than force. Using your muscles too hard or holding a half-halt too long makes you stiff, and causes a horse to stiffen, hollow his back, and resist.

In a good half-halt, your sacrum and tailbone drop down, flattening your lower back a little, with a slight "tucking" motion of your pelvis. Your seat "opens", which allows the horse to round up his back and deepens your seat. Your knees release as your legs sink down and back under your seat, making a stronger contact on your horse's barrel. Your spine briefly lengthens, your shoulders widen, and your elbows sink. A deep breath helps to engage the deep, inner muscles which engage your seat and create a correct half-halt.

Because half-halts are very brief, you probably won't feel everything happening at once. Try concentrating on only one part of your body (such as your seat) during several half-halts, then on another part (back, legs, shoulders, etc.). While a half-halt can be very strong, it is *not* a stiff, hard, muscular contraction, leaning back, or pulling on the reins. You should get a sensation of improved balance and increased energy, in yourself and in your horse.

Timing the Aids

Aids should be applied in brief pulsations in rhythm with the gait, not as a long, hard muscular effort. The *left leg and left direct rein aids* communicate with the *left hind leg* of the horse, and the *right leg and right direct rein aids* communicate with the *right hind leg.*

The horse can respond to an aid only if it is given at the right point in the stride. For most purposes, this is when the hind leg is pushing off the ground and about to swing forward through the air. When working on a curve or circle or in a ring, the aids are most often timed with the movement of the inside hind leg.

Although you can learn to time the aids by watching the horse's shoulders, this is not as satisfactory as learning to feel the timing, because it makes you look down. Learn to feel the movement of the hind legs, which is transmitted to your seat through the horse's back,

TIMING LEG AIDS

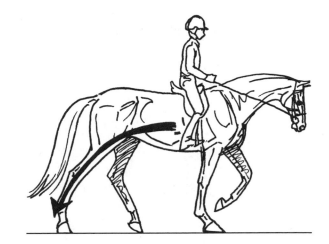

Leg aid affects
hind leg on the
same side

Apply leg aid as hind
leg pushes off

and to recognize the moment when each hind leg is about to push off,
in each gait.

Tips for learning to time aids correctly:

- **Focus on one leg at a time,** preferably the inside hind leg. When
  you can identify the motion of one hind leg, try the other one.

- **Have someone lead your horse at a walk,** so you can ride safely with your eyes closed for several minutes. You may notice motion you were unaware of before. Say, "Now" as you think the inside hind leg is pushing off, and have a helper check your accuracy.
- **For more forward movement or greater engagement,** apply a leg aid as the hind leg (on the same side) is on the ground and pushing off, so it can respond with greater thrust and by swinging more forward through the air.
- **To move laterally,** apply the leg aid as the hind leg is pushing off, to convert the step into a sideways step.

TIMING AIDS IN POSTING TROT

Using left leg aid as left hind leg is pushing off; posting on right diagonal

Using left leg aid as left hind leg is swinging forward; posting on left diagonal

- **To shorten or stop the motion of a front or hind leg,** apply the rein aid as the leg (on the same side) is moving through the air, so that the horse can finish his step with a shorter stride or a halt.
- **In the trot,** posting on the *outside diagonal* (outside foreleg and inside hind leg) lets you feel the push of the inside hind leg as it helps you **rise.** Applying a brief inside leg aid as you *begin to rise* will affect the inside hind leg as it pushes off and swings forward.

If you post on the *inside diagonal* (inside foreleg and outside hind leg) you can apply an inside leg aid as you *sit*, catching the moment when the inside hind leg pushes off and swings through the air. This can be useful for leg-yielding in rising trot.

In sitting trot, it may help to "post mentally" on one diagonal or the other, in order to identify the movement of the hind legs.

- **In the canter,** the outside hind leg moves first, followed by inside hind and outside fore together, then inside fore. Applying leg aids in harmony with this motion ("outside-inside") helps in canter departs, to maintain the lead and the bend, keeps the hindquarters from drifting out, and helps to engage the hind legs at each stride.

PATTERN OF FOOTFALLS IN CANTER

Right lead   Left lead

- **The canter has an up-down motion,** like a seesaw. The "up" moment, when the forehand rises, is when the hind legs reach forward and strike the ground. The "down" moment, as the head and forehand drop, is when the hind legs swing backward and the weight moves onto the forelegs.

In the canter, the horse can rebalance himself best if you half-halt during the "up," as forehand rises. If you half-halt on the "down," the hind legs are already on the ground and moving backward; the horse cannot engage more on that stride.

TIMING AIDS IN CANTER

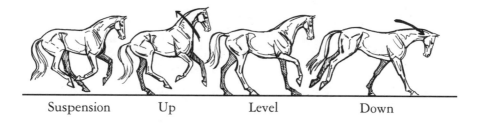

| Suspension | Up | Level | Down |

Putting the Horse on the Aids and on the Bit

A horse that is "on the aids" accepts all the aids, and responds promptly and generously to them. Because of the connection from the rider's seat and legs through his back and neck to the bit, he reaches out and seeks contact with the rider's hands. As the horse becomes more attentive and responsive, the rider's aids can become so subtle that they are nearly invisible.

In order to be on the aids, the horse must respond to seat, leg, and rein aids. Many riders put too much emphasis on riding the horse "on the bit," forgetting that this is not possible without the first two aids.

Seat Aids   Seat aids must be given in rhythm with the horse's swinging back. They can ask the horse to lengthen the "swings" (to lengthen stride), to put more energy into them, or to make them shorter, rounder, or smaller. A horse cannot respond to seat aids if his back is stiff and hollow. He must be ridden forward in rising trot or a light seat until he relaxes, brings his back up, and allows it to swing.

Leg Aids   Leg aids ask the hind legs for energy, forward movement, and engagement, and control the direction of the hind legs. The left leg influences the left hind leg, and the right leg the right hind leg.

The horse must be *"in front of the legs."* This means that he is always ready and willing to go forward promptly, when asked by the rider's leg aids. A horse that is sticky, stubborn, or resistant to going forward is "behind the legs"; his rider has no real control.

Rein Aids and Putting the Horse "On the Bit"   In order to respond to rein aids, the horse must accept contact with the bit with a soft, closed mouth and a relaxed neck, poll, and jaw. Discomfort, tension, or resistance show that he is not accepting the bit, often because the rider is not using his aids correctly.

A horse cannot be on the bit unless he is responsive to the rider's seat and legs. The leg aids generate energy and forward movement from the hind legs, which is transmitted through the horse's back; the seat regulates it; and the hands receive the energy.

When a horse responds correctly to leg aids, he moves with greater energy, and engagement. This causes his back to "round up" and swing, so the rider's seat can influence it. The energy and forward movement create a rounded arc (bascule) in his back and neck, like the arc of a rainbow. The horse raises his withers, arches his neck, and sends his poll forward, reaching forward and taking a soft, steady contact with the bit, accepting the bit with a relaxed poll and jaw, and a wet, closed mouth. He yields (gives) to the bit at the request of the rider by relaxing his jaw, softly chewing the bit, and flexing at the poll, which brings his face closer to the vertical.

If the horse is on the bit, he is always willing to stretch down, maintaining contact and staying round, whenever the rider allows him to take more rein.

Riding a horse on the bit has nothing to do with a "head set" (a fixed, vertical position of the head). "Setting the head" with see-sawing hands, severe bits, or control devices only creates a false frame, which prevents the horse from using his body and moving correctly, and going truly on the bit.

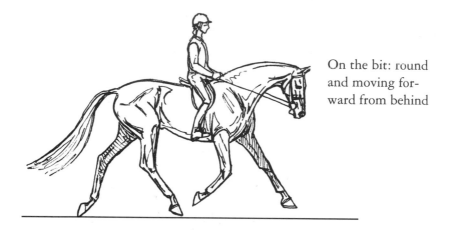

On the bit: round
and moving for-
ward from behind

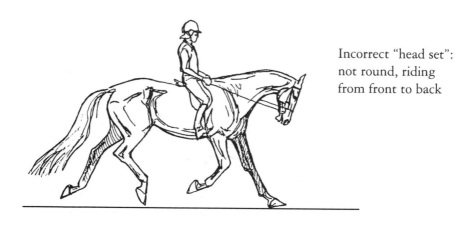

Incorrect "head set":
not round, riding
from front to back

Riding on the Flat

Warmup

A proper warmup is essential for every ride, to warm up and loosen the horse's muscles, dispel tension, and establish relaxation, attention to the rider, and a good working attitude. (Warmup is important for riders, too.) Some horses need extra preparation such as longeing before they are ready to work.

The warmup for a trained horse is like a brief review of the process of training. It begins by establishing *relaxation*, *regularity*, and *freedom of movement* with a good working tempo in a long frame, on straight lines, large circles, and changes of direction. It goes on to develop *contact* (including stretching down on contact) and put the horse *on the aids*, then works on *straightness* and *bending*. *Balance* and *suppleness* are addressed next, mainly through transitions and half-halts, which lead to increased *impulsion*, and finally, for horses that are capable of it, *collection*. It is important to work on each of these qualities in proper order, because each depends on the ones before it.

Stretching Down

Stretching "down and round" (also called "chewing the bit out of the hands") is an exercise to demonstrate and improve contact, relaxation, and roundness. Stretching down correctly teaches the horse to seek the bit and helps relax his back, neck, and poll. It confirms good contact and encourages a round, swinging back and relaxed neck.

Correct stretching down can only be done when the horse is on the aids, moving forward with a round, swinging back into correct contact.

To ask your horse to stretch down and round, keep sending him forward in rhythm with your legs and seat as you gradually allow him to take your hands forward and down, as far as they will go. If he is willing to stretch further, you can allow the reins to slip gradually through your fingers, but be careful not to drop the contact. The horse should "follow the bit down," maintaining contact, with his poll softly flexed; he may chew the bit as he stretches (hence the phrase "chewing the bit out of the hands"). When he has stretched down and maintained contact for a few strides, continue to support the rhythm with your seat and leg aids as you smoothly shorten your reins and bring him back to a normal frame.

To stretch down correctly, the horse must engage his hind legs and must keep his back up and round. If he disengages his hind legs, drops his back, or leans on the forehand, he may be down, but he is not round. Snatching at the bit, dropping contact, or poking his nose out are *not* correct stretching, and show that the horse is not properly on the aids. If you make the mistake of slackening the reins to encourage your horse to lower his head, he may learn to drop his head to *avoid* contact, which is the opposite of what you want!

Stretching down correctly is proof of good work. It should be used in warmup and during work to encourage relaxation, roundness, and good contact, as a rest and reward, and when finishing work, to allow the horse to stretch and relax his muscles.

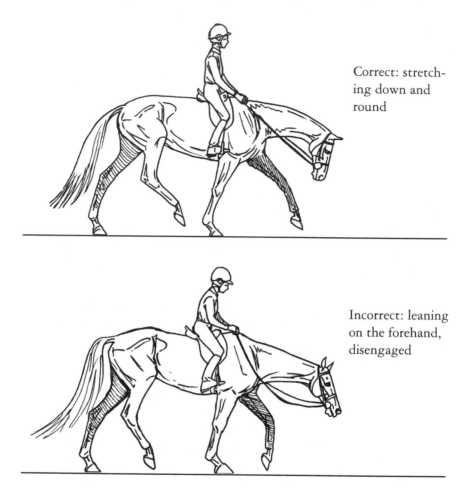

Correct: stretching down and round

Incorrect: leaning on the forehand, disengaged

Free Forward Movement

All good work is done with free forward movement, good rhythm, and regularity. "Free" means free from stiffness and constraint, *not* wandering aimlessly on a loose rein. "Forward" means the horse's willingness to move forward and "use himself" well: His hind legs reach forward with powerful strides, and he stretches his back and neck and reaches forward into the rider's hands. It does *not* mean going fast!

These qualities are essential to good gaits and movement, and must be preserved in any exercises you do. Free forward movement must be re-established by riding straight forward after any exercise that shortens the movement, or whenever the horse becomes tense, stiff, or starts to lose his rhythm.

Schooling Figures

The right choice of figures and exercises, correctly ridden, can improve your horse's straightness, balance, suppleness, and movement. Schooling figures are only of value when precisely ridden; if they are vague or uneven, you cannot monitor or correct your horse's movement and responsiveness. The figures you choose must be appropriate for your horse's needs and level of training; don't ask a young, green, or unbalanced horse to perform circles or figures that demand bending or collection beyond his capability.

Good preparation allows you to begin a figure at the designated point, with the horse balanced and moving well. You must continue to think ahead and ride each step accurately, to keep him tracking straight on the track of the figure, moving with regularity and balance, and to finish at the designated spot.

On large circles or curves, look approximately one quarter of the circle ahead. On smaller circles or figures, look at a point approximately halfway across the circle. When changing bend, straighten your horse for at least one stride before asking him to bend in the new direction. On completing a circle or figure, finish with the correct bend, or by straightening your horse in time to move smoothly into the next movement.

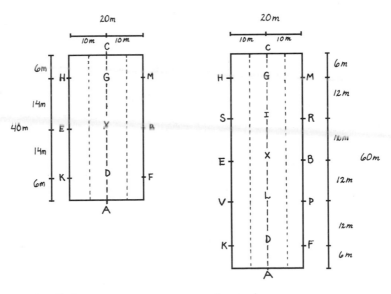

Small dressage arena   Large dressage arena

Inside and Outside

It is important to understand the concept of inside and outside, especially in lateral work. "Inside" refers to the direction in which the horse is bent, *not* the inside or center of the ring. "Outside" refers to the outside of the bend, *not* the outside of the ring or track.

There are certain movements in which the horse may be bent toward the track or the outside of the ring. In this case, the "inside" aids are still those on the side toward which the horse is bent, and the "outside" aids may be on the side toward the center of the ring.

Straightening the Horse: Riding "In Position"

In order to ride a horse straight, he must be aligned so that his hind legs follow directly behind his front legs and he moves on one track.

A horse (seen from above) is shaped like a triangle; his shoulders are narrower than his hindquarters. When ridden along the side of a ring, he tends to move with his outside shoulder and hip parallel to the fence, causing him to move crookedly.

To move straight, his shoulders and front legs must be brought inward enough to line up with his hind legs. This is called "riding in position"; it creates a very small bend to the inside. "Position left" is used when riding on the left rein (counterclockwise), and "position right" when riding on the right rein (clockwise).

To ride in position, ask for a tiny bend with your inside leg at the girth, and just enough inside rein to ask the horse to flex at the poll very slightly to the inside. Your outside leg behind the girth and outside supporting rein are very important, as they keep the horse from overbending or falling out with his hip or shoulder.

If you ride toward a mirror in position correctly, you will see the horse's front legs only; his hind legs are behind them. His head will have a very slight flexion to the inside.

Bending and Lateral Balance

Bending is another aspect of keeping the horse straight, with his hind legs following in the tracks of his front legs.

When moving on a curved track, the horse's inside hind leg must engage and bend its joints more, and his outside hind leg must swing farther. The muscles on the outside stretch farther, while those on the inside of the bend soften.

POSITION AND STRAIGHTNESS

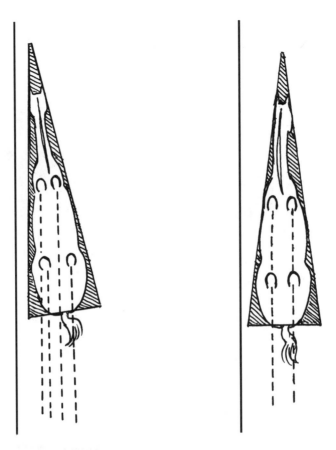

Horse moves crookedly when outside shoulder and hip are aligned with the track

Riding in "position right": horse is bent slightly to the right, bringing shoulders in line with hind legs

When bending correctly, the horse's hind legs follow in the tracks of his forelegs, he looks in the direction of the bend, and appears to bend evenly from his poll to his tail. He engages his hind legs (especially the inside hind leg), which rounds his back, and keeps his weight in the center, "standing up" instead of leaning through turns, which improves his balance.

Bending: The horse bends around the rider's inside leg, softening on the inside and stretching on the outside, showing roundness, engagement, and free forward movement. *Photo: C. H. Hamilton III*

Riding the Horse into the Outside Rein

Riding the horse "into the outside rein" enhances control, straightness, bending, and good movement. It is especially evident (and easier to learn) on turns and circles, but also applies on straight lines. To do this, the horse must be on the aids and must have learned to move "forward and out" from an inside leg aid.

Your inside leg, close to the girth, asks the horse to engage his inside hind leg, and reminds him not to fall in. Your outside rein has an especially important role: It receives and regulates the rhythmic forward thrust from the hindquarters, keeps the outside shoulder from bearing out and leaving the track, and controls the amount of bend in the horse's neck. The horse should "fill the outside rein" and become rounder and more elastic. Your inside rein indicates the direction in which he should look and move. Your outside leg, behind the girth, reminds his outside hind leg to stay on the track of the circle instead of skidding outward.

Your outside rein contact must be steady and elastic, so you can easily regulate the movement, bend, and balance with brief squeezes in rhythm with the gait. The outside rein can only regulate what it receives; if your leg fails to send your horse forward and out, and there is no stretch into your outside hand, you have nothing to work with. If you hang or pull on the outside rein, lose your balance, or drop the contact, it is impossible for the horse to stretch into your outside rein and respond correctly.

The inside rein should be used softly; pulling or "cranking" your horse's head and neck inward overpowers the effect of the outside rein and confuses your horse, and it makes him crooked and hard to control. If you think you need a stronger inside rein aid, try using a more effective inside leg instead.

Releasing the Inside Hand

A momentary release with the inside hand is used as a reward, to encourage relaxation, or (for more advanced horses and riders) to test balance, rhythm, and self-carriage. If done correctly, it rewards or calms the horse while he continues to work, without disturbing his rhythm or balance. Releasing incorrectly (too far, for too long, out of rhythm, with the wrong hand, or dropping contact with both hands) allows the horse to fall on his forehand, interrupts the work, and may teach the horse to quit working whenever he is rewarded.

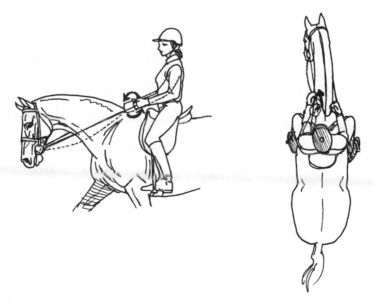

Release with inside rein: inside hand moves forward, down, and back to contact in circular motion

To release the inside rein, your inside hand, holding the rein, reaches forward toward the bit in a circular motion, with a gentle rub of your knuckles against the horse's neck, then smoothly returns to contact, while your outside rein maintains the same steady contact. Be careful to keep your balance and only extend your arm and elbow; *don't* lean forward, or open your fingers and let the rein slip through. The circular motion should be fairly large at first; to keep it smooth, try counting "one, two, three, four" with the rhythm of your horse's gait. Later, the circular release can be smaller and more subtle.

Lengthening and Shortening Stride

Lengthening and shortening stride is an important exercise for jumping as well as for flat work. It is important to learn to lengthen and shorten stride in all gaits while maintaining good balance, rhythm, and the same tempo.

When lengthening stride in any gait, the horse must reach farther and cover more ground at each stride, maintaining the same tempo instead of "running" faster with short strides. His "frame" (outline) lengthens as his legs reach farther, but he must not lose his balance and lean on the forehand. A good lengthening feels as if the tempo is slower, not quicker, with more power and roundness in each stride.

Horses can be asked to lengthen stride before they are trained and strong enough to perform extended gaits. True extended gaits require greater impulsion (thrust) from the hindquarters, and a greater degree of strength and balance.

To lengthen stride, your leg aids ask the hind legs to push off more strongly. As the strides become longer, the horse's back and neck stretch, and your hands and arms should allow the head and neck to stretch forward somewhat and lengthen his frame, but not enough to let him fall on his forehand. Don't lean forward, lose contact, or fall backward.

After a lengthening, the horse must be brought back to a working gait by rebalancing and shortening back to a normal stride and frame. Use half-halts in rhythm, and keep him moving forward and round as he rebalances.

Lengthening Stride in Walk   Use alternate leg aids to ask each hind leg in turn to push off and take a longer stride (left leg as the barrel begins to swing to the right; right leg as the barrel begins to swing

LENGTHENING STRIDE

Lengthening stride
correctly

Incorrect: Quickening
with short strides

Incorrect: Running
on the forehand

left). Don't overdo the lateral motion or sway from side to side, or the horse may begin to pace.

Lengthening Stride in Trot   To lengthen stride in rising trot, use both legs together as the inside hind leg begins to push off (if posting on the outside diagonal, while you are sitting).

To lengthen stride while sitting, the horse's back must be round and swinging. Engage your seat actively to ask for a bigger swing at each stride.

Lengthening Stride in Canter   To lengthen stride in canter, allow your seat to follow the "roll" of your horse's back at each stride. Engage your seat and apply your inside leg at the girth at the moment when your seat is moving forward, as the hind legs are engaging. Allow the horse to lengthen his frame, but don't lean forward, drop contact, or let him lean on the forehand.

Shortening Stride

To shorten his strides, a horse must rebalance himself, engaging his hind legs under his body, and shifting his weight back to his hindquarters. He should keep the same rhythm and tempo as he shortens and rebalances, instead of slowing down, losing his energy and impulsion, or "propping" his forelegs in stiff, "braking" strides.

To ask your horse to shorten stride, use half-halts in rhythm with the gait, with brief, rhythmic squeezes on the outside rein. Sit up and maintain your balance, and keep your legs back under your seat and on your horse's barrel, to encourage him to engage his hind legs. If you try to shorten stride by pulling on the reins, or lose your balance instead of rebalancing properly, your horse will learn to resist your hands, hollow his back, and stiffen against you instead of shortening correctly.

Rein-Back

The rein-back is a four-beat backward movement, in which the feet are raised and set down almost simultaneously in diagonal pairs; each forefoot is raised and set down an instant before the diagonal hind foot. (The pattern of footfalls is: right front, left hind, left front, right hind.) The horse should move backward in a straight line, with his hind feet in line with his front feet. He should bend his joints and raise his feet well at each step, instead of dragging himself backward with stiff legs. In a good rein-back, the horse remains on the aids and on the bit, and is willing to move forward immediately at any time.

The rein-back requires the horse to put more weight on his hindquarters and bend the joints of his hind legs more. This can improve his engagement and balance, but can easily overstress his back, hocks, and stifle joints, especially if it is practiced too much or incorrectly, or if it is forced.

Riding a correct rein-back correctly requires balance, timing, and feel, never force. Your horse must be on the aids, with his back round, and in front of your legs. At the halt, your legs and seat ask him to move, but you "close the door" with a holding (non-allowing) rein aid. As the horse meets your holding hands, his forward movement becomes a rein-back; his impulse to move forward is let out backward.

As soon as the horse begins to yield and move backward, your hands must lighten without losing the contact. Both legs (an inch or two behind their normal position) act as supporting aids, keeping the horse straight as he steps back. Your body should stay in a vertical balance, without leaning forward or backward, but you should lighten your seat a little by transferring some of your weight to your thighs. This allows your horse to round up his back and engage his hind legs, so he can step backward easily. If you lean back, drive your seat bones into his back, or pull, you will cause him to hollow his back, resist your aids, and rein-back badly, if at all.

To stop the rein-back and move forward, "close the back door": Sit deep, engage your seat and leg aids, and lighten the rein contact. In a good rein-back, your horse should remain balanced and in front of your legs, so that he is willing and able to move forward *immediately* at any time.

Faults in the rein-back include: the horse anticipating, resisting, or hurrying the movement; resisting or evading the bit; moving crookedly; or backing with inactive or dragging front or hind legs. These are usually caused by rider faults such as halting or reining back "all in the hands"; sitting too heavily or out of balance; failure to use supporting leg aids; or leaning forward.

Transitions

As your balance, timing, and aids improve, your horse's transitions should become increasingly prompt, smooth, and better balanced.

Good transitions improve a horse's balance, engagement, suppleness, and impulsion, put him in front of your legs, and make him light.

Prepare your horse for each transition with half-halts, to make him attentive and on the aids, with hind legs engaged, back rounded, and on the bit. The quality of a transition depends on the quality of the last stride of the previous gait. If the gait is not quite right, take a few strides to correct it before making a transition.

Trot-Walk-Trot

This exercise consists of approximately ten strides of trot, three strides of walk, then ten strides of trot. It can improve your horse's balance, impulsion, and responsiveness, but you must stay in balance and time your aids correctly. Start with posting trot; on the last five strides, sit the trot, use half-halts, and prepare to walk. On the *first* step of walk, immediately rebalance and ask for the trot. At first, your horse may not understand that he must trot, walk, then immediately trot again. With a few repetitions, he will learn to rebalance in the trot to be ready to walk, and to "keep his motor running" by maintaining impulsion and balance during the brief walk phase.

Halt-Trot

To trot from a halt, without walking steps, you must use repeated half-halts to engage your horse's hind legs, build his energy, and contain it until he really wants to move forward. Practice trot-walk-trot transitions until he is awake, on the aids, and in front of your legs. Then halt and give brief half-halts until you feel his energy building. When you close your legs, engage your seat, and ask for trot, think of your horse "springing" into a trot, with power from his hindquarters going through his round back and neck into your hands. You must soften your fingers to allow him to go forward, but without slackening the reins or falling forward; keep the contact. Breathing deeply helps you stay elastic, balanced, and light, as well as powerful.

Trot-Halt

To halt from a trot without walk steps, you must half-halt effectively and rebalance the trot for several strides, until your horse is able to engage his hind legs, shift his balance back, and tuck his hindquarters under him as he completes the last step of trot. Because a horse stops with one diagonal pair of legs, then the other, your rein aids must be given as a "one-two," timed with the outside and inside shoulder.

Canter Departs

There are three types of canter departs, which require progressively higher levels of riding and training. All three must be executed with clear, coordinated aids, and at the right level of training. The horse should always be prepared for a canter depart with one or more half-halts.

Canter departs are developed progressively. A very green horse usually canters from the trot, using an angled canter depart and outside lateral aids. As he becomes better balanced and responsive to the aids, he can canter from a working trot, with diagonal aids and a straighter canter depart. A trained, supple, well-balanced horse can canter from the walk, using inside lateral aids, which result in a more precise depart, and a straighter, more collected canter.

Outside Lateral Aids   Outside lateral aids are leg and rein aids on the same side (outside). The horse's head is flexed slightly at the poll to the outside, and the outside leg is applied about 4 inches behind the girth. This aid activates the outside hind leg and frees the inside shoulder, helping the horse to take the inside lead. It is clear and simple for green or unschooled horses, but it produces an outside bend and a crooked canter.

CANTER AIDS

| Outside lateral aids: outside leg, outside rein | Diagonal aids: outside leg, inside seat bone, inside rein | Inside lateral aids: inside leg, inside seat bone, inside rein |

An *angled canter depart* reinforces the outside lateral aids, especially for green horses. The horse is angled slightly into the rail before asking for the canter. The visual aid of a wall or corner guides him into a slight turn as he begins to canter, making it easier to take the inside lead. It also discourages him from running onto his forehand.

Diagonal Aids   The diagonal aids for a canter depart are the outside leg, applied about 4 inches behind the girth, and inside rein aid. The outside leg activates the outside hind leg to begin the canter, and the inside rein indicates the lead and asks the horse to look in that direction. This is a natural step from outside lateral aids and an angled depart, as it uses the familiar outside leg aid, but results in a straighter canter depart and canter. Its disadvantages are the lack of a true bend (looking in the direction of the lead is not bending), and lack of precision in beginning the canter.

A more sophisticated version of diagonal aids prepares the horse with outside leg behind the girth, then adds a slight push with the inside seat bone, along with the inside rein. This is a more precise aid, resulting in a better balanced depart and more prompt response. It also prepares the horse for the more advanced inside lateral aids for the canter.

Inside Lateral Aids   Advanced canter departs are executed with inside lateral aids, which allow you to address the balance, bend, and engagement, and to ask the horse to strike off more precisely with his hind legs. They establish a slight bend (or "position"), which indicates the lead. This is important in cantering from the walk, in the counter-canter, and in changes of lead.

For an inside lateral depart, the horse must be on the aids. Prepare him by asking for a slight bend in the direction of the lead you want, using half-halts. Your inside leg, applied close to the girth, inside direct rein aid, and a slight push of your inside seat bone ask for the canter, while your outside aids (outside leg behind the girth, and outside rein) act as supporting aids.

Precise timing is crucial in this canter depart. The horse begins a canter depart by balancing for an instant on his *outside* hind leg. This is followed by the diagonal pair (inside hind and outside fore together), then the inside fore. The outside hind leg must be well engaged to support the horse as he begins the canter. You must time your aids at the instant when he is balanced on his outside hind leg. In the trot, this is

Canter depart: The horse balances on his outside hind leg. Notice the engagement of the inside hind leg, and the upward lift of the forehand.
Photo: C. H. Hamilton III

when the inside diagonal (inside foreleg and outside hind) touch down. In the walk, it is when the inside shoulder begins to move backward.

Downward Transitions from Canter

Downward transitions from the canter require especially good balance, suppleness, and timing. The horse must stay round as he engages his hindquarters more, shifts his balance back, and "sits" into the downward transition. If asked to "come back" when he is unbalanced, hollow, or at the wrong point in the stride, he cannot make a good transition, especially to the walk. Ask for the downward transition as the horse's leading leg reaches forward, while his hind legs are in the air and his back begins to round. Give short, clear half-halts, keeping your upper body tall and vertical and your legs back under you. Tipping forward or leaning back, letting your legs swing forward, and pulling makes your horse stiffen against you with a hollow back, spoiling any chance of a round, balanced, and correct transition.

Canter-Trot-Walk Transitions   At first, ask the horse to shorten his canter for several strides, then trot for several steps, and then walk. This allows a little more time to rebalance in the trot before the transition to walk. As you and your horse become better at this, decrease the number of trot steps between canter and walk.

Canter-Walk Transitions   Canter-to-walk transitions (without any intermediate trot steps) require balance and timing, *not* harsher aids. You must shorten and balance the canter for several strides, then give the same aid as for the canter-trot transition clearly and strongly, but without pulling or hanging on the mouth.

Changes of Lead

Changes of lead require good balance, straightness, and timing. The horse must rebalance himself and straighten (get rid of the old bend), bend slightly in the direction of the new lead, and push off into the canter without losing his balance or rhythm.

Before you can begin changes of lead, your horse must be able to make good canter departs on either lead, and good transitions from canter to trot. At first, he may need to trot for six or seven strides or longer, in order to rebalance and be ready to depart on the new lead. As his balance, straightness, and transitions improve, he can perform more advanced changes of lead.

Change of Lead through the Trot   In a change of lead through the trot, the horse is brought back to the trot for two or three strides, then restarted into the canter on the opposite lead. It is often executed when changing the rein on the long diagonal. The horse must be straight and balanced, and must not rush through the trot or the canter depart.

Through the Walk (Simple Change of Lead)   The horse is brought back to the walk for two or three steps, then restarted into the canter on the opposite lead, with no trot steps. It requires good canter-walk and walk-canter transitions, and a high degree of straightness, balance, and suppleness.

Counter-Canter

Counter-canter is a canter on the outside lead. The horse is slightly bent toward the side of his leading legs (see "Inside and Outside," p. 60.). Counter-canter improves the horse's balance, straightness, and

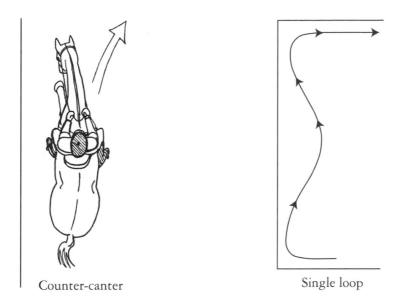

Counter-canter   Single loop

suppleness, and prepares him for flying changes. The horse must not be overbent or forced to canter on a turn that is too difficult for his level of training, balance, and suppleness.

To ride a counter-canter, start by riding a regular canter (on the correct lead) "in position," with the horse flexed to the inside only enough to make him straight. Your normal bending aids (inside leg at the girth, outside leg behind the girth, outside supporting rein and inside bending rein, with slightly more weight on the inside seat bone) keep the horse in the same lead and maintain the bend in counter-canter.

If you ride a single loop, maintaining the bend or position toward the side of the leading leg, your horse will be in counter-canter (for instance, cantering on the right lead through a gentle left turn) during the loop. You should feel as if the horse "stands up" and remains vertical during the corner, the single loop, and the next corner. You can progress to a deeper single loop, then to changing the rein while maintaining the same lead and bend, and finally to cantering around the ring and in circles in counter-canter.

Be careful not to lean sideways, overbend the horse toward his leading leg, or bend him the wrong way in counter-canter, and don't ask for too tight a turn for his balance and level of training.

Flying Change of Lead (Change in the Air)

This is an advanced movement in which the horse changes leads during the suspension phase of the canter. He must change front and hind leads together, and must maintain his rhythm, balance, and forward movement. To make flying changes, the canter must have good impulsion and suspension or "jump," but must also stay balanced, straight, supple, and calm. Failure to change both front and hind legs results in a disunited canter (an irregular, unbalanced canter with front legs on one lead and hind legs on the other). Speeding up, bucking, hesitation, or too much lateral movement are serious faults in the flying change.

To ask for a flying change, prepare the horse with half-halts, straighten him, then give the aids for the new lead just before the moment of suspension (as the leading foreleg strikes the ground). You must stay in balance, but your seat lightens a little to allow the back to round up as the horse changes his lead. Don't lean too far forward, tip sideways, or give too strong a leg aid.

Flying changes are advanced movements that require good preparation, balance, and coordination. A horse must be able to do good simple changes of lead (through the walk) and counter-canter fluently before he can learn to do flying changes.

Lateral Work

In lateral movements, the horse moves sideways as well as forward. Lateral work can improve straightness and lateral balance, make the horse more responsive to leg aids, and help to strengthen and supple him on both sides.

Lateral work can benefit a horse only when it is correctly taught and ridden; if done incorrectly or overdone, it can damage his training, make him stiff and resistant, and cause physical damage. When doing lateral work, remember:

- The horse must keep his rhythm, balance, and free forward movement. If he becomes tense, hollow, irregular, or loses his desire to go forward, abandon the lateral exercise and ride him forward until free forward movement is re-established.
- Always end a lateral movement by riding straight forward with free, forward movement in good rhythm.
- You must ride in good balance (especially lateral balance), without leaning, twisting, or collapsing to one side. You must also learn how to apply your left and right aids evenly, instead of overusing

the aids on your stronger side. This requires a ground helper with an educated eye, preferably your instructor.

• If your horse has difficulty with a lateral movement, he may not be physically ready for it. Try a simpler version of the exercise, and don't ask for too many steps at once. Force will only spoil the movement and set his training back.

Lateral Movements

Review the basic lateral work taught at the C Level: "forward and out," turns on the forehand, and leg-yielding at walk and trot. These form the foundation for more advanced lateral work. (See the USPC C Manual, pp. 112–118.)

Leg-yielding along the track. The horse is straight, with only a slight flexion at the poll, to the outside. *Photo: C. H. Hamilton III*

Leg-Yielding

Basic leg-yielding is done from the quarter line to the track, keeping the horse's body parallel to the long side of the ring. When your horse performs this easily in both directions, you can progress to:

Leg-Yielding along the Wall   The horse moves forward and sideways at an angle to the wall (no more than 30 degrees). His body is straight, and his head is flexed slightly at the poll away from the direction in which he moves.

Leg-yielding along the wall may be performed with the head toward the wall, or the tail toward the wall. (*Don't* confuse with shoulder-in.)

Leg-Yielding on the Diagonal   The horse moves forward and sideways along a diagonal line. His body is straight and parallel to the long

Leg-yielding on the diagonal, moving from left to right. The horse is straight, with a slight flexion at the poll, to the left. Notice the engagement of the inside hind leg as it crosses in front of the outside hind leg. *Photo: C. H. Hamilton III*

side of the ring, and he flexes slightly at the poll, away from the direction in which he moves.

In a variation of this exercise, the horse is asked to leg-yield from the wall to the center line or quarter line, to straighten for a stride, and then to leg-yield back to the wall.

(*Don't* confuse with half-pass, a more advanced movement.)

LEG-YIELDING

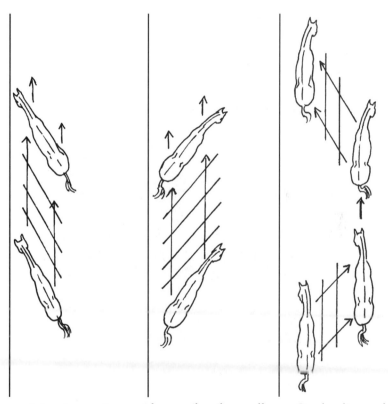

Along rail, head to wall   Along rail, tail to wall   On the diagonal

Shoulder-In

The shoulder-in is one of the most important exercises in classical dressage. It can supple and straighten the horse, develop his muscles and the carrying power of his hind legs, and improve engagement and collection, but *only* if it is taught and ridden correctly. If ridden incorrectly, it can damage his training, create resistance, and cause him to twist his hind legs as he moves, which can lead to soreness. Shoulder-in is also useful to counteract shying and other disobedience.

In the shoulder-in, the horse is bent around the rider's inside leg, looking away from the direction in which he is moving. His shoulders are brought about half a step inside the track of the outside hind leg, so that his outside shoulder is in front of his inside hind leg. His inside legs cross in front of the outside legs. With each step, his inside hind leg reaches diagonally forward under his body, lowering his inside hip and carrying more weight.

Incorrect attempt at shoulder-in. The rider is trying to push the horse sideways by twisting her body and dropping her left shoulder; her right leg is too far forward. The horse appears stiff and unhappy, and his hindquarters have drifted out, losing the bend. *Photo: C. H. Hamilton III*

A better shoulder-in. The rider is better balanced, with more effective leg aids, riding the
horse into the outside rein. The horse moves
correctly on three tracks, showing more roundness and better bending. (However, his jaw
could be more relaxed.) *Photo: C. H. Hamilton III*

To ride shoulder-in, you must first bend your horse around your
inside leg, using the usual bending aids. (Riding a circle or a corner
helps to establish the bend before beginning the shoulder-in.) Your
inside leg (at the girth) sends the horse forward and sideways, asking
him to bend and to engage his inside hind leg. The outside leg
(4 inches behind the girth) keeps his hindquarters from drifting out.
Your outside rein is especially important, controlling the degree of
bend in the neck, and maintaining the balance and frame, while your
inside rein gives direction and guides the horse's shoulders to the
inside.

SHOULDER-IN

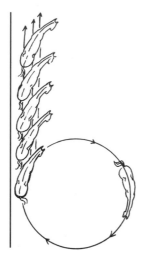

1. Outside supporting rein (regulates bend)
2. Outside leg behind girth (holds hindquarters on track)
3. Inside rein (positions forehand and maintains bend)
4. Inside leg at girth (bends horse and maintains lateral movement)

Circle, followed by shoulder-in

Aids for shoulder-in

Incorrect: Inside rein overbends the neck

Shoulder-in on three tracks

The most common problem in shoulder-in is falling out through the outside shoulder and bending in the neck only, *which is caused by rider error.* Using too much inside rein, "cranking" the horse's head sideways with an incorrectly applied inside indirect rein, and failing to control the bend with the outside rein are the most common rider faults. Your outside leg must keep the outside hind leg moving forward and prevent it from drifting out or stepping sideways, and your outside rein must keep the outside shoulder in front of the inside hind leg.

After the shoulder-in, always ride straight forward to establish free forward movement.

Shoulder-Fore Shoulder-fore is a preliminary exercise that prepares the horse for shoulder-in. It is ridden with the same aids as shoulder-in, but with less bend. Shoulder-fore has less collecting effect than shoulder-in, but it can be useful as an intermediate step between leg-yielding and shoulder-in. It can also be useful in straightening the canter, especially for horses that are not yet able to canter in shoulder-in without becoming stiff.

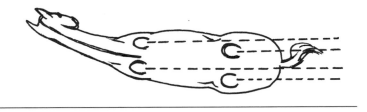

Shoulder-fore

Spiraling inward and outward on a circle (decreasing and increasing the circle) is a good exercise to develop shoulder-fore and later, shoulder-in.

- Spiral inward (decreasing circle): Ride a 20-meter circle, bending the horse correctly on the track of the circle. Gradually reduce the size of the circle (no smaller than 10 meters) by pushing the hindquarters inward with your outside leg behind the girth. At the same time, swivel your seat slightly to the inside and move both hands toward the inside (but *don't* cross the outside rein over the neck). Your outside rein comes against the neck, while your inside rein gently leads the horse's shoulders inward. Your inside leg must keep the horse bending, instead of falling in.
- Spiral outward (increasing circle): Use inside leg aids (in rhythm with the gait) to send your horse gradually back out to the larger circle. Your outside rein and outside leg control how much he moves outward at each step. *Don't* try to push him outward by

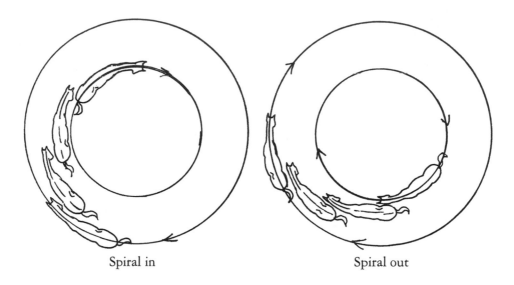

Spiral in   Spiral out

"cranking" his neck with a strong inside indirect rein; use your inside leg at the girth instead.

The horse must keep the same bend while spiraling in and out.

Haunches-In (Travers)

In the haunches-in (or travers), the horse remains bent around the rider's inside leg, but moves *in the direction of the bend*. His front legs remain on the track, and he looks in the direction in which he is going, while his hindquarters are carried slightly to the inside. Like the shoulder-in, haunches-in is a collecting and suppling movement, which develops the strength and carrying power of the horse's hind legs, and his ability to carry weight on his hindquarters.

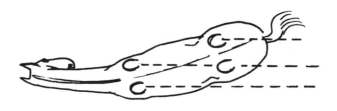

Haunches-in (travers)

The aids for the haunches-in are positioned the same as in the shoulder-in, but the emphasis is different. The outside leg, behind the girth, pushes the outside hind leg inward, under the body, while the inside hind leg maintains the bend, asking the horse to soften his ribs and to engage his inside hind leg. The inside rein (indirect rein, in the direction of the horse's outside hip) asks the horse to keep looking straight down the track, and the outside rein regulates the bend.

When starting to ride haunches-in, it helps to begin with a 10-meter circle. As you complete the circle, use your inside leg and rein to keep the bend, while your outside leg asks the hindquarters to stay to the inside as the horse moves down the track. Don't ask for too much bend at first, and be careful not to overdo haunches-in, especially in horses that have a tendency to move crookedly with their hindquarters to the inside.

TURN ON THE HAUNCHES

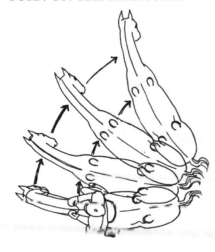

Aids for turn on the haunches:

- Outside leg behind girth (prevents hindquarters from swinging out)

- Outside supporting rein (regulates bend and forward movement)

- Inside seat bone

- Inside leg at girth (asks for bend, engagement, and activity of inside hind leg)

- Inside rein (maintains bend, leads forehand in direction of turn)

Turns on the Haunches and Half-Pirouettes

The turn on the haunches is a schooling movement which may be executed at the halt or walk. The forehand moves in even, regular steps around the horse's inside hind leg, maintaining the rhythm of the walk, and the horse bends in the direction of the turn. In the turn on the haunches, the horse's hind legs may move in a small circle, with the horse moving slightly forward.

In the pirouette (an advanced movement, performed in collected walk or canter), the horse's hind feet are lifted and set down nearly "on the spot" as the horse turns. Turns on the haunches and pirouettes may be executed as quarter turns (90 degrees), half turns (180 degrees), or full turns (360 degrees).

Turns on the haunches prepare the horse for pirouettes, which are more advanced movements, executed in a collected gait. In a pirouette, the inside hind leg should be raised and set down on the same spot, in the regular rhythm of the gait.

Turn on the haunches. The horse bends in the direction of the turn. (Balance of both horse and rider could be improved if the rider looked up and ahead.) *Photo: C. H. Hamilton III*

Faults in the turn on the haunches include: backing up; losing the rhythm of the gait, pivoting on the inside hind leg; uneven, hurried, or irregular steps; and failure to bend in the direction of the turn.

Turn on the Haunches in Motion   This is a variation of the turn on the haunches. It can be executed in walk, trot, or canter, while the turn on the haunches is performed only at a halt or in walk. The forelegs move around the hind legs, which describe a small circle; the horse is bent in the direction of the turn.

The advanced form is called "passade" (a turn on the haunches executed as a half-volte, or a half-circle of 6 meters). It is an intermediate step between the turn on the haunches and the pirouette.

Turn on the haunches in the walk. The front legs move around the hind legs, which describe a small circle, maintaining the rhythm of the walk. The rider demonstrates correct aids.
Photo: C. H. Hamilton III

The aids are the same as for the turn on the haunches. When beginning this turn, start with a large circle and ask for only a few steps at a time. Be careful to maintain the balance and the rhythm of the steps, and not to overbend the horse to the inside.

This movement can be used to increase the engagement and "carrying power" of the inside hind leg, when working toward pirouettes, renvers, and half-pass, and to improve balance and control for jumping turns at the canter.

Renvers (Haunches-Out, Tail to the Wall)

Renvers, or haunches-out, is the same as haunches-in (travers), except that the horse moves with his hindquarters on the track and his shoulders toward the inside of the arena. He is bent around the rider's inside leg, and looks in the direction of the movement. ("Inside" refers to the bend, *not* to the center of the arena.)

The aids are the same as for haunches-in; only the horse's position in relation to the track differs.

Renvers, like haunches-in, is a collecting movement that supples and straightens the horse. The renvers is more difficult than the travers or haunches-in because the horse does not have the rail or wall next to his shoulder as a reference point. Don't ask for too much bend or too many steps at first, especially if the horse finds the movement difficult. Renvers is a good exercise for horses that tend to travel with their hindquarters carried to the inside.

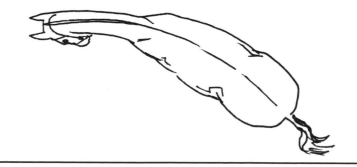

Renvers (haunches out)

HALF-PASS

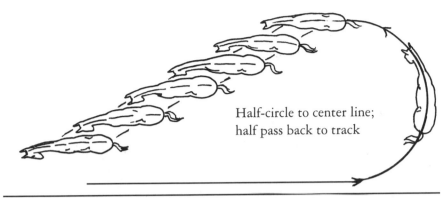

Half-circle to center line;
half pass back to track

Aids for half-pass:
- Outside leg behind girth (asks for lateral movement of hind leg)
- Outside supporting rein (regulates bend and forward movement)
- Inside seat bone
- Inside leg at girth (maintains bend and activity of inside hind leg)
- Inside rein (maintains bend and leads forehand in direction of movement)

Half-Pass

Half-pass is a lateral movement executed on the diagonal, instead of along the wall. The horse moves forward and sideways at each step, remaining parallel to the long side of the arena, with his forehand leading slightly. As in haunches-in and travers, the horse is bent slightly in the direction of the movement, around the rider's inside leg. (*Don't* confuse half-pass with leg-yielding!)

In the shoulder-in, the inside hind leg provides most of the thrust. In half-pass, the outside hind leg must step under and propel the horse forward and sideways. The half-pass helps the horse engage his hindquarters and gather himself. After a half-pass, you can take advantage of the increased engagement of the outside hind leg by straightening the horse and using the extra impulsion of the hindquarters to send the horse energetically forward.

To prepare for a half-pass, ride a 10-meter half-circle to the center line. Maintain the same bend and apply the same bending aids (inside leg at the girth, outside leg behind the girth, inside rein leading the forehand toward the inside, and outside rein supporting and controlling the bend), but shift a little more weight onto your inside seat bone. Don't lean, twist, or collapse one hip; use repeated outside leg aids to send the outside hind leg forward and sideways. Keep the horse parallel to the track, with the forehand slightly ahead of the hindquarters. If he begins to lose his bend or rhythm, or if his hindquarters begin to get ahead of his forehand, ride straight forward.

Half-pass, left to right. The horse shows good balance, lateral reach, and harmony between horse and rider, but should be bent more to the right. *Photo: C. H. Hamilton III*

Faults in the half-pass include loss of rhythm, short, stiff steps, haunches leading, falling in with the inside shoulder, and losing the bend to the inside.

CHAPTER 3

Riding over Fences

THE JUMPING SEAT

The jumping seat is similar to the dressage seat in some ways, and different in others. Good flat work is essential to good jumping, whether schooling a green horse, getting a good performance from an experienced horse, or solving problems in horse or rider.

Light Seat

The light seat is a seat halfway between the dressage seat and the jumping seat. It is useful in schooling jumping horses on the flat and over cavaletti and gymnastics, when you frequently change from flat work to jumping, for hacking and cross-country riding, and for riding young horses whose backs are not yet developed enough to carry the rider in a dressage seat. It offers security but allows you to be light on the horse's back.

In a light seat, your seat bones stay in contact with the saddle, but your upper body is angled slightly forward. This places more of your weight on your thighs, knees, and stirrups, and lessens the pressure of your seat bones in the saddle. Your stirrups should be shorter than dressage length (at the ankle point), but not as short as for jumping larger fences.

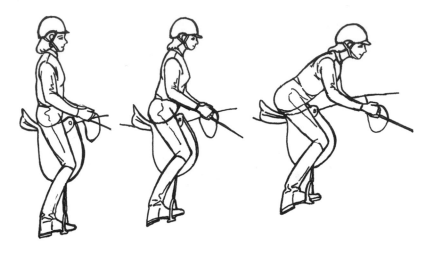

Dressage seat   Light seat   Jumping seat

Jumping Seat

The jumping seat is the position used over fences. It is in no way a rigid, "posed" position; the rider's position changes to adapt to the balance of the horse at the moment. In jumping, shorter stirrups are necessary for balance and security; they create greater angles at the ankle, knee, and hip joints. These angles help absorb the thrust of the takeoff and the shock of landing, and allow you to stay in balance.

The legs remain in place against the horse's side, but the upper body angle changes to go with the movement and balance of the horse. As in all seats, the rider's angles must be balanced: feet under the center of balance, with stirrup leathers vertical. The hips and seat are behind this vertical line; the head, shoulders, and knees are ahead of it.

The seat can be divided into four parts: lower leg, base of support, upper body, and arms and hands. All parts must work together to create a functional whole.

Lower Legs

General   Lower legs and feet must be placed under the center of the body, with stirrup leathers vertical. While the joints and angles of the legs must be flexible, they should remain securely in place on the horse's sides, even when the upper body angle changes.

Stirrup Placement   Stirrup irons are placed under the ball of the foot (at the balance point of the foot). Irons should be perpendicular to the horse's side, crossing the foot at an angle. The angle of the foot depends on rider's conformation; approximately same angle as that of rider's knees and thighs.

Feet and Ankles   Heels must be down, but must sink downward and backward, not pushed down and forward or jammed down, locking the ankles. Ankles must flex under the rider's weight, and absorb thrust and shock. They should not be rolled inward or outward; both cause stiffness.

Calves   They must be stretched down and back, inner calf in contact with horse.

Knees   Knees should be flexible, not pinching; gripping knees cause pivoting, unsteady lower legs.

Stirrup Length   Correct stirrup length for jumping varies with the size of the jumps. At the basic adjustment (for ordinary jumping, up to 3'), the stirrup should hang to the point of the ankle bone. Stirrups should be raised one hole for each foot the fences are increased in height.

Distribution of Contact   Contact should be distributed equally among inner thigh, inner knee, and inner calf (excessive grip with one part makes the others loose).

Base of Support (Thighs, Seat, and Pelvis)

Seat   Weight more toward the front of the seat bones than in other seats. Shorter stirrups result in seat suspended over the seat of the saddle, but seat bones should remain close to the saddle (not forward over pommel).

Distribution of Weight   In three-point contact, weight is distributed between inner thighs and seat bones. In two-point contact, weight is distributed between inner thighs and knees; seat bones are clear of saddle.

Upper Body

- Hip joints: open and close freely; hip joints control the angle between the upper body and the legs.
- Back: flat, straight (neither excessively hollow nor rounded).
- Chest: carried high and open (not contracted at upper chest and collar bones).
- Shoulders: Shoulders and collar bones hang wide and freely over ribs (shoulders not hunched, rounded, or contracted).
- Head and eyes: Eyes look ahead to focal point over center of fence. Head balanced (not looking down or tilted to side).

Arms and Hands

- Straight line from elbow to bit: important for contact and correct release. May be broken upward, but not downward.
- Upper arms: move freely from shoulder joints; close to body.
- Elbows: flexible; close to the body. Elbows out indicates too-long reins, flat hands, and tension in upper arms, shoulders, and chest.

Jumping with good form and balance. Rider demonstrates good angles at ankle, knee, hip, and upper body, but line from elbow to bit is broken slightly upward. *Photo: Hamilton*

- Wrists: straight.
- Hands: holding reins in a soft fist, with fingers closed (open fingers can lose grip on the reins or can be sprained). Knuckles between vertical and 30 degrees inside vertical.

The Rider's Angles

In jumping, the angles of your legs and body work together to absorb the thrust of takeoff and the shock of landing, and enable you to control your position and balance. The major angles are the ankle, knee, and hip joints, which control leg and body position and balance; and the shoulder and elbow joints, which control hand and arm placement, contact, and release.

These angles must close and open automatically, almost like a reflex, as your horse jumps. Correct angles depend on correct stirrup length, a balanced position, and freedom from excessive muscle tension, which locks the joints and causes you to compensate with position faults such as rounding the back.

Jumping without stirrups, showing good form, balance, and excellent leg position. *Photo: Hamilton*

Gymnastics develop your ability to use your angles correctly and to allow the horse to close and open your angles as he jumps.

Half-Halts in Light Seat and in Jumping Seat

Half-halts can be used in a light seat and in a jumping seat, as well as in a dressage seat. A jumping rider must be able to use half-halts effectively to call for the horse's attention, to rebalance, to shorten stride, and to engage the hindquarters. However, the way you half-halt must help your horse's jumping, not interfere with it.

Half-halts are most effective in a light seat, because your seat bones are in contact with the saddle.

Here are three types of jumping half-halts:

HALF-HALTS IN JUMPING SEAT

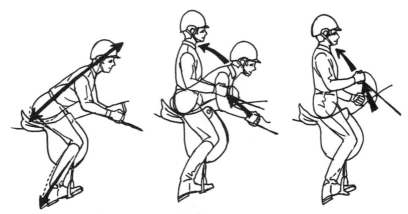

Lengthening spine   Opening hip angle   Opening hip angle with
in half-seat   upward lift on one rein

Half-Halt in Half-Seat   Your seat bones sink back and downward, as your spine briefly lengthens, *keeping the same body angle;* your legs stay under you, sinking back and down into your stirrups and your horse's sides. This half-halt rebalances you while going forward, and calls for the same response from your horse. It can be used in a half-seat or a light seat, when galloping, or during an approach, when sitting back too much could put you in danger of being left behind.

Opening the Body Angle (Sitting Up) Your body angle opens at the hip joints, and your shoulders come back over your seat, as you "sit up" momentarily into a more vertical position, as your legs sink back and down under your seat and into your horse's sides, and your hands momentarily "check" (resist or hold). This is a more powerful half-halt, acting on your horse's back and hindquarters. It is effective in balancing for turns, shortening stride, and engaging your horse's hindquarters. Caution: Misusing this half-halt, especially right before a fence, can put you behind your horse and cause you to be left behind when he jumps.

Half-Halt with Lifting Rein The most powerful half-halt, it combines sitting up (opening the body angle) with an upward lift on one rein. The rein (usually the outside rein) is lifted *briefly* upward (not pulling backward); this changes the action of the bit upward into the corner of the mouth and encourages the horse to raise his head and neck. This half-halt acts strongly on the horse's back, hindquarters, and head and neck, for maximum response in rebalancing and "coming back." It is used as an emergency aid, to rebalance a strong, heavy horse that leans on the forehand, and to correct a horse that bucks, bolts, or hangs toward the in-gate or the stable. Caution: This half-halt must be used with good judgment, or it can spoil the horse's mouth and training.

Releases over Fences

A correct release allows your horse to make a good jumping effort, stretching his head and neck in a good bascule, while allowing you to stay in control. You should ride with a correct automatic release most of the time, but must be able to use other releases correctly when the situation requires it. (See USPC C Manual Chapters 1–3.)

Automatic Release (Jumping on Contact, Following through the Air) For control and communication during the jump and immediately after; turning in the air or on landing; correcting horses that drift in the air or require extra control on landing.

Note: The most advanced release; if not executed correctly, it can interfere with the horse's jumping efforts and cause poor jumping and loss of confidence.

Bridge For extra support when jumping cross-country, especially banks, drops, and downhill fences; gymnastics; galloping fences.

Automatic release: The rider keeps a light, steady contact, with a straight line from elbow to bit. (However, slightly too-long reins have caused her to overflex her elbows in order to maintain contact.) *Photo: Hamilton*

Note: Rein length, length of bridge, and hand placement are important. Can restrict rider's ability to move one hand sideways (leading rein).

Short Crest Release   Intermediate step between long crest release and automatic release; provides support for rider's hands and arms and prevents interference with horse's mouth; for verticals, turns in the air, or on landing; drop or downhill fences; basic and intermediate riders.

Note: Rein length, hand placement, closed fingers are important. Rider must *not* "drop" horse by releasing before takeoff.

Long Crest Release   For maximum freedom of horse's head and neck over wide oxers, gymnastics, certain exercises when schooling green horses, or reschooling horses that have been overrestricted when jumping; as an exercise for beginning jumping riders, or a corrective exercise for certain rider problems.

Note: Rein length, placement of hands, keeping fingers closed, and pressing firmly forward and down with forearms are important. Rider must remain balanced over saddle and reach with arms, must *not* lunge forward or lie down on the neck. Rider must *not* "drop" horse by releasing before takeoff.

Long Crest Release, Holding Mane or Neckstrap   For beginning jumping riders; in emergency situations (if left behind, to prevent jerking on the mouth).

Note: This release affords the least control, and should rarely be used by advanced riders.

Releases: Special Techniques

Driving Hold for Automatic Release   A special way of holding the reins, which can help you follow the balancing gestures of the horse's head and neck more accurately, and develop a better automatic release when jumping on contact. The rein comes into the hand between the thumb and first finger, with the end of the rein coming out of the little finger. Keep your wrists straight and allow the horse to stretch your arms and elbows forward as his neck and head stretch out and down over a vertical, spread, or gymnastic jumping line.

The driving hold is not as effective as a normal rein hold in controlling the horse on the approach, but it is an excellent exercise for advanced riders.

Slipping the Reins   An emergency measure used to keep from interfering with the horse in the event of a peck or stumble, if the rider is left behind, and sometimes on drop fences. The rider keeps his position (or in case of a peck, stumble, or extremely steep descent, may even lean back).

Driving hold helps rider refine technique of following horse's head and neck gestures

Slipping the reins

Knot in end of reins

To slip the reins, open your fingers and allow the horse to pull the reins through as far as necessary, even to the buckle. On landing, you must quickly gather your reins and readjust them to a normal length. Because of the delay and temporary loss of control this causes, slipping the reins should be reserved for emergencies.

In situations where the need to slip the reins may arise (jumping cross-country or steeplechasing), the end of the rein should be tied in a knot, so that the reins cannot part at the buckle if you should slip them to their full length.

TYPES OF OBSTACLES AND THEIR EFFECTS

Vertical Fences

Vertical fences require a short, high jump, with accuracy and balance. The horse must jump up and "curl around" a vertical, and must jump cleanly. Large verticals are usually jumped best from a collected stride. Balance, impulsion, and accurate distance are especially important, and the pace should not be too fast. It is easier to turn in the air or to jump at an angle over verticals than over spread fences.

Because a vertical fence encourages a horse to shorten his stride and jump with a shorter arc, the horse may land close to the fence, which increases the distance to the next fence.

TYPES OF OBSTACLES AND JUMPING ARCS

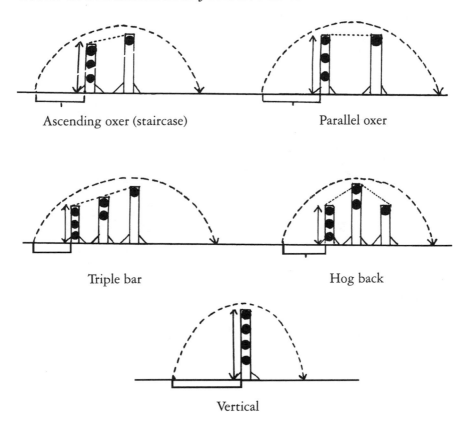

Ascending oxer (staircase)   Parallel oxer

Triple bar   Hog back

Vertical

Spread Fences

Spreads require a longer, wider jump with greater scope. The horse must extend himself to jump out and across a spread fence, which requires scope and power, and results in a longer arc. The rider must be careful not to restrict the reach of the horse's head and neck, which helps him extend his forelegs, or to sit down and cause him to drop his hind legs too early. When jumping a spread, a horse tends to lengthen his stride and may "flatten out" and get on the forehand; this uses up ground and may cause the distance to the next fence to "ride short."

Most horses jump spreads best from a slightly lengthened, powerful stride. It is unwise to jump a spread fence from a long takeoff spot, as this adds to the width of the fence and increases the chances of hitting the back rail.

The horse jumps with a good bascule over an ascending oxer.
Photo: Hamilton

Spread fences with height as well as width demand scope, power, and a clean, careful jumper. The horse must get his forehand and front legs up enough to clear the first element, must extend himself enough to get across the spread, and must fold up his hind legs to clear the back rail. The rider must ride a bold but accurate approach, and must stay off the horse's back and avoid interfering with him throughout the jump.

Rider interference, jumping high but not wide enough, or miscalculating the takeoff and descending early can cause a horse to jump into a spread. For safety, the last element of a spread may only be a single pole.

There are many types of spread fences, with different characteristics:

- Ascending oxer (step oxer, staircase): the easiest spread; its upward sloping shape gives the horse more time to fold his legs, while the back rail is easily seen. An inviting fence for green horses.
- Triple bar: like ascending oxers, the upward sloping shape allows more time to fold the legs. The width of a triple bar tends to encourage horses to land with a long stride.
- Hog's back: the shape of the fence encourages a round arc and a good bascule. A hog's back must never be built so that the back rail is obscured.

- Parallel oxer (front and back elements same height): requires a more powerful jump with extra scope, as if there were a higher rail at the center of the spread. The horse must fold front and hind legs equally well, and jump both elements carefully.
- Square oxer (equal width and height): the most difficult type of oxer, requiring a big, powerful jump with scope, width, and height. Requires good folding of both front and hind legs.
- Swedish oxer (cross oxer): if jumped in the exact center, it is similar to a parallel oxer, with front and back elements the same height. If jumped at a point where the first element is lower than the back elements, it creates an ascending spread. This is an imposing fence that requires scope and accuracy.

Spreads with Water

Water Jump   A wide, shallow ditch or artificial pool filled with water, usually with a small, slanting brush fence on the takeoff side. The far edge is marked by a white board. Sometimes a single rail is placed over the middle of the water, which encourages the horse to jump it properly.

WATER OBSTACLES

Liverpool triple bar

Water jump with small brush and pole over water

Water jump

True water jumps are spreads with little or no height. The horse should take off close to the edge, so as not to make the spread wider. They are usually jumped best from a slightly lengthened stride, but the horse must stay in balance and not fall on his forehand. The rider must allow the horse freedom to stretch fully over the water, but must *not* drop contact before takeoff, which can cause a refusal.

Liverpool A spread built over water, it is primarily a mental test; a liverpool is no more demanding than an ordinary ascending spread of the same dimensions, but it is imposing in appearance. However, an inexperienced horse or rider may look down into the ditch or water, which is distracting and can cause a refusal. You must ride positively, have the horse well in front of the legs, and *not* drop contact on the approach. Liverpools should be jumped from a slightly lengthened, powerful stride with the horse well in hand, not from a flat, over-extended stride.

Types of Obstacles in Combinations

The types of obstacles in a combination affect the way a combination "rides" because of their characteristic arcs, takeoff and landing points, and their effects on the horse's stride. Various combinations of obstacles may require extra balance, accuracy, or ability to shorten or lengthen stride.

The distances between elements of a combination are critical. A distance that is too difficult for the horse or rider, or made tricky by the type or size of obstacles, is dangerous. Start with two-stride combinations set with "easy" distances, adjusted to fit the horse's natural stride; this gives the horse some margin for error. You should only increase the difficulty of the obstacles and/or the distances when you are sure of the horse's (and the rider's) capability and confidence.

The distances given in the following examples are average distances for a 16-hand horse with a 12-foot stride, jumping fences approximately 3'3" to 3'7". You must know your own horse's ability, characteristics, and length of stride, and adjust distances accordingly.

Vertical to Vertical This combination requires balance, engagement, and accuracy. The horse must land and rebalance, and take a medium-short, round, well-balanced stride to jump the second element clean. If he lands short or loses impulsion after the first element, he may have to take an extra long stride and may take off too far back or jump flat at the second vertical. It is important to rebalance immediately on landing.

DISTANCES IN COMBINATIONS WITH VARIOUS TYPES OF OBSTACLES

		One stride	Two strides
Vertical-vertical		24'–26'	34'6"–36'
Vertical-staircase		23'–25'	34'–35'6"
Vertical-parallel		23'6"–25'	34'6"–35'6"
Staircase-vertical		24'6"–25'	34'6"–36'
Staircase-staircase		22'6"–24'6"	33'6"–35'6"
Staircase-parallel		23'–24'6"	34'–35'6"
Parallel-vertical		24'6"–25'6"	34'6"–35'6"
Parallel-staircase		22'6"–24'	33'–35'
Parallel-parallel		23'–24'6"	34'–35'

Vertical to Oxer   The horse must land from the vertical in balance but going forward with a driving stride to jump the spread successfully. If he lands short, loses impulsion, or falls on his forehand, he will have trouble adjusting his stride to take off accurately, but with scope enough to clear the oxer. A wider oxer or one with height and spread make this more difficult.

Oxer to Vertical   This combination demands excellent balance control. The oxer encourages the horse to land with a long stride, possibly on the forehand; he must rebalance quickly and may have to shorten stride to be ready to jump up and "curl around" the vertical.

Oxer to Oxer   Requires scope, balance, and accuracy. The first oxer may encourage the horse to land on the forehand; you must rebalance without overshortening his stride, and take off accurately but with power enough to clear the oxer.

Unusual Fences

Airy Fences   Fences without a ground line, or with little or no "filler," are difficult to judge. The horse must be attentive and careful, and must be ridden positively to a good takeoff distance. Horses may overjump these fences or may "dwell" (hesitate) in the air, which can affect the distance to the next fence.

Spooky or Unusual Fences   Spooky or unusual fences command a horse's attention, and tend to make him "back off," shorten stride, and jump high and short, or even refuse. They must be ridden positively but not too fast, with the horse well in front of the legs. Dropping the contact can cause a refusal or a hesitant, awkward jump.

GRIDWORK AND GYMNASTICS

Gymnastic jumping and ground poles (also called gridwork) can help to develop a horse's coordination, accuracy, and a good jumping style, and correct certain problems. It also focuses the horse's attention, steadies his stride, and can be used for variety and to keep him interested.

Riders benefit from gymnastics too, especially in rhythm, balance, timing, and confidence. Advanced riders should ride gymnastics without stirrups, to develop a secure seat and leg, and automatic timing.

Basic gymnastics (including distances for horses and ponies) are covered in the C-1, C-2, and C-3 jumping sections of the USPC C Manual.

General Considerations

Gymnastics can only accomplish their purpose if they are safe and suitable for the needs and level of horse and rider. They must be properly constructed and accurately measured, and must use suitable obstacles and ground poles that will not roll under a horse's foot and cause an accident. "X"-type cavalettis must not be used, because the danger of injury to riders and horses, and unused cups should be removed from standards. Poles should be substantial and easy to see, and standards and obstacles must not be capable of trapping a horse's leg.

You will need one or more dismounted helpers to adjust poles, obstacles, and distances for gymnastic exercises.

Horses should wear bell boots (some also need exercise bandages or galloping boots) for gymnastics and pole work, because of the increased possibility of overreaching. As in all jumping, the rider should check his stirrup length, girth, helmet, and chin strap before beginning gridwork.

Gymnastic jumping is more physically demanding than it appears, because it requires multiple efforts and intense concentration. Horse and rider must be well warmed up first. Be aware of the horse's (and rider's) fitness and fatigue level, and *stop* jumping before performance and/or attitude begin to deteriorate.

Gymnastics and ground poles should be approached in a slow but impulsive trot or canter. A fast, uneven, or unbalanced approach increases the chances of mistakes and magnifies problems. When possible, grids or gymnastics should be set so that they can be approached from the left or the right, alternating directions.

Ground Pole Work

Ground poles can be used for attention and variety, to stabilize the stride, improve suppleness, increase activity, and to teach the horse to adjust his strides. They are also used in connection with jumps to teach the horse to take off at the right distance and to jump straight. Quiet work over and around ground poles can help to relax a horse that tends to rush fences.

In these examples, spacing is based on a 16-hand horse with an average stride. You must adjust the spacing to fit your horse's stride, so that his feet fall in the middle of the spaces between the poles. Poles should be 10 to 12 feet long and 3 or 4 inches in diameter.

Ground pole exercises:

- Random poles: place poles at random around ring; ride over poles in all gaits, on straight lines and at angles; ride poles as a "course." Develops relaxation and obedience in green horses and horses that tend to rush poles or fences.
- Walk grid (4 to 6 poles, 3' to 3'6" apart):
  - Walk through, alternating directions.
  - Raise poles to 6 inches, for more roundness and greater bending of joints of hind legs.
- Trotting grid (6 poles 4' to 4'6" apart):
  - Trot straight through, alternating directions.
  - Raise poles to 6 inches, for more impulsion and roundness.
- Trotting grid (6 poles 8 to 9 feet apart):
  Above exercises, plus:

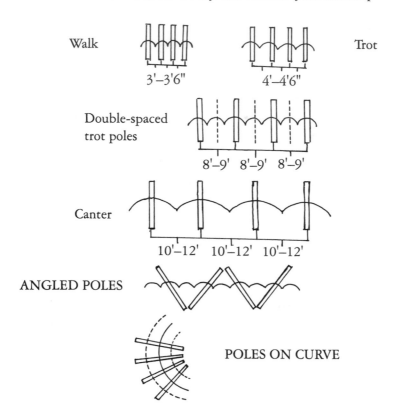

- Circles or figure 8s over alternate poles (in walk).
- Ride serpentine between poles (in walk).
- Circles over pairs of poles (in trot).
- Ride angled line through grid, lengthening stride in trot.
- Cantering ground poles (both directions):
  - Canter grid (6 poles 10 to 12 feet apart): Canter straight through in light seat, allowing horse to "rock" you over each pole.
  - Canter pole(s) on circle: Canter 20-meter circle with single pole, looking ahead to the next quarter point. Add a second pole halfway around the circle. Good for steady stride, correct distances, suppleness, and balance.
- Poles on a curve (center of poles 4'3" apart):
  - Ride curve at inside in walk, with accurate bend so horse steps into center of each space (both directions).
  - Ride curve at center in trot (both directions).
  - Ride curve slightly outside of center, in trot with longer strides. Don't ask for longer stride than horse can do well!

EXERCISES USING GROUND POLES

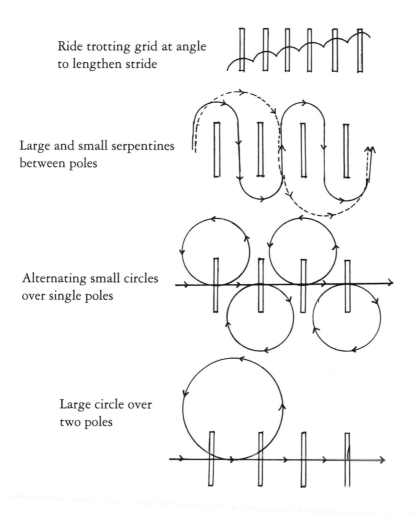

Ride trotting grid at angle
to lengthen stride

Large and small serpentines
between poles

Alternating small circles
over single poles

Large circle over
two poles

Ground poles in connection with fences:

- Trot poles to small fence (cross-rail), or before gymnastic: three to six ground poles spaced at 4'6"; takeoff distance (last ground pole to base of fence) equals twice the trot pole distance (9 feet).
- "Three-way" trot poles to fence or gymnastic: Three trot pole grids (spaced as above); center grid leads to fence or grid, with additional grid angled to each side. Rider may choose to angle right or left over trot poles, or go straight over grid and fence. Good for turning and for horses that anticipate or rush fences.

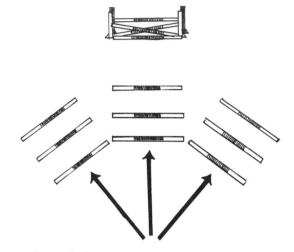

Three-way trot poles with fence

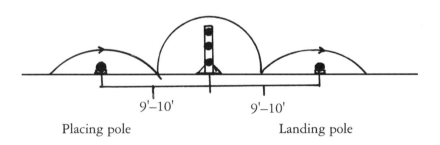

9'–10'   9'–10'

Placing pole   Landing pole

- Placing pole: Ground pole placed approximately 9 feet (correct distance varies) in front of fence. Horse steps over ground pole and arrives at correct takeoff spot.
- Landing pole: Ground pole placed 9 to 10 feet (correct distance varies) from fence on landing side. Horse must look at landing spot, adjust his landing, and rebalance over pole. Helps to develop bascule and balance on landing, and discourages rushing after the fence. Also teaches rider to rebalance on landing.
- Guide Pole: Ground pole placed perpendicular to fence, on takeoff and/or landing side, to prevent a horse from drifting to one side during approach, in the air, or on landing. A chute (two guide poles placed about 6 feet apart) may be used to keep the horse straight on approach. Do not use a chute on the landing side, as there is a danger of the horse landing on one of the poles.

Exercises for Straightness and Turns

Ideally, a horse should jump each fence straight over the center, turn in either direction, and land on either lead with equal ease. He should also fold his legs evenly, without "dropping a leg," twisting, or drifting to one side, as these can cause him to hit a fence. Horses that habitually jump crookedly may be trying to spare a weak or unsound leg; they should be checked by a veterinarian.

Exercises for the crooked or uneven jumper include:

- Guide poles or a chute on the ground before a fence.
- Single guide pole (not a chute) on landing side of fence.
- Angled poles (angled against the top rail as an inverted "V").
- Jumping fences on an angle (away from horse's preferred direction).
- Jumping fences on a curve or circle; turning in the air.

Gymnastic Distances

Distances between the elements of a gymnastic affect the horse's length of stride, takeoff point, balance, and rhythm. The distance can make a gymnastic easy, difficult, or impossible. A small variation in distance (as little as 6 inches per stride) can make a big difference in difficulty. Distances should be accurately measured, not estimated by "eye" or by pacing them off.

A distance may be "easy," short, or long. An "easy" distance is tailored to the horse's natural stride, considering the size and type of obstacles, and the jumping arc they produce. Easy distances develop confidence (in horse and rider) and confirm the habit of taking off at the correct spot.

Short distances require the horse to shorten his stride and maintain his balance between fences. They encourage a horse to jump "up and around" the fence, to be quick and careful with his front end, and to engage his hocks more. This results in a rounder jump with more power off the ground, a better bascule, and better folding of the forelegs. Shortened distances also help teach bold horses to wait and maintain their balance, and to jump with impulsion instead of speed.

Too short distances can be discouraging and even unsafe; horses may get in too close and hesitate or stop, and some horses will try to leave out a stride if the distance is too short for them.

EXERCISES TO CORRECT CROOKED JUMPING

Guide pole on landing

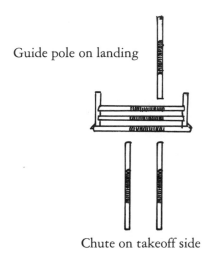

Chute on takeoff side

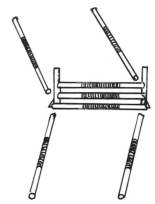

Chute on takeoff side with angled
poles on landing side to encourage
landing on designated lead

Open vee

Longer distances allow the horse room to lengthen his stride; they favor scope and a longer, flatter takeoff and jumping arc. However, a longer distance can also allow a horse to go on the forehand, increase his speed, and jump fast and flat, or "chip in" with an extra short stride. The rider must keep the horse in balance, maintain the rhythm, and get the horse to lengthen his stride correctly to prevent such problems.

Because of the effects of distances, green horses or horses (or riders) lacking in confidence need gymnastics with easy distances. The next step is to jump slightly shortened distances, to develop better balance, engagement, and jumping form. Long distances are used less, and must be adjusted and ridden correctly, to avoid developing undesirable habits.

APPROACHES TO FENCES

The approach to a fence determines how the horse will jump it. Good approaches demand good riding and control, which must be developed by proper schooling in flat work. To ride a good approach, you must be focused, organized, and ride with clear intent. Indecision, loss of concentration, or last-minute changes can upset and demoralize your horse, and lead to bad jumps, refusals, and loss of confidence.

The elements of an approach are: line, pace, impulsion, balance, and distance.

- *Line* is established by your eyes. It extends from the beginning of the approach, over the center of the fence, to a "target" or focal point. A line may be straight, angled, or curved, and may include more than one obstacle.
- *Pace* is the speed, rhythm, and tempo at which you jump. The pace must be appropriate for the horse, the jump, and the situation. Maintaining a regular and even pace is more efficient, smoother, and easier for the horse, and makes it easier to see distances and jump in stride.
- *Impulsion,* or energy and desire to go forward, is indispensable for jumping. The horse must be reliably "in front of your legs." Impulsion must be channeled into the best pace, rhythm, balance, and line, or it can degenerate into uncontrollable energy.
- *Balance* refers to the balance of both horse and rider. The horse must be in the right balance for the jump; you must be in balance with him, and influence his balance. Certain situations, such as jumping large verticals, sharp turns before or after the fence, uphill or downhill slopes, jumping at speed, or slippery footing, make good balance especially critical.

Lines of Approach

An approach may be straight, angled, or curved. Single fences and the first fence in a line are usually (but not always) ridden off a turn or an opening circle. When a fence is followed by a turn or a bending line to the next fence, line and rebalancing *after* the fence become critical. This is especially important when speed counts, as in a timed jumpoff.

Your inside and outside aids (both legs and both reins) create a "channel" that keeps the horse moving straight and accurately along your chosen line. Your aids must be ready to prevent or correct crookedness, sideways movement, drifting out, or falling in, while sending your horse forward in rhythm.

Straight Approach   A normal approach is a straight line for at least three strides before the fence, and leads directly over the center. Sometimes it is necessary to jump a fence at a point other than the center, in order to jump from good footing or for a better line to the next fence. Accuracy requires concentration and straightness.

Long, straight approaches (seven strides or longer) require good rhythm, timing, and the ability to keep a steady pace and *wait* for the jump. Many horses (and riders) tend to increase their pace, lean on the forehand, and hurry on a long approach, which can result in an overbold approach and an impossible distance.

Bending Approach   A bending approach is on an arc, bending line, or circle; you can adjust the distance by tightening or widening the arc. On a bending approach you must establish pace, rhythm, balance, and impulsion early. Your outside and inside aids are especially important, to keep your horse from bearing out, letting his hindquarters swing out, or falling in. Look ahead at the jump as you ride the curved line of the approach; over the jump, look ahead to where you are going.

This exercise develops your eye for a distance on a bending approach:

Set up a 25-meter circle, with "gates" (a pair of cones or standards) at three of the quarter points, and a pair of standards with a ground pole at the fourth. Canter the circle; as you pass through each gate, look ahead to the next. Ride each quarter as an even arc, using your aids to keep the pace even and prevent your horse from falling in or

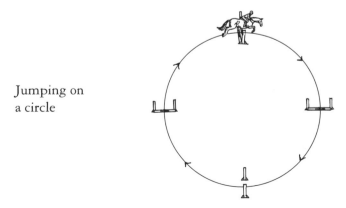

Jumping on
a circle

ANGLED APPROACH

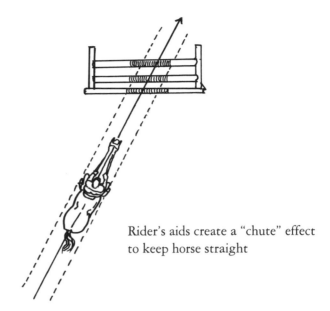

Rider's aids create a "chute" effect
to keep horse straight

bearing out. Work in each direction, then raise the fence to a cross-rail, then a simple vertical. This exercise teaches you to jump "automatically" as you look ahead to the next fence, and prepares you and your horse for turning in the air.

Angled Approach   An angled approach follows a line that crosses the fence at an angle. It is used to save ground, or to line up for the next fence. Because an angled approach can invite a runout, it must be ridden very accurately and positively. Choose a focal point to aim for, and define your line clearly, using leg and rein aids on both sides to "channel" the horse straight along the line. The pace should be steady but not too fast. Impulsion, with the horse reliably in front of the legs, is essential.

LEADS AND JUMPING

Leads are important for balance and safety in turns and approaches.
    Although a horse can jump from either lead on a straight line, turning on the wrong lead handicaps his balance and maneuverability, and

can result in an inaccurate approach or even a fall. When a horse is on the correct lead, his inside hind leg is engaged well under him, and he can balance better through turns. On the wrong lead, his outside hind leg is farther forward, and he cannot turn as sharply or as fast. A disunited canter is worst of all; he is uncoordinated, on one lead in the hind legs and the other lead in front, and may bear out, break to a trot, or even fall if he tries to turn sharply.

Schooling for leads and lead changes in jumping depends on good flat work. The progressive steps are:

Canter Departs on Designated Lead, along the Rail and in the Open, without the Visual Aid of the Rail or a Corner   Establish correct lead on a circle before jumping at canter.

Improving Balance, Engagement, and Maneuverability in the Canter   Ride circles, turns, and figures of varying size, changing leads through the trot (later the walk) when changing direction. Increase and decrease the circle (in both directions). Ride approaches to fences from turns and circles.

Counter-Canter   Develops straightness, balance, and preparedness for flying changes. Practice counter-canter on straight lines and wide, easy turns before and after fences.

Landing on a Designated Lead   Start by trotting a fence on a circle; then trot the fence and canter away from it on the circle. Do it first in your horse's preferred direction, then in his harder direction.

Turning and Changing Leads over a Jump   Horses often change leads naturally over a jump, because the effort of lining up their hind

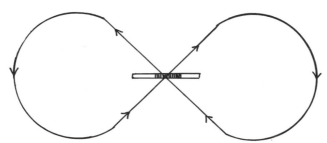

Figure-eight over pole or fence for flying change of leads

legs to jump often causes them to switch leads. You can jump a single vertical as a figure-eight exercise (see diagram), alternating leads.

Flying Change of Leads   The horse changes leads in the air, during the moment of suspension. The horse must change "clean" (hind legs and front legs both change at once) and smoothly, without bucking or speeding up. If he changes only in front, he will be disunited. Some horses will correct themselves and change behind in the next stride or two, but this doesn't always happen.

On an experienced horse, you must rebalance (half-halt), straighten the horse, then give the aids for the new lead:

- New outside leg, about 4 inches behind the girth.
- New inside leg, close to the girth.
- (New) outside supporting rein.
- (New) inside rein indicates direction (opening rein).
- Keep your weight in the center; *don't* lean sideways!

You must give the aids at the right time in the canter stride. Rebalance and straighten the horse on the "up" (as the forehand rises). Ask for the new lead on the "down" (as the head and neck reach out and down); the horse is going into the "jump" or suspension phase, and can change when all four feet are off the ground.

Flying change of leads

Never lean over the inside shoulder, pull the head sideways, or spur a horse roughly to try to make him change—this unbalances and upsets him, and can make him buck or rush off.

Flying changes come easily and naturally to some horses, and are more difficult for others. If a horse is green or awkward at changing leads, consider the following:

- You may be making it hard for him to change leads. Are you stiff, out of balance, or throwing your weight from side to side? Are you hanging on his mouth, or unclear with your aids or timing?
- Your horse may not be straight, balanced, or advanced enough in his canter work to do flying changes yet. Go back and review the previous canter work before asking for flying changes.
- He may need more impulsion and better engagement to make the change. If his canter is flat, lacking "jump," his back is hollow or he is "strung out" and disengaged, he cannot change leads.
- He may not understand what you want. Try making several simple changes (through the walk) at the same spot, gradually decreasing the number of walk steps to a single stride, then ask for the flying change in the same place. You can canter a figure 8 over a ground pole, giving the aids for the flying change when the horse is in the air over the pole. When he does change correctly, reward him immediately and generously, and *end the lesson!*

JUMPING TURNS

To turn accurately, a horse must engage his hind legs (especially the inside hind leg) well under his body, and must have balance and impulsion. Horses often slow down, lose impulsion, or become unbalanced during turns, which can lead to loss of time, a bad jump, a runout, or even a fall. Turns in jumping, especially at speed, require good riding and a horse made balanced and "turnable" by correct flat work.

Riding Jumping Turns

In a jumping turn, balance and engagement are all-important. If the horse is on the wrong lead, disunited, or on the forehand, his hind legs are not placed safely and surely, he lacks power, and worst of all, he can easily slip or even fall.

Lateral balance is important, too. It is natural for a horse making a fast turn to lean inward, but if he overdoes this, you can both lose your balance.

When a horse has trouble in a turn, he is likely to bear out (widen the turn), fall out through his outside shoulder, overbend in his neck, slow down, or break his rhythm and gait. All of these cost time, balance, and impulsion, and can spoil your approach to the next fence.

When riding jumping turns, your body balance, leg aids, and rein aids are all-important.

Seat and Balance   The tighter the turn, the more vertical you should be, from your feet to your head. This helps you use your weight and balance to keep your horse engaged and balanced. Turning your eyes and rotating your center in the direction of the line adjusts your balance, acts as a seat aid for turning, and makes your rein and leg aids more effective. Leaning excessively forward or inward can throw your horse onto his forehand and unbalance him.

Leg Aids   Your inside leg, close to the girth, asks your horse to engage his inside hind leg, to maintain impulsion, and not to fall inward. Your outside leg, stretched back and down, with the heel down, about 4 inches behind the girth, prevents the horse from bearing out or allowing his hindquarters to "skid" to the outside. Both legs help to maintain the bend and the canter lead, and keep your horse moving forward with impulsion.

Rein Aids   Both inside and outside reins must act together, in order to keep the horse moving forward along the line you have selected. The outside rein regulates the pace and is especially important to prevent bearing out or overbending the neck; the inside rein indicates the direction of the turn and asks for the bend. The inside rein can be used in a brief upward correction for a horse that falls in or leans on his inside shoulder.

Turning in the Air

Turning in the air can help you save ground, land on a particular lead, or get a better line to the next fence or turn. It is an important skill for riding jumpers or courses in which turning tightly or speed is a factor, and can also be used to correct a horse that drifts sideways or anticipates a turn on landing.

Start with a simple vertical fence (turning across a spread makes it wider, and increases the chances of hitting the back rail). Select your line carefully, and know exactly where you want your horse to go as he lands. A good beginning exercise is to set up a fence on a

Turning in the air

circle, placing pairs of cones or standards at the quarter points (see page 112).

To turn in the air:

- **Look** ahead, in the direction of the turn, toward your next focal point. Never look down, as this unbalances you.
- **Lead** the horse's head in the direction of the turn by applying an opening rein with your inside hand. Move your hand sideways (never backwards!); you may also rotate your inside hand briefly (as if "thumbing a ride"). The other hand releases normally (at first, you may need to rest the other hand on the horse's crest for support).
- **Shift** your weight *slightly* toward your inside knee, keeping the outside leg slightly back. Both legs should stay well under you, and your weight should shift only a little; if you allow your heel to come up or displace your weight too much, you become unbalanced and unsafe.

Roll-Back Turns

A roll-back turn is a short turn of 180 degrees or more. It is a variation of the turn on the haunches, performed at speed. The horse must engage both hind legs, but especially his inside hind leg, well under his body. His forehand swings around, making a wider circle than his hind legs, which turn in a very small circle. If he performs the turn well, he comes out of the turn with good balance, extra engagement, and

ROLL-BACK TURN

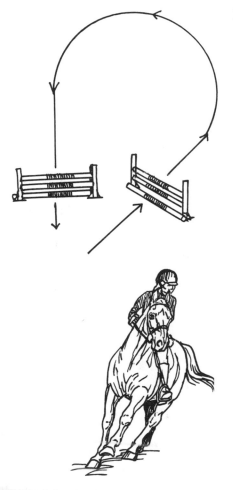

Riding a roll-back turn:
- Open hip angle (to maintain balance and increase effectiveness of aids)
- Look in direction of turn
- Outside leg behind girth (keeps haunches from "skidding" to outside)
- Outside supporting rein (regulates bend, prevents horse from bearing out through outside shoulder)
- Inside leg at girth (asks for engagement of inside hind leg, maintains impulsion)
- Inside rein (leads forehand in direction of turn)

power. If he loses engagement or his hind legs swing outward, he may bear out, lean over his inside shoulder, lose rhythm and engagement, or change to a disunited canter. All of these errors cost time, balance, and the ability to move forward and jump well.

To ride a roll-back turn, you must open your hip angle and sit up, with your seat bones in the saddle and your legs under your seat. Keep your outside leg back (with the heel down) to control the hindquarters, swivel your seat, and look in the direction of the turn. Your inside leg keeps the inside hind leg engaged. Use a firm outside rein to keep your horse from bearing out or overbending his neck, and use your inside rein to lead your horse through the turn. Although you must sit down and open your hip angle, be sure to stay in balance, and don't get left behind as your horse drives forward out of the turn.

A good exercise for roll-back turns is to ride a 15-meter half-circle in reverse (leave the track at an angle and turn back to the track). Ride this first in trot, then in canter (canter on the lead you will turn toward, after leaving the rail). Later, set a fence on the track and ride a roll-back turn to the fence.

Turning Problems

The following problems often crop up in jumping turns:

Loss of Impulsion, Slowing Down   This is how a horse protects himself when he is not balanced or athletic enough to turn properly, or if he senses indecisive or weak riding. Your legs (especially inside leg) maintain impulsion and engagement; you must use good judgment about how tightly your horse can turn, considering the footing, pace, and his experience and ability.

Bearing Out (Going Wide)   A horse bears out to avoid the difficulty of a tight turn, especially if he is unbalanced laterally, going too fast, or if his rider fails to use his outside aids effectively. To correct this, you must be in good balance (it helps to sit up straighter than usual), with an effective outside leg and outside supporting rein. Pulling the horse around with a strong inside rein often causes bearing out.

Falling in over the Inside Shoulder (Leaning In)   The horse loses his balance inward. This comes from lack of engagement of the inside hind leg, too much weight on the forehand, and often from bending to the outside; it can be caused by pulling the horse around with the reins with insufficient inside leg. The horse needs to engage his hind legs, rebalance himself, and "stand up" around the turn; this takes effective half-halts, inside leg at the girth, and sometimes a corrective upward lift on the inside rein.

Hindquarters "Skidding" to the Outside   The horse loses his balance inward, with inadequate engagement and too much weight on the forehand. He may "dig" with both hind legs together ("rabbit hopping"), instead of engaging his inside hind leg; this can cause him to

TURNING ERRORS

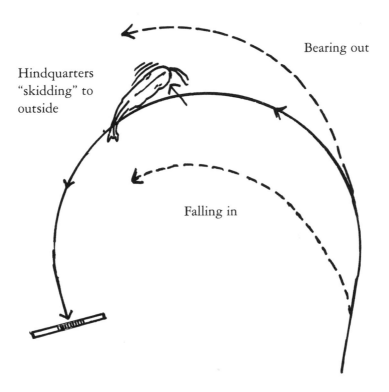

Bearing out

Hindquarters "skidding" to outside

Falling in

change to a disunited canter, slip, or even fall. It also costs speed, power, and balance.

Your outside leg, about 4 inches behind the girth, keeps the hindquarters in line and prevents them from skidding. Use effective half-halts, inside leg for better engagement, and sit up in a more vertical position on tight turns to control the hindquarters and turn in balance.

TYPES OF COURSES

Different types of courses are designed for various purposes, and test certain qualities in horses and riders. While you may or may not compete over all the following types of courses, you should understand their purpose and be able to ride appropriately over each (at a suitable height for the horse).

Hunter Courses

Hunter courses are designed for a smooth, flowing performance of the horse, demonstrating an even pace over fences simulating those found in the hunting field. In competition, the horse is judged on his performance, manners, and way of going. An even, steady pace, consistently good takeoff distances, good jumping style, long, low movement, and overall smoothness and ease of performance are paramount.

Hunter courses may be in the ring or over an outside course. There are usually about eight fences, simple verticals and spreads of moderate size. Typical hunter fences are natural rails, gates, walls, coops, brush, and logs. A hunter course typically includes a one or two-stride in-and-out (combination) and ascending oxers, but triple bars and square oxers are prohibited.

Because fences are set at standard distances (based on an average 12- or 13-foot stride), riders do not walk the course before competition, but ride it "off their eye."

Hunter seat equitation course

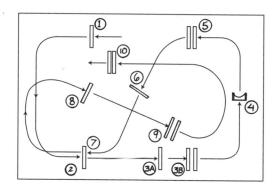

Working hunter course

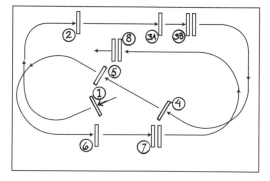

Equitation Courses

Equitation courses are designed to test the skills of the rider. In an equitation class, the rider is judged on his own and his horse's performance over the course, including correct takeoff distances, accurate lines and turns, form and style, and maintaining an even pace over the course. The rider must be both effective and smooth, with aids as subtle as possible.

Equitation courses may be held over hunter- or jumper-type obstacles, including verticals and spreads up to 3'6", one or more combinations and at least two changes of direction. Course designers include tests of technical ability (related distances, bending lines, and combinations), precision (narrow fences), and control (ability to lengthen and shorten stride smoothly, to ride a specific line, and to turn accurately). The horse is expected to be on the correct lead in all turns, so ability to land in the correct lead and execute smooth flying changes is important.

Show Jumping (Jumper) Courses

Show jumping classes are held over a course of show jumping obstacles, including verticals, spreads, double and triple combinations, and many turns and changes of direction. The purpose is to jump cleanly over a twisting course within a time allowed; jumping faults are incurred for knockdowns, disobedience, and time faults for exceeding the time allowed. Tied entries jump over a raised and shortened course; if entries are tied in the jumpoff, the fastest time wins. Riders walk both the course and the jumpoff course before a competition, to plan their ride.

Jumper courses are highly technical, requiring boldness, scope, power, accuracy, and control; speed is also a factor, especially in jumpoff courses and speed classes (in which time counts in the first round). A jumper must jump big, bravely, and fast, but he must also be careful and accurate to avoid knockdowns, and must be balanced and rideable in order to rate and turn accurately. A jumper rider must ride the best line to each fence, saving ground with well-planned turns and lines, and must adjust his horse's stride for each fence and distance, while avoiding knockdowns. In a jumpoff, he must balance the need to go as fast he can and turn as tight as possible, against his horse's ability to jump cleanly.

Show jumping
course

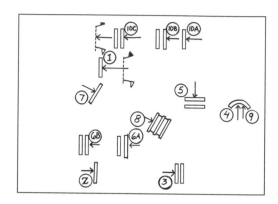

Timed jumpoff course
(dotted lines indicate
deleted obstacles)

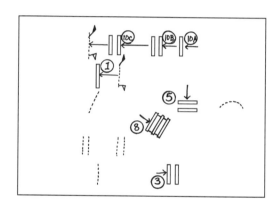

Stadium Jumping Courses (Combined Training)

Stadium jumping is the third phase of a combined training event. Its purpose is to demonstrate the horse's flexibility, suppleness, soundness, and rideability after the speed and endurance test.

The stadium jumping test is a single round over show jumping–style obstacles, with a maximum time allowed based on a standard pace appropriate for the level of competition. Knockdowns and disobediences incur penalty points. While exceeding the time allowed incurs penalty points, it is not a speed event, and there is no bonus for extra speed. There is no jumpoff; the penalty score is combined with the score from the other phases to determine a winner.

Stadium jumping courses are set in the open whenever possible, and often incorporate natural terrain features such as slightly rolling terrain. They are usually more open than a typical show jumping course, and slightly longer: about 400 to 500 meters, with 10 to 15 jumping efforts. Double and triple combinations may be included (depending on level), and obstacles incorporating banks, ditches, or water may be used. The fences are of medium size (usually smaller than show jumping fences), but the distances, turns, and design of the course require a supple, obedient horse and an accurate ride, while the time allowed requires a forward moving pace and accurate lines and turns.

A stadium course must be ridden at a suitable pace (325 to 350 meters per minute, depending on level of competition), staying within the time allowed while jumping a clean round.

CHAPTER 4

•••••••••••••••

Riding in the Open

REVIEW OF CROSS-COUNTRY FUNDAMENTALS

To ride and school safely in the open, over more demanding cross-country fences, a secure seat and effective control are crucial. The sound fundamentals that you have worked hard to develop in yourself and in your horse are your basis for galloping, jumping, and schooling over cross-country fences, and for activities such as combined training events, fox hunting, or hunter paces.

Safety

Safety is the first consideration when riding cross-country. Safety starts with good preparation of horse, rider, and equipment; it requires knowledge and solid skills; and most of all, it depends on good judgment and experience.

- *Never* ride or jump cross-country alone.
- Ride a horse you can control safely in this situation.
- Equipment: You need the right equipment, it must be in absolutely sound condition, and you must check each item for fit and security before you start.
  - ASTM/SEI safety helmet, properly fitted, with chin strap snugly fastened; safe and functional riding attire (see USPC D Manual

126

or *USPC Horse Management Handbook* for details). Some riders also prefer to wear a body protector. Because standards have not been established for body protectors as of 1995, the USPC does not currently require them. Nonslip gloves are important.

- Jumping-type whip (no wrist loop), spurs (blunt). Stopwatch is optional but useful.
- All-purpose, eventing, or jumping saddle, fitted to horse and rider.

An overgirth adds security, but must be put on correctly. Stirrup bars must be open and unobstructed by overgirth.

HORSE AND RIDER EQUIPPED FOR CROSS-COUNTRY JUMPING

Horse
- Jumping, all-purpose or event saddle
- Girth with split end and loops for overgirth
- Overgirth (placed so as not to restrict operation of safety stirrup bars)
- Breast collar
- Running martingale with rein stops (optional)
- Nonslip reins
- Noseband that does not restrict expansion of nostrils
- Galloping boots
- Bell boots
- Shoes and/or studs suitable for ground conditions

Rider
- ASTM/SEI helmet
- Long-sleeve or polo shirt
- Breeches
- Boots (blunt spurs optional)
- Nonslip gloves
- Stick (no wrist loop)

- Bridle properly fitted, with bit suitable for your horse for cross-country control. Nonslip reins, knotted at the end. Noseband must not interfere with expansion of the nostrils.
- Martingale or breastplate, if worn, correctly adjusted for your horse.
- Bell boots, galloping boots, or exercise wraps provide protection for your horse's legs.
- Check your horse's legs, feet, and shoes before riding cross-country.
- Be aware of footing, terrain, and ground conditions, and check the takeoff and landing before jumping an obstacle.
- Use good judgment about your own capabilities, those of your horse, and anyone riding with you. Be aware of your horse's fitness and fatigue level, and how he is feeling and performing.

Rider Fitness

You cannot gallop, jump, or school cross-country safely and effectively unless you are fit enough to ride well for as long as it takes to get the job done. Riding in a galloping position for any length of time is surprisingly tiring; your muscles must be strong, supple, and accustomed to doing their job, and you must be aerobically fit in order to take in enough oxygen. When you are unfit, you pant, your muscles ache, and your arms and legs feel like rubber; you become loose, unbalanced, and insecure, and your control and judgment deteriorate. Fitness is not just a matter of being competitive; it is essential for participating safely in this sport!

Cross-country riders need to be "riding fit" (muscles accustomed to this type of riding) and aerobically fit, (which may require fitness work in addition to riding). You must also use good judgment about what you can and should do at your present level of fitness.

Review of Seat and Position

The cross-country seat is adapted for galloping, negotiating natural terrain, and jumping solid fences at a cross-country pace. The most important factors are security, balance, and your ability to adjust for different speeds, obstacles, uphill and downhill, and natural conditions you may meet.

GOOD CROSS-COUNTRY POSITION

- Eyes up
- Shoulder over knee
- Hands low, using bridge
- Stirrups correct length
- Lower leg on horse's side
- Heels well down

WEAK, UNSAFE CROSS-COUNTRY POSITION

- Eyes down
- Standing up forward, over pommel
- Stirrups too long
- Reins too long; hands flat
- Knees pinching; lower leg slipping back
- Stirrup on toe; heels up

A good cross-country seat is fundamentally the same as a good basic jumping position, but there are some practical differences. Major points are:

- You must be able to ride in two-point contact (seat above the saddle), three-point contact (seat in the saddle), and a light seat (seat in the saddle with upper body angled forward), and be able to shift easily from one seat to another.
- Your feet and legs must stay underneath you, while your knee and hip angles open and close to adjust to the motion of jumping, galloping, and negotiating changes in terrain. Your stirrup leathers should stay vertical to the ground, even though your body angle

may change greatly. This is especially important in keeping your balance and absorbing shock when landing from a jump.

- To keep your legs safely under you, you need a secure, well-placed lower leg. Your inner knees and calves must lie firmly on your horse's side. They can only do this if your heel is well down and back, with your weight sinking into your ankles.
- In cross-country riding, the stirrup is placed just behind the ball of the foot, for extra security.
- The stirrups must be short enough to create the proper angles in your ankles, hips, and knees, and for you to ride in a good galloping position. Too long stirrups open your angles, causing your leg to pivot backward, and can lead you to stand up forward, lean on the horse's neck, and get ahead of your horse, all of which are dangerous! They also make it extremely difficult to control a strong horse at the gallop. Too short stirrups put you higher above your horse and may cramp your muscles, but it is better to ride a little too short than too long.

This rider shows confidence and a secure and effective cross-country seat, while allowing her horse freedom to use himself well. *Photo: Ed Lawrence*

- A cross-country rider must be in balance with his horse. Your horse can gallop and jump most easily when you are "with" him (your center of gravity is directly over his center of balance). However, it is safest to ride very slightly "in behind him," for security, balance, and control. This helps you to keep your horse in front of your legs, to keep him moving reliably forward and prevent hesitation or a refusal. It makes you more secure when adjusting to changes of balance and terrain at speed, and can help you stay with your horse if he should jump awkwardly, hit a fence, or stumble. You must never be ahead of your horse, especially when approaching a fence and when jumping. Getting ahead is dangerous, especially over cross-country fences; it can handicap your horse when jumping, and can cause a refusal, fall, or serious mistake. If you are ahead of the motion, any sudden change of balance (such as your horse hitting a fence or landing more steeply than you expected) can send you over his head.

This rider's eyes are up and her arms and hands are excellent. However, her pinching knee has caused her leg to pivot backward and her heel to come up, throwing her shoulders too far forward and leaving her vulnerable if her horse should stumble, hesitate, or need rebalancing on landing. *Photo: U.S. Pony Clubs, Inc.*

- You must allow your horse freedom to use his head, neck, and balance, and avoid interfering with his efforts, especially when jumping and recovering after a fence. Even if your balance is behind your horse, you can extend your hands and arms, or slip your reins (see p. 93). Rigid, pulling, or unyielding hands cause horses to become stiff, heavy, and hard-mouthed.

Control

Control in the open, especially galloping and jumping, depends on your security and position (especially stirrup and rein length), your fitness, your horse's training, and most of all, on your judgment and experience.

Important factors in control are:

- To stay in control you must stay in balance. Use a stirrup length short enough to give you a firm leg and good control of your balance. Don't topple forward, lean on your horse's neck, or let your legs slip backward.
- Your reins should be short enough to maintain a steady contact when your hands are just above and in front of the withers. Reins that are too long allow your horse to become unbalanced or to ignore you; if your reins are too short, you will hang on your horse's mouth, and may get pulled forward.

Galloping position, using a bridge

- Use a bridge (see USPC C Manual, p. 29, for details) when galloping and jumping, and especially when riding a horse that gets strong or pulls. When your hands are properly placed, with the correct length of rein, the bridge steadies your hands and makes the horse pull against himself, instead of against you. A bridge can also give you support when landing from a drop fence or a jump into water.
- Keep your horse paying attention by asking him to "come back" from time to time by slightly shortening his stride. Never let him gallop flat out; he may become unbalanced or overexcited and get out of control, and may run into a fence, an obstruction, or rough ground.

CROSS-COUNTRY CONTROL

Sitting up and rocking back; opening hip joint

Pulley rein: Brace one hand on neck
Lift up briefly with
other hand
Rock shoulders back

- To bring a horse back, sink down into a three-point position, keep your legs on his sides, push your heels down, and "rock back," opening your hip angle and bringing your shoulders back each time you give a rhythmic squeeze on the outside rein. If your horse does not "come back" for an ordinary rein aid, give a brief lift on one rein, and if necessary, use a pulley rein.
- Use a bit that your horse respects, but don't rely on severe bitting for control. Overbitting is just as dangerous as underbitting; remember that horses pull against and run away from pain.

Balance and Control

In cross-country work, a horse has a natural tendency to get more and more on his forehand when galloping, going downhill, after landing from a jump, and especially when he is tired. If he moves too much on the forehand, his balance "runs away with him": he must move his legs faster to keep up with his balance, and going faster puts him even more on the forehand. This can handicap him when he needs his balance most: on turns, hills, approaches to jumps, takeoff and landing, and changes of terrain and footing.

You must be aware of your horse's balance so you can help him. A horse that is moving in good balance (even at speed) engages his hind legs well at each stride, which makes him feel round and bouncy, as if he were jumping through a gymnastic. He "has his hocks under him," and keeps his balance where he has control of it, so he can turn, adjust his stride, or jump easily, and he feels secure and sure-footed.

An unbalanced horse takes long, flat strides; his hind legs swing far out behind him, but don't engage well under his body. He may lean on the bit and pull, or may move with his back hollow and his head high, with short, quick strides. He feels uncontrolled and irregular, and may slip, skid, or stumble on turns or going downhill. He has speed, but not true impulsion; this makes him hard to rate, and he may take off too early or too close to his fences, and tends to jump flat, hit his fences, and land heavily. A horse going fast and unbalanced into a cross-country fence (especially if his rider is unbalanced, too) is an accident waiting to happen!

To help your horse stay balanced at speed, you must restrain his speed somewhat, while asking him to engage his hind legs more. Stay in balance yourself, with your stirrup leathers vertical to the ground, and your legs under your center of balance. Open your hip angle and bring your shoulders back a little, keeping your legs firmly on his sides, until you feel him respond. You must find "the spot" at which you and your horse are in balance together, and the state of balance in which your horse moves easily and feels maneuverable.

Well-balanced cross-country gallop

Poorly balanced, leaning on the forehand, unsafe

Caution: A horse that is seriously unbalanced may be tired, lame, or too inexperienced for the speed and the job he is trying to do. Pushing on with a horse that is not up to what he is being asked to do is abusive, and is asking for an accident.

KNOWLEDGE OF PACE

C-3 Level Pony Clubbers are expected to have a basic knowledge of pace or speed at the gallop, including galloping at 250, 350, and 400 meters per minute. Advanced riders should refine their sense of pace and ability to rate the horse more accurately to these speeds, and to faster paces of 450 and 520 meters per minute. The basics of measuring pace, and also adapting pace to various types of terrain, are found in the USPC C Manual (pp. 137–143), and should be reviewed.

Galloping Position

The galloping position is essentially the same as the cross-country jumping position, except that you may shorten your stirrups another hole and "close down" over your stirrups when working at 520 meters per minute. Use a bridge, with your reins shortened enough to maintain a steady, firm contact when your hands are tucked into the sides of his crest. Your balanced galloping position helps your horse to keep his own balance, and puts you in a position from which you can best control him.

Your horse must always be warmed up thoroughly before galloping, and he must not be galloped too long or too often for his fitness, or on hard ground.

Measuring Distance and Time

To develop an accurate sense of pace, you will need to measure out an 800-meter track (half a mile, or 874 yards, or 2622 feet), or you could lay out a 400-meter track and go around twice. Post a marker (a flag, post, or something easy to see) every 100 meters.

The easiest way to learn to recognize a pace is to ride alongside an experienced rider who can show you just how fast you must go.

You will need a stopwatch (the type of stopwatch used by event riders is convenient, as it has large buttons and a digital readout that is easy to see). Make sure you know how to work the watch before you time yourself.

Although in a combined training event you would start from a standstill from the starting box, when timing your pace you should start about 50 yards before the first marker, so that you have reached your chosen pace when you start to time yourself. Start your watch at the first marker, and check your pace at each 100-meter marker.

The following chart will help you identify the time for the various paces:

TIMES AND MPH FOR VARIOUS PACES AT THE GALLOP

PACE (APPROX.)	MILES PER HOUR	TIME FOR 800 METERS ($^1/_2$ MILE)	TIME FOR 100 METERS
250 mpm	9 mph	3 min. 20 seconds	25 seconds
350 mpm	13 mph	2 min. 20 seconds	17.5 seconds
400 mpm	15 mph	2 min.	15 seconds
450 mpm	18 mph	1 min. 40 seconds	13 seconds
520 mpm	20 mph	1 min. 30 seconds	11.25 seconds

Tips for Riding at a Galloping Pace

- To ask your horse to gallop, use your legs in rhythm with his movement to extend his stride. Don't let him scramble with short, quick strides.
- A steady average pace is less fatiguing and less likely to result in injury to a horse than going very fast and frequently pulling up, then speeding up again. You will have to slow down in certain conditions (such as steep slopes, rocks, or mud) and make up time by going faster where the going is good, but don't use up your horse unnecessarily by excessive speed and severe changes of speed.
- On a cross-country course, choose landmarks located at given distances (such as the halfway point). Calculate what your time should be at the marker (considering the terrain and conditions and the Time Allowed). On course, you can check your watch at the marker to see if you are running slow, ahead of time, or right on your plan.
- Even if you are running slow, *the way your horse feels matters more than the time*! Never get so caught up in trying to make the time that you push your horse at a faster pace than he can handle.

CROSS-COUNTRY JUMPING

At the C Levels, you learned how to develop the skills you and your horse need to jump different types of cross-country fences. As you advance, you can jump the same types of fences, but with a greater degree of difficulty, and add new types of fences.

The Horse's Jumping Form

Cross-country jumping horses must jump with good balance and in safe, functional, and efficient form. Good jumping style allows a horse to jump bigger and more safely, with minimum stress on his legs, wind, and muscles. It also helps a horse to remain in balance and to recover quickly from the effort of jumping, changes of terrain, or unexpected occurrences such as a slip or hitting a fence. Most of all, good jumping form is safer for both horse and rider, and diminishes the chances of hitting a fence, making a mistake, or falling.

Poor jumping: flat, hanging knees, rider tipping forward

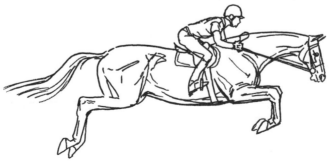

Good jumping: round, balanced, and in good form

The basics of good and faulty jumping form are discussed in the USPC C Manual.

Cross-country jumping, especially at speed, tends to encourage horses to jump fast and flat. Schooling over gymnastics and cross-country fences should focus on teaching the horse to maintain his balance and roundness, while moving confidently and reliably forward to his fences. He must also be schooled to keep and improve his responsiveness and attention to his rider, to jump straight, and to land in balance and rebalance quickly and easily, and to lengthen and shorten stride.

Problems in Cross-Country Jumping

Problems may be related to one or more of the following factors:

- Terrain: Uphill and downhill terrain and changes of terrain require more effort, change the horse's balance, and can alter the jumping effort required for an obstacle.
- Confidence and experience: Inexperience, rider hesitation, or a previous bad experience with a certain type of fence can sap a horse's confidence. Horses need to learn how to handle different types of cross-country fences through patient, progressive schooling. Some horses are temperamentally unsuitable for this type of work.
- Pace: Speed tends to make horses jump flat, and can compound balance, timing, and control problems. A sensible pace is appropriate to conditions, the fences, terrain and footing, and the horse's and rider's capabilities and fitness.
- Control: Some horses become overexcited, strong, or difficult to control, especially when jumping at speed or in company with other horses. Effective bitting (sometimes in conjunction with a particular noseband or martingale) and, especially, good riding are essential.
- Fatigue: A tired horse tends to gallop on the forehand, jump flat, hit his fences, and land heavily, and is harder to balance; he has less energy and scope than when fresh. Fitness, proper conditioning, and intelligent management of pace are important in staving off fatigue and jumping safely when a horse is tiring.
- Balance: Terrain, speed, fatigue, and rider balance all may encourage a cross-country horse to run on his forehand. Jumping off the forehand can cause takeoff errors and makes it more difficult to recover from a mistake.

- Rider error: Poor balance, timing, or presentation at the fence, or interference with horse's jumping efforts can defeat even the best jumper.

Jumping Various Types of Cross-Country Fences

Galloping (Steeplechase) Fences

Galloping fences are designed to be jumped at a faster pace (but *not* a racing pace). They are usually made of brush and slant away from the takeoff side, which makes them easy to judge and to jump. The Steeplechase phase of a three-day event consists of eight to ten steeplechase fences, to be jumped at a gallop. The horse must find a suitable galloping pace, balance, and rhythm, and jump these fences in stride, so that he moves and jumps efficiently, taking less out of himself.

Speed, length of stride, and easy, slanting fences all encourage a horse to move on his forehand and jump flat. When a horse has jumped one or more galloping fences, it can be difficult for him to come back and jump round over a different type of fence. Don't encourage this by allowing him to jump too fast, flat, or carelessly over steeplechase fences.

Steeplechase-type fence, jumped with flat arc

To ride galloping fences, you should shorten your stirrups to the maximum height for you (usually one or two holes higher than normal cross-country length). Close down over your stirrups, but keep your weight centered a little behind your stirrups. This is "insurance" in case your horse makes a bobble while jumping at speed. If you are even the least bit ahead of him, you will be off! Adjust your reins to a good galloping length, and use a bridge.

When riding a galloping fence, keep the horse in good balance and let him move forward to the fence, but don't encourage him to race or to overextend himself. One way to learn to ride galloping fences is to ride and jump alongside an experienced rider who can set the pace. If you do so, you must stay beside him and not forge ahead or drop back, as both horses usually take off together. While this can be a tonic for a lazy horse, it can be too exciting for many horses.

Angles, Corners, and Zigzags

Angles, corners, and zigzags require planning, obedience, and an accurate approach. Such fences invite a runout, so you must be clear about the line you will ride, the point at which you will jump, and the line you take after the fence. Ride a consistent line of approach, without weaving or changing your mind. Indecision, drifting, or looking down can spell disaster!

Angles, corners, and zigzag fences can be built easily with stadium jumping equipment. This helps you break them down into simple components and easy steps, before jumping fixed cross-country fences. Practice riding schooling fences at angles, and keeping the horse in a "channel" between your left and right aids, on the approach and afterward.

ZIGZAG FENCE WITH DITCH

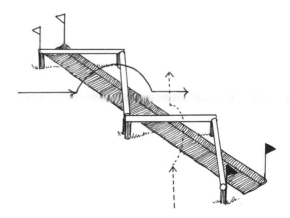

Best approach: ditch on takeoff side; adjacent panel acts as a wing

Zigzag Fences These often have an imposing appearance, but are really a series of narrow fences, connected. Walk the line you have selected, and remind yourself on which side you will need stronger aids to keep your horse jumping straight.

Angles   Angles should be jumped as single fences first. When the horse goes straight and jumps at an angle reliably in either direction, you can move on to variations of angles, such as a pole angled over a ditch, forming a V. When planning your approach, try to jump as close to the center of the V as possible, not out where it is wider. Avoid creating a false ground by jumping it so that the ditch is on the far side.

ANGLE FENCES

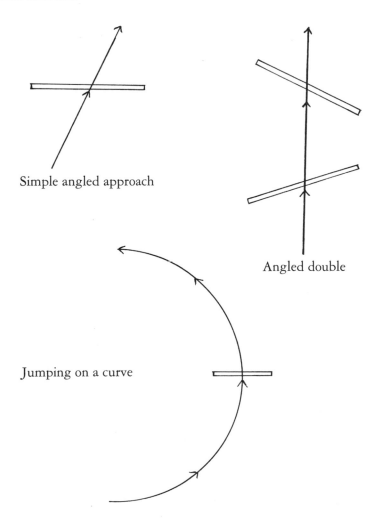

Simple angled approach

Angled double

Jumping on a curve

Long Angled Fences The long "V" can be jumped as an option fence. If you can, begin by jumping through the "V" out toward the ends, where you can ride it as an angled combination of one (or even two) strides. You must choose an accurate line which minimizes the angle of both fences; if you miscalculate, the first fence is easy, but the second can result in a refusal or runout. From this, you can move inward, jumping it as a bounce. Walk this line carefully and ride it accurately!

CORNER OPTION FENCE

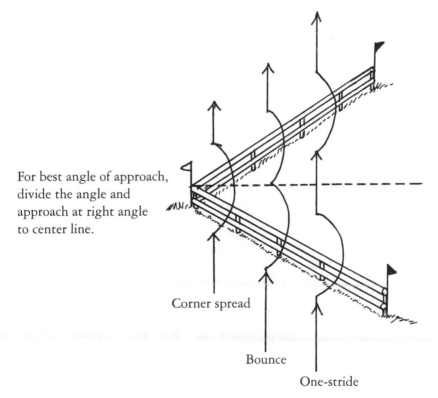

For best angle of approach, divide the angle and approach at right angle to center line.

Corner spread

Bounce

One-stride

Corners Jumped As a Spread These are the most difficult type of angled fence, as they ride as a parallel oxer, and the narrow end invites a runout. If you drift even a little, the spread may be impossibly wide, or you may incur a runout or a swerve in the air. Use firm supporting aids on the narrow side of the fence, to keep the horse from drifting or falling out in that direction, and use your eyes positively to define your chosen line.

Option Fences and Combinations   Require forethought and planning. You can build variations of option fences out of stadium jump materials, which allows you to practice almost any type of combination you might encounter. This is safer and more versatile than starting out over fixed obstacles. As with corners and angles, break them down into their components, and practice the components by themselves before combining them.

As a result of your previous work, you should know your horse's capabilities and weaknesses. Does he have a big jump? If so, the option of the single larger fence may be your best choice. Is he limited in scope, but handy? He may handle a trappy turn better than a maximum-size fence. Is he unreliable about jumping certain types of fences, or from a short or long takeoff distance? In schooling at home, you should work on his weak points and on types of fences at which he is inexperienced or needs confidence. In competition, choose the options that make the most of his abilities and avoid his weaknesses whenever possible.

Distances vary considerably in cross-country combinations, as they are influenced by the size and type of fences, the terrain, and the angles and possible routes of approach. In general, cross-country combinations are usually set slightly longer than their counterparts in the ring, because the horse will be moving at a stronger pace outside. When evaluating distances, remember that factors that tend to make a horse lengthen his stride (such as a slight downhill grade, or a long gallop beforehand) may make the distance ride shorter than it appears.

When riding a combination, you need balance, impulsion, and rhythm, and your horse must go straight. It is usually better to have a bit more impulsion than you need than not enough, but don't let it escape into speed. Most combinations need to be ridden with a balanced, bouncy stride; it may help to imagine that you are riding through a gymnastic as you approach the first element.

Bounce Fences   These are a variety of combination, and are often found in conjunction with option fences. A cross-country bounce is set at a longer distance than those in the schooling ring, because of the extra pace and impulsion.

BANK AND DITCH COMBINATION

Approach in balanced, round, but not over-extended canter	Rider's angles close and open with horse's motion	Be careful not to get behind or ahead of the motion	Maintain contact without interfering with horse's use of his head and neck	Keep leg firmly on to keep horse moving forward

BOUNCE FENCE

Rider remains balanced over his leg as his angles open and close with the motion of the horse

Bounce fences require a horse to engage his hind legs and jump off his hocks with impulsion and accuracy. Approach a bounce as if you were riding a gymnastic, and keep the rhythm. Don't commit your body very far forward at a bounce; instead, keep your balance more central, over your feet, and let your horse rock you as his front end rises, dips, rises again.

Bullfinch

A **bullfinch** is a specialty fence, consisting of a large hedge with a thin screen of twigs extending up from it, sometimes as high as 6 feet. The horse is supposed to jump the lower part of the hedge and go right through the screen of greenery. If a horse has never seen a bullfinch before, he may think he is supposed to clear the whole thing, and he may well decide that it is impossible!

Bullfinch

To teach a horse to jump bullfinches, start with a hedge or brush box, and stick several tall but wispy branches into it. At first, jump through the space between the branches; later, put them closer together, so that the horse brushes easily through them.

Even when a horse is used to bullfinches, you should ride them very positively, with a straight approach and plenty of impulsion. If you falter, a stop or a runout is a likely consequence.

Drop Fences

Drop fences are fences with a lower landing. At the C-3 Level, you jumped simple banks, steps, and drops; now you will encounter fences with more height and a drop on the landing side. The horse is usually not aware of the drop until takeoff, or until he is nearly across the obstacle. It is important to keep him reliably in front of your leg and on the aids during the approach; if you drop the contact or lean forward, he may drop his head, see the drop, and hesitate or refuse.

A drop should not be ridden too fast and flat, or the horse will jump with too flat an arc and may stumble or have trouble regaining his balance on landing. On the other hand, if you overshorten his stride or lose impulsion on the approach, he may hesitate and then lurch over with a steep, nearly vertical landing. An impulsive, springy trot, or a round, bouncy canter is the best approach.

When a horse jumps down a drop, you have to cope with an extra-long descent, much like landing from a big fence. You may also have to absorb more shock on landing. Bridge your reins, slide your leg and foot forward, ahead of the girth, and keep your head and eyes up. Keep your stirrup leathers perpendicular to the ground, and stay back over them; on a big drop, you may have to lean well back. In this case, let the reins slip through your fingers to the knot at the buckle (see "Slipping the Reins," p. 98).

Jumping a drop off a ramp or ledge is like riding a step or jumping down off a bank. It is best approached in a steady, impulsive trot. As with a drop fence, be prepared to sit in the middle or even to lean back if necessary, and to slip your reins.

Drop Jumps into Water

Drops into water present some special problems. The horse cannot judge the depth of the water he is jumping into, or see the bottom, so he must be ridden positively to the fence, and must not be allowed to drop his head or get behind the legs. Landing in water exerts a sudden, strong drag on the horse, slowing him suddenly. If you jump into water too fast or while sitting forward, this effect is magnified and can send you right over the horse's head! In addition, the horse must make a strong effort to recover his balance and stride in the water; this often feels like a buck or a jump, and can further unseat a rider already loosened by the drop. Finally, the horse must exit the water, often over an additional jump out. You must be able to ride in strongly, keep your balance during the drop, landing and recovery, and reorganize the horse in time to jump out safely. This takes an extremely secure seat and good timing.

DROP INTO WATER

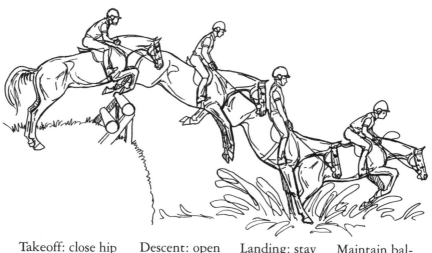

| Takeoff: close hip angle but don't get forward | Descent: open hip angle; slip reins | Landing: stay back, vertical to ground | Maintain balance during recovery |

When jumping a drop into water, the approach and seat are essentially the same as for a large drop. A strong leg position, with the heel well down and the leg in front of the girth, is an essential part of your "safety seat." Stay back as you descend and land; keep your balance in the center of the horse, with your feet still a little in front of you, during the recovery, and regain your reins as quickly as you can.

Before jumping drops into water, practice water crossings and jumping into and out of water, as described in the USPC C Manual. Practice drop fences and steps also, until you are confident and competent in leaning back over your legs, slipping your reins, and recovering your reins and balance on landing.

CHAPTER 5

Longeing

Ground training is a most important part of horsemanship. Good ground training teaches obedience, respect, trust, and cooperation, and helps to establish a good working relationship between trainer and horse. It can improve a horse's movement, help develop his muscles correctly, and affect his attitude and behavior under saddle as well as in the stable.

Whenever you handle a horse, you are practicing ground training. If you insist on certain behavior at some times and ignore it at others, this confuses the horse and undermines his training and respect for you as his handler. Good horsemanship and successful training require correct and consistent handling at all times.

Before a horse can be trained to longe or be schooled in any of the methods described here, he must be properly trained to lead, to stand still when asked to, and to respond to simple signals and voice commands. (Please review these subjects in the USPC D and C Manuals.)

LONGEING

This chapter includes more about longeing equipment and techniques, training horses to longe, and longeing to improve the horse. Longeing to train the rider (longe lessons) is covered in Chapter 6.

An introduction to longeing, including equipment, safety, and basic principles, is found in Chapter 10 of the USPC C Manual. Before you can progress to more advanced longeing at the B, HA, and A Levels, you must know this material and have practiced the basic skills until you can perform them with ease.

LONGEING YOUNG HORSES

Longeing puts lateral stress on a horse's legs and joints, which increases with speed and on smaller circles. Young horses' immature bones and joints are especially vulnerable to injury from too much or incorrect longeing, or from accidents if the horse acts up. They are also more easily overstressed mentally by too long or demanding training sessions. Work in hand and free longeing are less stressful and safer for immature horses than longeing too much or too soon. When longeing young horses, always use protective boots on all four legs, and keep training sessions short.

Foals should not be longed, as they are especially vulnerable to neck injuries if pulled violently sideways. Yearlings can be longed at slow gaits for short periods, but must not be overstressed. Two-year-olds (and some yearlings) have nearly reached adult weight, but their bones and joints are still immature. They can be longed lightly, but it is better to vary the training program with work in hand, free longeing, and ground driving, instead of daily longeing.

IMPROVING LONGEING TECHNIQUE

Good longeing is largely a matter of communication between trainer and horse, using body language, gestures, timing, tone of voice, and a consistent vocabulary of commands. This relates to the way horses naturally communicate with each other. Besides commands, cues, and learned responses, you communicate qualities such as confidence, relaxation, authority, energy, and awareness. Negative attitudes such as fear, anger, impatience, inattention, and indecisiveness are also easily picked up by the horse.

Body Language

Your body language (posture, gestures, and the way you use your body) convey your mood and intentions to your horse. This is also communicated by touch, through your handling of the longe line and whip.

Mental Attitude Body language starts with mental attitude. Clear intent is especially important. This means making a clear decision about what you intend to do and what you intend the horse to do. Your attitude of quiet confidence and clear, positive intent gives the horse confidence and encourages him to accept you as his leader.

Posture and Movement Your posture and the way you move communicate your attitude and intentions to the horse. A submissive posture (eyes lowered, head turned away, shoulders rounded, backing away from horse) conveys a non-threatening or even fearful attitude. An aggressive posture (looking directly at horse with shoulders squared, head up, moving toward horse) conveys dominance or even an attack. It is easier to get a horse to move in balance if you are balanced than if you slouch or lean. Deep breathing improves your posture and helps you project confidence and calmness.

BODY LANGUAGE

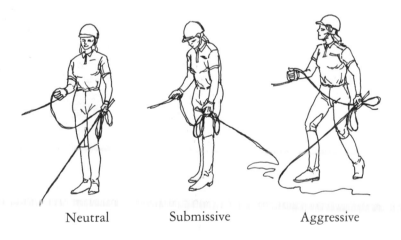

Neutral   Submissive   Aggressive

Gestures Gestures are movements of your body, limbs, and whip. Horses understand gestures, as they use them in communicating with other horses. A gesture may be small or large, gentle or vigorous, all of which affects the horse's reaction to it. The longe whip serves as an extension of your arm; it accentuates any gestures you make. Some horses react more strongly to gestures (particularly whip gestures) than others.

Some gestures used in longeing include:

- **Pointing toward the hindquarters:** sends horse forward or asks for increased activity in hindquarters.
- **Pointing toward a point in front of the head:** encourages horse to stop or reverse.
- **Pointing toward horse's shoulder:** encourages horse to move outward on the circle.
- **Moving arm and/or whip in a back-to-front gesture:** encourages forward movement and more activity in hind legs.
- **Raising hand or whip:** calls for attention, may appear threatening.
- **Lowering the hand and/or whip toward the ground:** diminishes threat; encourages relaxation.
- **Shaking the whip:** draws attention to the whip; threatening.

Body Placement   Your placement in relation to the horse is most important in longeing. (See USPC C Manual, pp. 294–295.) Your leading hand and the longe line form one side of the "control triangle"; your other hand and the longe whip are the second side, and the horse is the third side. Your position, at the point of the triangle, should normally be opposite the horse's girth.

Any change in the control triangle is a signal to the horse. Moving toward the rear sends him forward, as if being chased from behind. Moving toward the front tends to make him slow down, stop, or reverse. Moving toward the horse sends him outward on the circle and makes him more aware of your gestures and control, while moving backward increases the distance between you and the horse, and diminishes the effect of the aids.

When longeing, you must be aware of the "control point." This is a point on the horse (usually located slightly behind his shoulder) at which he reacts to your body placement and movements. You normally stay opposite the control point; getting behind the control point drives the horse forward, and getting ahead of this point encourages the horse to slow down or stop.

Handling the Longe

The longe line is a means of communication between handler and horse, as the reins are in riding. Light contact should be maintained at all times when longeing.

Importance of Posture and Hand and Arm Position As in riding, "good hands" in longeing depend on good posture; balance; and shoulder, arm, and hand position. Good balance and posture make it easier to keep your balance, handle the longe line well, and longe safely. If you slouch or lean forward, you are unable to give clear and correct rein aids, and can be pulled off balance by a resisting horse. Leaning back against the horse causes a heavy pull on the longe; this should only be used as a momentary defensive measure when a horse pulls hard or tries to bolt.

The long muscles of your back and the muscles at the back of the upper arm stabilize your arm and help you resist if a horse pulls. Your upper arm should hang close to your ribs, with a natural bend at the elbow. The forearm, wrist, and hand should be held so that the longe forms a straight line from your elbow to the cavesson. Carrying your longe hand too high is tiring and makes your touch stiff; dropping your arm too low pulls downward against the horse. Bending the wrist or pulling the longe hand inward causes a continuous pull and may teach the horse to pull against you.

Rein Aids on the Longe The longe line should be treated as a rein, both in maintaining a light, steady contact, and in giving rein aids. As in riding, rein aids should be applied as a brief change of pressure in a specific direction, *not* as a pull or jerk. It is important to keep the horse moving forward on the track of the circle, in order to maintain the contact.

Specific rein aids and their effects are discussed in the USPC C Manual, pages 290–292.

Practice letting out the longe (allowing it to run through your loosened hand) as the horse moves out onto a larger circle, and taking in the longe (picking up additional folds), until you can do this easily with either hand. For safety, *always* keep the excess longe in folds, not loops that could coil around your hand, and never let the longe slacken dangerously or drag on the ground.

Handling the Whip

The longe whip is a means of communication, not an instrument of punishment. It serves as the primary driving aid in longeing, assisted by the voice, taking the place of the rider's leg aids.

The whip must be handled quietly and fluently, so as not to cause excitement, confusion, or fear in the horse. Waving a whip around, using it too often, awkwardly, or too severely, may cause a horse to become confused, to panic, or to ignore whip signals. The horse should respect the whip but never fear it.

Most longe whips have a stock about 6 feet long, and a lash 5 to 6 feet long. Some whips are longer, in order to be able to touch a horse at a distance of 15 feet or more. (To lengthen a whip, you can attach a 6-foot braided bootlace to the end of the lash.) A longe whip should be balanced so that it is easy to handle. Practice using a longe whip (especially an extra-long whip) without a horse until you can handle it fluently with either hand.

The longe whip may be used in several ways:

Pointing the Whip   Most whip signals are given by pointing the tip of the whip toward a precise spot, or by moving it in a gesture. The whip acts as an extension of your arm.

Running Out the Lash   The lash may be run out toward a specific point on the horse, keeping it close to the ground. This is accomplished with a quick turn of the wrist.

Touching with the Whip   Touching the horse with the lash of the longe whip is a strong driving aid to send the horse forward. The lash may be lightly tossed upward, run out to lightly flick the horse, or (rarely) applied with a stinging snap. This last should be used only as a last resort, to stop a serious disobedience.

The lash should usually be applied on the barrel, at a spot close to the girth, where a rider's leg would touch the horse. If used on the hind legs or hindquarters, it encourages forward movement but may provoke kicking. Using the whip on the shoulder (to correct cutting in) should be reserved for experts, because of the danger of striking the horse in the head or eye.

For safety, the lash should be kept close to the ground and applied in a forward and upward direction. Striking downward or swinging the lash wildly can cause it to wrap around the horse's legs or get caught on the tack or under his tail, with dangerous results. The lash must *never* be used near a horse's head, because of the danger of striking him in the eye.

Snapping the Whip   Occasionally an audible snap or crack may be necessary to send a recalcitrant horse forward. This should be done well behind the hindquarters and close to the ground, by moving the tip of the whip forward, then quickly backward.

Importance of the Circle

Longeing is work performed on a circle. You can only evaluate and improve a horse's movement when he works consistently on a round circle of a given size. If he keeps changing the shape and size of the circle, his movement is inconsistent and you have less control.

In the early stages of longeing, the handler walks in a small circle as the horse works in a larger circle (parallel longeing). This keeps you closer to the horse, where your signals are more effective. In more advanced training, you pivot in the middle of the circle, providing a fixed center point for the circle.

Going Forward on the Circle The first requirement is to establish forward movement on a circle, even if this requires parallel longeing or help from an assistant. If the horse hangs back, hesitates, or turns around, longeing cannot be accomplished.

Roundness of the Circle A longeing circle must be perfectly round. Horses may change the shape of the circle by cutting in or falling out. They usually do this at the same place (often toward the stable, or away from a spooky object).

Tips for handling circle problems:

- Falling out: Longe in an enclosed ring (preferably a round ring), or create a barrier (using safe materials) on the side where the horse pulls outward. Correctly adjusted side reins help keep a horse from falling out through the outside shoulder. Before he reaches the spot where he falls out, begin applying direct rein aids in rhythm with the steps of his inside hind leg. In difficult cases, the double longe may help.
- Cutting in: Before the horse reaches the point where he usually cuts in, send him forward by using the longe whip in rhythm with his inside hind leg. When he tries to cut in, point the whip toward his shoulder and say, "Out." It may help to shorten the longe line and move closer to the horse (parallel longeing).

Size of the Circle A longeing circle must be large enough for the horse to move evenly and in good balance for his stage of training, but small enough for good control. The smaller the circle and the faster the gait, the harder it is for the horse to keep his balance and track correctly. Longeing on too small a circle, especially at fast gaits, puts extra stress on joints and muscles and increases the risk of injury, especially in immature or unfit horses. However, too large a circle makes it harder to keep control.

In early training, the longeing circle should be about 60 feet to 20 meters (66 feet) in diameter. As the horse's balance and strength improve, he may be longed on slightly smaller circles at the walk and trot (approximately 15 to 18 meters in diameter). Sometimes the beginning of a canter circle may be briefly 25 to 30 meters, to establish contact and balance.

Tracking Correctly on a Circle   Tracking correctly (tracking "straight") on a circle means that the horse's hind legs follow in the tracks of his front legs. This keeps his neck and spine properly aligned and allows him to bend correctly.

Horses often move crookedly on circles. A horse may carry his shoulder to the inside, swing his haunches out, or carry his hip to the inside. Many horses bend their necks too much to the inside or the outside. To some degree, this is due to the one-sidedness that is found in all horses. This problem must be addressed in order to strengthen and supple the horse, and develop his ability to move correctly in both directions. Start by establishing your circle in a slow, even lazy rhythm to allow the horse to establish the track before asking for engagement or more forward movement. Only when the horse is secure can you improve straightness in tracking on the longeing circle.

Tips to improve tracking straight on the longeing circle:

- Correctly fitted side reins discourage a horse from looking out of the circle, bending his neck too much to either side, or "popping" a shoulder. Longe on a large enough circle (approximately 20 meters). Too small a circle makes crookedness worse.
- Use the longe whip to encourage the horse to engage (reach farther forward) with his inside hind leg at each stride. Crookedness is often related to poor engagement of the inside hind leg.
- Keep the speed slow and the rhythm and tempo steady. If a horse leans inward instead of staying vertical or "standing up" and tracking properly, he is going too fast for the size of the circle.
- Horses that swing their haunches out may benefit from work with a double longe, which helps to keep the hindquarters in line (see p. 165).

LONGEING EQUIPMENT

Basic longeing equipment (including longe lines, whip, cavesson, and snaffle bridle), its fitting, and use are introduced in the USPC C Manual. Other longeing equipment includes surcingles or rollers, side reins, and various types of bitting and training devices.

Surcingle or Roller

A surcingle or roller is a band equipped with rings for side reins, long reins, etc. Used over a saddle, it provides attachments for side reins. Used alone, it may be used to provide an attachment for side reins, or to accustom a green horse to girth pressure.

When used alone, a surcingle should be fitted as carefully as a saddle, avoiding pressure on the spine or digging into the shoulder blades; a saddle pad is advisable. When used over a saddle, the stirrups should be removed. Be careful not to pinch the horse's skin between the girth and surcingle.

Side Reins

Side reins are used for limbering-up exercises, to help a horse find contact with the bit, to influence the position of the head and neck, and to develop self-carriage in a comfortable frame. The horse learns to yield or "give" to the bit and side reins, and to accept the head and neck position they create. Properly adjusted side reins encourage a horse to keep his neck and spine correctly aligned. They stabilize the base of the neck, which discourages "rubber-necking," or over-bending the neck sideways.

Types of side reins include:

SIDE REINS

Solid

Elastic end

Rubber rings

Solid Side Reins   Made of leather or webbing without stretch or give. Some trainers prefer solid side reins because they provide a positive connection to the bit. However, care must be taken to avoid letting the horse lean on them or get behind the bit.

Side Reins with Rubber Rings   Rubber rings inserted in the side reins provide some give, especially if the horse tosses his head. However, they add weight to the side reins.

Elastic End Side Reins   Elastic ends allow more stretch than rubber rings, for a lighter and more elastic contact with the bit. Although these may be useful for extremely sensitive horses, many trainers believe they encourage horses to pull.

Adjustment of Side Reins

Side reins must be adjusted correctly for their purpose and for the horse's level of training. They should not be used in the walk, as they may inhibit the balancing gestures of the horse's neck, shorten his stride, and spoil his walk. During warmup, side reins should be adjusted quite long if used at all, so that they do not inhibit the horse's ability to stretch his neck and back. Side reins must never be shortened so much that the horse is forced to retract his neck or to carry his face behind the vertical.

Normal-length side reins are adjusted so that the horse makes contact with the bit when his head and neck are in a normal position for his conformation and level of training. His face should be about one hand's breadth in front of the vertical.

Longer side reins are used in the early stages of training. They are adjusted so that the horse can stretch his neck and lower his head, and make contact with the bit with his mouth approximately on a level with the point of his shoulder.

Shorter side reins are adjusted to maintain contact when the horse works in a shorter frame in collected gaits, with his face at or near the vertical. They are used only for advanced horses, and only for short periods of concentrated work. Shorter side reins do not create collection; instead, they are adjusted to conform to the horse's increased ability to shift his balance to the rear, lower his haunches, and stay collected.

Both side reins should be of equal length. Shortening the inside side rein makes the horse appear to bend, but instead may encourage him to fall out through the outside shoulder and to overbend laterally in

ADJUSTMENT OF SIDE REINS

Basic adjustment: head at normal height for horse, face slightly in front of vertical

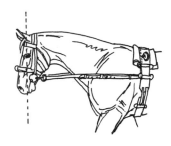

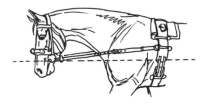

Long adjustment: mouth level with point of shoulder, face slightly in front of vertical

Short adjustment: mouth level with point of hip; face at or near vertical

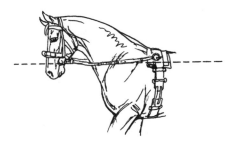

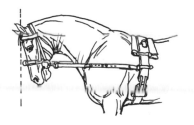

Incorrect adjustment: flexion behind poll, face behind vertical

the neck ("rubber-neck"). This can inhibit the engagement of his inside hind leg.

Always adjust both side reins before attaching them to the bit. As soon as the side reins are attached, the horse should move forward. Some horses, if forced to stand still with short side reins or during adjustment, may lean on the bit, get behind the bit, or become upset, even to the point of rearing.

When a horse has finished working, the side reins should be removed so he can stretch freely while cooling down.

Caution: Side reins must *never* be used when jumping, as they restrict a horse's use of his head and neck over a jump and can cause a jab in the mouth, loss of confidence, or even a fall.

Sliding Side Reins (Lauffer Reins)

Sliding side reins run from an upper surcingle ring through the bit ring and back to a lower surcingle ring on each side, forming a triangle. They should *not* run between the horse's front legs to the girth, as this can cause the horse to overflex, carry his neck too low, and get behind the bit.

SLIDING SIDE REINS

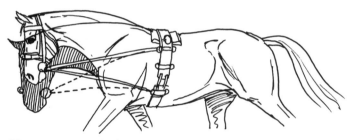

Horse can stretch down while maintaining contact

Sliding side reins allow a horse to maintain contact with the bit in a range of positions, particularly as he lowers his head and stretches his neck. Unlike regular side reins, they do not tighten or loosen as he changes the position of his head and neck. They can be useful for horses that have too high a head carriage, are tight in the back, and do not know how to stretch forward and down.

Sliding side reins should be adjusted so that the horse can make contact with the bit when he carries his neck slightly arched, with his face at or slightly in front of the vertical. Early in training, they are attached to the middle and lower surcingle rings. At a later stage, they may be attached to the upper and middle rings.

Caution: Sliding side reins are advanced training equipment and must be used only by trainers who understand their proper adjustment and use, and have advanced longeing skills.

Training Devices

All training devices like side reins and draw reins are intended to develop a specific head and neck carriage. Training devices work by applying pressure when the horse deviates from the desired head and neck position, and reducing or eliminating pressure when he returns to it. In theory, the horse should learn to move in a correct posture and should develop the muscles that facilitate this way of moving.

Unfortunately, the use of such devices is not simple, and the results are not always good. A horse may "set his head," assuming a fixed head and neck position that relieves the pressure, but if he does this with his back hollow or his hind legs trailing, his balance, movement, and muscle development suffer. If a device is adjusted incorrectly or too tightly, the horse cannot find relief from the pressure. This causes tension, stiffness, and pain and can ruin his movement and attitude. It also leads to defenses such as leaning on the bit, retracting the neck, overflexing, shortening the stride, and even to violent resistances like rearing or falling over backward. Incorrect use of bitting devices is abusive, and can cause muscle soreness, physical damage, or serious accidents.

Because of the dangers of these devices, they should be used only by experts who are extremely knowledgeable about horse training, movement, and muscle development. Any training device must be introduced tactfully, adjusted gradually to the point where it works best, and the horse must be longed correctly, with careful attention to rhythm, relaxation, engagement of the hind legs, and good movement. Most experts who are capable of using such devices without causing harm have little use for gimmicks; unfortunately, they are too often used by less knowledgeable trainers in search of a quick fix. In such hands, they are all too easily abused.

Elastic poll pressure devices are one commonly used (and abused) training device. These apply pressure on the poll and the bit in a downward and backward direction, with some elasticity. They encourage a horse to lower his head and flex his poll and neck. Disadvantages: Although the give of the elastic makes these devices less rigid than some others, they can encourage a horse to overflex, flex behind the poll, pull on the bit, or become heavy on the forehand, especially if misadjusted or if the horse is not longed correctly.

The *chambon* is another commonly used device. It applies pressure to the poll and mouth when the horse raises his head; the horse is free to stretch forward and down. The purpose of the chambon is to develop the back muscles. Correct use of the chambon encourages a horse to

TRAINING DEVICES

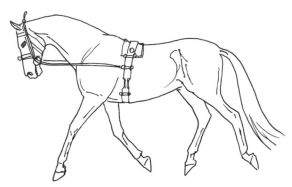

Elastic poll pressure device

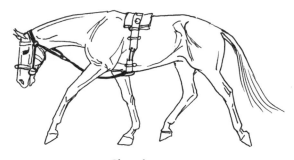

Chambon

lower and extend his head and neck, while raising and rounding his back. Disadvantages: Chambons can cause soreness in the neck muscles. The horse may go on the forehand if not longed correctly. It takes weeks of correct and consistent work to develop the muscles and movement so that the horse carries himself and does not go on his forehand. The horse must be taught to respond correctly to the pressure of the chambon (lowering his head) in hand; otherwise he may resist violently when he feels the pressure, even to the point of rearing and falling over backward.

The *gogue* is a variation of the chambon which can be much more restrictive, especially if misused. Pony Clubbers should not use gogues at any level, and the use of restrictive devices is strongly discouraged.

LONGEING WITH THE BIT

For ordinary longeing, it is best to attach the longe line to the nose ring of a properly fitted longe cavesson. This permits good control without endangering the horse's mouth, or interfering with the contact. However, it is sometimes desirable to longe with direct contact with the horse's mouth. This must be undertaken only by a handler who is experienced in longeing correctly, and only with a horse that is well trained to longe. Longeing a green or difficult horse with the longe attached to the bit can pull severely on the mouth, causing pain, damaging the horse's training, and injuring the mouth.

There are two methods of attaching the longe to the bit. The longe must be unfastened and changed to the inside whenever you change directions.

Longe Attached to Bit and Noseband   The safest method for the horse's mouth is to fasten the longe to the inside bit ring, and also to attach it to the side of the noseband (see diagram). This permits direct contact with the bit, while preventing the bit from being pulled sideways through the mouth. This method also transfers some of the pressure to the noseband, instead of to the bit alone. It can be used with a regular cavesson, flash noseband, or dropped noseband. It requires a longe line with a buckle end, or a snap end large enough to encompass the noseband as well as the bit ring.

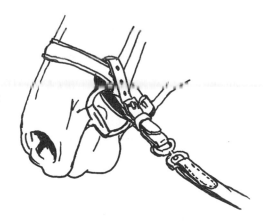

Longe attached to bit
and noseband

Longe over Poll (Gag Bit Effect)   The longe is run through the inside bit ring (from outside to inside), over the poll, and fastened to the bit ring on the opposite side. *Caution:* This arrangement acts as a gag bit, pulling the bit upward into the corners of the mouth and pressing against the poll. It is quite severe, and must be handled carefully to avoid injury to the mouth.

Longe over poll: gag bit effect (severe)

This method is used when maximum control is needed, such as when longeing a strong-willed horse that pulls, or when safe control is essential, as when giving a longe lesson. It must only be used by a handler who is expert at longeing, and has excellent hands.

Do not run the longe line through the inside bit ring, under the jaw to the other bit ring. This draws the rings together, pulls on the outside of the jaw, and causes the bit to pinch and hit the roof of the mouth, making the horse uncomfortable and crooked.

Do not attach the longe to the inside bit ring alone; the bit can be pulled sideways, right through the mouth, which can injure the mouth and damage the bridle.

DOUBLE LONGEING

The double longe is often used in preparation for long-reining or ground driving. It can be helpful in longeing horses that persistently swing the haunches out, travel crookedly, or turn in to face the handler.

Double longeing requires two longe lines or long reins, a longe cavesson, and a surcingle. For safety's sake, the tail should be tied up in a mud knot, to avoid catching the longe line under the tail.

Caution: Before double longeing, the horse *must* be accustomed to feeling the pressure of a longe line around his hindquarters, croup, hocks, and tail, on both sides, without fear or resentment.

DOUBLE LONGE

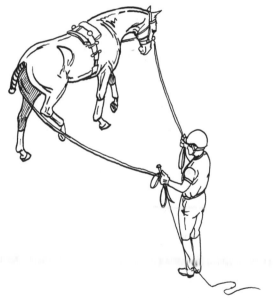

Tail tied up to prevent catching longe on tail

In double longeing, the inside longe line is attached to the inside ring of the longe cavesson and runs straight to the trainer's hand. The other longe is attached to the outside cavesson ring, and passes through the middle or lower surcingle ring, around the hindquarters, and back to the trainer's hand. (If no surcingle is available, tie a ring to the stirrup or girth at shoulder height.) When changing direction, the horse must be stopped and both longe lines reattached in the inside and outside position.

Caution: The longe lines or long reins should not be fastened together, as this creates a dangerous loop in which the handler and/or horse could become entangled. Be careful not to allow the extra folds of longe line to hang down in dangerously large, sloppy loops.

The horse is started off in a straight line with the trainer walking behind. After the horse has become accustomed to the two lines and thoroughly accepts them, the trainer gradually walks on a smaller circle to accustom the horse to the pressure of the outside line as outside aids affecting the gaskin, hock, and quarters in general. As work proceeds, the circle can be carefully increased.

The inner longe is handled as usual, keeping a light contact with the inside of the horse's nose. The outer longe must be handled with a light, steady contact along the horse's side and around his hindquarters, to keep his hind legs following in the tracks of his front legs. The horse's head must not be pulled to the outside. *Caution:* Don't let the outside longe drop too low, where it could become entangled in the hind legs, or lift it high enough to get caught under the tail.

LONGEING FOR VARIOUS PURPOSES

Longeing for Exercise

Longeing can be used to exercise a horse in place of riding. Because longeing is harder work than it appears, and is especially stressful on unfit or immature joints, you must assess the horse's level of fitness and keep the longeing workload within his limits. Twenty minutes should be the maximum for a fit horse; young or unfit horses should be longed for ten minutes or less, increasing gradually as the horse's fitness increases.

Always longe on good footing, warm up slowly, and warm down at the end of the session. Work equally in both directions (or slightly more in the horse's difficult direction), and use a timer to keep track of how long he is worked in each direction and the total time.

Longeing to Settle a Fresh Horse

Longeing can settle a fresh horse or relax a tense horse before riding. This is especially important when a student's horse is too fresh to ride safely. It is best to longe with the saddle and bridle in place (with a cavesson and side reins added). *Caution:* Fresh horses may kick, so follow safety procedures carefully, and be alert!

Start out as quietly as possible (at a walk, if the horse will cooperate). If the horse is very fresh, it is better to allow him to trot slowly than to fight him about walking. Do not allow bucking and running, because it increases the risk of injury, and because a horse should associate longeing with steadiness and good behavior, not wild, undisciplined behavior. Instead, emphasize developing steady rhythm and tempo, relaxation, and free forward movement. If a horse needs to run, buck, and play, it is safer for him and better for his training to turn him out than to let him run and buck on the longe.

Longeing an Unfamiliar Horse

When longeing an unfamiliar horse, your primary goals are to assess his movement, attitude, and level of training, and to establish a rapport that will allow you to work with him. Safety precautions are always important, but especially so when working with an unfamiliar horse. Be very careful not to get into a position in which you could be kicked, and treat an unfamiliar horse as if he were a green horse until you ascertain otherwise.

Before longeing, show the horse the longe whip, then run it gently over his body, noting his reactions. Practice parallel leading with halts and transitions, to see if he responds to voice commands. You can then proceed to parallel longeing, then regular longeing. Note which direction is easier and which is more difficult, and be alert to keep him from stopping and turning around when working in his difficult direction.

As you longe, assess the horse's balance, movement, acceptance of the bit and side reins, and response to your aids and signals. Consider his temperament and willingness to cooperate with you.

Some categories a horse might fall into are:

- **Well-schooled:** familiar with longeing, supple and responsive, able to move correctly in all gaits; accepts the aids and responds correctly.

- **Balance and movement problems:** obedient but stiff, crooked, or unbalanced (usually more so in one direction). May not be able to canter safely on the longe.
- **Green:** unbacked, or never longed before.
- **Problem horses:** difficult attitude (tense, "hot," fearful, stubborn, lazy, etc.) or bad habits (balking, bolting, turning around, kicking, etc.).

LONGEING TO IMPROVE THE HORSE

Longeing for Obedience and Discipline

Longeing is a good way to teach a horse to pay attention, respond to signals, and learn how to learn. It provides a safe way to establish obedience, respect, and rapport, especially in difficult or spoiled horses.

When longeing for obedience, you must read the horse's intentions accurately. Remember the three-second rule: For a horse to associate a behavior with reward or correction, reinforcement must take place within three seconds or less. You must be prepared to reward or correct instantly, depending on the horse's behavior. One well-timed reinforcement can work wonders; rewarding or correcting even a few seconds too late will have negative results.

Work on one behavior at a time (for instance, moving forward promptly in response to a voice command). Be clear and consistent in giving signals, and be ready to act instantly. If the horse resists or acts up, you may need to escalate your corrections (for instance, from pointing the whip to snapping it, a light touch, or even a sharp crack). Be ready to reward instantly and generously as soon as the horse begins to move in the right direction.

Longeing to Improve Movement

Longeing may be used to improve the horse's gaits, balance, and movement. Good longeing technique, along with careful observation and an "educated eye" for movement, can lead to improvement in muscle development and performance under saddle.

The following qualities are basic to good movement. They are progressive and should be taught in the order in which they are presented, as each depends on the foundation of the previous ones.

Rhythm and Tempo   Clear rhythm and good working tempo come first. "Running" gaits are tense and quick, with short strides; too slow a tempo goes with lazy, dragging gaits and a broken or shuffling rhythm. An inconsistent horse that changes from slow to quick and back again cannot move well. When a horse finds the right working tempo, his rhythm becomes clear and steady, he can swing his legs freely in rhythm, and he breathes evenly. This leads to relaxation and better movement.

To improve rhythm and tempo, keep the circle round and consistent in size. Counting to yourself helps to emphasize the rhythm and helps you time your aids correctly. Watch the inside hind leg; the aids (half-halts or whip signals) should be applied as the inside hind leg pushes off and swings through the air.

For a tense, quick horse, longe at a slower trot on a slightly smaller circle (about 18 meters). Encourage a slower tempo with gentle half-halts in rhythm with the motion of the inside hind leg, and quiet, soothing voice aids. For a lazy horse, point the whip toward the inside hind leg each time it swings forward, and use a stimulating voice command such as a cluck or the word, "Come" or "Hup."

Relaxation, Calmness, and Looseness   Good working relaxation depends on both mental calmness and athletic relaxation or "looseness" of the muscles. This is only possible when the horse develops a steady working tempo. Mentally tense horses need to calm down and to pay attention to the trainer, instead of overreacting to distractions in the environment.

To develop calmness, the trainer's attitude and demeanor are especially important. Breathe deeply, use a quiet, soothing tone of voice, and apply rein aids with a gentle, relaxed touch, in rhythm with the gait. If possible, longe in an enclosed ring, away from distractions.

Athletic relaxation and looseness of the muscles develops only when the horse warms up and settles into a good working tempo. Watch for the following relaxation signs, which indicate that he is becoming physically and mentally relaxed:

- The eyes are soft and the ears are not held stiffly.
- Taking a deep breath, like a sigh.
- Blowing the nose in a long, gentle snort.
- Stretching down with the neck and head and relaxing the back.
- Chewing the bit softly.

Forward Movement and Engagement   Forward movement comes from engagement (the reaching forward of the hind legs at each stride), and from the horse's desire to move forward. Good engagement provides impulsion or thrust; it also results in a swinging back that transmits power from the hind legs and can carry a rider better, and in better balance.

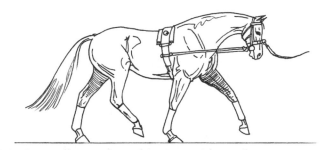

Moving well: round, tracking up, with good engagement

Moving poorly: hollow back, overbent, moving with stiff, constrained steps

Do not be in a hurry to ask for tracking-up until after relaxation and a slow, steady rhythm have been established. Tracking-up and subsequent engagement develop gradually as the horse builds confidence and strength.

To move forward better, the horse must take longer, more powerful strides with his hind legs—*not* run faster with short, quick steps. A horse can only reach farther as the hind leg swings through the air, not when it is grounded and bearing weight. Point the whip at the inside hind leg as it pushes off the ground and swings forward to encourage a longer stride in the same tempo.

Engagement and forward movement require work; a tired, sore, or lazy horse will move with short strides and poor engagement. Tense, quick, running strides, inconsistent tempo, and tension in the back prevent good engagement. A lazy horse may need to be enlivened with strong driving aids (stepping toward the hindquarters, snapping the whip, or touching him with the lash) to develop his desire to go forward.

Stretching and Use of the Back   In order to carry a rider comfortably, a horse must move with a swinging back that is slightly rounded. This is caused by the engagement of the hind legs at each stride, the downward stretch of the horse's neck, and the use of the abdominal muscles. It requires a good working rhythm and tempo, relaxation and looseness of the muscles, and free forward movement.

Stretching down is a good exercise to develop a rounded, swinging back. To do this, the horse must accept the bit and stretch his head and neck down in a slight arch, seeking contact with the bit. Increasing the engagement of the hind legs (while maintaining the same balance, rhythm and tempo) encourage him to stretch down in a "rainbow" arc, with a round, swinging back and a softly rounded neck.

Correct stretching down: round, well engaged

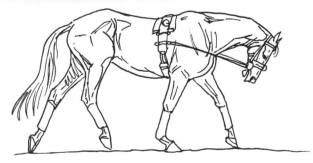

Incorrect: hollow, disengaged, leaning on forehand

Stretching down can be encouraged by the use of sliding side reins, which allow the horse to keep contact with the bit without tightening as he stretches. Use a leading rein in an outward and downward direction, while encouraging greater engagement of the hind legs by pointing the whip at the inside hind leg as it swings forward.

When a horse stretches correctly, he stays in balance and engages his hind legs—falling onto the forehand *is not correct stretching.* His head and neck should not poke stiffly out and down in a straight line, nor should the underside of his neck bulge. His hind legs should engage more, not less, and he should seek contact with the bit instead of evading it.

Balance and Transitions   Work on the longe requires more balance than ordinary movement. Young and unschooled horses often have trouble keeping their balance on the longe line, especially at the canter. A well-balanced horse "stands up" or remains upright, bending around a circle. Leaning inward, pulling, stumbling, or breaking gait show that the horse is out of balance, going too fast for the size of the circle. Fear, tension, or lack of engagement may cause a horse to rush, which further handicaps his balance. Only a well-schooled horse should be cantered on the longe.

Balance on the longe requires good engagement of the hind legs (especially the inside hind) and appropriate speed for the size of the circle. The horse must learn to bring his hind legs under him and shift his balance to the rear, so that the hind legs carry more weight instead of simply pushing it forward. This requires strength and coordination, as well as engagement, rhythm, and correct tempo.

To help a horse improve his balance on the longe, he may be fitted with side reins, adjusted correctly for his conformation and level of training. These discourage him from falling in or out with his shoulders, and act as a passive restraint on his speed. The longeing circle should be small enough to discourage excessive speed, but large enough for the horse to track correctly and bend comfortably at his stage of training. Longe at a slow trot, using half-halts in rhythm with the inside hind leg, until he remains upright instead of leaning or pulling.

Frequent transitions, correctly executed, will improve balance and strengthen the hindquarters. The horse must balance and rebalance himself for each downward transition and push off with his hindquarters in each upward transition. Try trotting for ten to twelve strides and walking for three or four strides, repeating these transitions several times in both directions. With repetition, the horse learns to stay in balance in the trot in order to be ready to walk, and to keep his engagement in the walk as he anticipates the trot transition.

Before a horse is able to canter on the longe, he must develop strong enough muscles to strike off into canter and stay in balance in canter on a circle (20 meters or larger). If he leans or travels crookedly at the trot, he is not yet ready to canter. More work on transitions, engagement, and tracking correctly on the circle will gradually develop his balance and strength. Before cantering a horse on the longe, be certain you have accurately assessed his level of training, and the stability of his balance in trot.

Suppleness, Straightness, and Lateral Balance   Suppleness refers to a horse's ability to shift his balance forward, backward, and laterally. It is not simply flexibility, which is the ability to bend the joints. Although a supple horse must be flexible, a horse can become too flexible and "rubbery" (especially in the neck) if he loses his forward movement or is pulled sideways.

Straightness (in longeing) refers to the horse's ability to track correctly (the hind legs following in the tracks of the front legs). It also relates to his ability to engage and to carry weight equally with both hind legs and with both shoulders. Horses are not naturally symmetrical; like people, they all have one side that is stronger and easier to use. One of the goals of training is to develop the horse as evenly as possible, to overcome this natural crookedness. This requires frequent changes of direction, and extra attention to the correctness of the work on the horse's weaker side or difficult direction.

Correctly adjusted side reins, longeing on a circle of appropriate size, keeping the circle round, and frequent changes of direction are all helpful in developing suppleness. (See "Importance of the Circle," p. 155.)

Spiraling in and spiraling out on a circle is an exercise to improve lateral balance and suppleness. Starting with a 20-meter circle, the horse is brought in on a smaller circle (approximately 15 meters) by applying a direct rein repeatedly, in rhythm with the gait, while taking in the longe line a little at each stride. Longe several times around the 15-meter circle, then send the horse gradually back out to a 20-meter circle by pointing the whip toward the girth at each stride (as the hind leg pushes off and swings forward), while letting the longe out. The horse should move forward and out slightly at each stride, not outward all at once. The exercise should be practiced in both directions, with emphasis on the horse's more difficult side.

Improving Acceptance of the Bit

Longeing can be used to educate a green horse to accept the bit, and to give to it, or to improve a horse with problems in this area. (First, make sure that the horse's mouth is comfortable and that he has no painful teeth.) The horse should be fitted with a smooth snaffle bit with a comfortable, moderately thick mouthpiece, a saddle or roller, and side reins of equal length. Don't overtighten the throatlash or noseband, as this can inhibit correct flexion and relaxation of the jaw.

Sliding side reins may be helpful for horses that are tense, high headed, or tight in the back; horses that are oversensitive in the mouth may do better with elastic side reins. Use a longe cavesson, to avoid interfering with the contact or pulling on his mouth.

After warming up without side reins, adjust the side reins so that the horse can make contact with the bit when the front of his face is about one hand's width in front of the vertical, with his mouth at approximately the level of the point of his shoulder. Longe at a trot with a steady, not too fast tempo, and encourage the horse to take longer strides with his hind legs, without quickening or rushing. As he engages his hind legs more, he will stretch his back and reach out and down with his head and neck. If the side reins are correctly adjusted, the horse makes his own gentle contact with the bit.

It is particularly important not to overshorten the side reins, or to cause the horse to "set his head," retract his neck, or overflex. However, side reins adjusted too long make it impossible for a horse to make contact with the bit while moving in good balance.

Signs of progress include:

- Gently chewing the bit, which produces foam in the mouth.
- Stretching the neck and back, showing more roundness in the back, while continuing to reach well forward with the hind legs.
- A more steady and consistent, but not rigid, head carriage.
- Indications of relaxation, such as a rhythmically swinging tail, breathing in rhythm with the strides, and gently snorting or "blowing his nose."
- Progression to self-carriage as a result of meeting and giving to the side-reins.

Improving the Canter

For most horses, cantering on the longe is more difficult than trotting, as it requires more balance, strength and suppleness. Correct longeing can greatly improve the horse's canter work under saddle. It must be introduced gradually, however, and kept within the horse's capabilities.

Before cantering on the longe, the horse must longe well at the trot, tracking correctly and moving with good balance, impulsion, and correct bend. He must not lean or pull against the longe, or travel crookedly. He may be fitted with side reins, adjusted for normal longeing (face about a hand's width in front of the vertical). More advanced horses can canter with shorter side reins (face nearly vertical, mouth on a level with the point of the hip), but they must be able to maintain good forward impulsion and balance in a more collected frame.

Practicing a series of transitions (trot–walk and walk–trot) improves the horse's balance and impulsion in preparation for the canter. Asking him to strike off into canter from a walk or collected trot results in a better balanced canter than if he runs into it from a fast trot. The horse should strike off into canter on a circle smaller than 20 meters, then move outward, correctly bent, to canter on the larger circle. Give a clear signal that means "Canter," not a signal that could be mistaken for a command to speed up the trot. If he misses the canter depart, bring him back to balance in a walk or collected trot before trying again.

Keep the circle round but large enough for good balance at the canter (at least 20 meters). You may need to revert to parallel longeing in order to make the circle large enough and to stay closer to the horse, so he is more aware of your aids. Longeing in a ring with a fence or a barrier supports your outside aids and helps to prevent the horse from pulling or falling out.

Emphasize the "jump" in each canter stride by gesturing with your whip toward the inside hind leg as it reaches forward. If the horse hollows his back, his engagement suffers, the canter becomes "flat," and it may degenerate into a four-beat canter. Too restrictive side reins, trying to slow the canter down too much, or cantering on too small a circle for the horse's level of training, can lead to this problem. (For more about canter work on the longe, see p. 179.)

TEACHING A HORSE TO LONGE

Teaching a horse to longe (whether a green or unbroken horse or a trained horse that has never been longed) requires confidence, patience, and experience in training and handling horses, as well as in longeing. You will also need a safe place to work (an enclosed ring with good footing), and an assistant can be very helpful.

The early stages of longeing are of vital importance, as this is where you make your first real impressions on the horse, gain his respect, and teach obedience to the voice. This lays the foundation for future progress. Longeing can be a great help in developing a well-mannered horse, as well as strengthening muscles, increasing balance and impulsion, and bringing an unbroken horse into condition for riding.

Equipment

A longe cavesson is essential equipment, for control and to avoid damaging the horse's mouth, along with a 30-foot longe line (*not* the type with a chain end), and a longe whip. Boots or bandages are necessary to protect the legs, in case the horse makes mistakes or moves awkwardly at first. Later, you may need a saddle or surcingle, snaffle bridle, and side reins.

Prerequisites

Before you can begin training a horse to longe, he must have been taught good manners during ground handling, tacking up, and so on. He must be taught to lead from both sides, and to halt, walk, and trot in response to voice commands. He should be accustomed to seeing a longe whip, and being gently touched with the whip all over his body.

Introduce the longeing equipment first (during grooming is a good time). Adjust the cavesson; try on boots or bandages, and let the horse see and sniff the longe whip before rubbing it gently over his neck, body and legs. Work patiently and quietly, and make it a pleasant experience. This should be repeated as often as necessary, until the horse accepts the equipment with an unconcerned attitude.

Using the longe equipment, practice leading and transitions, responding correctly to voice commands, especially halting. Work from both sides, and on a circle in both directions.

Next, practice parallel leading (leading from a distance of 4 or 5 feet, then 10 to 12 feet from the horse) on both sides. (For more about parallel leading and parallel longeing, see the USPC C Manual, p. 278.)

Procedure (with Assistant)

The easiest way to begin longeing a green horse is to work with an assistant. (The assistant must be an experienced horseperson who can lead correctly and who will follow directions.) The assistant can help give the horse confidence and prevent mistakes, and helps establish control. However, one drawback is that the horse's attention may be divided between the assistant and the trainer, instead of on the trainer alone.

The assistant's job is to keep the horse on the track of the circle, and to assist the trainer in any way necessary. This must be done as unobtrusively as possible, without distracting the horse's attention from the trainer's signals. The assistant never speaks to the horse, but may give the horse a reward (a tidbit) when directed by the trainer. Eventually, the assistant "fades away" by doing less and moving farther from the horse, until the horse is longed entirely by the trainer.

The assistant leads the horse from the outside of the circle, using a lead line attached to the same ring on the cavesson as the longe line. (If the horse tries to turn into the circle, the assistant may walk on the inside.)

To move the horse forward, the trainer should give the voice command, "Walk on," and point the whip at the horse's hocks. If necessary, repeat the command and the gesture with the whip. The assistant should move forward with the horse, keeping the lead loose; if the horse does not understand, the assistant leads him forward. When halting, the trainer should give the voice command, "And Whoa," step slightly forward (opposite the horse's shoulder), and quietly move the whip forward, so that it points to a spot in front of the horse's head. As the command "Whoa" is given, the assistant simply stops walking; if the horse continues to move, he runs against the pressure of the assistant's lead line and the longe line. By walking on the outside of the circle, the assistant can keep the horse from turning in or out. (Some horses work better with the assistant on the inside. However, it is easier for the horse to see the trainer's signals when the assistant is on the outside.)

Practice walking and halting at various places on the circle, with the trainer giving all voice commands and words of praise. When the horse is responding consistently to voice commands without any help from the assistant, the lead line may be tied around the horse's neck, while the assistant continues to walk alongside without holding the lead. If necessary, the lead line may be used to make a correction. When the horse responds correctly, the lead line may be removed and the assistant is no longer needed.

Practice longeing at a walk, halting, and walking on in both directions, with the assistant and eventually with the assistant "fading away." Keep the training sessions short (10 to 15 minutes), to avoid going beyond the horse's short attention span. Since the best reward is stopping work, always end the lesson with something that the horse does well.

Once the horse learns to walk, halt, and walk forward on the circle without an assistant, he can be introduced to trotting and further longe work as described below.

Procedure (Single Handler)

If you don't have an assistant, or if you prefer to work by yourself, you can teach a horse to longe by progressing from parallel leading to parallel longeing, and eventually to true longeing. Without the help of an assistant, it is even more important to work in an enclosed area of suitable size (ideally, a round pen or longe ring about 60 feet in diameter).

Begin by parallel leading (leading from a distance of 4 to 10 feet), walking a circle of a size that results in the horse moving on a 60-foot circle. Practice halting and walking on, using the voice commands described above. Then move out to a distance of 10 to 15 feet and switch to the position for parallel longeing (see diagram). In this position, you can point or gesture with the whip more effectively to keep the horse moving forward on the 60-foot circle.

When longeing a green horse, it helps to stay slightly behind the control point to keep him moving forward.

When the horse moves forward on the circle easily for several revolutions, prepare to halt. Move forward, ahead of the control point, and quietly move the whip so that it points at a spot in front of the horse's head, as you give the command, "And Whoa." Keep the whip low and quiet (omit the whip gesture if it worries the horse). If the horse does not stop, guide him straight into the wall or a corner, so that he has to halt without turning. Walk out to the horse to reward him with a pat and perhaps a tidbit; never bring him in toward you to halt him, or he may learn to turn in whenever he wants to stop working.

You can gradually let out the longe and move farther away, but you will probably need to continue parallel longeing with a shortened longe line for a while, in order to stay close enough for good control. (But walk a circle that is round and large enough to keep the horse working on a 60-foot circle.)

Trotting

When the horse walks on and halts promptly in response to voice commands, you can introduce trotting. Give the command "Trot," and point the whip toward his hocks, or give it a small shake if necessary. Repeat if necessary, and praise immediately when he trots.

Let the horse trot several times around the circle; if he is slightly tired, he will be more willing to walk when you ask him to. Give the command "And Walk," and move forward, slightly ahead of the control point, keeping the whip low and quiet. You can give brief, gentle "check and release" aids with the longe line, but try to use voice commands and body language, and avoid pulling on the longe any more than absolutely necessary. Pulling inward too much may make the horse turn in or bend his neck sideways instead of teaching him to come back to the walk on command. If he has difficulty learning this, go back to the walk and practice until the horse halts more easily.

Lengthening and Shortening Stride within a Gait

The horse should be taught to lengthen and shorten stride within a gait on command. To increase the stride, use a short, sharp "cluck" or a command like "Come" or "Hup" once with each stride, and point the whip toward the horse's inside hock as the hind leg swings forward. To slow down the gait, use a command like "Easy" or "Steady," and give short, repeated half-halt aids in rhythm with the gait. It may also help to push the horse outward toward the corner or wall, or to move him in on a slightly smaller circle, just enough to encourage him to shorten his stride a little. Praise him immediately when he responds even a little. At first, the horse will probably slow down or speed up the tempo when asked for a change of speed. With practice and correctly timed aids, he will learn to lengthen and shorten his stride instead of simply speeding up or slowing down.

Cantering on the Longe

Don't try to canter a green horse on the longe until he is working well at the trot (see "Improving the Canter," p. 174).

To ask for a canter, shorten the longe and go back to parallel longeing, but walk a circle of a size that lets the horse move on a circle slightly smaller than 20 meters. Prepare the horse with repeated trot–walk and walk–trot transitions. Give the voice command, "*Canter*," and make a circular gesture with the whip, moving it forward and upward toward his stifle. As he strikes off into canter, allow him to move outward onto a 20-meter circle, or a somewhat larger circle if necessary. Praise him immediately if he canters, and encourage him to keep cantering, even if only for a few strides.

If the horse has difficulty taking the canter, do not try to drive him into a canter by making him trot faster. This produces a rushing, unbalanced trot, from which it is almost impossible to canter correctly.

One way to overcome this problem is to longe the horse over a single ground pole or a small jump. This often causes him to land cantering in the correct lead. As he canters on, shift the circle slightly, to avoid jumping the obstacle again.

Cantering on one lead is a sign of one-sidedness. Cantering on the wrong lead is usually a sign of poor balance (it also may be caused by the trainer pulling the horse's head inward as he begins the canter). The horse needs more suppling work at the trot in his difficult direction. If caused by a momentary lapse of balance or a mistaken signal, bring the horse back to a better balanced trot or walk and try again. Do not allow him to continue on the wrong lead. Do not try to make him change leads without first bringing him back to a balanced trot.

Cantering disunited (on one lead in the front legs and the other in the hind legs) often happens when a horse is too much on the forehand or when his head is pulled inward. As his hind legs swing to the outside, he is likely to go disunited. (This can also happen when a horse tries to execute a flying change and fails.) A disunited horse should be brought back to the trot and rebalanced before cantering again. He needs more work on tracking correctly, and on "standing up" (remaining vertical and bending) instead of leaning inward. Enlarging the longeing circle may help.

HANDLING LONGEING PROBLEMS

Longeing Away from Home   You may need to longe a horse to settle him in a strange place or before a competition. Before you can longe safely away from home, your horse *must* be well schooled at home, and you should be able to longe him safely in the open. At a competition, clinic, or rally, there may be very little safe space in which to longe. Sometimes the only available space is not level. Use good judgment about where you longe and whether longeing is feasible at all, given the footing and conditions. Do not monopolize the schooling area or longe in an area that is too busy to be safe. You may have to longe in a smaller circle than usual (if so, do less than usual, because the work is harder for your horse), or in the open.

Especially in the open, keep the work slow and emphasize steady rhythm, stretching, and quiet obedience. Keep his attention on you by timely use of transitions, voice commands, longe, and whip, and watch for signs of relaxation and loosening up (chewing the bit, blowing his nose, and stretching his neck and back). Discourage bucking and playing.

Don't overdo longeing, especially when warming up for a competition.

Disobediences If a horse bucks or bolts, place one foot in front of you, bend your knees and keep your shoulders back. Use short, strong half-halts and firm voice commands. A horse that kicks should be corrected with a sharp, displeased voice and a swift upward jerk on the longe line.

A horse whose obedience is questionable should always be longed in an enclosed ring, with no riders present. Don't allow him to drag you around! If a horse is too strong for you to hold, let him go rather than take chances with your safety or his.

Never longe a rider unless you are sure the horse being used is consistently obedient.

Evasions The horse that does not go forward and the horse that comes in on the circle (often practiced simultaneously) are evading your control and the work of longeing. Use the command "Out," and point or shake the whip at his shoulder, as you step forward on the line of the whip, then drive him forward from behind. Increasing or decreasing the size of the circle for one round may also help.

A more serious type of evasion is turning the head in and swinging the quarters out, sometimes swinging around to face the trainer. This type of evasion is more common when a horse is worked without side reins, which is a good reason for using them. He should be fitted with correctly adjusted side reins, with the outside side rein short enough to discourage him from bending his neck too much and popping his outside shoulder out. Send him forward strongly, so that he cannot shorten stride, hesitate, or stop. In difficult cases, the double longe may be helpful.

If the horse succeeds in stopping, facing you, or begins backing away, follow him until he is stopped by reaching a wall or other barrier, then step back, opposite his hindquarters, and send him forward. You may need to shorten the longe, move closer to him, and move in a circle (parallel longeing). Horses usually try this evasion in the same spot, so be aware of any hesitation or shortening of stride as he approaches that point and send him forward. Be careful not to get ahead of the control point, which can provoke this behavior.

Some horses stop and whirl around, especially after changing directions or when longed in their difficult direction. Stop the horse and reposition him (lead his head around until he is facing in the correct direction), then send him forward. This action must be taken promptly and firmly, but not roughly; avoid "rewarding" the horse with a rest or release of pressure until he is moving forward again in the direction he should.

Stubborn Horse When longeing a calm but stubborn horse (one that refuses to move forward, frequently stops, or has no respect for the whip), stop and analyze the situation. Make sure there is nothing nearby that distracts or worries the horse. Go back to parallel longeing or even parallel leading, to establish the basic idea of longeing. Use the whip close enough to his hocks to make him respect it and move forward. Stay close enough to reach the horse with the whip, even if you have to walk a large circle.

If nothing else works, try having an experienced rider ride the horse on the longe line, applying leg aids each time you give a voice command.

Lazy Horse A lazy horse avoids the work of longeing (and therefore, its benefits) by putting forth the least effort he can get away with. It is all too easy to fall into a pattern of nagging, so that you do more and work harder while the horse pays even less attention to you. Instead, insist on a prompt response to your aids by using the whip immediately when he fails to respond, as sharply as necessary to command his attention and awaken his energy. Shorten the longe and walk a circle (parallel longeing) so that you are close enough to reach him with the whip. It may be necessary to hit him once across the rump, hard enough to make him respect the whip.

Lazy horses do better when kept busy with frequent transitions and different exercises, and in fairly brief sessions.

Bored Horse Horses easily become bored with longeing, because of the repetitive nature of the work. A horse that suddenly becomes uncooperative may be bored. Keep longeing sessions short; keep the horse's attention by varying gaits, making frequent transitions, changing directions, and spiraling in or out. Longeing over a single ground pole can also restore a horse's interest. Try longeing in different locations, and avoid a fixed routine.

Rushing Horse   If a horse rushes or won't stop, check your body language and your handling of the whip; make sure you are not unknowingly "chasing" him forward. Keep the whip quiet and pointing toward the ground, or reverse it so that it trails behind you. Shorten the longe and move closer to him, walking a circle (parallel longeing). Move forward, opposite the horse's neck, and use voice commands along with repeated half-halts, timed with the swing of the inside hind leg. Making the circle slightly smaller may help slow him down.

To stop a rushing horse, move with him, use a "body block" or direct him into a fence, wall, or corner (which must be too high to jump), giving a voice command to halt just before he is forced to stop.

One-Sided Horse   If a horse longes well in one direction but consistently resists in the other, treat him as though he were a green horse when longeing in his difficult direction, asking for only a little work at a time. When he becomes more comfortable longeing in his difficult direction, he should be worked *slightly longer* on that side to achieve equal suppleness on both sides.

A one-sided horse should be checked by a veterinarian, to determine whether lameness, soreness, or faulty vision in one eye might be the cause of his difficulty.

Frightened or Difficult Horse   Do not attempt to longe a really frightened or extremely difficult horse. If a longeing session degenerates into a rodeo performance, the danger of injury to both you and the horse is too great, and the horse will learn nothing of value.

Problems Caused by Handler   Many longeing problems are caused by the handler's mistakes or lack of skill. In these cases, the solution is to improve yourself. Some common handler errors are:

- Not teaching control, as in "Whoa" or "Halt" first.
- Nagging.
- Incorrect technique with longe or whip.
- Dwelling too long on one thing or exercise.
- Poor timing; misreading the horse.

CHAPTER 6

• • • • • • • • • • • • • • • •

Teaching Horsemanship

U.S. Pony Club instructors teach *horsemanship*, which is more than just riding. Horsemanship means teaching skills and knowledge, and especially the attitude, responsibility, and feeling for horses that makes a true horseman or horsewoman. Sharing knowledge and helping others learn and grow is an important part of horsemanship. This helps not only your students, but their horses and ponies as well.

B Pony Clubbers teach D- and C-Level riders in unmounted and mounted classes. HA and A Pony Clubbers teach all levels, including dismounted lessons, work on the flat and over fences, and coaching and preparation for rallies and other competitions. *The USPC C Manual of Horsemanship*, Chapter 11, covers an introduction to teaching, including what makes a good teacher, safety checks, helping students prepare for inspection, dismounted instruction, and acting as an assistant.

We always teach best what we know best and care about most. Your riding experience will give you insights and ideas to pass on to your students. As you prepare and teach a lesson, you will often find that it helps you understand the topic better yourself.

TEACHING AND LEARNING

Types of Learning

There are several types of learning:

Cognitive Learning facts and knowledge. (Example: learning the parts of the horse.) **Conceptual learning,** which is related to cognitive learning, is learning concepts or ideas and reasons. (Example: learning safety rules and reasons for them.) Most schoolwork emphasizes cognitive and conceptual learning.

Affective Learning related to "affect," or feelings and attitudes. (Example: learning to treat a pony kindly.)

Motor Skills Learning physical skills and movements. (Example: learning to post the trot.)

Problem-Solving Learning to use one's intelligence and creativity to solve problems, both individually and while working with others. (Example: learning to handle an uncooperative pony.)

Social Skills Learning to interact with other people. (Example: learning to be a helpful, cooperative member of a pony club.)

All types of learning are important, but in riding instruction, sometimes skills and cognitive learning (learning facts) can be overemphasized. The attitudes and values (affective learning) a child develops through learning horsemanship may be more important than how high he jumps or whether he passes a particular rating level. They also increase his ability to work with others, to take responsibility, and to solve problems.

Learning Styles

There are several different learning styles. Although we all learn in many ways, each person has a dominant style in which he learns best. Good teachers use a variety of teaching techniques, in order to appeal to as many learning styles as possible.

Verbal Learning through words. Some people understand best when they hear a verbal explanation, read about a subject, or discuss an idea.

Visual   Learning through seeing. Visual learners understand best when they see a picture or watch a demonstration.

Kinesthetic   Learning by doing or feeling. Kinesthetic learners need to experience what they learn. Some subjects (such as sitting the trot) require kinesthetic learning.

> We learn:
> 10 percent of what we read;
> 20 percent of what we hear;
> 30 percent of what we both see and hear;
> 50 percent of what is discussed with others;
> 80 percent of what we experience personally;
> 95 percent of what we teach to someone else.
> —William Glasser

Teaching Methods

The method you choose depends on the subject, the ages and needs of your students, the teaching situation, and the resources available. It is best to use more than one method, because some people understand better with one method than another. Any method you use must be safe, clear, and organized, and must keep your students' interest.

Explanation   When telling how to do something, keep it short and simple, to keep students interested and avoid confusion. Be positive: tell how to do it, not how *not* to do it.

Demonstration   If you're showing how to do something, your demonstrations must be brief, clear, and to the point. Practice first to be sure you can demonstrate correctly, and always show good safety procedures as well as the procedure you are teaching. Make sure all your students can see, and explain the steps as you do them.

Skill Drills   Repetitive exercises or practice, used in mounted lessons, develop motor (physical) skills (such as half-seat position at the trot). Developing the correct motor skills takes the right kind of practice. Use repetitions of an exercise instead of making students hold a position or continue an exercise so long that fatigue sets in. Be creative; vary exercises to keep practice interesting and fun.

Questions and Discussion   Asking questions can strengthen students' grasp of what they already know, and lead students to *discover* what you wish to teach them. By starting with simple questions that students can answer easily, you can ask "leading" questions that lead them to new ideas. Because the students make discoveries themselves, this is a powerful teaching tool.

Discussing a subject should cause students to think about it, to organize their knowledge, and to put it into a practical situation. In Pony Club rating tests, discussing the performance or topic with the Examiner lets the Pony Clubber present practical knowledge of the subject, instead of merely repeating memorized words or ideas.

Group discussions work best when all members of the group have at least some knowledge of the subject, or on topics about which people have questions and opinions, such as horse behavior. Don't let one or two students dominate the discussion or answer all the questions; use a "round robin" method or call on each person so that everyone has a chance to contribute.

Practical Lesson   Students learn by doing, usually with a brief explanation and/or demonstration first. This works well for teaching hands-on skills such as grooming, bandaging, etc. You must have enough equipment for everyone, a safe place to work, suitable horse(s), and supervision of all students while they are working. Having students work in teams or pairs may help.

Lecture   Best for introducing a new topic or information on a subject the group is interested in; only for older students and dismounted instruction. Lectures should be *brief, clear,* and *interesting.* Disadvantages are that students may become bored, may not understand, and may "tune you out," and you do not get as much feedback from your students as in other methods. Lectures tend to be used too often; they can be one of the least effective methods of teaching, especially in mounted and practical situations.

Role Playing and Skits   They help students to view reality from another point of view and encourage creativity, expression, and social skills (interacting with other people). This method can be great fun, especially for younger Pony Clubbers. Role playing is a good way to demonstrate horse behavior.

Games and Contests   Games can motivate students while making learning and practice fun. They should involve skills or knowledge you want to encourage (such as keeping all ponies on the rail, or learning parts of tack), and must be fun for *all* participants, not just the winner. Don't overemphasize competition at the expense of good horsemanship and teamwork. Above all, games must be safe and suitable for the level of the riders.

These are only a few of the instructional methods you might use. Be flexible and creative, and pay attention to each student's response to the methods you choose.

Your Students

Every student is an individual, with his or her own needs, abilities, interests, and reasons for riding or being in Pony Club. The more interested you are in your students, the easier and more rewarding it is to teach them. Try to put yourself in your students' place. Would you like to have yourself as a teacher? How easy would it be to learn from you?

Good instructors tailor their teaching to the age and level of their students, without ever talking down to them.

Pony Clubbers range from young children to young adults. Because skills and learning ability develop gradually, different age groups have different characteristics. However, each child develops at his or her own rate. Some will be farther ahead or slower to develop in certain areas than the average for their age group.

Young children (age six to nine) are developing gross motor skills (skills involving large muscle movements) and coordination. They usually have lots of energy and enthusiasm, like to have fun, and need to be kept busy. However, they have short attention spans and can get bored or physically tired quickly. They need help with strenuous or complicated tasks, such as carrying heavy objects and tacking up.

Preteens (age ten to twelve) have better coordination and are developing fine motor skills (skills requiring small or detailed muscle movements). They have longer attention spans than younger children, but not as long as teens or adults. Preteens are usually very much involved with and influenced by their peer group. They may have lots of energy that needs an outlet, but some can be shy and sensitive, especially to criticism.

Teenagers are in a process of change, physically, mentally, and emotionally. Some have growth spurts, and may have difficulty in coordination while learning to cope with their changing bodies. Teens may sometimes feel and act like adults, and at other times like kids. Teenagers are developing and testing their values, beliefs, and goals. They expect honesty and high standards from teachers and leaders, and their respect must be earned, not demanded. Teenagers, especially at the upper levels, are able to handle much more responsibility than younger children. They need to be involved in the process of setting goals and rules, rather than having these dictated to them.

Goal Setting

Goals are important for teachers and students. They tell you where you are headed and how you know when you get there. They also help you stay motivated along the way.

When planning a lesson or course, goals (educational objectives) tell what you expect your students to accomplish. To be useful, goals must be clear and specific. For instance, "riding better" is too vague. "Riding with good balance and position at posting trot" is a more specific goal.

Large goals (such as passing a Pony Club rating test) must be broken down into smaller subgoals that can be attained step by step. This gives a student many small successes along the way, leading to larger accomplishments. They also build confidence and motivation. Setting a goal so high that it seems unattainable, or concentrating only on a goal far in the future, can be discouraging.

Goals must be important to the student. If you set goals that are not important to your student, you will be in conflict and you probably won't get very far. For instance, if competition is important to you but not to your student (or vice versa), you are both likely to be disappointed. Children should be involved in the process of setting goals. Each child has his or her own motivation, goals, and reasons for riding or being in Pony Club. If your teaching helps your students reach their own goals, you will both be successful.

Physical Education

Like other sports, teaching riding requires a knowledge of the human body and how it works. Instructors must study human anatomy and kinesiology (the study of movement) as much as horsemanship and equitation. The popularity of fitness and sport science has made more people aware of fitness and physical training. However, less research has been done about how the human body is used in riding than in other popular sports.

As an instructor, it is important to know how to assess and teach physical skills, and how best to develop your students' abilities. Devising an exercise to strengthen the proper muscles is much more effective than nagging a rider to correct a bad habit.

We all have an imperfect sense of what our bodies are doing, and have unconscious habit patterns that feel natural and normal to us, even when they are incorrect. For instance, a person who habitually tilts forward may believe that he is sitting straight up when he is actually leaning forward; when he sits up correctly, he may feel "all wrong," as if he were leaning backward. In addition, human bodies are not perfectly symmetrical; we all have a stronger and a weaker side. This can cause problems in balance, position, and crookedness. Instructors must help their students become more aware of how they use their bodies, and must realize that repeated mistakes do not mean that a student is lazy or disobedient.

Some riders are naturals, gifted with athletic ability, coordination, and "feel." Riding skills come easily to them, but they may not understand how or what they do. Those who lack the gifts of the natural can become excellent riders, but they need good instruction and may have to work harder. Attitude, desire, and the willingness to work hard— not physical talent—are what ultimately determine how far a person will go in horsemanship.

Sport Psychology

Sport psychology is a recent innovation in the teaching and coaching of all sports, including riding. It focuses on the mental and emotional side of sports and competition, including teaching and learning, motivation, goal setting, problem solving, and developing the most effective mindset for training and competition. Sport psychology techniques have helped riding instructors, competitive coaches, and riders from beginners through Olympic competitors, and the field is growing rapidly. Sport psychology can be especially helpful in dealing with the pressures of competition.

You can learn more about sport psychology through books, audio tapes, and seminars. Some colleges offer courses in sport psychology.

WHAT IS GOOD TEACHING?

If you think about the best teachers and teaching you have had, you will probably find that many of the ideas listed below were essentials. You may be able to think of other aspects of good teaching that are important as well.

Safety First! Always put safety first, for humans and for horses. Learn (and keep learning) about safety procedures, and use safety checks. Plan and practice emergency procedures, and always know how and where to get assistance quickly whenever and wherever you teach.

Establish safety rules and procedures, and insist that they are followed. Don't make exceptions, or allow anyone to ride with unsafe attire or equipment, ever!

Consider the age, experience, physical condition, and abilities of each rider. Teach only what students can handle at the present. *Never* overface a rider or horse! Fear, fatigue, and confusion interfere with learning and cause accidents.

Use your own best judgment. If you have an uncomfortable feeling about letting a student do something, don't!

Know Your Subject In order to teach anything, you must understand it. Motivational speaker Les Brown says, "You can't teach what you don't know, and you can't lead where you don't go." To teach riding at any level, you must have experienced it yourself. Teaching "over your head" is foolish and embarrassing; in riding, it is dangerous! For some subjects, knowing your subject may mean researching or looking it up.

Be a Model Your students will do what they see you *do*, not what you *say*. Be properly turned out (boots, breeches, neat shirt, and ASTM/SEI safety helmet for riding lessons; neat, appropriate clothes and footwear for unmounted lessons).

Never smoke, chew gum, or use crude language when teaching. Set the kind of example you want your students to follow.

Discipline and Respect Safe horsemanship requires discipline: self-discipline, to set a safe example; disciplined riders, who pay attention and respond to you promptly, especially in an emergency; proper and safe behavior from nonriding spectators and helpers; and well-schooled horses that are under control. Riding is too dangerous a sport for sloppiness or lack of discipline.

Discipline doesn't mean punishment or shouting orders; rather, it means having a clear, positive authority and being in charge. To have discipline, you must first establish ground rules, which must be reasonable and easily followed. Your students (and others) must understand that it is important for safety that they pay attention and do as you say.

Discipline also implies respect: respect for the horse, for others, and for oneself. Being punctual, polite, considerate, and neatly turned out shows respect for the instructor, students, and those who make riding and Pony Club possible.

Be Interested in Your Students   Know each student as an individual. Find out about special problems they may have (such as learning disabilities, physical, or emotional problems). Discuss each student's goals, what he enjoys, and what he finds difficult.

Be patient. What comes easily to one student may be hard for others. Each student has his or her own abilities and learns at his or her own rate.

Understand your students' fears: physical fear (fear of falling or getting hurt) and mental fear (fear of failure, embarrassment, or looking foolish). Never embarrass or degrade a student, or allow others to do so; discuss fears and problems privately.

Accepting a student's fear, without judgment or criticism, is the first step toward conquering it. "Pushing" a fearful student or denying the fear can make it many times worse, and can create a very dangerous situation. Remember that *safety* must come before achievement.

Be Fair, Be Honest, Be Positive!   Students respect teachers who are fair and honest. Fairness means treating students equally, and having respect for every student and horse, regardless of abilities. Give equal attention to each member of the class, and never play favorites.

Be specific in what you praise: "Your seat is more secure and less bouncy" is more helpful than a meaningless "Good." When you ask a student to try an exercise or training technique, evaluate the results honestly. If your way doesn't work, admit it and try something else.

Teach in positive terms as much as possible. Tell students how to do something, not how not to do it. Avoid negatives like "don't" or "stop"; these can put the wrong idea more firmly into a student's mind! Above all, reinforce and build on the good things about your students, their riding, and their ponies, instead of tearing them down with negative criticism. Remember that skills are learned through success, not failure.

Break Material Down into Simple Steps   Anything is easier to learn when it is broken down into small steps (subskills), and each step is taught thoroughly before going on to the next. This method develops solid skills and builds confidence through success at each step. Trying to teach too much at once or moving ahead too fast can be overwhelming and unsafe. Bypassing essential steps or skimping on correct basics handicaps a student in later work, and is dangerous!

When teaching any subject, ask yourself what skills and knowledge are needed first. Review and test these "basics" before going on to the next step. If a student has trouble, ask yourself if one of his basics is weak, or if the step is too big. Breaking it down into smaller, simpler substeps will help. Remember that each student (and horse) learns at his or her own rate. Don't rush a slow student through the basic steps, or hold back one who quickly masters several steps.

Use Variety to Keep Lessons Interesting Keep your students' interest by using a variety of teaching methods and exercises. Different methods appeal to different types of learning. Use your creativity and sense of humor!

Find different ways to say the same thing, and express new ideas. Listen to other instructors, read, and write down new exercises or techniques. Ask questions, use analogies, and relate riding to everyday things, such as riding a bicycle.

Include some independent work in each class. Help students set goals to work on during a period of "free riding," and discuss their work afterward. Give students "homework," or exercises to practice on their own.

Use games and challenges (safe and appropriate for level) to encourage skills and horsemanship while having fun.

Cavaletti, ground poles, cones, and markers can be used for variety and to create interesting exercises. Always use safe equipment, properly spaced for the size and stride of the ponies.

Set Ground Rules Students cooperate better if they understand *in advance* what is expected of them in any situation. This is especially important with a new student or class. People feel unfairly treated if they are criticized for breaking a rule if they were not told about it first, and ignorance of safety rules is dangerous.

Keep ground rules simple, clear, and few in number. Always give reasons for them. Instead of lecturing, have the group discuss reasons for rules, or even have them formulate the rules themselves. Posting a sign with barn safety rules, or giving students a written list of rules can help reinforce the rules, but does not take the place of good instruction.

TEACHING TECHNIQUES

To teach well, you must know your material, prepare, and present it in an organized way, using safe and suitable teaching methods and exercises.

Resources

The *USPC Manuals of Horsemanship (Book 1, D Level,* and *Book 2, C Level)*, in addition to this book, are excellent references for teaching subjects for different levels. You should also review the USPC Standards of Proficiency for the level you are teaching.

A good instructor is well read and stays informed of new developments in riding, training, and horse knowledge through books, publications, videos, and educational opportunities such as clinics. Recommended books, videos, and resources are listed in the USPC Standards, the current USPC Reading List, and in Appendix B of the USPC C Manual.

Consulting with other instructors or an expert is another good way to gather information on a subject. Remember that new skills and ideas must be safe and appropriate for your students, and must fit into the USPC Standards. You may also need to practice an exercise or ride a student's horse in order to have firsthand knowledge on which to base your teaching.

Progression

Good teaching is *progressive*; it moves from simple to complex, and from basic to more advanced. Major subjects and large goals are broken down into smaller topics and subgoals, and these in turn are broken down into smaller lessons and steps to be mastered. This applies to a course of study (such as the USPC standards), to subjects (such as bandaging), and to lessons.

It is important to know which skills and knowledge are basic and fundamental to your subject, and which should come later.

Evaluating Students' Level

When starting work with a new student, especially one beyond the beginner level, you must evaluate his or her basic skills and knowledge, ask questions, and find out whether any of his or her basics are weak or misunderstood. *Never* assume that a rider's skills in one area must be good because of what you see in another area (for instance, don't assume that he understands and uses the aids correctly because he has jumped a certain height). Before introducing new work, always review the basics and evaluate how well the rider understands and performs them for his or her level, before introducing new work.

Failure to learn and practice correct fundamentals becomes a serious handicap to a rider, hurts his progress, and can endanger him, his horse, and those around him.

Lesson Planning and Organization

Being organized saves time and makes it easier for students to learn and for you to teach. Poor organization and planning wastes time and leads to confusion and unsafe situations. It can leave students bored and frustrated, and may lessen their respect for the teacher. Be prepared; review the material and plan your lesson. Divide your lesson into sections and steps, and teach the basics first. Have your teaching area and any equipment set up ahead of time. Keep track of the time, and start and finish on time.

No matter how well you plan, you must adapt your teaching to your students' needs and the conditions *at that time*. You may find that a student needs extra help or more confidence, a pony needs further schooling, or the class needs more review and practice before you can safely go on with the lesson you had planned. Weather, ground conditions, and the teaching environment can change, and people and horses sometimes have bad days. Be aware of how your students and horses are feeling and performing, and be ready to modify your plans to make the lesson safe and positive.

Write out a lesson plan, or at least notes on what you plan to teach and what you will need to teach it. A few notes written afterward help in planning the next lesson, recording students' progress, or for a substitute teacher.

A well-organized lesson includes the following steps:

Preparation This includes gathering information on lesson material, lesson planning, and physical preparations (collecting equipment, setting up the ring). It also includes necessary information on students, level, and horses, and safety preparations (tack safety checks, survey of teaching area, and any necessary preparation of horses and/or riders, such as longeing or turnout).

Warmup Ten to fifteen minutes of progressive exercises are needed to warm up horses and riders and get them physically and mentally ready to work. Remember to vary the exercises and change gaits and directions frequently.

Review and Evaluation   Observe and evaluate riders as they perform skills they already know and review last lesson's work. Are they competent and confident? Are there any problems? Do they need more practice or review? If riders (or horses) are not ready to go on to the lesson you have planned, adjust your plan accordingly.

Explanation   Explain the day's objective—what you will teach and why.

For new work, explain the step or exercise, what it will accomplish, and why it will help. Keep your explanation clear, short, and simple. Don't lecture!

Demonstration   Demonstrate, on the ground or mounted, (or have an assistant demonstrate) if possible. Visual aids (diagrams, posters, blackboard, marker board, or even drawing in the dirt) can be helpful. Make sure that everyone can see, and that your demonstration is clear, short, and safe.

Application (Trial)   Students apply or try out the new work. This is usually done individually, as it is easier to watch each student closely, and in order to give help or make corrections. Try to devise an exercise or method which is simple to perform and gives students the best chance of success.

Critique   Discuss the student's performance and how it went. Be positive; praise any success or effort in the right direction. Suggest ways to improve, and why they might work better.

Practice and Evaluation   Practice the exercise again, in both directions. Developing "muscle memory" takes repetition. Reinforce what is correct about the exercise; if you dwell on mistakes, it may fix them more firmly in the student's mind.

Summary   Review the day's objectives and success. Discuss problems and how to correct them. Assign "homework" or practice. Ask questions, and ask if students have questions. Ask students what they have learned.

Review the lesson yourself, and make notes on what you taught, how it went, and what should be covered in the next lesson.

Sample Lesson Plan, Mounted Lesson

Topic: _____   Level: _____

Class Size _____ Time: _____   Location: _____

Students' Names and Ages: _____   Assistant(s): _____

Equipment Needed: _____   References: _____

Objectives: (How will you know when objectives are achieved?) _____

LESSON PROCEDURE:	NOTES TO REMEMBER	(APPROXIMATE LENGTH)

   A. Safety Check

   B. Warmup

   C. Review and Evaluation

NEW MATERIAL	NOTES TO REMEMBER	(APPROXIMATE LENGTH)

   A. Explanation

   B. Demonstration

   C. Application (Exercise)

   D. Critique

   E. Practice and Evaluation (Exercise)

   F. Summary

   G. Homework or Practice Assigned

Other Notes on Lesson: _____

_____

_____

_____

TEACHING MOUNTED LESSONS

Voice and Communication

Students must be able to hear and understand your instruction. It takes practice to develop a well-controlled voice that carries well and enunciates clearly, especially outdoors.

In order to be heard at a distance, you must learn to *project* your voice correctly. Shouting or raising your voice is very stressful, makes you sound angry, and can strain your vocal cords and make you lose your voice.

Voice projection requires proper breathing. Most people take shallow breaths most of the time, using the upper chest. To project your voice, you must use your diaphragm and abdominal muscles, and breathe from deep down in your chest as you speak.

To learn to project your voice, practice outdoors or in a large indoor arena. Ask a helper to stand at a distance (100 feet or so) and tell you how well you can be heard.

1. Place one hand over your lower abdomen, below your navel.
2. Take a deep, slow breath, feeling your lower abdomen "fill" and press against your hand as you inhale.
3. Speak a simple phrase such as "Prepare to trot," as you press your hand against your abdomen. Speak slowly and send each syllable out "from the diaphragm."
4. For contrast, try raising your voice. You can feel the strain on your throat and vocal cords; your helper can tell you which method is easier to hear.

Voice is very directional. Place yourself upwind, facing your class, and aim your voice at your students. If you turn away or speak toward the ground, your students cannot hear you.

Think before you speak. If you use fewer words and simple phrases, it is easier to make each one heard. Talking too much and too quickly makes your speech an indistinct babble. It isn't necessary to fill every moment with instruction. Students need some quiet time in order to process and practice what you have told them.

Vary the tone and speed of your voice, to add expression and enthusiasm, or to emphasize action or pace. Avoid speaking in a monotone or sing-song rhythm. Enunciate your syllables more clearly than in ordinary conversation; don't mumble. Your tone of voice conveys as much as your words, to horses as well as to students.

Look up and out, and make eye contact with your students. This projects confidence and authority, and makes you easier to understand. You can reinforce your words with gestures, body language, and other nonverbal communication. This helps students understand even if they fail to hear everything you say.

Horse Awareness

The safety and effectiveness of your teaching depends to a great extent on your awareness and how well you work with your students' horses. Being a lesson horse is one of the hardest jobs for a horse, as he must tolerate some inevitable rider mistakes during the learning process. Good teaching is considerate of the horse and should improve his training as well as help the student ride better.

Horses used for teaching must be safe and suitable, whether they are lesson horses or owned by students. You must be able to evaluate a horse's level of training and the rider/horse combination, and be sure they can work safely with each other. Sometimes this requires riding the horse yourself.

As an instructor, you are responsible for the safety and well-being of both the horses you use and the riders you teach. You must make sure that each horse is handled, ridden, and worked in a way that is appropriate for him. Be aware of the fit and suitability of tack, and the horse's fitness and fatigue level.

Monitor each horse's behavior and attitude throughout the class. Your ability to "read" a horse's mood or intentions is an important safety factor. If you notice a behavior trend (such as a horse beginning to act nervous, irritable, bored, or uncomfortable), take action right away. Don't ignore the behavior until it becomes a serious problem.

Teaching Mounted Group Lessons

Mounted group work may be taught in several ways:

- **As a ride** (working in line behind a leader).
- **Open order:** All riders maintain the same gait, direction, and exercise, but they may pass safely, circle or cut across to maintain a safe distance.
- **Individual work** performed in turn, with the rest of the riders lined up on the rail or in the center.

- **Riders working independently** (for riders at a suitable level, able to work safely and productively on their own).

It is easier to control a group lesson in a clearly defined area. Arena markers (corners, center line and quarter line markers, and dressage letters) help to define figures and where movements are to be executed.

Learn to scan your class, frequently checking each student's technique and control, and giving your attention to the whole class, instead of getting overly involved with one student. If you have an assistant, use him or her to give extra help to individuals when necessary. Learn and use students' names, and be sure to observe and communicate with each student individually, even if briefly.

Working as a ride is good for students and horses. Riders must pay attention, use their aids to adjust pace and spacing, and ride accurate corners, lines and figures. Horses learn to adjust pace and balance, respond promptly, and work quietly in company. Working as a ride behind an experienced leader can enhance control, especially when a class has a variety of levels and abilities.

Always establish ground rules for safety, and explain your terms and words of command. Make sure your students (and you!) know left from right and understand your directions. Choose an experienced, competent leader who can set a steady pace and ride figures accurately.

Here are some standard terms and practices for group riding classes:

Spacing   Maintain a minimum of one horse length between horses (more at faster gaits). Shorten stride or go deeper into a corner to maintain a safe distance. Specify whether students may pass, circle, or cut across the ring to maintain spacing, or whether they must keep their places in line.

Passing   If passing is permitted, it must be done only to the inside. Never squeeze between a horse and the rail.

Track   Riders should ride on the outer track (next to the rail) unless told to do otherwise.

Direction:
   "On the right rein" means clockwise (right hand toward inside).
   "On the left rein" means counterclockwise (left hand toward inside).

"**Track right**" means turn right on reaching the track.

"**Track left**" means turn left on reaching the track.

When working independently, or when an exercise results in one or more riders changing direction, pass left shoulder to left shoulder.

Halting, Making Adjustments   If a rider must stop, he should do so at the center of the ring, out of the way of those continuing to work.

Directive Terms:

"**Leading file**" means the leader.

"**Form a ride**" means to form up in line behind a leader, keeping one horse length spacing.

"**Whole ride**" or "**all**" means all together.

"**In succession**" or "**in turn**" means one at a time.

"**Go large**" means return to the outer track and continue in the same direction (on the same rein).

Words of Command   Words of command tell riders four things:

Who is being given the command ("Whole ride," "In succession," or the rider's name, etc.).

What to do ("Turn left," "Prepare to canter," etc.).

When to carry out the command ("Ride, tr—OT," "Canter NOW," etc.). "Leading file, begin" tells the leader to begin the exercise.

Where to carry out the command ("At the K marker," "as you cross the center line," etc.).

Commands must be clear and well timed. Give the preparatory command ("Leading file, prepare to turn left at the E marker,") in plenty of time, pause, then give the "do it" command ("Turn left NOW") when the rider arrives at a good place to begin the exercise. If you give a command hastily or too late, the riders will not have enough time to prepare and may act too late or apply their aids roughly. This can also result in dangerous bunching of horses.

Give students plenty of time to prepare for transitions, and use your tone of voice to help them (and the horses) understand your commands. Your voice should rise when you ask for an increase of pace, and fall for a decrease of pace, and give cadence when needed.

Teaching Beginners

Teaching beginners is an important job, because a student's early experiences with horses and riding can make or break his or her riding career. Good teaching of beginners includes the following goals:

- **Safety:** a safe experience, teaching basic safety practices and the reasons for them, and establishing a safety-conscious attitude.
- **Confidence:** developing self-confidence, trust in the instructor, and confidence in the pony.
- **Familiarization:** becoming familiar with pony, tack, procedures, and vocabulary.
- **Technique:** learning basic techniques, such as mounting and dismounting, basic position, holding the reins, applying simple aids, etc.
- **Control:** learning to control the pony, using simple aids.
- **Pony Care and Handling:** learning safe and simple basics of handling and caring for the pony, and to treat the pony kindly and responsibly.
- **Enjoyment:** a pleasant experience, tailored to the student's age, personality, and individual needs.

What You Will Need

- Student must wear safe and suitable attire (not necessarily riding clothes), including properly fitted ASTM/SEI safety helmet and safe footwear. (See USPC D Manual, p. 283.)
- A suitable horse or pony—quiet, patient, and not too big.
- Tack fitted to pony and rider; neckstrap; lead line; (longeing equipment if teaching longe lesson).
- A safe place to work, preferably an enclosed ring (60 × 120 feet is a good size).
- Review the USPC D Manual, especially Chapter 2, "D-1 Riding," and Chapter 5, "Handling, Leading, and Tying."
- If teaching a class, assistants to help students with their ponies and to lead ponies.

Introductory Lesson

An introductory lesson should be short, simple, safe, and fun. Its purpose is to introduce children to the instructor and the pony, develop confidence, and teach what they need to know to have a safe and fun lesson. An introductory lesson should include a tour of the stable, tack-room, and so on, and safety rules and reasons. It may be dismounted (teaching safety and pony nature, basic handling, simple grooming, tacking up, etc.), or may include mounting and dismounting, basic position, holding the reins, and walking (on a lead line). It is easier and safer to teach the first lessons as private lessons or very small leadline groups, placing the student in a riding class only after he has good basic control and can follow directions. If you must teach an introductory lesson to a group of students, you will need good organization, good control of your class, *and assistants to help you.*

Some Tips for Teaching Beginners

Review the USPC D-1 Level material, especially safety, pony handling, and basic riding (found in the **USPC D Manual**).

Keep lessons short, simple, and skill-specific. Everything is new to a beginner, and he can be overwhelmed if you try to teach too much at once.

Teach students why things must be done a certain way, but keep reasons brief and simple.

Stay close enough to the student and pony for safety and to encourage confidence. (Use a lead line or longe line until students can manage their ponies safely by themselves.) Don't leave a beginner alone in charge of a pony, mounted or dismounted.

When teaching a group, be aware of group control, spacing, pony behavior, and attention to all riders. Don't get stuck on one rider and forget the rest. You must anticipate pony behavior to keep beginning riders safe, as they lack the knowledge, experience, and control to do this themselves.

Don't ask beginners to perform an exercise or to ride for too long. Unaccustomed muscles tire quickly, so allow frequent short rest breaks.

Develop a wide range of exercises and activities you can choose from, which can be done at slow gaits. This keeps students interested while gradually building foundation skills and practice time. Allowing students to progress to faster gaits too quickly (because they ask to or you run out of ideas) is unsafe and leads to poor learning and abusive riding.

Keep lessons fun by teaching in small, easy steps, praising any improvement, and using games, creativity, and your own and your students' sense of humor.

Emphasize horsemanship, especially kindness, consideration, and responsibility for the pony.

Teaching Jumping

Teaching jumping requires a knowledge of safety, good basic horse-manship on the flat, and knowledge and experience in jumping. You must understand the foundation skills and progression in the training of both horse and rider over fences. Teaching jumping requires an educated eye for cause and effect in the performance of horse and rider, and the effect of different obstacles, combinations, and gymnastics.

It is especially important to understand the foundation skills and progression of skills in teaching jumping. Overfacing students or horses, or permitting students to try more advanced jumping than they are prepared for is *dangerous*! The *USPC Manual of Horsemanship* (D, C, and B and A Levels) are organized into progressive skill levels, with recommended jumping activities for each level. Instructors should review the jumping skills for the level they are teaching, and also for the previous level.

Before a rider can jump safely at any level, he must have:

- **Safe attire** and safe, properly fitted tack suitable for jumping.
- **Suitable horse or pony,** sound, well schooled, and capable of jumping at the level required.
- **Solid basics at his level,** including a secure and correct seat, effective control and use of aids, nonabusive riding, and good balance in full seat and half seat (jumping position).
- **Confidence** and desire to jump.

Prepare students and horses for jumping by:

- Proper warmup on the flat.
- Checking tack, girth, and helmet chin strap.
- Adjusting stirrups to proper jumping length.
- Jumping warmup, including ground poles, cavaletti, or low fences.

Use safe equipment and jump only on good footing. Remove unused cups from standards, and store extra equipment safely out of the way.

Build solid-looking, inviting fences with safe lines and distances. Gymnastics and courses must be suitable for the horses' size, stride, and training level, and the riders' capability.

Measure distances, and check distances in gymnastics by riding through with ground poles, before raising fences. For mixed classes, set two gymnastics, one for ponies and one for horses.

Make exercises progressive: Evaluate students' performance and horses' behavior over a ground pole, cavaletti grid, or low cross-rail. Horses that rush, weave, or trip over a low pole need further schooling or a better approach before fences are raised. This is a good way to check distances, too.

Encourage rhythm, relaxation, free forward movement, straightness, and good jumping form in horses and ponies. Relate correct work on the flat to its effect on jumping.

Teach riders the importance of a correct and secure seat, good balance, use of aids, eye control, and release. Relate rider position (and errors) to the horse's performance over fences.

Make sure that the rider can develop sufficient impulsion to jump the fence or gymnastic, and that he has control.

If you see a trend developing (such as a horse starting to rush, hang back, or run out), correct it immediately even if it means going back to an easier exercise. If you ignore such tendencies, they get progressively worse and may become dangerous.

Know when to stop. Finish jumping before riders and horses get tired, and their jumping deteriorates. Don't allow children to overjump their horses (including after class and at home).

Teaching Longe Lessons

Longe lessons allow a rider to concentrate on improving his riding, without having to control his horse. Their purpose is:

- To build confidence.
- To improve suppleness, eliminate stiffness, and help the rider follow the horse's movements more accurately.
- To improve a rider's balance, security, and correct position.
- To develop a secure, correct, supple, and independent seat, from which the rider can apply his aids correctly and easily.

Longe lessons can be useful for students of all levels, as long as the instructor is sufficiently skilled, the horse is suitable, and the length and demands of the lesson are appropriate.

The instructor must always pay attention to the following:

Confidence Persisting in spite of fear and tension prevents progress and leads to soreness, bad experiences, greater fear, and potentially dangerous situations. If a student is afraid or tense, go slower!

Balance   The rider needs to find a correct balance, with his weight evenly distributed over both seat bones and a balanced pelvis. If he tips forward, backward, or off to the side, especially in transitions, go back to a slower pace and re-establish correct balance.

Suppleness   Suppleness is related to balance and confidence. Loss of balance will cause a rider to tighten his muscles or grip in an effort to stay on the horse; fear or lack of confidence will cause stiffness. Stiffness can disrupt balance.

Whenever confidence, balance, or suppleness are lost, go back to a slower pace, an easier exercise, or even halt, in order to re-establish correct fundamentals.

Be aware of fitness and fatigue level. Longe exercises are tiring; many short repetitions with brief rest periods are better than prolonging an exercise to the point of exhaustion. (This also applies to the horse, who must not be longed too long in one direction or too long or hard in any session.) Longeing a rider until he is so tired that he "gets it" is very hard on both horse and rider, is unsafe, and afterward, the rider usually doesn't know what he did correctly.

Requirements for longe lessons:

Safe longeing area with good footing, preferably an enclosed ring, with a minimum of distractions. Other riders should not be riding in the immediate area.

Suitable horse or pony, obedient and well trained to longe, and accustomed to being used for longe lessons. His gaits must be regular, steady and comfortable, and he must respond to the instructor's commands. *Never try to teach a longe lesson on a green horse!*

Instructor with knowledge and experience in longeing, able to longe the horse with complete control, maintaining even gaits and making smooth transitions.

Correctly fitted longeing equipment, including:

- Longe line and longe whip; boots or bandages for horse.
- Saddle that fits both horse and rider. The saddle may be fitted with a pommel strap (safety strap), which the rider may hold to secure his or her position.
- Snaffle bridle.
- A longe cavesson, fitted correctly over the bridle (noseband fastened inside bridle cheekpieces), is the best choice of headgear.
- Side reins may be used to help maintain a steady balance and frame, but only on well schooled, experienced horses, and *only* by

instructors who can fit them correctly and understand their proper use. (Longeing with side reins is an advanced skill, and is not appropriate for most Pony Club longe lessons. Incorrect use of side reins can damage the horse's training and can be dangerous.)

- Both instructor and rider should wear safe and suitable attire, including correctly fitted ASTM/SEI safety helmet.

The procedure is as follows:

Longe the horse first without the rider, in both directions, until he is settled and obedient.

If side reins are used, they must *always* be unfastened before the rider mounts or dismounts. This is a safety measure that allows the horse freedom of his head and neck, and prevents the rider from getting caught in the side reins while mounting or dismounting.

When the horse is ready, halt and let the rider mount and adjust his stirrups. He should ride on the longeing circle with reins and stirrups (on the longe line) until he is relaxed and confident. At this point, the reins can be secured over the horse's neck and are no longer needed. However, they should always be within reach in case of emergency.

At the halt, show the rider how to rest his hands lightly on the pommel, and how to hold the pommel or safety strap if he begins to lose his balance or feel insecure. **Emphasize that he must never grab the reins to save his balance.**

At the walk, let the rider get used to the longeing circle and begin to feel the movement of the horse. Encourage him to breathe deeply, to sit deep and tall, to look up and out, and to notice the way the horse moves his seat bones.

Do some simple exercises that help the rider to get used to riding without reins. Examples:

- Large arm circles, one arm at a time.
- Reaching forward to stroke horse on neck, then back to stroke behind the saddle.
- Arm circles and shoulder circles, both arms at once.
- Stretching both arms up over head, then touching knees, then toes.
- Side swings (see USPC D Manual, pp. 50–55 and 89–97).

Let the rider practice at posting trot and sitting trot with stirrups, to build confidence. Keep the trot slow, steady, and rather lazy.

The next stage depends on the rider's level and needs, and the instructor's judgment. Some students will need further work with stirrups, in order to develop confidence, balance, and security. Others will be ready to go on to work without stirrups.

Depending on the rider's level and fitness, the rest of the longe lesson may consist of more exercises, position work, transitions, and variations of pace. Remember to work equally on both sides, for the benefit of both horse and rider. Give frequent short rest breaks, to avoid overstressing the rider's muscles and his concentration. Longeing is hard work; ten minutes may be plenty for a novice, and twenty minutes is quite demanding for a fit, experienced rider and horse.

When a student is ready to work without stirrups, cross the stirrup irons over (pull the leathers out and fold them flat). Work at the walk until the rider is confident and comfortable in the correct position. Practicing leg exercises (leg stretches, ankle circles, etc.) and repeating some easy loosening exercises help develop confidence and a secure seat. Remind your student to secure his seat and reposition himself when necessary by holding the pommel or safety strap, rather than by tensing up and gripping with his legs.

Exercises to develop good balance and position without stirrups:

- At halt or walk, stretch both legs slowly downward, slightly backward, and out to the side from the hip joint. Hold for a few seconds, then release and let legs return to the horse's side. Be careful not to arch the back, tip forward, or exaggerate the stretch. This helps to lower the knees, flatten the thighs, and improve the rider's leg position.
- Bring knees and thighs off the saddle (sideways), then allow them to fall back into position. Don't take them too far off or hold for too long, or cramping may result. This emphasizes the balance on the seat bones, and allows the legs to hang correctly under the body.
- Hold the arms out to the side and somewhat to the rear. Without body movement, bring each heel back and up alternately to touch the hands, in rhythm with the horse's strides. (Be careful not to kick the horse's sides.) This exercise helps to flatten the thighs and lower the knees.
- Sitting trot, posting trot, and half-seat without stirrups. (See USPC C Manual, pp. 49–52.)

Only advanced riders on experienced longe horses should be allowed to canter on the longe. These riders may practice canter transitions and exercises at the canter for short periods.

For advanced riders, it is useful to practice transitions and work in all gaits with the hands in a riding position, as if holding reins. Always be aware of position, balance, and suppleness. Only a rider whose position is basically correct and supple will be able to stay in balance. If a rider becomes insecure or loses his balance and position for any reason, the horse should be brought back to a walk while the rider corrects his position. Even fit, experienced riders should take frequent short rest breaks, which can be used for discussion.

SAFETY IN TEACHING HORSEMANSHIP

Safety is always the first consideration when teaching and working with horses. This is especially important with students who have their own horses or ponies and ride on their own between lessons. Only good safety education and making a habit of safe practices will keep students (and others) safe.

You, as the instructor, are responsible for the safety of your students. Use your best judgment, and don't hesitate to recheck something, or to modify an exercise or activity to make it safer, explaining why the change was necessary. You must set an example for your students in safety and good horsemanship, as they will copy what you do, not what you tell them to do.

Safety requires knowledge, experience, proper procedures, and planning to avoid accidents. All good instructors continue to learn about safety, just as they continue to learn about horses and horsemanship. The following section is only a beginning. In addition, you should be familiar with the USPC Standards, the USPC Horse Management handbook, the current USPC Reading List, and special safety rules for your own stable and riding activities. First aid and CPR training are essential for riding instructors, and could save a life!

Safety Checks

Safety checks are essential for safe riding and teaching, every time you or your student gets on a horse. They also are an important responsibility for instructors. If you fail to check a student's tack or allow him or her to ride with unsafe equipment, it could lead to an accident causing injury to the rider, horse, or both. Students should be taught to make a thorough safety check themselves before mounting, but this should always be double-checked by the instructor.

Safety checks include formal tack and safety inspections at all Pony Club lessons, rallies, competitions, and other functions, and your own personal safety check of your students, their tack and attire, their horses, and the environment every time they ride.

Details that must be covered in a tack and safety inspection are described in the *USPC Horse Management Handbook*, the USPC Standards, and the USPC C Manual (pp. 303–306.) The following checklists includes teaching environment and other factors you should know about for a safe lesson, and emergency procedures.

A Safety Checklist for Riding Instructors

I. Teaching Environment

    A. Weather (consider: wind, precipitation, storm coming, extreme heat or cold, heat/humidity index, wind-chill factor).

    B. Ring or teaching area:
        1. Clear of obstacles, distractions, or hazards (take down jumps when teaching beginners).
        2. Suitably fenced, with gate closed.
          a) No rings should be enclosed by rope or wire, nor should these materials be used for gates.
          b) No posts or projections protruding to inside of ring.
          c) Gate closed; easily seen; does not invite horse to jump out; no diagonal supports above gate (which can catch rider's arm or leg).
        3. Suitable size, location, and type of area for students, size of class, and type of lesson.
        4. Safe footing.

    C. Equipment, obstacles, etc.:
        1. Suitable for class and lesson or activity.
        2. Safely constructed (no sharp edges, protruding points; easily visible to horses; fixed or balanced so as not to fall over or roll; constructed so horse cannot become trapped in obstacle).
        3. Correctly set, with suitable distances, ground lines, and footing.
        4. Jump cups removed from standards when not in use.

    D. General:
        1. Avoid noise and distractions (traffic, construction, mowing, etc.).
        2. Spectators, pets, and other nearby activities under control.

3. Other horses nearby are distracting; they should not be loose in area, tied to ring fence, or allowed to disturb lesson.

II. Horses and Ponies

A. Suitable for rider (size, temperament, training level, experience).
B. Suitable for lesson or activity.
   1. Serviceably sound.
   2. Capable of performing lesson requirements safely.
   3. Fit and prepared for demands of lesson.
C. Instructor should be familiar with horse (evaluate horse and rider combination; ride horse if necessary).
D. Free from bad habits or dangerous behavior (shown by previous behavior); free from disabilities or unsoundnesses that could cause accidents.
E. How is horse acting/feeling at present?
F. Preparation of horse for lesson (turnout, longeing, instructor ride first if necessary).

III. Tack (Must Meet USPC Standards for Tack and Safety Inspections)

A. All equipment clean, supple, in good working condition and good repair.
B. Saddle
   1. Fit: No pressure on spine; 2 to 3 fingers clearance at withers; no pinching at shoulders; balanced correctly.
   2. Girth:
      a) Tighten gradually to safe level.
      b) Overtightening a girth is as bad as too loose a girth.
      c) Check before mounting, after 10 minutes of work, and before jumping.
   3. Stirrup bar catches in open position.
   4. Stirrups: correct size for rider.
      a) Too small can trap foot; too large can let foot slip through.
      b) Safety stirrups recommended for small, lightweight riders.
   5. Saddle pad: smooth, pulled up in front, correctly secured.
C. Bridle
   1. Bit correctly adjusted for comfort and control; curb chain flat (not twisted) and adjusted for correct action of bit.
   2. All buckles closed; strap ends through keepers and runners.
   3. All bridle parts sound, strong, and supple, with sound stitching; correctly adjusted for comfort, security, and control; no rubbing or pinching.

4. Noseband correctly adjusted (comfortably snug, not cranked tight; admits two fingers); throatlash moderately loose, but bridle secure.

5. Reins correct length; no dangerous loop that could catch rider's foot.

D. Breastplates, martingales, boots, and bandages

   1. Control devices (martingales, etc.) used only by riders educated in their correct use; suitable for horse, level of rider, and activity.

   2. Correctly adjusted to individual horse, for security, comfort, and effectiveness.

   3. Safety Equipment:

      a) Always use rein stops with running martingale.

      b) Rubber ring at neckstrap of martingale prevents strap from dropping too low near horse's legs.

      c) Boots and/or bandages correctly put on and securely fastened; suitable for activity.

IV. Riders

A. Correctly and safely dressed for riding (according to situation, whether formal or informal):

   1. Boots or riding shoes with heel and smooth, one-piece sole (no hiking boots, shoes without heels, or soles with ripples, ridges, or deep tread).

   2. ASTM/SEI certified headgear, properly fitted, chinstrap fastened.

   3. Riding pants, breeches, or jodhpurs that allow correct position.

   4. Shirt (short or long sleeves, not sleeveless or tank top) or sweater worn tucked in—no loose-fitting clothing.

   5. Appropriate clothing for weather (neck warmer, ear warmers, layering in winter; short sleeves, sun protection, ventilated helmet for hot weather; no long or loose scarves. Gloves optional but a good idea.

   6. No jewelry that could catch on horse or tack (rings, bracelets, earrings, hair combs, etc.). No sharp objects in hair or pockets. No waist packs.

   7. No chewing gum or candy in mouth (can cause choking).

   8. No wrist loops on crops.

B. Instructor should be familiar with rider and his or her level of experience, capability, and riding history. Evaluate riders, take history, and keep notes!

C. Any disabilities, fears, physical or emotional problems that instructor should be aware of? Is rider on medication? Any medical restrictions?

D. How is rider feeling today? Is rider mentally/physically prepared to ride? What is his or her level of fitness? Any problems or distractions?

E. Is rider familiar with and confident about riding this horse? About this lesson?

F. Has rider mastered prerequisites for this lesson? What skills or basics are necessary to perform successfully?

G. Can instructor communicate effectively with rider? Does rider have enough discipline and attention span to listen, follow instructions, and ride safely?

Emergency Procedures for Riding Instructors

I. Before an Emergency Occurs

1. Establish emergency procedures; post procedures and have staff, parents, or responsible adults familiarized with them.

2. Have simple first aid and emergency equipment on hand:
   a) Fire extinguishers, hoses, buckets.
   b) First aid kits (human, equine).
   c) Blanket and pillows (can be used to keep injured person still until medical help arrives.

3. Have a means of communication for emergency (phone, portable phone, CB, emergency signal). Post emergency numbers (911, Fire, Emergency Service or Ambulance, Police, Veterinarian) and how to report an emergency (including directions to facility) by the telephone. Be sure everyone knows how to call for help and report an emergency.

4. Record emergency numbers for students' parents and obtain signed permission for treatment in case of emergency.

5. Take First aid and CPR training, and maintain your certification.

6. Consult with emergency personnel in your area—fire chief, paramedics, civil defense—regarding your facility and emergency plans. This is especially important in areas that may be threatened by flood, brush fire, tornado, or other natural emergencies.

7. Have a designated area where people are to report to in case of an emergency. Conduct fire drills and practice emergency procedures!

II. Specific Emergency Procedures

A. Falls:
  1. *Stop* the class. (Teach all riders to stop immediately if a rider falls or a horse gets loose.) Other riders halt or emergency dismount; remain under control while instructor helps fallen student. Catching horse is secondary priority.
  2. Keep fallen rider *still* while you check for injuries. Don't pull him up on his feet.
     a) If rider appears possibly injured, follow emergency procedures:

        CHECK: Is rider *conscious*? Able to speak? Check if rider is breathing or has no pulse

        CALL: Send someone to call 911 or Emergency Service immediately, then

        CARE: Begin CPR. If rider is *bleeding seriously*, apply direct pressure to wound.

        Do not move victim! Bring help to where he is. Reassure him.

        Do not attempt to move limbs, take off helmet or boots, get victim up, and so on—just keep him still and as comfortable as possible.

        The most qualified first-aid person should remain with victim; send someone else to report accident, send for help, and take charge of other riders.
     b) If rider appears uninjured:

        Don't dramatize the situation, but do allow time to regain composure.

        Ask if he knows what happened and why.

        Explain how to prevent a recurrence before having him try again.

        Watch out for fear, shock, or delayed reaction.

        Include the rest of the class in explanation of what happened and how to prevent it. Sometimes watchers are more scared than the one who actually fell.

        Allow time to rebuild confidence, and set rider up for success with easier activities before trying same activity again.

        If you must school the horse, do so in a positive manner, not a rough-riding session. Change horses if necessary for rider's confidence.

Never embarrass the rider or allow others to do so. Don't blame the horse, either!

B. Loss of Control

1. *Stop* all other horses, to prevent incident from involving others and escalating. This may help stop the runaway horse, too.
2. Call instructions—short, simple, and clear: "Sit up!" "Pull up!" "Circle!" A calm, commanding voice well projected may get through to a scared rider and may even help control the horse. Shrill, panicky screaming makes a bad situation worse!
3. Move to block the horse, but be careful not to cause him to dodge and spill the rider, or injure you or any other person.
4. On the trail—*Stop all other riders!* Leader reverses to face the ride and keeps control; does not leave the ride. Instructor may follow runaway, but at a safe pace—do not chase or horse will go faster. Try to get rider to circle horse to regain control.

C. Injured Horse

1. The most experienced horse first-aid person should deal with the horse. Keep spectators and unqualified people away!
2. Keep the horse as calm and quiet as possible while you assess the situation. The calmer you are, the better for the horse.
3. Protect yourself and any helpers from injury. An injured or upset horse can hurt you unintentionally and compound the emergency. Restrain the horse as necessary, but don't take on more than you can handle.
4. Send for the veterinarian if indicated. Staff, students, boarders, and others should be taught how to call for help. Tell them exactly what to say (nature of injury, etc.).
5. Keep the horse quiet and apply appropriate first aid until the veterinarian arrives. Take and record vital signs.

HANDLING TEACHING PROBLEMS

General Suggestions for Handling Problem Situations

Good communication works both ways: from teacher to student, and from student to teacher. Parents must also be included. It is important that students (and parents) feel that they can communicate with you, especially when a problem arises. To do so, they must feel that you are fair and honest, that you care about them, and will listen to what they say. This helps them accept communication from you, trust you, and believe what you say.

Many small problems can be prevented from becoming big ones by clear, positive communication early on. Saying nothing and hoping a problem will go away often allows it to get worse.

For good communication, especially about problems, you must make time to talk with students and parents, and listen to their concerns. Choose an appropriate time when you can listen well, giving your full attention. If this is not possible during a lesson, set up a time when you can meet. It may help to paraphrase what you have heard, to see if you understood it (for example, "As I understand it, you are saying————. Have I understood you correctly?"). When handling a problem or enforcing a rule, use positive, not negative statements, and look for ways to solve problems, not to place blame. Avoid scolding, sarcasm, and labeling or name-calling. Instead, state the effect of the behavior ("When you talk instead of paying attention, you can't hear me, and that isn't safe"), and the consequences ("So we will have to stop the class until everyone is ready to pay attention"). Logical consequences work better than punishment, and reinforcing good behavior (with a smile or praise) works best of all.

Common Teaching Problems and Some Solutions

RIDING GROUP OF MIXED ABILITIES
- Assign an experienced rider as leading file.
- Try to find a common subject all can benefit from (for instance, leg aids), and teach it on several levels. Novice riders can learn from watching more experienced riders, and the better riders can benefit from demonstrating correct work.
- Be careful to give attention to all riders, not just a few.
- An assistant instructor can give extra help to those who need it.
- When you must focus on one or two riders, give the others something meaningful to do.

UNFIT PONY OR RIDER
- Allow a slower pace, nonstrenuous activities, and frequent rest breaks.
- Explain to the rider about fitness and why he must limit his activities.
- Make recommendations on how to begin the conditioning process.

INEXPERIENCED RIDER WITH GREEN HORSE OR PONY

- Emphasize the need for patience by the rider, and a gradual training process.
- Recommend that the rider allow a more experienced person to ride the horse regularly.
- Do not allow sitting trot or any activities beyond the horse's level.
- Encourage the horse to find its balance through free, active gaits and lots of walking.
- Give frequent periods of rest and relaxation; don't go on working past the horse's attention span or level of fitness.
- Suggest books on training of young horses.

UNSAFE OR INAPPROPRIATE TACK

- Make temporary adjustments (see p. 446) if possible. Never allow a student to ride with unsafe equipment.
- If the saddle can't be made safe and nothing else is available, allow the student to ride bareback if capable.
- Ask if another rider might loan his tack or mount for some riding time.
- Make sure the student and his parents understand what is unsafe and what to do about it. Be tactful, positive, and helpful!

BORED OR UNINTERESTED CHILD

- Is the rider bored because he is in a class that is not challenging enough? Is he uninterested in riding? Ask the child to express his feelings about the class. Discuss the problem with parents; is there pressure on the child to ride against his will?
- Assign an assistant instructor for individual help.
- If child is shy, introduce him or her to a "buddy" and have them work as a pair. (Have the entire class work in pairs to avoid emphasis on the problem child.)
- Try mounted games.
- If a bored student is capable of moving up, try him or her in a more advanced group.

CHILD UNWILLING TO TRY NEW ACTIVITIES

- This may indicate fear and/or lack of confidence. Often the child is afraid he will be forced to do something he is afraid of.

- Break skills down into small steps. Allow the child to learn each step at his own speed until he is confident enough to combine them.
- Assign an assistant instructor for extra help and modified activities, until the child is ready to join the group.
- Explain to the student that he will *never* be expected to do something he isn't ready to do, and that it is okay to stop at any point in an activity.

FEAR

- Fear may be physical (fear of falling or getting hurt), mental (fear of failure, embarrassment, or looking foolish), or both. Fear may or may not be based on a previous bad experience.
- Fear is real. Give the student permission to acknowledge his fear. Never deny it, ridicule it, or make him afraid to express his fear. Covering up fear makes a rider stiff and incapable, and his horse will feel it.
- Physical fear requires a slow, gradual process of building (or rebuilding) confidence. Make sure the activity is safe and that the rider has a quiet, reliable horse. Break skills down into easy steps, and build up many small successes. When the rider begins to feel bored with an exercise, encourage him to stretch his own limits a little at a time, by trying just a little more than he is comfortable with. He must push himself—if you push him, you may increase his fear.
- Mental fear is related to stage fright or performance anxiety. Like physical fear, it doesn't help to deny it or to say that there is no reason to be afraid. Some students become more comfortable with mental fears if they practice doing what they are afraid of (competing, performing in front of an audience, taking tests) in gradual stages. Sport psychology techniques are often helpful.

OVERMOUNTED STUDENT

- Assess the situation and decide whether this horse/rider combination can work safely at any level. If you feel it is unsafe, don't allow the student to continue to ride.
- Can the horse be made more controllable by longeing, turnout, a change of equipment, or being schooled by a more experienced rider? Is a change of horses possible?

- Limit activities to a safe level (avoid fast gaits, work in the open, etc.).
- Discuss the problem with the student and his parents. Be sure they understand the danger to the child and to others. Seek solutions, such as borrowing a more suitable mount for Pony Club activities.

LOSS OF TEMPER, RUDENESS, OR ABUSIVE RIDING

- Call a halt immediately. Have the rider dismount and take time to settle down before he continues to ride or handle the horse. Be firm, clear, and calm, but insist on compliance.
- Discuss the incident with the rider in private. Does he understand why his behavior is wrong and what the consequences are? What led to it? How can he prevent this from happening in the future?
- Most such incidents occur when a rider is overwhelmed by fear, frustration, or embarrassment, or is unable to control his horse well enough for the activity. While it is tempting to berate a rider for such behavior, yelling, name-calling, and public humiliation do nothing to teach him better behavior, and may make it worse.

INTERFERING PARENT

- Parents sometimes try to intervene in a lesson situation because:
  - They are concerned for their child's safety or welfare.
  - They want their child to get the most out of the lesson.
  - They believe they are helping.
- Establish ground rules with parents at the beginning. Listen to their concerns and explain how these will be taken care of (safety, attention to each child, individual goals, etc.). Explain that it is distracting to students (and therefore unsafe) if anyone besides the instructor tries to give instructions during a lesson, and that you cannot teach if this is happening.
- Some children are distracted when their parents watch their lessons. Suggest that parents leave during the lesson, but come back to watch their child show what he/she has learned at the end of the lesson.
- Enlist the parent for another activity (helping with unmounted lessons, lunch, or building jumps, etc.).
- Suggest some ways parents can help their child progress, such as supervising practice at home, videotaping, and so forth.

PART TWO

······················

The Horse

CHAPTER 7

Systems of the Horse

This chapter introduces the basics of equine anatomy (the systems of the horse) and physiology (how they function). A system is a combination of parts that work together to perform one or more functions. Although each system has its own unique role, all systems are interdependent and rely on each other. To better understand horse care, nutrition, conditioning, and especially various ailments, we must understand how these systems work.

In addition to the anatomy and physiology of the various systems, major diseases and conditions that affect each system are listed. For details on these ailments, please see Chapter 12.

SYSTEMS OF MOVEMENT: THE SKELETAL AND MUSCULAR SYSTEMS

The skeletal system is the framework of the body; its major functions are support, protection of vital organs, and movement. The joints, held together by ligaments, permit movement; muscles, attached to bones by tendons, move the bones. The foot and lower leg contain special structures adapted for movement, absorbing shock, traction, and protection of the foot.

(The anatomy and function of the foot and lower leg are discussed in Chapter 8 and Chapter 9.)

THE SKELETAL SYSTEM

Bones

The skeleton consists of approximately 206 bones. Bones provide the framework of the body, levers for movement, attachment points for muscles, and protection for vital organs and the spinal cord. Bones are living tissue, with blood vessels and nerves. They contain protein and most of the mineral content of the body, especially calcium and phosphorous. Red blood cells are produced in the marrow of the bones.

Joints

Joints are where bones meet. Some joints are immovable (like the joints of the skull); others permit a little movement or a wide range of movement.

JOINT

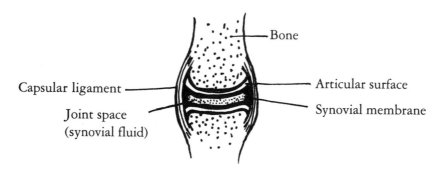

BURSA

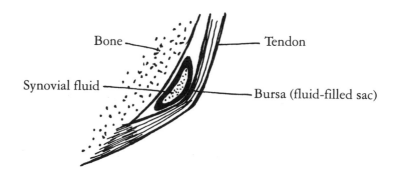

Ligaments are strong bands of connective tissue which hold joints together. Each moveable joint is enclosed in a **joint capsule** made of ligament, which contains **synovial fluid** or "joint oil" to lubricate the joint. A **bursa** is a fluid-filled capsule that protects a joint or a prominent bone end, such as the elbow or hock.

Cartilage

Cartilage is smooth and firm but flexible. It forms certain structures (like the ears and nose), and covers the articular surfaces of bones in joints, to allow the bones to move smoothly and to help absorb shock.

In some cases, cartilage provides a matrix or form in the immature bone, which turns to hard bone as the animal matures. This is true of the joints of the skull, and of the epiphyseal plates ("growth plates") found at the ends of most long bones. Radiographs of the epiphyseal plates, particularly those of the radius and carpal joints, are sometimes used to determine whether a young horse is mature enough to begin serious work.

Axial and Appendicular Skeleton

The **axial skeleton** includes the skull, spine, and ribs; the **appendicular skeleton**, the front and hind limbs.

The **axial skeleton** includes:

- Skull (including mandible or lower jawbone, teeth, and hyoid bone).
- Vertebral column:
  - Seven cervical (neck) vertebrae; the first is called the atlas and the second is called the axis.
  - Eighteen thoracic (chest) vertebrae.
  - Six lumbar vertebrae.
  - Five sacral vertebrae (fused together in the sacrum).
  - Eighteen to twenty-three coccygeal (tail) vertebrae.
- Rib cage:
  - Eighteen pairs of ribs (each connected to a thoracic vertebra).
  - Sternum (breastbone)

Diseases and Conditions Affecting the Skeletal System

- Osteomalacia
- Epiphysitis
- Rickets
- Arthritis

SKELETAL SYSTEM

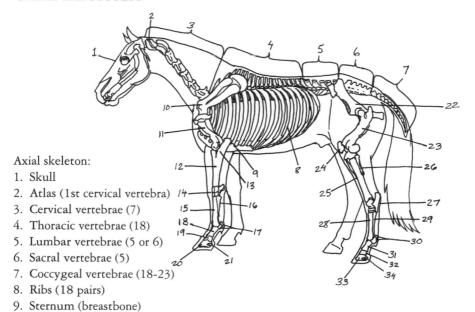

Axial skeleton:
1. Skull
2. Atlas (1st cervical vertebra)
3. Cervical vertebrae (7)
4. Thoracic vertebrae (18)
5. Lumbar vertebrae (5 or 6)
6. Sacral vertebrae (5)
7. Coccygeal vertebrae (18-23)
8. Ribs (18 pairs)
9. Sternum (breastbone)

Appendicular skeleton:
Forelimb
10. Scapula (shoulder blade)
11. Humerus (arm)
12. Radius (forearm)
13. Ulna (elbow)
14. Carpal (knee) bones
15. Large metacarpal (cannon) bone
16. Small metacarpal (splint) bones
17. Sesamoid bones
18. 1st phalanx (long pastern bone)
19. 2nd phalanx (short pastern bone)
20. 3rd phalanx (coffin or pedal bone)
21. Navicular bone

Hind limb
22. Pelvis
23. Femur (thigh bone)
24. Patella
25. Tibia
26. Fibula
27. Tarsal (hock) bones
28. Large metatarsal (cannon) bone
29. Small metatarsal (splint) bones
30. Sesamoid bones
31. 1st phalanx (long pastern bone)
32. 2nd phalanx (short pastern bone)
33. 3rd phalanx (coffin or pedal bone)
34. Navicular bone

THE MUSCULAR SYSTEM

There are three main types of muscle:

- **Cardiac muscle:** found in the heart.
- **Smooth muscle:** found in autonomic systems such as the digestive tract.

- **Skeletal muscle:** muscles that move the bones, usually acting in pairs.

Muscles

Muscles are made up of **muscle fibers**, which are arranged in **bundles**. Muscle fibers are controlled by **motor nerves,** which stimulate them to **contract** or "fire" by means of an electrochemical reaction. When muscle fibers contract, the muscle shortens, exerting a pull. The more muscle fibers involved, the stronger the pull. Because muscles can only pull, not push, skeletal muscles usually work in pairs; one muscle group **flexes** (bends) a joint, and another **extends** (straightens) it.

Tendons

Tendons are strong, fibrous connective tissue that connect muscles to bones. Some tendons are wide, flat sheets; others are thick bands or long cables. A **tendon sheath** protects a tendon where it crosses a joint; like a joint capsule, it contains synovial fluid, which lubricates it.

Fascia is a thin, tough, and fibrous connective tissue. It encases muscles and lies in wide sheets. Some muscles and tendons are attached to fascia, especially in areas like the back.

Major Muscles and Muscle Groups

Some of the major muscles and muscle groups are:

MUSCLES OF THE HEAD AND NECK
- **Masseter:** Large muscle of the jowl, used in chewing.
- **Brachiocephalus:** Long muscle running from poll to upper arm, helps to extend and raise the forearm.
- **Rhomboid and Splenius:** Muscles at the top of the neck, running to the shoulder blade. Well developed when the horse carries his head and neck well.
- **Trapezius:** Muscle at the top of the neck and behind the withers; carries the saddle.

BACK AND TRUNK MUSCLES
- **Longissimus dorsi:** Deep muscle of the back.
- **Latissimus dorsi:** Muscle running along back and down the barrel to the back of the shoulder blade. Supports the saddle.

MAJOR MUSCLES

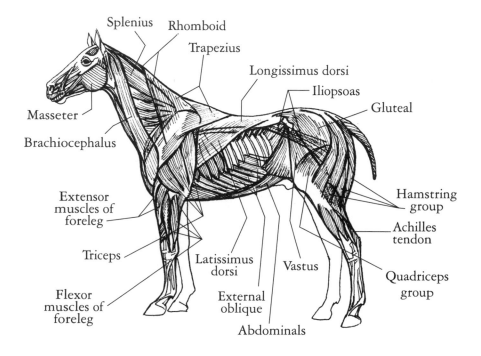

- **Internal and external obliques**: Muscles of the ribs, which aid in breathing.
- **Abdominals (abdominal obliques and rectus abdominus)**: Aid in breathing; also help to raise the back and bring the hindquarters under.
- **Iliopsoas**: Deep muscle from underside of lumbar spine to femur (thighbone) and pelvis; important in engaging hindquarters.

HINDQUARTER MUSCLES
- **Vastus**: Muscle from hip to stifle; flexes hind leg.
- **Gluteal Muscles**: Large muscles of hip; extend the femur.
- **Quadriceps group**: Muscles on the front of the femur (thighbone); flex the hind leg and bring it forward.
- **Hamstring group**: Muscles running around the back of the hindquarters; extend the hind leg and push the body forward.
- **Achilles tendon**: Large tendon above the hock; extends the hock.

FORELEG MUSCLES
- **Triceps:** Large muscle from elbow to bottom of shoulder blade; straightens elbow and foreleg.
- **Extensor muscles of lower leg:** Muscles of the forearm that extend the lower leg.
- **Flexor muscles of lower leg:** Muscles of the forearm that flex the joints of the lower leg.

Diseases and Conditions Affecting the Muscular System
- Azoturia, "tying up" syndrome.

THE CIRCULATORY SYSTEM

The main function of the circulatory system is transportation. It carries oxygen from the lungs to all cells, and carbon dioxide from the cells to the lungs. It also transports nutrients and water from the digestive tract to all cells, and carries waste from cells to the kidneys. Hormones and defense cells are also carried in the blood. The blood and lymph bathe the cells in fluid and maintain the heat of the body.

The Blood

Blood is a fluid made up of several substances:

- **Plasma:** the fluid part of the blood, which contains serum and cells that aid in clotting.
- **Red blood cells:** cells containing hemoglobin, which carries oxygen and carbon dioxide. They are produced in the bone marrow.
- **White blood cells:** defense cells, which act against harmful germs in case of disease or injury.

The Heart

The **heart** is a hollow muscular pump, made of cardiac (heart) muscle inside a protective cover called the **pericardium.**

The heart has four **chambers or internal compartments:**

- **Left and right atria** (upper chambers).
- **Left and right ventricles** (lower chambers).

CIRCULATORY SYSTEM

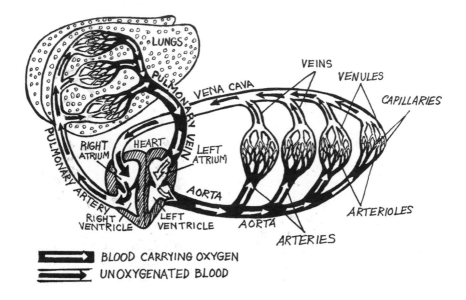

The heart pumps the blood by contracting (squeezing) to drive blood from one chamber to another, and outward through large arteries. **Deoxygenated blood** (which is dark red and depleted of oxygen, and carries carbon dioxide from the cells) arrives at the right side of the heart through the **vena cava**, a large vein. It collects in the **right atrium** (the upper chamber), and is pumped into the **right ventricle** (lower chamber) through a one-way **valve**. It is then pumped through the **pulmonary artery** to the **lungs**, where carbon dioxide is exchanged for oxygen.

The **bright red, oxygenated blood** comes back into the **left atrium** of the heart through the **pulmonary vein**. It is pumped through a one-way **valve** into the **left ventricle (lower chamber)**, which pumps the blood out through the **aorta**, the main artery of the body, to all parts of the body.

Blood Vessels

- **Arteries** carry blood away from the heart. The **aorta** is the largest artery. Large arteries branch out into smaller **arterioles** and finally into tiny **capillaries.**
- **Veins** carry blood back to the heart. Smaller **venules** and **capillaries** combine into larger veins, which eventually flow into the **vena**

MAJOR BLOOD VESSELS

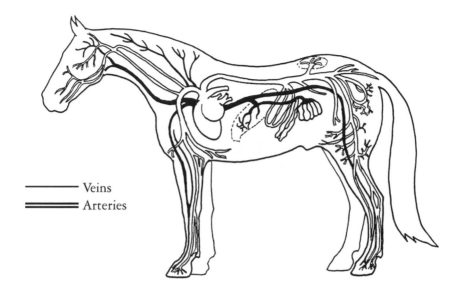

Veins
Arteries

cava, the largest vein, which carries deoxygenated blood back to the heart.
- **Capillaries** are tiny blood vessels only one cell thick, in which oxygen and nutrients are absorbed by the cells, and carbon dioxide and waste products are taken into the bloodstream.

Oxygen, carbon dioxide, and nutrients pass from the cells into the bloodstream, or from the bloodstream into the cells, through the cell membrane transport systems.

The Lymphatic System

The lymphatic system consists of:

- **Lymph:** A clear fluid containing white blood cells, which bathes all the cells of the body.
- **Lymph vessels:** Thin-walled vessels that transport the lymph throughout the body.
- **Lymph nodes:** Bean-shaped masses of lymphatic tissue, which act as filters and produce **lymphocytes** and **antibodies** (defense cells) to cope with infection.

LYMPHATIC SYSTEM

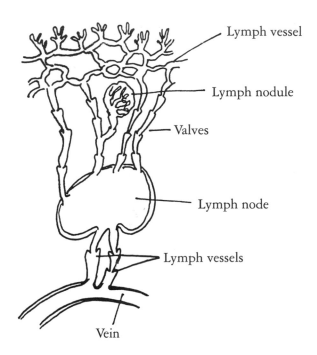

Lymph vessel

Lymph nodule

Valves

Lymph node

Lymph vessels

Vein

Points to Remember

The heart is a muscle, and like all muscles must be kept toned to work efficiently. Like all muscles, the heart must be brought into condition gradually (as in interval training).

A fit heart beats more powerfully, so it can beat fewer times per minute to pump the same amount of blood as an inefficient heart. That is why athletes have a lower heart rate than non-athletes. Since the heart muscle can only rest between beats, fewer beats per minute allows more rest between beats. (However, this should not be confused with an abnormal, sluggish heart.)

Each heartbeat pumps blood out of the heart and into the aorta, then outward through the arteries. Therefore, if an artery is cut, the wound spurts blood with each beat. If a vein is cut, there will be a continuous flow of blood from the wound.

Arterial blood pumped away from the heart is oxygenated (carrying oxygen) and is bright red. Venous blood, which is returning to the heart, is deoxygenated and is darker.

Diseases Affecting the Circulatory and Lymphatic System

- Equine infectious anemia
- Equine viral arteritis (EVA)
- Passive edema of the legs (stocking up)
- Lymphangitis

THE RESPIRATORY SYSTEM

The major function of the respiratory system is to take in oxygen and to deliver it to the blood. Oxygen is essential to every cell; if the body is deprived of oxygen for more than a few minutes, death results. The respiratory system also removes carbon dioxide, a waste product of metabolism, from the blood.

The Upper Respiratory System (Head and Throat)

Nostrils Horses can only breathe through the nostrils, not through the mouth. The hairs inside the nostrils help to trap dust and foreign matter.

Nasal Cavities Air passages lined with mucus membrane, separated from the mouth by the hard palate and (farther back) the soft palate.

RESPIRATORY SYSTEM

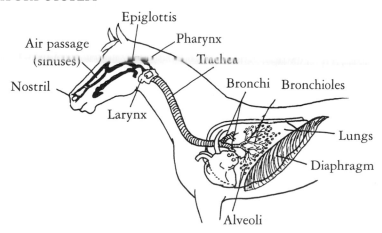

RESPIRATORY FUNCTION

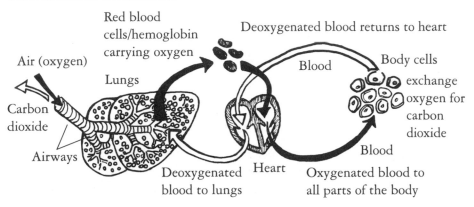

Nasal Turbinates   Very thin, curling bones inside the nasal passages, covered with mucus membrane. The large surface area helps to warm incoming air before it reaches the lungs.

Sinuses   Air-filled cavities in the bones of the skull, connecting to the nasal cavities; they reduce the weight of the skull and help to warm air as it passes inward.

Pharynx (Throat)   A common passage for food and air; leads to the larynx.

Larynx (Voice Box)   A box of cartilage, located between the branches of the lower jaw. It contains the vocal cords, which produce sound. The larynx controls the air as it goes in and out, and prevents food, water, and foreign objects from entering the lungs.

Epiglottis   The flap that covers the **glottis** (the opening into the windpipe) when the horse swallows.

Trachea (Windpipe)   Long tube made of rings of cartilage, which runs from the larynx to the lungs.

Lower Respiratory Tract

Lungs   Two large, elastic organs which fill the chest cavity.

Bronchi   The windpipe divides into two tubes or "bronchi," with one branch going to each lung. Inside the lung they divide into many smaller passageways called bronchioles.

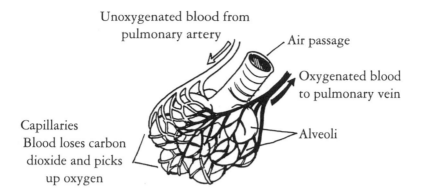

Unoxygenated blood from pulmonary artery

Air passage

Oxygenated blood to pulmonary vein

Capillaries
Blood loses carbon dioxide and picks up oxygen

Alveoli

Alveoli Small air sacs only one cell in thickness, like bunches of grapes, at the ends of the bronchioles. Carbon dioxide and oxygen are exchanged through the walls of the alveoli into the many blood vessels of the lungs.

Pleura The protective covering of the lungs.

Diaphragm A large sheet of muscle that runs from the underside of the backbone to the ribs. It is the primary breathing muscle, although the muscles of the ribs and abdomen also help.

Breathing

Breathing is the process of moving air in and out of the lungs.

In breathing, the diaphragm contracts and flattens and the ribs expand, making the chest cavity larger. This pulls air in through the nostrils and down into the lungs. As the diaphragm relaxes, it expands and the rib cage contracts, pressing against the lungs and expelling the air. The muscles of the rib cage, trunk, and abdomen also help in this process.

At the gallop, the abdominal muscles work strongly to bring the hind legs forward under the body at each stride. This pushes the abdominal contents (the intestines) forward against the diaphragm and lungs, causing the horse to exhale in rhythm with each stride.

Points to Remember

The respiratory tract contains mucus, which is normally thin and clear. In various respiratory diseases, the amount and quality of the mucus may change.

A **nasal discharge** refers to mucus or matter coming from one or both nostrils. A clear discharge may be normal, especially when the horse first begins work on a chilly morning. A thick, white, reddish, or yellow discharge points to some kind of infection. A discharge from only one nostril usually means that the problem is a sinus infection, a foreign body, or a bad tooth on the side of the discharge. A discharge from both nostrils usually means a generalized respiratory infection.

A **cough** is a forceful expulsion of air to clear the respiratory tract of some foreign material. This includes excess mucus, which the body produces in some diseases.

Diseases and Conditions Affecting the Respiratory System

- Influenza
- Rhinopneumonitis
- Strangles
- Heaves (emphysema)
- Roaring

THE DIGESTIVE SYSTEM

The function of the digestive system is to take in (**ingest**) food, break it down into useable form, extract most of the nutrients from it, and excrete the waste. The digestive system consists of a long tube (over 100 feet long in most horses) running from the mouth to the anus. It also includes the teeth (which grind food) and certain organs like the pancreas and liver, which help in the processing of nutrients.

Parts of the Digestive System

Mouth   Teeth bite off feed (as in grazing) and begin the mechanical breakdown (by chewing). **Saliva** (from salivary glands) is added to moisten the food and to begin to break down starches.

Tongue, Pharynx, and Epiglottis   These aid in swallowing. The pharynx is the area between the **hard palate** (roof of the mouth) and the opening to the esophagus. The **epiglottis** is the flap that covers the opening to the windpipe during swallowing.

Esophagus   A muscular tube, which carries food to stomach. Food can move only one way (toward the stomach).

DIGESTIVE TRACT

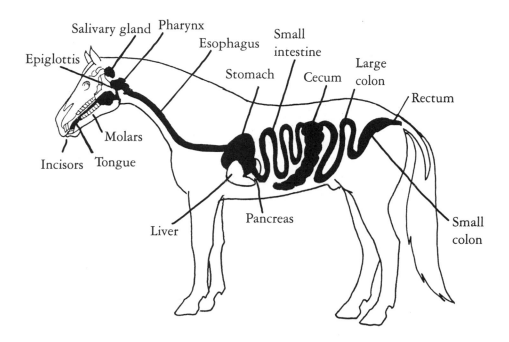

Stomach A muscular sack, holding approximately two to four gallons, which churns the food and saliva to a liquid form. It works best when no more than two-thirds full. **Hydrochloric acid** and the enzymes **pepsin, renin,** and **lipase,** are secreted in the stomach and further help the chemical breakdown.

The **pyloric valve** controls the flow of food from the stomach to the small intestine. The most liquid part of the food passes through first: water, carbohydrates, proteins, and fats, in that order.

Small Intestine Consists of three parts:

1. **Duodenum:** approximately 3 feet long. Ducts from the pancreas and liver secrete digestive juices (pancreatic juice, containing the enzymes trypsin and amylase, and bile) into the duodenum. This changes the food from an acid concentration to a more basic form, and the added enzymes further aid in the breakdown of proteins, fats, and starches.
2. **Jejunum:** the main part of the small intestine; approximately 20 feet long. Most proteins are absorbed into the bloodstream from here.

3. **Ileum:** the final part of the small intestine; about 6 feet long. At the end of the ileum is a valve that controls the flow of food into the cecum.

The lining of the small intestine is covered with **villi**, small hairlike projections that increase the surface area for absorption of nutrients.

Large Intestine   Consists of four parts:

1. **Cecum:** a large pouch approximately 4 feet long; it holds about 8 gallons. It contains bacteria that break down cellulose through fermentation, and that manufacture some vitamins.
2. **Large colon:** a tube 10 to 12 feet long. Some further digestion takes place here, chiefly absorption of carbohydrates derived from cellulose broken down in the cecum.
3. **Small colon:** a tube 10 to 12 feet long but smaller in diameter. Some water is extracted here, and the remaining waste material is formed into fecal balls or manure.
4. **Rectum:** a "holding chamber" approximately 1 foot long; it ends at the anus (a sphincter muscle).

Pancreas   Produces pancreatic juice (which contains enzymes and is alkaline, to counter the acidity of the stomach) and **insulin,** which controls blood-sugar levels.

Liver   Converts amino acids into proteins, stores glycogen (a form of sugar or energy), regulates the nutrients carried in the blood, and produces bile (a digestive fluid).

Points to Remember

Peristalsis is the muscular contractions that move food along the digestive tract, mixing it with digestive juices. Peristalsis produces **gut sounds.** Lack of gut sounds or abnormal gut sounds may be indications of colic or digestive disorders.

The manure can give an indication of how well the digestive tract is working. For example:

• Whole grains in the manure mean that feed is not being chewed properly. This could be due to bad teeth or to "bolting" the feed.

- Hard, dry fecal balls may indicate that the horse is not drinking enough water.
- Diarrhea can be due to many causes, including parasites, lack of digestive enzymes, bacterial infection in the gut, change of diet, or nervousness.
- Parasites can sometimes be observed in the manure.

Diseases and Ailments Affecting the Digestive System

- Colic
- Choking
- Laminitis
- Enteritis

Feeding Principles and Physiology of the Digestive Tract

Good feeding practices depend on a knowledge of the horse's digestive system and how it works. (Information about the digestive system and its physiology can be found in the USPC C Manual, Chapter 5.) Following are some important feeding practices, and the physiological reasons for them.

FEEDING PRACTICES	REASONS
Feed small amounts often, not a large amount all at once.	The horse has a small stomach that works best when no more than $2/3$ full.
Horses should have water at all times except when overheated. A horse may drink up to 20 gallons of water per day.	The horse's digestive system needs water for saliva, digestive juices, transportation of food through the digestive tract, and absorption of nutrients.
Feed only clean, high-quality feeds; never moldy, spoiled, or contaminated feed, or grass clippings.	Spoiled or unsuitable food may produce toxins or gas, causing colic. Horses cannot vomit, so they cannot easily get rid of unsuitable food.
Roughage should make up the larger part of a horse's daily ration.	The horse's digestive tract is designed to handle fibrous plant matter and requires sufficient roughage for good digestion.

FEEDING PRACTICES	REASONS
Horses must be prevented from overeating concentrates. Store grain and supplements securely where horses cannot get into them.	The horse's digestive tract and feeding behavior are designed for continuous grazing on fibrous plant materials. Concentrate overload can cause colic or laminitis.
Changes in feed must be made gradually over 10 days or more.	Beneficial bacteria in the gut help to digest certain nutrients. These are specialized to handle specific foods and take up to 10 days to adjust to a new kind of food.
Cut grain ration by 50% or more on idle days, particularly when horse is confined to stall.	Full grain ration without exercise can cause serious metabolic disorders (azoturia, tying up syndrome) when exercise is resumed.
Discourage horses from bolting feed.	Too rapid eating may result in choking, and does not break feed down into easily digestible particles.
Check teeth and have them floated when necessary.	Teeth must be in good condition to break feed down into easily digestible particles.

THE URINARY SYSTEM

The urinary system includes the kidneys (and their associated blood vessels), ureters, urinary bladder, and urethra. It filters out waste materials and excess water from the blood, which are excreted as urine. It also must return all necessary proteins, minerals, and electrolytes to the system, and acts as a buffer in maintaining the proper pH (acidity) of the blood.

Parts of the Urinary System

Kidneys   There are normally two kidneys, but an animal can survive with only one working kidney. Each kidney contains millions of **nephrons** (a system of tiny tubules and capillaries), in which filtration takes place.

Blood is circulated through the kidneys through the renal veins and renal arteries, which are connected to the aorta and the vena cava.

URINARY SYSTEM

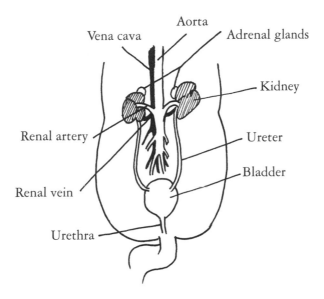

Ureters   Tubes that carry waste (in the form of urine) from each kidney to the urinary bladder.

Urinary Bladder   A muscular sack that stores the urine until it is excreted.

Urethra   The tube that takes the urine from the urinary bladder to the outside. In a male horse, it goes through the penis. In a female, the external opening is within the vulva.

Points to Remember

Although the kidneys excrete wastes, it is equally important to save the important nutrients; otherwise the body would be in a constant state of depletion.

The kidneys work *only* by filtering the blood. They do *not* pick up waste from the large intestine.

The kidney has a tremendous ability to compensate. Some individuals are born with only one kidney. The remaining nephrons simply work overtime to maintain the normal body state. In fact, approximately 75 percent of a kidney must be nonfunctional before blood chemistry will reveal a problem.

Kidney disease is very rare in horses.

THE NERVOUS SYSTEM

The nervous system provides "command and control" functions for the body by receiving, sorting, and transmitting nerve impulses.

The nervous system has three parts or branches:

Central Nervous System   Includes the brain and the spinal cord.

Peripheral Nerves   Include the nerves which run to the muscles and all parts of the body. These include:

- **Sensory nerves:** nerves that receive stimuli (a stimulus is a change in the environment, such as heat, cold, touch, sound, smell, taste, etc.) and transmit them to the brain.
- **Motor nerves:** nerves that transmit instructions to the muscles.

NERVOUS SYSTEM

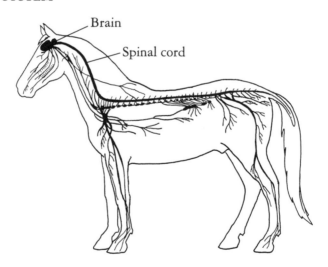

Brain

Spinal cord

NERVE CELLS

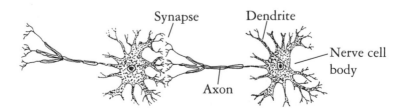

Synapse   Dendrite

Nerve cell body

Axon

Autonomic Nervous System It controls the functions of the internal organs of the body. This allows the heart to beat, the lungs to breathe, digestion to take place, and so on without the need for conscious awareness. The **sympathetic** and **parasympathetic** systems operate reflexes and "automatic" reactions, such as shivering from cold.

Nerve Cells and Their Functions

The basic nerve cell is called a **neuron.** The body of the cell has branches called **dendrites,** and long fibers called **axons.** The junction between one neuron and another (where one neuron's axon touches another's dendrite) is called a **synapse.**

The nervous system works like a relay system. Information is passed from muscle to neuron, or from one neuron to another through chemicals. Some chemicals stimulate muscles to contract; others inhibit or stop contraction (or the muscles would be in a continual state of spasm). A chemical called **acetylcholine** stimulates muscles. Another chemical called **acetylcholinesterase** prevents the constant action of acetylcholine.

Points to Remember

Many pesticides (including certain fly sprays, some dewormers, and flea and tick dips used on dogs) are **cholinesterase inhibitors.** These are cumulative; they build up in the system. If an animal receives too much of a cholinesterase inhibitor (possibly by being exposed to an overdose or a combination of these products), it can block the release of cholinesterase in his nervous system, resulting in muscle spasms or seizures due to the continuous flow of acetylcholine. It is important to read the ingredients and product warning labels, and follow directions carefully when using fly spray, dewormers, and certain tranquilizers.

Diseases Affecting the Nervous System

* Tetanus
* Equine encephalomyletis
* Rabies
* Botulism

THE ENDOCRINE SYSTEM

Hormones are chemical substances produced by ductless glands, and carried in the bloodstream. They stimulate certain organs and body processes. The major endocrine glands, the hormones they produce, and their major effects are listed in the table on the following page.

THE REPRODUCTIVE SYSTEM

The functions of the reproductive system include sexual behavior, mating, gestation or pregnancy, birth, and lactation (production of milk). The reproductive, endocrine, and urinary systems are interrelated.

The Reproductive System of the Stallion

The reproductive organs of the stallion are designed to produce sperm and to place it within the mare where it can unite with an egg.

Sperm are the male reproductive cells.

MALE REPRODUCTIVE SYSTEM

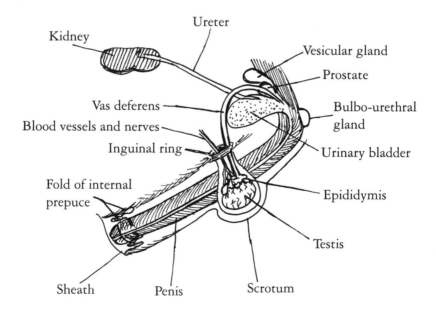

The **testes** (or testicles) are the organs in which sperm are produced and stored. They function best at a temperature slightly lower than the internal body temperature, so in mature males, they are located outside the body in a sac called the **scrotum.**

ENDOCRINE GLANDS, HORMONES
& EFFECTS OF HORMONES

Gland	Hormone	Acts on	Effects
Pituitary	FSH	Ovary	Stimulates follicle development.
	LH	Ovary	Stimulates ovulation and development of "yellow body" in ovary.
	Prolactin	Mammary glands	Milk production.
	GH	Overall metabolism	Growth.
	TSH	Thyroid	Stimulates thyroxin secretion.
	ACTH	Adrenals	Stimulates cortisol secretion.
	Vasopressin	Arteries	Raises blood pressure.
	Oxytocin	Uterus	Stimulates contractions in foaling.
Pancreas	Insulin		Controls level of blood sugar.
Thyroid	Thyroxine		Controls rate of metabolism.
Adrenal (cortex)	Cortisone		Controls levels of salt, sugar, and water in blood and tissues.
Adrenal (medulla)	Adrenaline		Stimulates sweating; increases blood flow to muscles.
Ovary (follicle)	Estrogen	Uterus and reproductive system	Causes estrus behavior and condition of reproductive organs.

(Continues)

ENDOCRINE GLANDS, HORMONES
& EFFECTS OF HORMONES

Gland	Hormone	Acts on	Effects
Ovary (yellow body)	Progesterone	Uterus and reproductive system	Prepares reproductive tract for pregnancy or diestrus.
Uterus	Prostaglandin	Yellow body of ovary	Stops yellow body secreting progesterone.
	PMSG	Ovary	Protects yellow body during pregnancy.
Testes	Testosterone	Reproductive system, overall	Male sex hormone; stimulates libido, sexual behavior, and secondary sex characteristics (muscle development).
Brain	Releasing factors	Pituitary	Stimulates pituitary to release its own hormones (FSH, LH, GH, ACTH, etc.).

Testosterone (the male sex hormone) is also produced in the testes. This hormone produces secondary sex characteristics (such as the enlarged crest and deeper voice of a stallion) and influences sexual behavior.

Before birth, the testes are located in the abdomen. They descend into the scrotum through the **inguinal canal.** Both testes should have permanently descended by the age of twelve months. A male having one or more testes retained in the abdomen or caught in the inguinal canal is called a **cryptorchid** (sometimes referred to as a "rig").

Castration (or gelding) involves the surgical removal of both testes. This makes the gelding infertile and removes the source of testosterone, so it usually (although not always) limits male sexual behavior. It is usually performed when the colt is a yearling, but may be done at other times at the owner's discretion.

During mating, sperm leaves the testicles through the **spermatic cord** and is delivered to the **urethra** (located within the penis). It is expelled during **ejaculation**.

The **penis** telescopes upon itself within the sheath. A substance called **smegma** accumulates within the folds of the sheath, on the surface of the penis, and in a pouch at the opening of the urethra. This should be removed by periodic cleaning.

The tranquilizer acepromazine causes the penis to relax and hang from the sheath. This facilitates cleaning, and is also a sign that the horse has been tranquilized. (Acepromazine has been known to cause paralysis of the penis.)

The Reproductive System of the Mare

The mare's reproductive system is designed to produce an egg, which unites with a sperm to form an **embryo**. It contains and nourishes the embryo while it develops (**gestation**), and expels it during birth (**parturition**). The reproductive system also includes the mammary system, which provides milk for the foal.

FEMALE REPRODUCTIVE SYSTEM

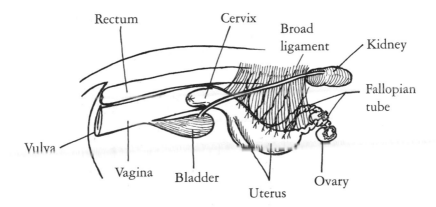

The **ovum (egg)** is the female reproductive cell. Eggs are produced in the **ovaries** (there are two, a right and a left). The ovaries also produce the female hormones **estrogen** and **progesterone**.

The **fallopian tubes** lead from each ovary to the uterus.

The **uterus** is the organ in which the embryo implants and grows during gestation. The end of the uterus located in the vagina is called the **cervix**. It is tightly closed, except during estrus.

The **vagina** is the passage from the uterus to the **vulva** (the external opening). The urethra also opens into the vulva.

The Estrus (Heat) Cycle

The pituitary gland signals the body to release **follicle stimulating hormone (FSH)**. This causes the ovary to develop a **follicle** containing an egg (ovum). The ovary then produces the hormone estrogen, which stimulates the follicle to open and release the egg (**ovulation**). Estrogen also stimulates receptive behavior, causing the mare to be receptive to breeding at the time of ovulation.

The remains of the follicle (which opened to release the egg during ovulation) is called the **corpus luteum (CL)** or **yellow body**. The corpus luteum secretes the hormone **progesterone,** which ends the estrus cycle in one of two ways:

- If the mare is bred and becomes pregnant, it continues to produce progesterone throughout the pregnancy, which helps to maintain the pregnancy and prevents the mare from coming back into estrus (heat).
- If the mare is not bred or does not become pregnant, it produces progesterone only for a few days. After that, the progesterone level drops off and the estrus cycle starts over again, beginning with FSH.

Gestation (pregnancy) lasts an average of 335 days.

The **estrus cycle** averages about twenty-one to twenty-four days, but the actual period of **estrus** (heat), during which the mare can conceive, lasts only three to five days. Mares are "seasonally polyestrus," which means that they go through many estrus cycles during a season.

The increased number of daylight hours beginning in late winter and early spring stimulates the production of FSH. The natural breeding season peaks in spring and early summer, ensuring that most foals are born in the spring, when better weather and natural nutrition are to be expected.

Most fillies begin cycling during the spring of their second year, but they should not be bred until they are three or older, as pregnancy puts a strain on an immature body.

Diseases Affecting the Reproductive System

- Rhinopneumonitis (contagious abortion)
- Equine viral arteritis (EVA)

THE SKIN

The skin is the largest organ of the body. It functions as a sheath for the body which protects against trauma, excessive radiation, and the entry of microorganisms. It also aids in thermoregulation (temperature control), excretes waste products, and synthesizes vitamin D. The skin contains sweat glands, sebaceous (oil) glands, and sensory nerves, which detect pressure, pain, and temperature. The hair coat, mane, and tail grow from the skin, and the hooves are composed of a specialized form of skin over a bony framework.

Parts of the Skin

There are three layers of skin:

- **Epidermis,** or thin outer layer of skin.
- **Dermis,** a thicker layer, containing most skin structures.
- **Subcutaneus,** a thin layer of fatty material just over the muscles.

The skin contains certain structures, including:

- Apocrine (sweat) glands.
- Sebaceous glands, which secrete sebum (skin oil).
- Hair follicles, which include the papilla or root, the hair shaft, and the tiny erector pili muscle, which can cause the hair to stand up.
- Blood vessels and nerves.
- The panniculus muscle, a large, thin sheet of muscle which lies under the skin. This allows the horse to twitch the skin to remove flies, and to shiver to create heat.

Points to Remember

The skin has a two-way function: It absorbs sunlight (from which it synthesizes vitamin D) and heat, and excretes salts and water through sweat. Excess heat is radiated into the air, and the outside air temperature and/or moisture in contact with the skin heats or cools the skin and the body.

The hair coat provides protection from cold, dampness, and insects. Specialized hair features such as fetlocks, the hair inside the ears, whiskers, and the mane and tail have protective roles. If this natural protection is removed, the horse will need extra care and is less suited to living and working outdoors.

The winter coat is longer and thicker, with extra long "guard hairs" which permit water to run off. The skin produces extra sebum (oil), which helps to waterproof the skin and hair coat.

The hairs of the body have tiny muscles that permit them to erect or stand up (called a "staring coat"). This increases the loft of the coat, trapping air close to the skin for warmth. A staring coat indicates a horse trying to keep warm, or a sick horse that may be having chills.

Growth and shedding of the winter coat are determined by the hypothalamus, a part of the brain which is affected by the shortening and lengthening of daylight, and the temperature.

The condition of the skin and hair coat is an indicator of the horse's general health. A healthy horse's skin is supple and pliable, and his hair coat shines with a normal amount of skin oil. Good grooming, nutrition, and general good health are necessary for healthy skin.

Diseases and Conditions That Affect the Skin

- Warts (papilloma virus)
- Sarcoid tumors
- Dermatophilosis (rainrot, rail scald, scratches, grease heel)
- Ringworm

CHAPTER 8

• • • • • • • • • • • • • •

Conformation, Soundness, and Movement

ANATOMY OF THE LOWER LEG AND FOOT

The structures of the lower leg are the same in the front and hind legs below the knees (carpal joints) and hocks (tarsal joints). The structures of the lower legs provide support, absorb shock, dampen vibration, and provide a rebound effect that helps each foot to leave the ground with less effort. The **stay apparatus,** a system of muscles, tendons, and ligaments at the front and back of each limb, allows the horse to lock his limbs and remain upright even while asleep. Although the structures of the lower leg are primarily bones, ligaments, tendons, and the specialized structures of the foot, it is important to remember that the muscles of the upper leg are connected to the tendons of the lower leg, and the whole leg works as a coordinated limb.

The Suspensory Apparatus

The suspensory apparatus is a system of ligaments in the lower leg, which support the fetlock joint. The suspensory apparatus carries most of the weight of the horse, especially at some phases of the stride. It prevents the fetlock joint from overextending or sinking too far toward the ground, and helps absorb shock. The elastic structures of the suspensory apparatus also contribute to a **rebound effect,** which helps the foot leave the ground at each stride.

The suspensory apparatus is the same in the front and hind legs.

Structures of the suspensory apparatus are:

Suspensory Ligament   Large ligament that runs down the back of the cannon bone from the back of the knee (carpal) bones, to the sesamoid bones, then separates into two lower branches which run diagonally forward to the common digital extensor tendon.

STRUCTURES OF THE LOWER FORELEG

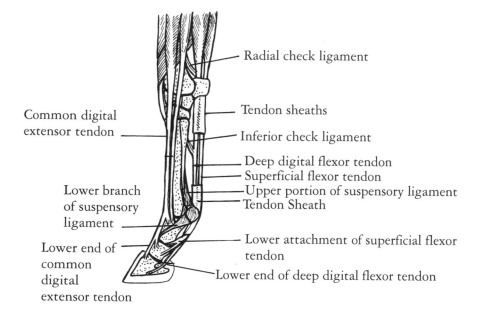

- Radial check ligament
- Tendon sheaths
- Inferior check ligament
- Deep digital flexor tendon
- Superficial flexor tendon
- Upper portion of suspensory ligament
- Tendon Sheath
- Lower attachment of superficial flexor tendon
- Lower end of deep digital flexor tendon

Common digital extensor tendon

Lower branch of suspensory ligament

Lower end of common digital extensor tendon

Other parts of the suspensory ligament system are a system of smaller ligaments that run down the sides and back of the fetlock joint and pastern bones to the coffin bone and navicular bone.

Check Ligament   Runs from suspensory ligament to deep flexor tendon.

Deep Digital Flexor Tendon   Inner tendon running behind the carpal bones, around the fetlock joint, and across the navicular bone, fastening to the underside of the coffin bone.

Superficial Flexor Tendon   Outer tendon, which runs from behind the carpal bones, and around the fetlock joint, and branches out to each side of the pastern.

Common Digital Extensor Tendon   Runs down the front of the leg to the top of the coffin bone.

Sesamoid Bones   Two small bones at the back of the fetlock joint that form a "pulley" through which the flexor tendons pass.

The suspensory apparatus is essential to the horse's ability to move and bear his own weight, even at a standstill. Injuries to the suspensory ligament cause serious problems because the horse places so much weight on this structure, and are slow to heal because of the limited blood supply to ligaments.

The Stay Apparatus

The stay apparatus is a system of ligaments, tendons, and muscles that can lock the major joints of the front and hind legs and hold them firmly in position, so that the horse can remain standing even when relaxed. The suspensory apparatus is part of the stay apparatus, and is the same in front and hind legs. The upper part of the stay apparatus differs in the front and hind limbs.

Stay Apparatus of the Forelimb   Includes muscles that attach the forelimb to the ribs and neck, muscles of the arm, elbow and shoulder, extensor and flexor muscles of the forearm and their tendons, and the suspensory apparatus of the lower leg.

Stay Apparatus (Reciprocal System) of the Hind Limb   Includes the major muscles of the hindquarters (hip to stifle, thigh muscles, gluteals [croup muscles], and hamstrings), ligaments of the stifle joint, tendons, and ligaments of the gaskin, hock, and suspensory apparatus.

The hock and stifle are **reciprocal** joints, which means that when one bends or straightens, the other must also. The stifle joint is constructed so that the patella (kneecap) can be lifted and locked over the end of the femur (thighbone) and held in place by the ligaments of the

STRUCTURES OF THE LOWER HIND LEG

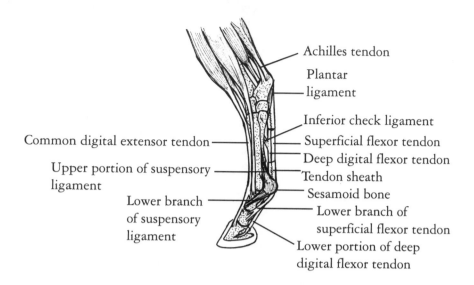

Achilles tendon

Plantar
ligament

Inferior check ligament

Common digital extensor tendon

Superficial flexor tendon

Deep digital flexor tendon

Upper portion of suspensory
ligament

Tendon sheath

Sesamoid bone

Lower branch
of suspensory
ligament

Lower branch of
superficial flexor tendon

Lower portion of deep
digital flexor tendon

stifle joint. This locks the stifle and hock, so that the horse can stand on the limb even when relaxed. The biceps femoris and quadriceps femoris muscles flex the stifle and unlock the patella.

Structures of the Foot

The foot has special structures to help it perform its essential functions: support, absorbing shock, traction for secure footing, and pumping blood back up through the lower leg.

Coffin Bone (Pedal Bone)   Major bone of the foot; supports the weight of the horse.

Navicular Bone   Small wedge-shaped bone which lies under the back of the coffin bone.

Navicular Bursa   Fluid-filled sac which cushions the navicular bone and the deep flexor tendon.

Deep Digital Flexor Tendon   Crosses the navicular bone and attaches to the underside of the coffin bone.

INNER STRUCTURES OF THE FOOT

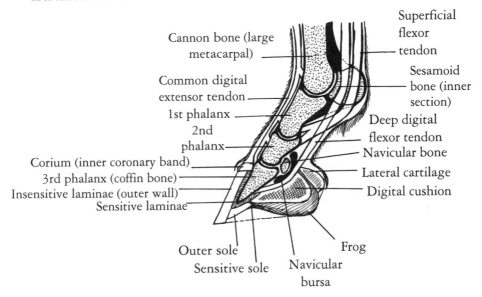

Cannon bone (large metacarpal)

Common digital extensor tendon

1st phalanx

2nd phalanx

Corium (inner coronary band)

3rd phalanx (coffin bone)

Insensitive laminae (outer wall)

Sensitive laminae

Superficial flexor tendon

Sesamoid bone (inner section)

Deep digital flexor tendon

Navicular bone

Lateral cartilage

Digital cushion

Outer sole

Sensitive sole

Navicular bursa

Frog

Digital Cushion   Spongy structure above the frog, containing blood vessels. Pressure on digital cushion helps to pump blood back up the leg with each step.

Coronary Band   Outer band of tissue at the hairline, from which the hoof grows.

Corium   The deep tissue beneath the coronary band, which produces the horn.

Wall   The hard outer shell of the hoof, made of tiny hairlike tubules called "**insensitive laminae**." The wall of the hoof supports the horse's weight. The wall angles backwards at each end, forming the **bars**. These aid in absorbing shock and allowing the foot to expand under pressure. Most of the horse's weight is borne by the walls of the feet.

Sensitive Laminae   Tiny hairlike tubules that grow from the surface of the coffin bone and interlock with the insensitive laminae of the wall. The sensitive laminae have blood and nerve supply. The inter-locking of these two types of laminae suspends the coffin bone in a strong, hard, protective casing that can flex under pressure.

Periople   Thin varnishlike outer layer of the hoof, which keeps moisture in.

Sole   The ground surface of the hoof, inside the wall. The outer layer of the sole is insensitive; the **sensitive sole** is the deep layer next to the underside of the coffin bone, which has blood and nerve supply. The sole should be arched or concave, not flat.

Frog   a rubbery, wedge-shaped structure that lies between the heels. The frog helps to absorb shock and helps to pump blood back up the leg by compressing the digital cushion at each step.

Lateral Cartilages   Wing-shaped cartilages that extend from the upper sides of the coffin bone and form the flexible bulbs of the heels. They aid in the expansion of the foot.

(Also see Chapter 9, "The Foot and Shoeing.")

GAITS AND MOVEMENT

Horses are athletes; they are only useful because of their ability to move. Good movement is efficient, athletic, and easier to ride; it allows a horse to reach his full potential. Poor movement is ugly, difficult to ride, and uncomfortable and damaging to horses.

Different breeds, types, and individual horses have different kinds of movement, which makes them suitable for a particular purpose. Regardless of type, all horses share the same basic anatomy and principles of movement. In addition, there are certain basic qualities which are essential to good movement and soundness in all horses.

The Phases of a Stride

A stride is a sequence within a gait during which all four legs complete a step. Each leg completes the following cycle of movement:

- **Swing phase:** begins when the foot leaves the ground. The leg swings backward, then flexes and swings forward.
- **Grounding (impact):** the moment when the hoof strikes the ground.
- **Support:** the phase during which the leg bears weight.
- **Thrust:** begins as the leg reaches a vertical position under the weight, and continues until the foot leaves the ground.

PHASES OF A STRIDE (HIND LEG)

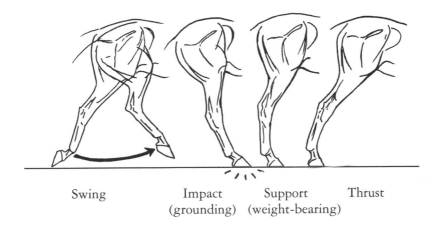

Swing	Impact	Support	Thrust
	(grounding)	(weight-bearing)	

How a Horse Moves

When a horse moves, his hindquarter muscles provide the power that pushes him forward. The deep muscles of the back and spine stabilize the back and transmit the thrust to the rest of his body. The neck muscles aid the head and neck in acting as a balancer, and the muscles of the neck, shoulder, arm and forearm move the forelegs and help to absorb shock. The abdominal muscles, along with deep inner muscles called the psoas group, draw the hindquarters and hind legs forward, engaging them under the body.

With every stride:

The muscles at the front of the hindquarters (hip to stifle and front of thigh) flex the hind leg and swing it forward under the body (swing phase). The degree to which the hind leg reaches forward under the body is called **engagement**. The greater the engagement, the greater the power of the stride.

The abdominal muscles (which run from the breastbone to the floor of the pelvis) flex the loin at the lumbar-sacral joint, and help to bring the hind legs forward under the body. The psoas group (deep muscles running from the underside of the lumbar spine [loin] to the floor of the pelvis and the femurs) also flex the loin and help to engage the hind legs.

The hoof strikes the ground (impact or grounding), and the hind leg bears weight (support). The muscles of the croup and back of the hindquarters (gluteals and hamstrings) straighten the leg, causing it to

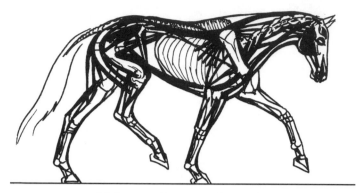

Major muscle groups in motion

push the horse's body forward (thrust) until the leg extends behind him and leaves the ground (breakover).

The muscles of the spine (several layers of deep muscles on each side of the back, connecting the vertebrae of the croup, loin, back and neck) help to stabilize the spine and transmit the power (thrust) to move the horse forward. These muscles, along with the hindquarter muscles, create a "chain of muscles" on each side of the spine, from hind leg to poll.

The nuchal ligament (cervical ligament) connects each of the seven cervical (neck) vertebrae to the withers (and to the dorsal ligament system which runs the length of the back). When the head is lowered, it pulls on the bones of the withers and back, affecting the horse's balance.

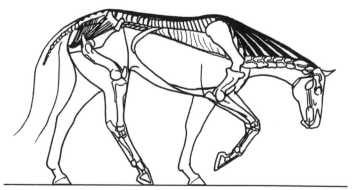

Nuchal ligament pulls on withers and dorsal ligament system when head is lowered.

The deep muscles of the neck stabilize the base of the neck and help the horse to arch his neck, raise his forehand, and change his balance. The muscles at the top of the neck raise and extend the head and neck. The muscles on the underside of the neck flex the neck downward; some help to extend the forearms. The lateral muscles (on the sides of the neck) bend the neck sideways.

The muscles of the shoulder, neck, and arm rotate the shoulder blades, and flex and extend the shoulder and elbow joints. Along with the forearm muscles, they help the forelegs flex, swing forward, absorb shock and carry weight. The suspensory apparatus also helps to carry the horse's weight, absorb shock and support the fetlock joint, and aids in the rebound effect which helps each foot leave the ground.

The forelegs are attached to the trunk by a "shoulder sling" of muscles, which absorbs shock and can help in lifting the ribs and forehand.

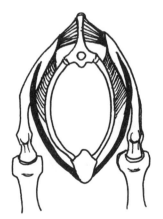

Muscles of the shoulder sling

The Circle of Muscles

The entire system of muscle groups is called the "circle of muscles." In good movement, the circle of muscles works in harmony; each muscle group performs its function and is neither overstressed nor underused. Poor movement breaks up the smooth functioning of the circle of muscles and puts more stress on some muscle groups. This is less efficient, hampers the horse's athletic ability, and may eventually lead to soreness, poor muscle development, and unsoundness.

GOOD MOVEMENT

Good movement depends on conformation, soundness, and correct muscle use. It is affected by shocing, footing, and by the way the horse is trained and ridden.

Normal Movement

Normal movement depends primarily on soundness and conformation.

CHART 8-1: NORMAL AND FAULTY MOVEMENT

Good Normal Movement	*Faulty Movement*
Sound: free from lameness, pain, or disability.	Lame, sore, or "off."
Symmetrical: both front and both hind legs move evenly, with the same height, arc, and length of stride.	Asymmetrical, uneven or unlevel. Abnormal arc of stride.
Straight and true: when viewed from front or rear, each foot travels straight, without deviating inward or outward.	Crooked: winging in, paddling, plaiting, interfering.
Free; the legs swing freely from the hip and shoulder.	Stiff, abnormally shortened strides.
Coordinated: steady, even, and well balanced.	Uncoordinated; unbalanced; stumbling.

CONFORMATION AND MOVEMENT

Conformation affects a horse's strength, athletic ability, and movement. Certain types of conformation favor different kinds of movement; some conformation defects handicap a horse in the way he moves.

Proportions

A horse's proportions (size or length of each part in relation to each other) affect his ability to move. Some examples include:

- Long muscles are able to move a limb farther than short muscles. Length in the neck, shoulder, forearm, croup, and from hip to hock helps a horse take longer strides for his size.

GOOD PROPORTIONS

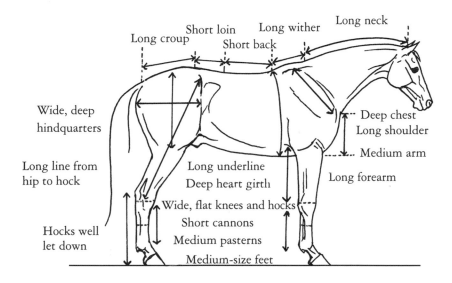

Long neck

Long wither

Short loin

Long croup

Short back

Wide, deep hindquarters

Deep chest

Long shoulder

Medium arm

Long line from hip to hock

Long underline

Deep heart girth

Long forearm

Wide, flat knees and hocks

Short cannons

Medium pasterns

Medium-size feet

Hocks well let down

Long forearm

- Shorter is usually stronger. Short, wide, well-developed cannon bones and flexor tendons are stronger than long, narrow cannons. A horse with a long back may have springy gaits and greater scope over fences, but a long back is less able to carry weight and more prone to injury than a short back. Long pasterns are more prone to injury than shorter ones, and they put more stress on the flexor tendons.
- In the front legs, ideal proportions are: long shoulder, short arm, long forearm, short cannon, medium pastern. This favors maximum length of stride, strength, efficiency, and range of motion. A short shoulder, long arm, short forearm, and long cannon causes a shorter, higher stride and is less strong.
- A long distance from hip to hock ("hocks well let down") indicates short, strong hind cannon bones and a more powerful hind leg.

Angles

The angles of the major bones affect the range of motion of the joints and the power and efficiency of the horse's stride. Some important angles are:

Hind Leg Angles   The hind legs act as levers, which push the body forward and carry weight, especially during transitions and collection.

HIND LEG ANGLES

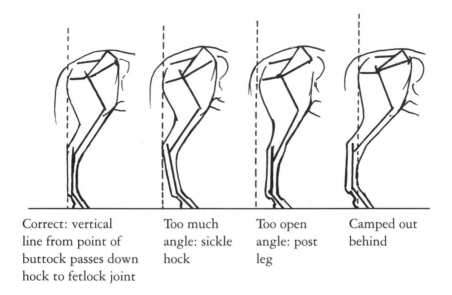

Correct: vertical line from point of buttock passes down hock to fetlock joint

Too much angle: sickle hock

Too open angle: post leg

Camped out behind

Correct angles make these levers more efficient in pushing and carrying weight.

In the ideal hind leg, a vertical line dropped from the point of the croup runs down the back of the hock, cannon, and fetlock joint. This gives the hocks the best angle. If the hock angle is too acute (sickle hocks or standing under), they are placed too far under the body to push effectively, and this puts extra stress on structures at the back of the hock. If the hock joint angle is too open (straight hock), it swings forward and backward efficiently but puts extra stress on the hock when carrying weight. If placed too far back, the hocks are less able to reach forward under the body, resulting in less engagement and power.

Shoulder Angle   The shoulder blade rotates with each stride, swinging the entire foreleg forward and back. A sloping shoulder has more range of motion and can swing the foreleg farther forward, which is important for long strides and to bring the knees up in jumping. It also absorbs shock, which makes the gaits smoother. An upright (straight) shoulder cannot swing the leg as far forward or up, resulting in a shorter, rougher stride.

Angle of Croup   The lumbar-sacral joint (the place where the loin ends and the croup begins) is important in balance and movement.

SHOULDER ANGLES

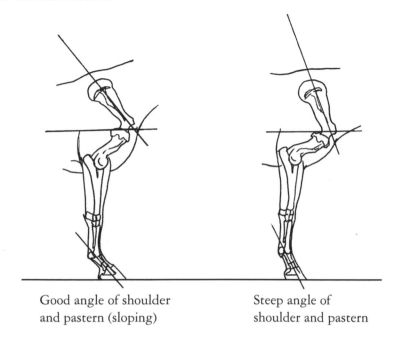

Good angle of shoulder
and pastern (sloping)

Steep angle of
shoulder and pastern

ANGLE OF CROUP

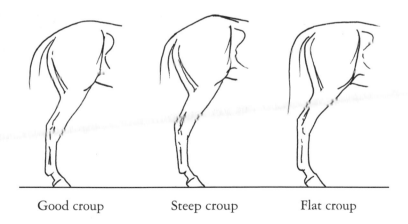

Good croup   Steep croup   Flat croup

The angle of the croup affects the horse's ability to flex this joint, tuck his hindquarters under him, and engage his hind legs for balance and power.

An ideal croup is long and slightly rounded, neither flat nor steep. This allows good angles, placement, and engagement of the hind legs. A very flat croup often goes with hind legs set too far behind the point of the buttock, which makes for poor engagement. A short, steep croup often goes with hind legs that "stand under" or have excessive hock angle (sickle hocks).

Angle of Pasterns   Pasterns should be of a medium angle, sloping enough to absorb shock, but not so sloping as to be easily injured or to allow the back of the fetlock joint to strike the ground.

Angle of Neck   The angle of the neck affects the way the horse naturally carries and uses his head and neck for balance. A low-set neck, which comes out of the front of the chest, results in a low head carriage and a tendency to move on the forehand. A neck set high with an upward angle ("swan neck"), encourages flexibility and collection, but makes it easy for the horse to carry his head too high and drop his back. The ideal neck depends on the type and purpose of the horse, but an average angle of neck is best for all-around balance and movement.

ANGLE OF NECK

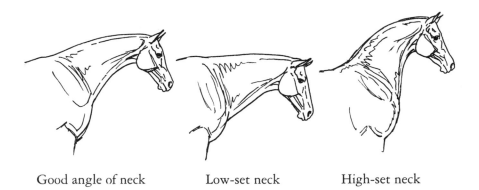

Good angle of neck   Low-set neck   High-set neck

Type of Muscling

A horse's type of muscling affects his movement and way of going, and the type of energy his muscles can deliver best. Fast-twitch muscle fibers deliver anaerobic energy for short but intense efforts; slow-twitch fibers deliver aerobic energy over a longer period. Although all horses have both slow-twitch and fast-twitch muscle fibers, some have a preponderance of one type.

Horses with short, thick, bunchy muscles (such as sprinters, stock horses, and draft horses) tend to have a preponderance of fast-twitch fibers. They tend to move with shorter strides but with great power.

Horses with long, flat, muscles (such as endurance horses) tend to have a preponderance of slow-twitch muscle fibers. They move with long strides and efficient movement that can be sustained over longer distances.

Midrange horses fall between the two extremes and are more versatile, having some ability to produce short, intense effort and some ability to carry a lower level of exertion over a distance.

For most breeds and types, middle-range muscling is preferred. However, when evaluating a horse, take into account the job he is bred and conformed to do. His type of muscling should be compatible with his purpose. Muscle tone and development reflects his current condition and training.

CONFORMATION AND SOUNDNESS

Conformation Points That Relate to Soundness

All good conformation is functional; that is, it helps the horse to be stronger, sounder, and perform better. However, some points are more directly related to strength and soundness:

- Straight legs (front and rear view).
- Legs correctly set.
- Correct angles of shoulder, pastern and hock.
- Short, wide cannon bones with clean, well-developed tendons.
- Large, clean, flat joints (especially knees, hocks, and fetlock joints).
- Well-shaped feet, size in proportion to horse.
- Short, broad, and well-muscled back and loin.
- Symmetry (both sides and limbs appear even and equally developed).

Conformation Defects and Their Effects on Soundness

No horse is perfect; a horse may have conformation defects, blemishes, or unsoundnesses. A **conformation fault or defect** is a structural problem, which may be hereditary. This makes horses with serious conformation faults poor candidates for breeding. Conformation defects are not unsoundnesses, nor do they always lead to unsoundness. However, serious conformation faults are undesirable because they make it harder for a horse to perform well, put more stress on certain parts, and make it more likely that injuries or unsoundnesses will occur, especially with hard work.

A **blemish** is an acquired defect which is unsightly but which does not affect the horse's usefulness, like a scar. Some conditions (such as splints) may be classified as unsoundnesses when they are acute and cause lameness, but may subside, leaving only a blemish once they have healed.

Unsoundnesses are conditions or injuries that cause lameness or otherwise impair the horse's health or ability to work. Certain conformation defects may weaken a part and predispose a horse to unsoundness, but a conformation defect is not an unsoundness and does not always lead to unsoundness.

(For more about conformation and unsoundnesses, please see the USPC C Manual, Chapter 12.)

CHART 8-2: CONFORMATION DEFECTS AND EFFECTS

Conformation Defect	Effect on Movement and Soundness
Base wide	More stress on inside of foot; may lead to ringbone.
Base narrow	Causes plaiting, possible interference or stumbling. More stress on outside of foot; may lead to ringbone.
Toes in	Causes paddling. More stress on outside of foot; may lead to ringbone.
Toes out	Causes winging in, possible interference. More stress on inside of foot, may lead to ringbone.
Over at the knee	Sometimes associated with contracted tendons. If severe, may cause stumbling.
Back at the knee (calf knees)	Extra stress on front of knee joint and flexor tendons. May lead to carpitis, carpal chip fractures, or bowed tendons under strenuous work.
Bench knees	Uneven stress on splint and cannon bones. May lead to splints, ringbone.
Knock knees	Uneven stress on splint and cannon bones and inside of feet. May lead to carpitis, splints, arthritis, or ringbone.
Standing under in front	Tends to move on forehand, may be prone to stumbling.
Camped out in front	Extra stress on flexor tendons and heels.
Sickle hock	Hock is less able to extend fully; more stress on plantar ligament. May lead to curb.
Straight hock (post leg)	Hock is less able to flex and absorb shock, making collected gaits more difficult. Extra stress on hock joint may lead to bone spavin, bog spavin, or thoroughpin.
Hocks camped out behind	Horse is less able to engage hocks well under body, making collection difficult and giving less speed and power.

(Continues)

CHART 8-2: CONFORMATION DEFECTS AND EFFECTS (Continued)

Conformation Defect	Effect on Movement and Soundness
Cow hocks	More stress on inside of hock and hind leg; may lead to bone spavin, bog spavin, or thoroughpin.
Bowed hocks	More stress on outside of hock and hind leg; may lead to bone spavin, bog spavin, or thoroughpin.
Straight stifle	Angle of stifle joint predisposes joint to stress, inflammation (gonitis), and locked stifle.
Contracted heels	Lack of frog pressure causes poor circulation; associated with navicular disease.
Flat soles	May be caused by coffin bone rotation due to founder; causes tender feet.
Upright pasterns	Increased concussion; may lead to concussion-related ailments such as navicular disease, sidebone, or ringbone.
Long, sloping pasterns	More stress on flexor tendons (may contribute to bowed tendons); fetlock joint may strike the ground, resulting in injury to sesamoid bones.
Straight shoulder	Less range of motion in shoulder and foreleg, causing short stride and less ability to fold knees well in jumping. Increased concussion.
Mutton withers	Difficulty in fitting saddle and holding saddle in place. May be combined with other faults such as short shoulder or being built downhill.
High withers	Difficulty in fitting saddle; prone to wither sores and galls.
Long back	Less ability to carry weight; more vulnerable to injury. However, may have more springy gaits and more scope over fences than short back.

Conformation Defect	Effect on Movement and Soundness
Short back	Prone to forging, especially if long legged.
Slab sided	Less room for heart and lungs; may lack endurance. Also, saddle may slip backward.
Flat croup	Often associated with hind legs set too far back (camped out behind), causing difficulty in engaging hind legs and in collection.
Short, steep croup	Hindquarters less powerful because of less length of muscle. Often associated with tipped pelvis, sickle hocks, or standing under.
High in hips (built downhill or overbuilt)	Horse tends to move on the forehand; difficulty in balance and collection. Saddle may tend to slip forward.
Ewe neck	Causes difficulty in flexion and carriage of head and neck (often high headed).
Short neck	Head and neck are less effective as a "balancer"; associated with short stride.
Too long neck (swan neck)	May be more difficult to ride on contact, with a tendency to raise or overflex neck and hollow the back. Roaring is more common in large horses with very long necks.
Parrot mouth	Horse may have difficulty in grazing because upper incisor teeth extend out over lower teeth. If molars are also misaligned, may have difficulty in chewing feed.
Undershot jaw	Lower incisors extend beyond upper incisors, making grazing difficult. If molars are also misaligned, may have difficulty in chewing feed.

CHART 8-3: COMMON UNSOUNDNESSES

Unsoundness	Location	Effects
Navicular disease	Navicular bone and navicular bursa	Causes soreness in heels, short stride, landing on toe. Bone spurs, arthritis, and degeneration of navicular bone may occur over time.
Sidebone	Lateral cartilages of foot	Cartilage becomes ossified and turns to bone, due to concussion or as part of normal aging process. May cause lameness at first; eventually subsides, leaving a blemish.
Ringbone	Pastern bones	Arthritis and new bone growth on pastern bone (nonarticular ringbone), pastern joint (high ringbone), or coffin joint (low ringbone). Often due to uneven concussion on one side of foot due to crooked legs.
Splints	Between splint and cannon bone, usually in front legs	New bone growth due to inflammation in interosseous ligament, caused by concussion or blow to splint bone. Usually subsides to blemish once healed.
Osselets	Bones of fetlock joint, usually in front legs	Arthritis of fetlock joint, causing new bone growth. May limit range of motion in fetlock joint. Common in race horses.

Unsoundness	Location	Effects
Carpitis	Bones of carpal joint (knee)	Arthritis of carpal joint; may have chip fractures or "joint mice" (tiny chips of bone loose in joint, causing inflammation). Associated with calf knees, especially in racehorses.
Bucked shins	Periosteum (bone covering) of cannon bone usually in front legs	Inflammation of periosteum, sometimes with microfratures, due to concussion, especially in young race horses. Usually subsides to a blemish once healed.
Bowed tendon	Deep digital or superficial flexor tendon and tendon sheath, usually in front legs	Strained tendon, with tearing of tendon fibers and tendon sheath, due to trauma. May heal enough to return to work, but scarring leaves a "bow" and is never as strong as before injury.
Sprained suspensory ligament	Suspensory ligament	Sprain of ligament, with tearing of ligament fibers due to trauma. Takes a long time to heal because of poor blood supply to ligament; easily re-injured.
Curb	Plantar ligament (at back of hock)	Sprain of plantar ligament due to excess strain on back of hock. Associated with sickle hocks. Usually subsides to blemish once healed.

(Continues)

CHART 8-3: COMMON UNSOUNDNESSES (Continued)

Unsoundness	Location	Effects
Bone Spavin	Bones of medial (inner) side of hock	Arthritis in hock joint due to stress, often associated with poor hock conformation or long term stress on hocks. Over time, bones may fuse, which relieves pain.
Bog Spavin	Joint capsule of hock (front surface of hock)	Joint capsule becomes distended with overproduction of synovial fluid due to stress on hock. May subside with rest. Usually a blemish rather than an unsoundness.
Thoroughpin	Joint capsule of hock (upper portion of hock)	Similar to bog spavin, except that it involves the upper part of the hock joint.
Corns	Ground surface of hoof, between bars and wall	Bruise caused by pressure of shoe in the wrong place, especially when shoe is left on too long and overgrown. May become infected (suppurating corn).
Hoof cracks		
Sand cracks	Outer wall of hoof, running down from coronary band	Due to dry feet, poor quality horn, or damage from excessive rasping. May require therapeutic shoeing, hoof dressing, and nutritional supplements to stimulate growth of horn.

Unsoundness	Location	Effects
Toe cracks	Outer wall of hoof, at toe, running up from ground surface	Often due to hoof splitting when trimming is neglected. May require therapeutic shoe, groove, clip, or other treatment to stop progress of crack.
Quarter cracks	Outer wall of hoof, at quarter (side), running up from ground surface.	May be due to neglected hoof trimming or unbalanced feet with excess "flare." Requires therapeutic shoeing, with clips, groove, or other measures to stop progress of the crack.

CHAPTER 9

• • • • • • • • • • • • • • •

The Foot and Shoeing

ANATOMY OF THE FOOT

The horse's foot consists of external and internal structures of the hoof, including bones, ligaments, tendons, blood vessels, and nerves. (The terms "hoof" and "foot" are often used interchangeably; here "foot" refers to the entire internal and external foot structure, while "hoof" refers only to the external structure. Please refer to descriptions and diagram in Chapter 8, pp. 254–57.)

FUNCTIONS OF THE FOOT

The design of the horse's foot allows it to perform several important functions: weight bearing, absorbing shock, pumping blood, traction, protection, and growth and repair.

Weight Bearing   The shape and structure of the hoof are designed to bear weight. The hoof wall is made up of tubules of horn; the inside of the wall is made of horny laminae, hairlike "leaves" that interlock with the sensitive laminae that cover the surface of the coffin bone, forming a strong attachment.

The horse's weight is carried mostly on the hoof wall, and on the frog when the hoof sinks into soft ground. The sole can bear some weight, but its main function is to protect the deeper structures of the foot. It should be concave, not flat.

Absorbing Shock   The foot is a major shock-absorbing mechanism, along with the joints and angles of the legs. Elastic structures like the frog, plantar cushion, and lateral cartilages, and expansion of the walls and heels, help the foot absorb shock as the foot strikes the ground. This reduces the concussion transmitted to bones and joints.

Pumping Blood   Because the lower leg and foot have no muscles to aid in pumping blood, and are located a long way from the heart, the pumping action of the foot during movement helps the circulation.

Blood enters the foot through the digital arteries. The blood vessels of the hoof run through the plantar cushion, an elastic structure located underneath the back of the coffin bone, between the lateral cartilages and above the frog. With each step, the plantar cushion is squeezed between the coffin bone, lateral cartilages, and frog, compressing the veins and pumping blood back up the leg toward the heart. One-way valves within the veins prevent the blood from returning to the foot.

This mechanism only works during movement; circulation is impaired when the horse is inactive for long periods.

Traction   The ground surface of the foot provides a nonslip surface on different kinds of ground. The frog helps to prevent slipping on hard ground; the arched shape of the sole helps to stabilize the foot on soft ground; and the front edge of the hoof digs into the ground as it breaks over.

Protection   The hoof is designed so that tough, insensitive outer structures protect the softer, sensitive parts inside. The hoof wall, sole, and frog are insensitive and can tolerate concussion, abrasion, heat, and cold. Each has a sensitive counterpart located deeper, which has a blood and nerve supply. The periople (the shiny outer covering of the hoof wall) seals the hoof, protecting the horn from loss of moisture. The outside of the coronary band is less sensitive than the inner coronary band, but is more sensitive than other outer structures of the foot.

Growth and Repair   The foot constantly repairs itself, replacing dead cells and those worn away by contact with the ground. The hoof wall grows from the corium, which is located beneath the coronary band and is like the nail bed from which fingernails grow. The corium produces horn tubules, which make up the horny wall of the hoof; it also produces the periople, or outer covering of the hoof.

The hoof wall grows downward at a rate of about ¼ to ⅜ inch per month. The rate of growth is affected by nutrition, metabolism, health, and climate; variations in any of these can result in "growth rings," which are visible on the hoof wall.

Under ideal natural conditions, the hoof should wear away at the same rate at which it grows. Often this is not the case, and the hoof may wear away faster than it can be replenished, or may grow faster than it wears down. The horse may then require shoeing or foot trimming.

THE HORSE'S FOOT IN MOTION

In order to evaluate a horse's movement and the effect of shoeing on his way of going, you must understand the basics of stride and movement.

Phases of the Stride

Each foot goes through four phases during each stride:

- **Impact or grounding:** the moment when the foot lands.
- **Support:** the phase of the stride during which the foot bears weight.
- **Breakover:** the foot rotates forward over the toe as it leaves the ground.
- **Flight phase:** the foot is carried through the air.

Foot Flight Patterns

The flight pattern is the path a foot takes as it moves through the air from breakover to grounding. Foot flight patterns are determined by leg conformation, the angle and length of the foot, the shape of the foot or shoe, and the weight of the shoe. The horse's breed or type, conformation, natural way of going, soundness, and the balance in which he is ridden can also affect foot flight patterns. The ideal flight pattern represents a sound horse with efficient movement.

To evaluate the flight pattern of each foot, watch the horse walk and trot on a hard, level surface, directly toward you, away from you, and from the side. When watching from front or rear, focus on one foot at a time; compare its flight path to an imaginary center line. From the side, note the height, shape, and length of the arc. It is easier to see the way the foot lands from the side or rear.

NORMAL FLIGHT PATH OF FOOT

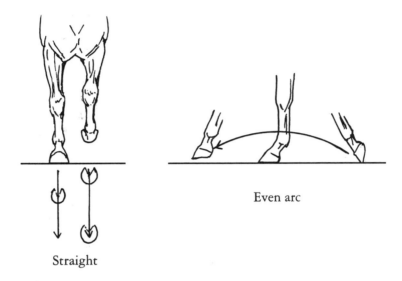

Even arc

Straight

The ideal flight pattern (viewed from front or rear) is straight and true, without deviating inward or outward. On a level surface, the hoof lands in lateral balance, without twisting, rocking, or one side landing first.

Viewed from the side, the ideal flight pattern is a balanced arc. The foot breaks over easily, and is carried at a moderate height (which varies according to breed). The first (upward) part of the flight pattern is equal to the second (downward) part. On hard, level ground, each hoof lands cleanly, with most of the weight on the back half of the foot.

Faulty flight patterns include:

Winging In The foot breaks over at the inside of the toe and deviates inward. Caused by toe-out conformation, it places uneven weight and concussion on the foot, and can cause interfering.

Winging Out The foot breaks over at the outside of the toe and deviates outward. Caused by toe-in conformation, it places uneven weight and concussion on the foot.

FAULTY FLIGHT PATTERNS

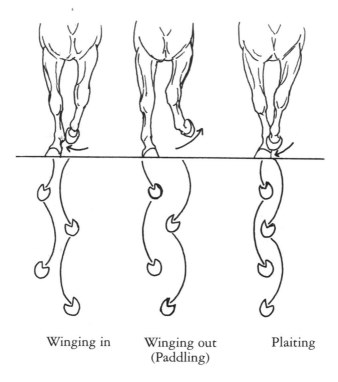

| Winging in | Winging out (Paddling) | Plaiting |

Plaiting   The foot deviates inward, and is placed close to the center line, almost in front of the opposite leg. Caused by base-narrow conformation, it places uneven weight and concussion on the foot and can cause interfering or stumbling.

Short Initial Arc; Long, Flat Landing   Characteristic of sloping hoof and pastern angle, with low heel and long toe. The hoof stays on the ground longer, requiring more leverage to break over, causing strain on the flexor tendons and navicular area. The first part of the arc is short and steep; the second part is longer and flatter.

Long Initial Arc; Short, Steep Landing   Characteristic of an upright hoof and pastern angle, with high heel and short toe. The hoof breaks over quickly and the first part of the arc is long and flat. The second part of the arc is short and steep, resulting in more concussion.

Decreased Arc in One Foot   Characteristic of a lame horse. The foot is carried in a shorter, lower arc, less weight is carried on the foot, and

ARC AND HOOF ANGLE

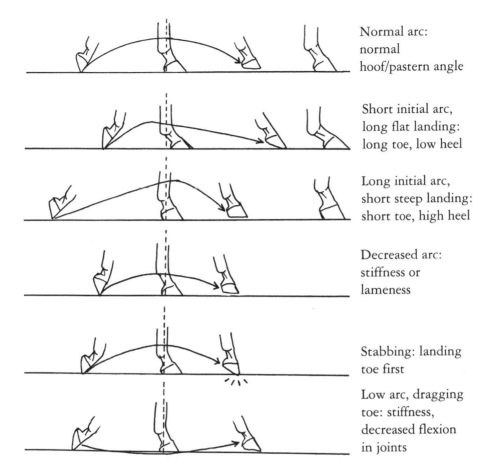

Normal arc: normal hoof/pastern angle

Short initial arc, long flat landing: long toe, low heel

Long initial arc, short steep landing: short toe, high heel

Decreased arc: stiffness or lameness

Stabbing: landing toe first

Low arc, dragging toe: stiffness, decreased flexion in joints

the joints of the leg bend less. If severe, the horse may barely touch the foot to the ground.

Excessively Low Arc ("Dragging the Toe") Characteristic of a horse that does not flex the joints of the leg sufficiently, often due to lameness, stiffness, fatigue, or moving in poor balance.

Landing Toe-first ("Stabbing") Characteristic of a horse trying to avoid landing on sore heels. The stride is short and steep, and the horse is prone to stumble.

SHOEING AND TRIMMING PRINCIPLES

Good trimming and shoeing aims to keep the horse sound and comfortable, allowing him to move as efficiently as possible for his job, within the limitations of his conformation. Some principles of good trimming and shoeing include the following.

Each horse must be shod or trimmed according to his own individual characteristics and needs.

WEIGHT AND CONCUSSION TRAVEL IN VERTICAL LINE

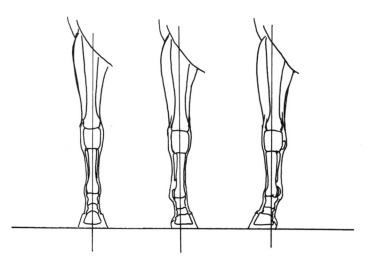

Straight, balanced leg and foot distribute concussion evenly

Toe-in: more stress on outside of foot and leg

Toe-out: more stress on inside of leg

Balanced hoof lands evenly

Unbalanced hoof strikes on one side first and rocks laterally

Weight and concussion (shock) travel in a straight up-and-down direction. A properly balanced foot distributes concussion and carries weight evenly, without overstressing any part. An incorrectly balanced foot places extra strain and concussion on the parts of the foot and leg that bear the most weight.

The feet should be trimmed (and shod) so that they best support the vertical column of the leg. Viewed from the side, a vertical line down the center of the cannon bone should touch the heel of the foot.

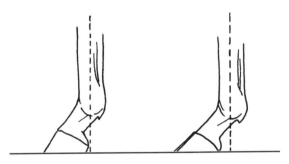

Correct: vertical line down center of cannon touches heel

Incorrect: long toe, low heel; foot too far forward

A foot should be trimmed so that it lands in good lateral balance (on a hard, level surface), without twisting, rocking, or landing on one side first.

The angles, balance, and placement of the feet affect the angles of the joints and limbs above them. Incorrect shoeing or trimming causes stress, which can result in injuries and lameness, not only in the feet.

The angle of the hoof should match the angle of the pastern. This keeps the bones of the pastern and hoof in alignment. A "broken backward" or "broken forward" angle places extra stress on bones, joints, tendons, and other structures.

Extra weight tends to increase the arc of the stride (making it higher and longer), concussion, and the effort needed to pick each foot up. If the horse wings in or out, extra weight will increase this tendency. In general, a horse should be shod with the least weight that is practical.

A horse's feet change according to his work, way of going, soundness, and other factors. The wear pattern shown by each foot (and/or shoe) is an important indicator of his soundness and way of going.

ANGLE OF HOOF AND PASTERN

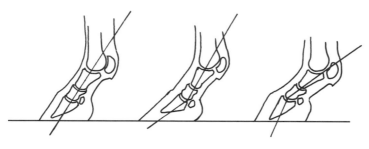

Correct: hoof angle
matches pastern
angle; bones aligned
normally

Broken-backward
angle: long toe,
low heel

Broken-forward
angle: short toe,
high heel

TRIMMING AND SHOEING TO CORRECT PROBLEMS

Proper trimming and/or shoeing can help alleviate certain soundness and way of going problems. This requires an expert evaluation of the horse's conformation, way of going, and problems, and skilled application of special trimming or shoeing techniques. The farrier, veterinarian, and trainer should work as a team in evaluating the horse, deciding on the best way to shoe him, and keeping him sound during work.

Corrective Trimming

Corrective trimming is used to correct certain defects of foot and leg conformation (especially crooked legs) while the horse's bones are still growing. The shape and balance of the foot is altered so that the leg gradually grows straighter. This is a gradual process that is carried out over many months.

Corrective trimming is most effective in foals and young horses under eighteen months of age. After the bones have matured and the epiphyseal plates have hardened, their shape does not change. Radical "corrective" trimming or shoeing in mature horses can force the bones out of their natural (although crooked) alignment, causing severe stress on bones, joints, and other structures, and often resulting in lameness.

Therapeutic Shoeing

Therapeutic shoeing is the use of special shoes and shoeing techniques to help a horse to heal an injury, or to cope with a chronic condition such as navicular disease, founder, or arthritis. It is usually done in consultation with a veterinarian.

There is a great variety of therapeutic shoes and shoeing techniques for various ailments and chronic conditions. Some horses may only need therapeutic shoes temporarily, for an acute condition such as a foot abscess. Others may require long-term therapeutic shoeing in order to stay sound enough to work.

Corrective/Therapeutic Shoeing

This type of shoeing is related to corrective trimming and therapeutic shoeing, but is less radical and is usually applied to less severe problems. It consists of adjustments in trimming and shoeing, and the use of specialized shoes, to correct defects in the horse's movement. The purpose is to help the horse move better and work in comfort, not to change his conformation or make his legs and feet appear straighter. Many horses need some degree of this type of shoeing, adapted to their needs by an observant and skilled farrier.

Problems such as interfering, forging, overreaching, stumbling, or dragging the toes can often be helped by special shoes or adaptations such as rolling the toe. Changes in the weight, angle, shape and type of shoe can make a significant difference in the way the foot breaks over, its flight pattern, and how it lands.

In some cases, corrective shoeing must be done at more frequent intervals than usual, such as every four weeks. The extra expense of special shoes and more frequent shoeing should be taken into account when considering the purchase of a horse that requires this.

It is important to know (and record) what size and type of shoes your horse wears, and to take notes on his hoof measurements, angles, and any soundness or movement problems. Remember that his feet may change over time, and so may his shoeing needs.

Types of Shoes

There are many types of shoes for different purposes. (Basic shoes and features are described in the USPC C Manual, Chapter 8.) Shoes may be made in special shapes, usually to correct a problem, or different materials, or with added features. Special shoes (which are usually custom-forged) include:

Bar Shoe   Therapeutic shoe used to apply or relieve pressure on certain parts of the foot. There are different types of bar shoes (straight bar, egg bar, heart bar, etc.).

TYPES OF SHOES

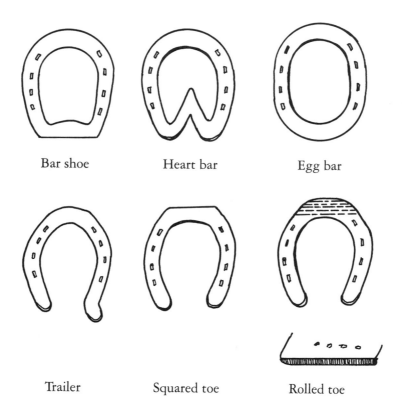

Bar shoe	Heart bar	Egg bar
Trailer	Squared toe	Rolled toe

Feather Edge Shoe   Shoe with the inside quarter beveled and angled; used to reduce the possibility of interfering and to limit the damage if the hose strikes itself.

Trailer Shoe   Hind shoe with one extended heel, used to help the hoof land straight.

Squared Toe   Shoe squared off at the toe, to prevent forging or overreaching.

Rolled Toe or Rocker Toe   Shoe with toe rounded or turned up slightly at the front. This makes it easier for the foot to break over and may be used to help prevent stumbling.

Other types of shoes:

Keg Shoe   Manufactured steel shoe, available in standard patterns and sizes; may be heated and shaped or modified.

Aluminum Racing Plate   Very light, narrow aluminum shoe for minimum weight, manufactured in several styles. They are very light but wear out quickly.

Aluminum Wide Web Shoe   Lightweight shoe with wide width to protect sole. More substantial and longer wearing than racing plates, with optional steel wear plate at toe. May be tapped for studs.

Polo or Rim Shoe   Concave, fullered shoe with higher inner rim. It allows the foot to break over easily in any direction.

OPTIONAL FEATURES

Pads

Pads are used to protect the sole, to reduce concussion, or for treatment of various problems. Oakum or other packing material is used between the sole and the pad.

Regular Pads   Leather or synthetic material; protects the sole, may reduce concussion.

Degree Pads   Wedge-shaped pads, thicker at the heel; used to adjust the angle of the hoof while protecting the sole and reducing concussion.

Rim Pads or Cut-out Pads   Pads that cover the edge of the foot and heels, leaving some of the frog and sole exposed. Used to alter the angle of the hoof and to reduce concussion.

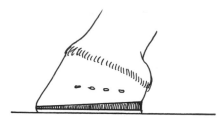

Degree or wedge pad

Clips

A shoe may have clips on the sides (quarter clips) or at the toe (a toe clip), which help it to stay on.

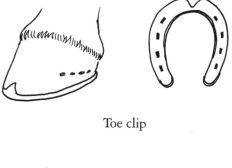

Toe clip

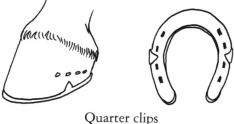

Quarter clips

Traction Devices

Traction devices may be added to shoes to prevent slipping.

Heels or Calks   These dig into the ground and help to prevent slipping, especially on grass. Often used on shoes for jumping horses or trail horses in the mountains.

TRACTION DEVICES

Heels or calks   Borium

Borium   A super-hard steel-alloy material welded onto the heels and toes of the shoe. Borium bites into hard surfaces like pavement, ice, or rock, to prevent slipping. However, it increases concussion and can inflict severe injuries if a borium-shod horse kicks another.

Tapped Shoes with Removable Studs (Screw-In Calks)   Shoes can be tapped (drilled) to receive screw-in studs or calks of various sizes and types. They are used for combined training, dressage, and show jumping, for security on different types of footing and conditions.

Studs should be used only when the horse and the activity require them, and under expert supervision, as they can cause injury if used improperly. It is important to use the correct length and type of stud for grass, soft footing, mud, or hard ground. When studs are used, the horse should wear bell boots for protection, in case he steps on himself.

Studs must be removed when the horse is not working on a surface that requires them. A special tool is used to insert, tighten and remove them. The holes should be plugged with cotton or rubber plugs, to prevent dirt from filling the holes and ruining the threads.

Types of studs include:

- **Road studs:** small studs for hard surfaces.
- **Bullets:** for use on ground that is fairly firm but soft on top.
- **Blocks:** square studs for soft, muddy ground.
- **Olympic:** largest, sharper studs for extremely slippery footing.

TAPPED SHOES AND SCREW-IN STUDS

  Small square
road stud

 Short pointed
stud

 Long pointed
stud

 Medium pointed
stud

 Long square
stud

 Screw-in plug

Cotton plug

 Shoe tapped to
receive screw-in
calk

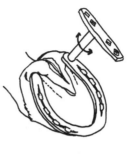 Using tee tap to
remove plug and
clean threads

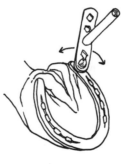 Base of tee tap serves
as wrench to insert
and tighten stud

 Shoe with stud in
place (on outside heel)

CHAPTER 10

Conditioning and Exercise Physiology

Conditioning horses for demanding athletic activities such as eventing requires an understanding of exercise physiology and modern conditioning methods. Above all, it requires experience and good judgment, in order to adapt the conditioning program to the individual horse and to day-to-day and week-to-week conditions. Close observation of the horse and the advice of an expert are essential.

The material in this chapter is based upon that covered in the USPC C Manual, Chapter 7. This material, especially the sections on thermoregulation, cooling out, and basic conditioning, should be read in conjunction with this chapter.

EXERCISE PHYSIOLOGY

The horse is an athlete by design. He is built to move, and every system contributes and collaborates with the other systems to produce movement, agility, speed, and endurance. To understand conditioning, it is important to know how the various systems operate during exercise. (Also see Chapter 7.)

Muscles and Energy Production

Skeletal muscles are the muscles that produce movement (locomotion). They work by contracting or shortening. Skeletal muscles can only pull; they cannot push. For this reason, many skeletal muscles operate in pairs; one muscle flexes or bends a joint, and an opposing muscle extends or straightens it.

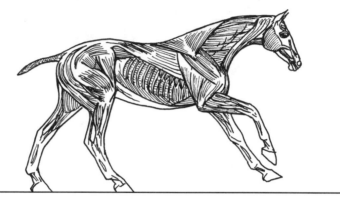

Skeletal muscles in motion

Muscles are made up of long, slender muscle cells, called **muscle fibers.** A muscle fiber contains thousands of tiny threadlike filaments called **myofibrils.** These in turn contain even smaller protein filaments of two types: **myosin filaments** and **actin filaments.**

Muscle fibers are arranged in **bundles** that resemble long strands. These bundles in turn make up the **muscle belly.** Some muscles are simple; others are complex, having several parts and functions. Muscles are connected to bones by tendons, tough bands of connective tissue. Muscle bundles and the muscles themselves are encased in **fascia,** a thin, tough connective tissue. Muscles are supplied with blood vessels (arteries, veins, smaller arterioles and venules, and capillaries). Glycogen and triglycerides, sources of energy for muscular contractions, are stored in the muscle fibers. Motor nerves control muscular movement; sensory nerves monitor the amount of tension and stretch in a muscle.

Contractions in muscle fibers are produced by a chemical reaction between the actin filaments and the myosin filaments, triggered by a motor nerve impulse. An individual muscle fiber contracts fully (fires)

MUSCLE STRUCTURES

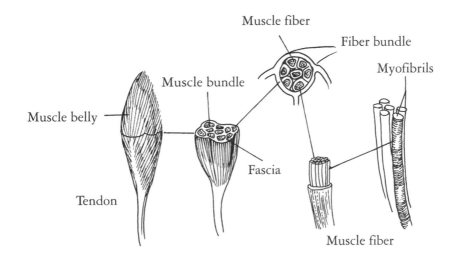

Muscle fiber

Fiber bundle

Myofibrils

Muscle bundle

Muscle belly

Fascia

Tendon

Muscle fiber

when it receives a nerve impulse; there is no partial contraction. However, a muscle may contract only a few fibers, many, or nearly all at once; the degree of tension in the muscle depends on how many fibers contract at once.

Muscle contractions require energy, which is produced in one of three ways: aerobic metabolism, anaerobic alactic metabolism, or anaerobic lactic metabolism. Each type of metabolism (energy production) produces a type of energy suitable for a particular type of exercise; horses use all three types in varying degrees, depending on the kind of work they do.

Aerobic Metabolism   Aerobic metabolism (energy production) uses oxygen and **glycogen** (fuel created primarily from carbohydrates and fats) to create energy to move muscles. It produces energy at a fairly low rate, which can be sustained for long periods of time. Examples of aerobic exercise include endurance and distance riding, foxhunting, and the roads and tracks phase of eventing.

Anaerobic Alactic Metabolism   Anaerobic means "without oxygen," and alactic means "without lactate." The anaerobic alactic metabolism produces energy using **creatinine phosphokinase** (a substance present in limited amounts in the muscle cells) and **glycogen**. It produces a short but intense burst of energy that lasts for only about ten to twenty

Myofibrils (relaxed)

Myofibrils (contracted)

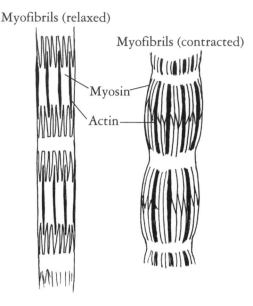

Myosin

Actin

seconds, and ends when the muscle's stores of creatinine phosphokinase is exhausted. This energy is used for brief, intensive efforts like short sprints, breaking into a run from a standing start, or jumping.

Anaerobic Lactic Metabolism   Anaerobic lactic metabolism pro-duces energy **without oxygen,** using glycogen (carbohydrates) as fuel. This process produces **lactate** (lactic acid), a toxic waste product. The lactate is carried away by the circulatory system, but as more lactate is produced than can be carried away, it builds up in the muscle tissues and results in a burning sensation and fatigue. Most activities that require strenuous exertion for more than twenty seconds involve anaer-obic lactic metabolism (racing, polo, dressage, show jumping, and eventing).

Types of Muscle Fibers

There are two types of muscle fibers: **slow-twitch fibers** and **fast-twitch fibers.** Every horse has some of both types, but some horses have a preponderance of one type. An individual horse's makeup of slow-twitch and fast-twitch muscles is part of his conformation, type, and genetic heritage; the number of slow-twitch and fast-twitch fibers does not change with conditioning.

Slow-Twitch Fibers   Slow-twitch muscle fibers are best suited for aerobic metabolism. Horses with a preponderance of slow-twitch muscle fibers are best suited for aerobic activities requiring endurance, such as distance riding and endurance racing.

Fast-Twitch Fibers   Fast-twitch muscle fibers use anaerobic metabolism to produce contractions of great strength but short-lived energy. Horses with a preponderance of fast-twitch muscle fibers tend to excel in sports requiring brief, strenuous muscular effort: sprinting, reining, polo, jumping, and dressage.

All-around athletes such as event horses should have a balance of slow-twitch and fast-twitch muscle fibers.

Effects of Conditioning

With conditioning, muscles increase in size and strength. The circulation becomes more efficient at delivering oxygen and nutrients and removing waste products, and the capillaries become larger and more numerous, so they can serve muscle cells and fibers more efficiently. The nerve pathways that govern muscular efforts become more efficient, and specific movements become easier, more fluent, and efficient. The muscles also become stronger and better able to tolerate the effects of lactate. Muscle tissue is the fastest to condition and shows the effects of conditioning sooner and more dramatically than other body tissues.

Cardiovascular System

During exercise, the cardiovascular system (heart and blood vessels) must pump blood through the blood vessels at an increased rate, to deliver oxygen and fuel to the cells and remove waste products. During exercise, the large skeletal muscles help to pump blood throughout the body by rhythmically squeezing the elastic blood vessels as they contract and relax with each stride.

During exercise, the heart rate increases dramatically, from a resting rate of about 35 beats per minute, up to 250 beats per minute or higher during maximum exertion.

Measuring Heart Rate   Heart rate during exercise can be measured most accurately by using an on-board heart rate monitor, a device that uses electrodes under the saddle or girth to read and display the working heart rate to the rider on a readout device. Methods that involve measuring the heart rate immediately after exercise (such as taking the pulse manually or with a stethoscope) are much less accurate, as the heart rate drops very quickly (within fifteen to thirty seconds) after pulling up from a gallop.

The Spleen   The horse's spleen serves as a reservoir for extra red blood cells, which are released into the circulation during exercise. This increases the blood volume and the amount of oxygen that can be transported during exercise. In addition, the spleen detects and screens out red blood cells that are used up or damaged, and removes them from circulation for recycling.

Effects of Conditioning   With conditioning, the heart becomes stronger and more efficient. It can pump more blood with each beat, can achieve a higher maximum heart rate, and drops to a normal resting rate more quickly. The capillaries become larger and greater in number, which makes the exchange of oxygen, carbon dioxide, nutrients, and waste product more efficient. The blood contains more red blood cells, which are higher in hemoglobin, making them better able to transport oxygen and nutrients.

Respiratory System

Exercise creates a greater demand for oxygen. The job of the respiratory system is to take in oxygen by breathing fresh air into the lungs, and to expel waste gases (chiefly carbon dioxide).

Gas Exchange   Gas exchange refers to the exchange of oxygen for carbon dioxide, which takes place in the alveoli and small blood vessels of the lungs.

Respiration Rate and Stride Rate   At the canter and gallop, the mechanics of the stride cause the horse to breathe once during each stride. This "locks" the respiration rate to the stride rate. At other gaits, the horse does not have to breathe in unison with each stride, but he is more aerobically efficient when he moves at a regular stride rate which allows him to breathe evenly in rhythm with his strides. At the trot, horses often breathe once every two strides.

At the canter and gallop, the movement of the hind legs, gut, diaphragm, chest, and neck are interconnected. During the first phase of the stride, the hind legs are gathered under the horse, the neck rises, the ribs expand, the gut contents move backward in the abdomen, and the diaphragm is drawn backward, creating more space in the lungs and causing the horse to inhale. During the second half of the stride, the neck is extended and lowered, the rib cage is compressed, the hind legs extend backward, and the gut contents move forward, pushing against the diaphragm and lungs and causing the horse to exhale. The horse can often be heard to snort with every stride.

BREATHING MECHANISM IN GALLOP STRIDE

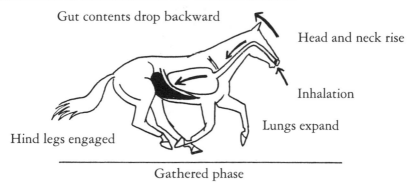

Gut contents drop backward

Head and neck rise

Inhalation

Lungs expand

Hind legs engaged

Gathered phase

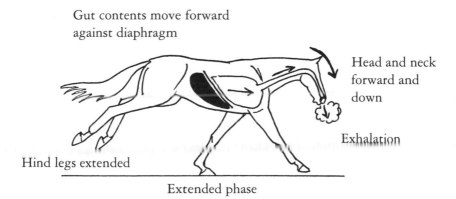

Gut contents move forward against diaphragm

Head and neck forward and down

Exhalation

Hind legs extended

Extended phase

Effects of Conditioning With conditioning, the respiratory system becomes more efficient at taking in oxygen and expelling carbon dioxide, and the horse becomes more aerobically efficient during exercise. This effect is noticed as improvement in "wind"; the horse can go farther at a faster speed without tiring or running out of breath.

CONDITIONING PRINCIPLES

Training Effect   Training (in the context of conditioning) refers to physical development, which takes place at the cellular level. All the systems of the body are involved in the training (conditioning) process, but some systems (muscular, cardiovascular, and respiratory systems) are more directly affected than others.

Demand   Work creates a demand for more oxygen and fuel in the cells of the body. The body adapts to this demand (over time) by increasing the number of red blood cells and improving its efficiency in delivering oxygen and fuel to the cells, removing waste products, and producing energy. In conditioning, the purpose of exercise is to increase demand enough to stimulate a training effect.

Progressive Loading   Progressive loading refers to small, measured increases in exercise. Only the right amount of exercise will have a training effect. Too little does not create a demand and stimulate conditioning; too much leads to overloading, injuries, and breakdowns.

Overloading   Overloading occurs when the body or some part of the body is subjected to work or stress beyond its limits. Instead of stimulating a training effect, injury or breakdown occurs. This will cause a setback in the conditioning process, and may result in permanent damage.

Rest   Rest is necessary for conditioning. A brief period of rest (recovery) between efforts allows the body to recover and prepare for a new effort. Rest between workouts is essential for replenishing, repair, and strengthening of body tissues. Insufficient rest results in overloading and damage.

Nutrition   Proper nutrition is essential to provide fuel for energy, protein for building body tissues, water for fluid balance and cooling, and essential vitamins and minerals to regulate metabolic processes. During conditioning, the horse's nutritional needs change with his work and condition.

As a horse's workload increases, his energy needs increase. A horse doing strenuous work requires a larger amount of feed, and a higher proportion of concentrates (grain) to roughage than for a maintenance ration. The ration must be at least 50 percent roughage in order to keep the gut functioning efficiently, but the roughage may need to be of a higher quality than for maintenance or light work. His protein requirements remain approximately the same, although growing horses and aged horses may need slightly higher levels of protein. (For more information on nutrition during conditioning, see Chapter 11.

Different Tissues Condition at Different Rates   Muscles show the effects of conditioning most quickly; visible effects may be seen in a few weeks. However, tendons, ligaments, and joints may take several months to strengthen, and hooves and bones require the most time (up to a year) to condition. Because of this, it is important not to mistake early signs of muscular conditioning for overall fitness and risk injuring less well-conditioned structures by too much strenuous work too soon.

Cardiovascular and respiratory conditioning develops endurance and "wind"; this takes place gradually over weeks and months.

Peaking   A horse's condition cannot continue to increase past a certain point, or remain at a high level indefinitely. Systematic training will improve it to a "peak" or optimum level, and then it declines somewhat. When conditioning for a particular event, it is important to pace the conditioning process so that the horse achieves peak condition at the time of competition and does not reach his peak too early or too late.

TYPES OF CONDITIONING

Aerobic Conditioning

Aerobic conditioning is conditioning carried out at a level **below the anaerobic threshold,** at which the horse can function aerobically (his muscles burn oxygen to produce energy). Aerobic conditioning increases the body's ability to deliver oxygen to the tissues efficiently, and to produce energy aerobically. This results in better cardiovascular efficiency and greater endurance.

Long, Slow Distance Work (LSD)   Long, slow distance work is aerobic conditioning. It usually involves trotting and slow cantering, with some periods of walking. As the horse becomes fitter, the distance traveled and the length of the workouts are gradually increased, rather than increasing the speed. Long, slow distance work lays the foundation for all other conditioning, providing a "base" of cardiovascular fitness and endurance.

Anaerobic Conditioning

Anaerobic conditioning is work carried out at a pace **above the anaerobic threshold** (the point at which muscles produce energy anaerobically, without burning oxygen). It is used to strengthen muscles and develop specific skills and speed. Anaerobic conditioning should be added only after the horse has developed a "base" of fitness through aerobic conditioning.

Some types of anaerobic conditioning are:

Skill Drills   Muscles must be prepared for the demands of a particular activity by practice in that skill. For instance, jumping horses need to jump, and dressage horses must practice specific movements. Skill practice conditions specific muscles anaerobically, and improves strength, coordination, and fluency in specific skills.

Speed Play   Speed play is an anaerobic training technique that helps to develop strength, coordination, balance, and quickness. It consists of brief sprints and changes of speed and direction in a random pattern, sometimes incorporating uphill and downhill terrain. It is especially useful for jumpers, eventers, polo ponies, and horses in specialties requiring quick responses.

Interval Training

Interval training is a conditioning method based on the principle of progressive loading. It consists of several work intervals at a measured speed and distance, which raise the horse's heart rate to a certain level. Each work interval is followed by a short rest period in which the heart rate is allowed to recover to a specified level (usually around 100 to 125 beats per minute). The number of "sets" (work and rest intervals) and the speed and distance of each work interval must be carefully determined, keeping in mind the horse's heart rate, recovery rate, and response to the conditioning process. It is the total amount of work, connected by recovery periods, that results in conditioning benefits.

Interval training is a powerful tool for developing cardiovascular fitness. Using interval training, a horse can do more fast work, aimed at more specific conditioning goals than in traditional galloping work, with less risk of injury. However, interval training requires precise measurement of speed, distance, and heart rate (preferably with an onboard heart rate monitor), and a high degree of experience, knowledge, and judgment.

Interval training for eventers, which is carried out at a controlled gallop, should not be confused with repeated short sprints, a technique used by some racehorse trainers to sharpen short-distance speed.

CONDITIONING PROBLEMS

Azoturia (Equine Exertional Rhabdomyolysis)

Azoturia (also called "tying up") is a serious metabolic disorder. It is most often seen in horses that are in work and fed a high grain ration that have had a day or two off but have not had their grain cut back while idle.

The technical term for azoturia is equine exertional rhabdomyolysis, which means a breakdown of muscle tissue due to exertion. Although it was once thought that the buildup of lactic acid in the muscles caused a spasm or huge "charley horse," recent research has shown that the problem has more to do with an electrolyte imbalance at the cellular or subcellular level. This prevents the affected muscles from relaxing. When electrolyte balance is restored, the muscles can relax, but serious damage may have been done to the muscle fibers during the period of contraction.

If a horse shows signs of azoturia, stop work at once and call the veterinarian. Restoring the cellular electrolyte balance can only be accomplished by *immediate* veterinary treatment; giving the horse electrolyte supplements will *not* help. Treatment includes administering fluids, anti-inflammatory drugs, a tranquilizer such as Acepromazine, and/or other muscle relaxants. The treatment aims to relieve the horse's distress and to minimize permanent physical damage to muscle tissue and the kidneys. Follow-up treatment will entail a suggested feeding and exercise plan following the acute phase.

Signs of azoturia:

- Unwillingness to track up, short strides and stiffness in the hind legs, which may worsen until the horse cannot move at all.
- Hard, tense, quivering hindquarter muscles.
- Sweating, restlessness, anxious expression.
- Dark-colored urine.
- Elevated temperature.
- Most often occurs when horse is first put back to work after a rest day or two, especially if grain ration was not cut back while idle.

Prevention of azoturia is easier than coping with the problem once it occurs. Some horses are more susceptible to azoturia than others, depending on conditioning, nutrition, environmental stress, genetic predisposition, temperament, and hormones. Although the last three factors are beyond the owner's control, good management can reduce the effects of the first three.

Management practices to prevent azoturia:

- Always adjust the feed schedule according to the work and exercise schedule.
- If a horse works on several consecutive days and then has a day off, he should be turned out for several hours of self-exercise rather than being confined.
- Always reduce the grain ration (to 50 percent or less) on days off.
- If a horse must suddenly be confined to a stall because of injury or other reasons, reduce the grain ration to a small handful, or eliminate grain from the ration entirely.
- Condition horses gradually and avoid overstressing horses beyond the limits of their fitness. Warm up slowly and warm down gradually after strenuous work.

Overtraining

Overtraining occurs when a horse is subjected to too much work and/or stress, and instead of improving, his condition deteriorates. Signs of overtraining include poor appetite, dull coat, weight loss, lack of energy, disinterest in work and/or sourness, and heat and/or filling in the legs. Overtraining pulls a horse's condition down rapidly and his immune system may be compromised; he is vulnerable to injury and illness.

Horses vary from day to day in training, but any of these signs point to a potential problem and should be taken seriously. The horse's workload should be cut back (particularly fast work) and his overall health and soundness should be checked. Sometimes more turnout time, hacking out, or a change of work will refresh the horse mentally and physically.

PART THREE

Horse Care and Stable Management

CHAPTER 11

Feeds and Nutrition

FEEDING DIFFERENT AGES AND TYPES OF HORSES

Horses' nutritional needs differ with the work they do and with other factors such as pregnancy, lactation, growth, and aging. It's also important to consider other factors such as those discussed below. Nutritional charts and recommendations are only guidelines, with a range of estimated nutritional requirements. Each horse must be fed as an individual, adapting the feeding program to meet his needs; those needs may change from week to week or even daily. There is no substitute for close observation of each horse and intelligent application of basic feeding principles.

Factors to Consider when Adjusting the Daily Ration

Current Condition   Does the horse need to maintain his present weight, put on weight, or lose weight? Is he getting fit, maintaining fitness, or letting down?

Physical Type   Tall, lean, "rangy" horses usually require more feed per 100 pounds of body weight than compact, chunky "easy keepers." Small ponies and certain individuals are prone to become overweight and need their feed intake carefully monitored to prevent laminitis.

Temperament   Is the horse high-strung and nervous, aggressive, or lazy? Feeding high-energy feeds can affect behavior and rideability, especially for school horses, small ponies, or horses ridden by inexperienced riders.

Appetite and Feeding Behavior   Some horses have excessive appetites and need their feed intake controlled to prevent too much weight gain. Shy feeders may refuse to eat when they are intimidated by other horses or disturbances. Picky eaters should be encouraged to eat by providing the most palatable feed frequently in small amounts.

Health   Horses that are ill, debilitated, or confined to a stall for long periods need special feeding. Follow your veterinarian's recommendations.

How the Horse Is Kept   Is the horse kept stabled, stabled with some pasture, or at grass? How much nutrition is provided by pasture grass?

Daily Work Variations   The grain ration *must* be cut back on rest days (to 50 percent of the normal ration, or less) to prevent azoturia. The horse should get some extra roughage to make up for the missing grain—about 3 pounds of grass hay for every pound of grain cut from his regular ration.

Seasonal Variations   Horses need more fiber and may need more energy to maintain their body heat during cold weather. The amount of work and turnout time may vary according to the season, and the feeding program should be adjusted accordingly.

Guidelines for Feeding Horses

Mature Idle Horses and Ponies (Maintenance Ration)   A maintenance ration is one that maintains the horse at his current health and condition, without allowing for additional needs such as work or growth. It contains enough protein for replacement of body tissues, and sufficient energy, vitamins, and minerals for normal body functions.

Idle horses and ponies (on long-term rest or not being ridden) often do best on a maintenance ration that is 100 percent good quality roughage (good hay or pasture), with free access to salt and water. Aged horses, "hard keepers," or horses kept on poor quality pasture

CHART 11-1: RECOMMENDED NUTRIENT CONCENTRATIONS IN TOTAL DIET FOR HORSES AND PONIES (DRY MATTER BASIS)

Type of Horse	Digestible Energy (Mcal/lb in total ration)	Crude Protein (% of daily ration)	Calcium (% of daily ration)	Phosphorous (% of daily ration)
MATURE HORSES AND PONIES				
Maintenance	.9 Mcal/lb	8.0%	0.24%	0.17%
Light work	1.2 Mcal/lb	9.8%	0.30%	0.22%
Moderate work	1.2 Mcal/lb	10.4%	0.31%	0.22%
Intense work	1.3 Mcal/lb	11.4%	0.35%	0.25%
AGED HORSES AND PONIES				
from	.9 Mcal/lb	9.8%	0.24%	0.17%
to	1.2 Mcal/lb	12.0%	0.24%	0.17%
MATURE BREEDING HORSES AND PONIES				
Stallions	1.1 Mcal/lb	9.6%	0.29%	0.21%
Pregnant mares	1.0 Mcal/lb	10.0%	0.43%	0.32%
Lactating mares	1.2 Mcal/lb	13.2%	0.52%	0.34%
GROWING HORSES AND PONIES				
Weanlings (6 months)	1.4 Mcal/lb	14.5%	0.56%	0.31%
Yearlings (12 months)	1.3 Mcal/lb	12.6%	0.43%	0.24%
Yearlings (18 months)	1.15 Mcal/lb	11.3%	0.34%	0.19%
2-year-olds	1.2 Mcal /lb	10.4%	0.31%	0.17%

Reprinted with permission from Nutrient Requirements of Horses, fifth revised edition. Copyright 1989 by the National Academy of Sciences. Courtesy of National Academy Press, Washington, D.C.

may need small amounts of concentrates. Small ponies and animals that tend to put on excessive weight should not have unlimited access to lush pastures.

Mature Horses and Ponies at Work   A horse or pony at work needs enough nutrients to meet his maintenance requirements, plus enough energy for the work he does, and protein, vitamins, and minerals to provide for maintenance and repair of tissues under increased stress. Protein and calcium requirements increase *slightly* with intense work. This should not lead horse owners to overfeed protein, which may do more harm than good.

Light work: nonstressful, fairly slow exercise (such as pleasure riding or easy trail riding), about thirty minutes to one hour per day. Light work is performed mostly at the walk, with some trotting and a little cantering.

Moderate work: a medium level of exercise (schooling and competing on the flat or over fences, lessons, schooling cross-country, longer or more strenuous trail rides), about one to two hours per day. Moderate work is performed mostly at the trot and canter, with some walking and galloping.

Hard or intense work: high level of exercise (eventing, foxhunting, polo, endurance, racing); intense work thirty minutes to 1 hour per day; three to four hours or more for endurance competition or foxhunting.

Energy is measured in megacalories (Mcal) and kilocalories (kcal). One kilocalorie equals 1,000 calories; one megacalorie equals 1 million calories.

CHART 11-2: ENERGY REQUIREMENTS FOR VARIOUS TYPES OF EXERCISE

Activity	Energy Required per Hour per Kilogram of Body Weight (above maintenance requirement), in Kilocalories (kcal)
Walking	0.5 kcal/hour
Slow trotting, some cantering	5.0 kcal/hour
Fast trotting, cantering, some jumping	12.5 kcal/hour
Cantering, galloping, jumping	23.0 kcal/hour
Strenuous effort (polo, racing, eventing)	39.0 kcal/hour

Adapted with permission from Nutrient Requirements of Horses, *fifth revised edition. Copyright 1989 by the National Academy of Sciences. Courtesy of National Academy Press, Washington, D.C.*

Aged Horses Aged horses may not digest and utilize feed as efficiently as younger horses, partly because of the gradual deterioration of their teeth. Feeding quality hay and crimped or rolled grains or pelleted feeds makes feed easier to digest with less efficient chewing. Aged horses may have slightly increased protein needs (up to about 12 percent), especially if they are under stress, and some may benefit from increasing the fat and energy content of the feed. An easy way to do this is to add one cup of corn oil to the daily ration.

Young Horses (Foals to Two Years) Young, growing horses have special nutritional needs for growth and development of strong bones. They are more vulnerable to deficiency diseases and nutritional imbalances than mature horses. The calcium/phosphorous ratio is especially critical, as overfeeding phosphorous or underfeeding either mineral can cause skeletal and joint problems. It is just as important not to overfeed young horses as it is to avoid deficiencies, and plenty of free exercise is essential.

Foals can be fed grain as soon as they will eat it, by sharing the mare's grain or in a "creep feeder" that gives the foal free access to grain but excludes the mare. As the foal grows and depends less on milk, it will need increasing amounts of grain and grass or good hay. The calcium/ phosphorous ratio should be at least 1.1 parts calcium to 1 part phosphorous; ratios of up to 3:1 are acceptable.

Weanlings need grain and hay or good pasture with protein levels of about 14 percent and calcium/phosphorous ratio of 1.1:1 to 3:1. Weanlings should show growth and weight gain, but pushing young horses for excessive gain and fast growth can lead to developmental orthopedic disease (DOD), especially if they are kept in stalls with limited exercise. Large pastures with free exercise reduces the risk of DOD.

Protein requirements gradually drop for yearlings (from 12.5 to 11 percent) and for two-year-olds (about 10.4 percent). Energy levels are slightly higher than those for mature, idle horses, but these also decrease. It is still important to keep calcium and phosphorous ratios correct (from 1.1:1 to 3:1), and to provide plenty of free exercise.

Breeding Stock Pregnant mares should receive a normal ration, sufficient to keep them in good flesh but not cause them to become overweight, for the first eight months of pregnancy. Their nutritional needs do not increase greatly until the last third of pregnancy. It is important to meet calcium and phosphorous needs, and to keep the calcium/phosphorous ratio in balance in order to build strong bones in the developing foal.

Lactating mares require the most feed volume, energy, protein, vitamins, and minerals of all horses. When producing milk, a mare will draw protein, calcium, and other nutrients from her own body if she does not receive adequate nutrition, and she may not produce enough milk for the foal if she is underfed. A lactating mare should be fed enough to keep her in good flesh, especially if she is bred back while nursing a foal.

At the peak of lactation (6 to 8 weeks after foaling), a mare can consume up to 3 percent of her body weight per day (30 pounds for a 1000 pound mare). She will need 1 Mcal energy per 100 pounds body weight, 13.2 percent protein, and extra calcium (.52 percent) and phosphorous (.34 percent).

Breeding stallions require extra energy (about 1.1 Mcal per 100 pounds body weight), especially if used heavily. Vitamins A, D, and E are important for fertility. Their protein and mineral requirements are about the same as other mature horses. It is important not to let stallions become unfit and overweight, as this can increase the risk of heart attack during breeding.

HORSE FEEDS

Horse feeds can be classified as roughages, concentrates, and supplements. There are many varieties within each category, each with its own characteristics and nutritional values.

ROUGHAGES

Roughages (hay and pasture) are feeds that are high in fiber and relatively low in energy. They are the most natural feed for horses, and should make up the greater part of any ration. Roughages take longer to consume than concentrates, providing the horse with the almost continuous "little and often" feeding and the fibrous plant material his digestive system requires.

HAY

Hay is a primary source of fiber and carbohydrates. The process of digesting fiber generates heat, so feeding plenty of hay helps horses maintain their body temperature during cold weather. Good-quality hay also provides protein, vitamins, and minerals, especially calcium.

Factors Affecting Quality, Palatability, and Nutritional Value of Hay

Type of Hay   Various plant species contain different levels of nutrients and vary in palatability. For instance, legume hays are higher in protein than grass hays.

Soil and Growing Conditions   Plants derive nutrients from the soil in which they grow. Drought, infertile soil or soil deficient in minerals can affect the quality of hay.

Stage of Plant Growth at Harvest   Hay should be cut before plants mature. After this point, they become coarse and stemmy, and less nutritious and palatable.

Harvesting and Curing   Properly harvested and cured hay retains most of its nutritional value. Weather damage, improper handling, or baling when wet can result in moldy, dusty, or less nutritious hay.

Moisture Level   Baled hay should have a moisture level of 12 percent to no more than 18 percent. Before cutting, the moisture level is usually 25 to 27 percent or higher; this must be reduced by proper drying. If the hay is baled or stored too damp, it develops mold, which can be toxic to horses.

Storage   Hay stored while damp generates heat, which can lead to spontaneous combustion. Hay exposed to weather during storage loses its nutritional value, at least in the outer layers of hay. Heat, overexposure to sunlight, and long periods of storage diminish vitamin levels, especially carotene and vitamins A and D.

Non-Nutritious Matter   Good hay is clean and free from weeds, trash, toxic plants, or foreign objects. Animal carcasses accidentally baled in hay can be a source of botulism, especially in large round bales. Alfalfa hay grown in the South, West, and Southwest must be checked for blister beetles, which are highly irritating and can be fatal to horses.

TYPES OF HAY

CHART 11-3: TYPES OF HAY AND NUTRITIONAL VALUES

Hay	Digestible Energy (Mcal/lb)	Crude Protein %	Fiber %	CA %	P %
Alfalfa, early bloom	1.02	18.0	20.8	1.28	0.19
Alfalfa, midbloom	0.94	17.0	25.5	1.24	0.22
Alfalfa, late	0.89	15.5	27.3	1.08	0.22
Bermuda grass, immature	0.95	12.5	34.0	0.30	0.19
Bermuda grass, mature	0.80	7.0	42.0	0.24	0.17
Birdsfoot trefoil	1.19	14.4	29.3	1.54	0.21
Clover	0.90	13.5	36.0	1.23	0.22
Fescue	0.86	11.8	23.9	0.40	0.29
Oat hay	0.79	8.6	29.1	0.29	0.23
Orchardgrass, immature	0.95	12.0	30.2	0.24	0.30
Orchardgrass, mature	0.80	8.0	33.6	0.24	0.27
Prairie grass	0.67	5.8	30.7	0.32	0.12
Timothy, prebloom	1.00	11.0	37.0	0.45	0.25
Timothy, midbloom	0.85	8.0	45.0	0.43	0.20
Timothy, late	0.75	5.0	54.0	0.34	0.13

Grass Hays

Grass hays contain more fiber and lower levels of protein than legume hays, so they are less likely to be overfed. Horses fed on grass hay are more likely to require supplemental concentrates, especially if they are growing, lactating, or working hard. There are many different varieties of grass hays grown in different regions of North America; some of the most common are timothy, orchardgrass, coastal Bermuda grass, prairie hay, and oat hay.

Legume Hays

Legumes are plants that utilize nitrogen, producing a higher level of protein than grass hays. They also tend to be higher in calcium. Because legume hays have higher nutrient levels, they are more likely to be overfed than grass hays. The legume hays are alfalfa, clover, and birdsfoot trefoil.

Types of Bales

Bales Wire bales (65 to 125 pounds) or string bales (35 to 50 pounds) are commonly available and easy to handle.

Large Round or Square Bales Weighing Several Hundred Pounds These are sometimes used for free-choice hay feeding in pastures or dry lots. However, mold and botulism can be serious problems if large bales are stored damp or get soaked with rain or groundwater.

Processed Hay

Hay (usually alfalfa) may be processed for ease in storage, handling and transportation, to reduce waste, and in order to combine it with concentrates for mixed feeds or complete rations.

Cubes (Range Cubes) Hay (usually alfalfa) chopped and run through a press, making cubes about 1½ inches square. Cubes reduce waste but result in less time spent in eating, which may lead to wood chewing. Horses fed hay cubes or pellets should have water available, to reduce the risk of choking.

Pellets Hay (usually alfalfa) ground and processed into pellets, often combined with grain as part of a complete pelleted ration. Pellets reduce waste and are convenient to store and transport, but result in less time spent in eating, which may lead to wood chewing. As with hay cubes, horses should have water available to reduce the risk of choking.

Chopped Hay (Chop or Chaff)   Hay chopped into short lengths; may be mixed with grain to slow down greedy eaters and add bulk to the diet. Commercially prepared chopped hay (sometimes with molasses added) is available in some parts of the country.

Silage   Produced by controlled fermentation of high-moisture forage, often used for cattle feed. Toxins produced in spoiled or moldy silage can be fatal to horses and are hard to detect; therefore, silage is not recommended as a horse feed.

Evaluating Hay Quality

Characteristics of Good-Quality Hay	*Signs of Poor-Quality Hay*
Low moisture content (12% to 18%)	Damp. Too high moisture causes mold, can cause spontaneous combustion.
Green in color	Brown, yellow or weathered in color. Gray or black indicates mold.
Sweet smelling, like newly cut grass	Musty, moldy or fermented odor.
Free of mold and dust	Dusty. Moldy hay is unacceptable.
Fine stems, high proportion of leaf to stems	Coarse, with woody stalks and more stems than leaves.
Cut before maturity: grass hays, before seed heads mature; alfalfa, cut early in bloom	Cut late: mature seed heads or gone to seed; alfalfa cut late in bloom.
Free from weeds, poisonous plants, trash or foreign objects	High weed content; poisonous plants; animal carcasses baled in hay.

Hay samples can be laboratory tested to determine the levels of nutrients. For information about hay testing, contact your county agent or nearest agricultural college.

OTHER ROUGHAGES

Beet Pulp

Beet pulp is a byproduct of the processing of sugar beets. It may be used as a roughage, especially for horses with heaves or allergies. It is usually shredded or pelleted. Because some horses find it less palatable than hay, molasses may be added.

Beet pulp is more digestible than hay, but contains more roughage than grain. The calcium content of beet pulp is higher than that of timothy hay but lower than that of alfalfa. Beet pulp is very low in phosphorous and B vitamins, and contains no carotene or vitamin D.

Beet pulp swells as it absorbs water or saliva. It must always be fed wet; eating dry beet pulp may cause choking. Shredded beet pulp should be soaked with an equal amount of water (1 part water to 1 part beet pulp). Pelleted beet pulp requires three times as much water (3 parts water to 1 part beet pulp.)

Pasture Grass

Pasture grass is the most natural food source for horses. Good pasture (with free access to salt and water) can meet all or nearly all of the horse's basic nutritional requirements. Along with carbohydrates, protein, minerals, and other vitamins, pasture supplies carotene (from green, leafy plants) and vitamin D (from sunlight), two elements that may be lacking in horses kept confined indoors. Pasture is especially important for broodmares, growing young horses, and idle horses.

Although pasture is a good food source for most horses, there are some exceptions. Overweight horses and small ponies can develop laminitis when grazing lush pastures, especially in the spring when the grass grows quickly and has high levels of water and protein. Overweight animals should have limited access to good pasture; they can be confined to a dry lot or overgrazed "diet" paddock.

Horses at moderate to hard work cannot get enough energy from pasture grass to meet their energy needs; they require supplementary feeding, usually concentrates. In addition, horses require plenty of grazing time to take in adequate nutrition from pasture. If a horse is frequently kept away from pasture for long periods, he will need supplementary feeding to make up for lost grazing time.

The quality of the pasture grass depends on many factors: the varieties of plants and grasses, soil fertility and mineral content, climate, weather and growing conditions, seasonal changes, weeds and other plants, and especially, heavy use or overgrazing.

To evaluate the nutritional value of a pasture, walk over it and note the main varieties of grass and the condition of the pasture. Soil testing (available through your local Cooperative Extension or agricultural college) may reveal a need for lime or fertilizer. Cutting down weeds and reseeding bare areas, rotating or resting pastures, and regular removal of manure can make a great difference in the quality of the nutrition available.

CHART 11-4: PASTURE GRASSES AND NUTRITIONAL VALUES

Forage	Digestible Energy (Mcal/lb)	Crude Protein %	Fiber %	CA %	P %	Dry Matter %
Alfalfa, late growth	0.31	5.0	5.6	0.40	0.07	23.2
Alfalfa, full bloom	0.25	4.6	7.2	0.28	0.06	23.8
Bermuda grass	0.33	3.6	8.7	0.15	0.08	30.3
Birdsfoot trefoil	0.19	4.0	4.1	0.33	0.05	19.3
Bluegrass	0.33	3.8	8.6	0.15	0.14	30.8
Brome, smooth, early growth	0.31	5.6	6.0	0.14	0.12	26.1
Brome, smooth, mature	0.40	3.4	19.1	0.14	0.09	54.9
Clover, early growth	0.22	4.1	4.6	0.44	0.07	19.6
Clover, full bloom	0.27	3.8	6.8	0.26	0.07	26.2
Fescue	0.32	4.7	7.7	0.16	0.12	31.3
Lespedeza	0.25	4.1	8.0	0.30	0.07	25.0
Orchardgrass, early bloom	0.24	3.0	7.5	0.06	0.09	23.5
Orchardgrass, midbloom	0.25	2.8	9.2	0.09	0.05	27.4

Forage	*Digestible Energy (Mcal/lb)*	*Crude Protein %*	*Fiber %*	*CA %*	*P %*	*Dry Matter %*
Ryegrass	0.23	4.0	4.7	0.15	0.09	22.6
Timothy, early growth	0.29	3.3	8.6	0.11	0.07	26.7
Timothy, midbloom	0.27	2.7	9.8	0.11	0.09	29.2

(For more about pasture management and maintenance, see the USPC C Manual, [Book Two], pp. 198–199.)

CONCENTRATES

Concentrates are feeds that are relatively high in energy and low in fiber; they include grains, mixed or processed feeds, and supplements.

GRAINS

Oats

Oats are the most widely fed horse grain in North America. Oats contain more fiber and less concentrated nutrients than most other grains, which makes them less easy to overfeed. They are quite palatable, and generally contain about 9 to 12 percent protein, and 1.3 Mcal energy per pound. Oats contain about three times as much calcium as phosphorous.

Oats should be clean, plump, and heavy, good-quality oats weigh 32 to 40 pounds per bushel. Avoid dusty oats or oats containing small black kernels that resemble mice droppings; they may be contaminated with ergot, a fungus that can be toxic to horses. Oats should be stored three to four months after harvest, to allow nitrogen levels to drop before feeding.

Oats may be fed whole, crimped (slightly crushed), or rolled (flattened). Crimping or rolling may improve digestibility for very young or aged horses.

Barley

Barley is similar to oats in nutritional value but is lower in fiber and somewhat more concentrated. Barley contains about 10 to 12 percent protein, and about 1.5 Mcal energy per pound. It is lower in calcium than oats, and about the same in phosphorous.

Because barley kernels are harder than those of oats, barley should be rolled (slightly crushed). It may be steamed or cooked before rolling.

Good-quality whole barley weighs approximately 48 pounds per bushel; rolled barley about 40 pounds per bushel. Like oats, kernels should be plump, heavy, sweet smelling, and free from dust.

Corn

Corn is the most energy-dense of the grains. It contains about 9 percent protein, and 1.6 Mcal energy per pound. Corn is low in calcium and high in phosphorous; it contains significant amounts of carotene. Corn is also low in lysine, an essential amino acid.

Corn may be fed as whole grain (shelled corn), cracked, rolled, or on the cob. Whole-ear ground corn contains the ground cobs as well as the grain; it contains more fiber and reduces the energy per pound to about 1.3 Mcals.

Good-quality corn is plump, clean, firm, and dry, and smells sweet, weighing about 56 pounds per bushel. The moisture content should be below 14 percent. It should not smell musty, have black spots, or feel sticky or oily. Corn should be checked under ultraviolet light at the feed mill for evidence of mold, which can cause moldy corn disease, resulting in brain damage and death.

In the past, some horse owners believed that corn was a "hot" feed and would cause horses to sweat, especially if fed in hot weather. This is not true; however, corn is highly concentrated and hence can easily be overfed. Overfeeding corn (or any other grain) can cause a horse to become overweight, which can lead to excessive sweating.

Bran

Bran is the ground-up outer coating of wheat kernels. It contains about 15 percent protein and 1.25 Mcal energy per pound. Bran is very high in phosphorous and low in calcium. Feeding large amounts of bran can cause overfeeding of phosphorous, which makes it impossible for the horse to utilize calcium and leads to calcium deficiency disease. For this reason, bran should make up no more than 10 percent of the total ration.

Bran is high in fiber and is laxative. It is often fed as a mash, cooked with hot water.

Good bran is light, flaky, and free-flowing. It should not contain dust, clumps, or cobweblike strands (evidence of weevils), or smell musty.

Brewers Grain

Brewers grains (usually corn and rye) are byproducts of the process of distilling alcohol. They usually contain about 25 percent protein, and about 1.25 Mcal energy per pound. They are higher in phosphorous than calcium.

Brewers grains are usually found as a component of commercially mixed feeds or pelleted rations, rather than fed alone. They are used as a source of protein, and are quite palatable to horses.

Oilseed Meals

Oilseed meals are ground from the seeds of certain plants. They are excellent sources of protein and fat. All are low in calcium and higher in phosphorous.

Soybean Meal   Ground soybeans. Contains about 45 percent protein and 1.55 Mcal energy per pound.

Cottonseed Meal   Ground cottonseed. Contains about 41 percent protein and 1.4 Mcal energy per pound.

Flaxseed or Linseed Meal   Ground flaxseed. Contains about 33 percent protein and 1.5 Mcal energy per pound.

Alfalfa Meal and Pellets

Ground or pelleted alfalfa is often used as part of commercially mixed feeds and complete feed rations. Alfalfa meal or pellets contain about 15 to 17 percent protein and 1 Mcal digestible energy per pound. Alfalfa meal is a good source of calcium (1.3 to 1.4 percent) and is low in phosphorous, so it can be used to balance other concentrates that are high in phosphorous and low in calcium.

Molasses

Molasses, a byproduct of the processing of sugar cane or sugar beets, sweetens feed, making it more palatable to horses, and keeps dust down. It is high in energy but supplies little or no protein or phosphorous.

Cane molasses is a good source of calcium. Molasses can be added to feed in dry or syrup form.

CHART 11-5: TYPES OF CONCENTRATES AND NUTRITIONAL VALUES

Concentrate	Digestible Energy (Mcal/lb)	Crude Protein %	Fiber %	CA %	P %	Fat %
GRAINS						
Barley	1.49	11.7	4.9	0.05	0.34	1.8
Brewers grain	1.15	23.4	13.7	0.30	0.50	1.0
Corn, shelled	1.54	9.1	2.2	0.05	0.27	3.6
Oats, grade 1	1.36	12.5	10.8	0.05	0.34	4.6
Oats, lower grade	1.32	9.1	11.2	0.10	0.31	4.6
Wheat bran	1.33	15.4	10.0	0.13	1.13	3.8
MEALS						
Alfalfa meal	0.91	15.6	26.2	1.25	0.23	2.8
Cottonseed meal	1.25	41.3	12.2	0.17	1.11	1.5
Soybean meal	1.43	44.5	6.2	0.35	0.63	1.4
MISCELLANEOUS						
Beet pulp, dehydrated	1.06	8.9	18.2	0.62	0.09	—
CALCIUM SUPPLEMENTS						
Dicalcium phosphate	—	—	—	22.0	—	—
FAT SUPPLEMENTS						
Vegetable oil/ corn oil	—	—	—	—	—	99.7
Hydrolyzed animal fat	—	—	—	—	—	98.4

MIXED FEEDS AND PROCESSED FEEDS

Commercially mixed feeds are formulated for different purposes, with different levels of nutrients. They may be grain mixes with various levels of protein and energy, or complete pelleted rations. When choosing a commercial feed, check the feed label and manufacturer's information on the type of feed, purpose, and nutrient levels.

Feeds intended for cattle, hogs, and other livestock should not be used for horses. Some livestock and cattle feeds may contain monensin or other antibiotics which are toxic to horses and can be fatal.

Sweet Feed

Sweet feeds are mixed feeds containing molasses, which increases palatability, dampens the feed, and prevents dust, and adds energy. The protein and other nutrient content of the feed depends on the specific mix.

Sweet feeds attract flies, so feed tubs should be kept clean and spilled feed cleaned up promptly.

Processed Feeds

Pelleted Feeds   Feed ingredients ground and pressed into pellets. May be mixed grain pellets, alfalfa meal pellets, or pelleted supplements.

Pelleted Complete Feed   Contains both grain and roughage (usually alfalfa, sometimes beet pulp) ground and pelleted. Complete feed pellets are intended to provide both roughage and concentrates.

Extruded Feeds   Feed ground and extruded into bits similar to kibble dog food. Extruded feed has greater volume and is less dense than pellets or grains. It takes a horse longer to consume the same level of nutrients, which may help prevent rapid eating and overeating.

Feed Label Information

Commercial feed labels must indicate the minimum percentages of crude protein and fat, and the maximum percentage of crude fiber. Vitamin and mineral levels are not required to be listed unless specific claims are made on the label, or the mineral content exceeds specified levels.

The label must also list the feed ingredients by their common names. However, manufacturers may use collective terms such as "grain products," "plant protein products," "animal protein products," "processed grain byproducts," and others. This lets manufacturers take advantage of computer formulation and use alternative ingredients to provide the same levels of nutrients.

Because the actual ingredients can vary from one batch of feed to another, it is nearly impossible for the horse owner to evaluate the quality of grains used in commercially processed feeds. It makes sense to buy from a feed company that has a good reputation for quality control.

Further information on commercial feeds, ingredients, and recommendations on nutrition is available from feed companies, dealers, and salespersons. Other sources of information are county agents, Cooperative Extension services, state horse specialists, and agricultural colleges.

SUPPLEMENTS

Feed supplements are concentrated substances that are added to the ration to make up a deficiency in a specific nutrient.

Horse owners should be aware that a balanced ration of high-quality feed usually meets horses' nutritional needs without feeding additional supplements. Supplements add to the cost of feeding, and can cause problems if they are overfed. Feeding more than one supplement or feeding excessive doses of any supplement can result in excessive levels of vitamins, minerals, or protein. Certain vitamins and minerals can be toxic when fed in excessive amounts, and an imbalance of minerals can cause problems just as serious as a deficiency. Feeding excessive protein can cause kidney problems.

Supplements may be helpful when feeding lower-quality hay or pasture is unavoidable (for instance, under drought conditions, when hay has been stored for a year or longer, or when it is impossible to obtain good-quality, green hay), or for horses under stress. When feeding supplements, it is important not to overfeed any vitamin or mineral. You should check the nutritional balance of the ration, and consult your veterinarian.

Types of Supplements

Vitamin Supplements These supply fat-soluble vitamins such as vitamins A, D, E, and K, usually in powder or pellet form. Storage for long periods or exposure to heat, light, and air can cause vitamin supplements to deteriorate. They should be stored in an airtight container away from sunlight, and should be used within thirty to sixty days.

Mineral Supplements   These include calcium supplements (dicalcium phosphate, bone meal, limestone), other minerals (phosphorous, selenium), electrolytes, and trace minerals (usually supplied in mineralized salt).

Mineral imbalances and overdoses can cause serious problems, so mineral supplementation should not be undertaken without checking the mineral levels supplied in the ration, and the advice of your veterinarian.

Electrolytes are minerals (potassium and salts) that help to maintain the correct fluid balance in the blood. Heavy sweating, especially during hard work in hot weather, may cause the loss of large amounts of electrolytes, which need to be replaced. This is best done by offering water with electrolytes added (mixed according to manufacturer's directions). Plain water should also be offered, as some horses may refuse to drink electrolyte water and may become dehydrated. Ask your veterinarian for advice before giving electrolytes. (For more about electrolytes, see Chapter 10, "Conditioning and Exercise Physiology.")

Protein Supplements   Sometimes helpful for horses with increased need for protein, such as weanlings and yearlings, pregnant and lactating mares, aged horses, and horses under stress. Protein supplements include vegetable protein sources (such as soybean meal, oilseed meals, and legume meals) and milk protein (dried skimmed milk or milk replacers). Excess protein is converted to fat or excreted through the kidneys; excessive protein levels can cause kidney problems.

Fat Supplements   A source of concentrated energy, they help to produce healthy skin and shiny hair coat. They are often used to promote weight gain and to achieve a "bloom" on the coats of show horses. Corn oil and wheat germ oil are two common sources of fat. Fats can turn rancid and lose their palatability if stored too long or exposed to heat and light.

BALANCING A RATION

A balanced ration is an amount of a mixture of feeds that provides a horse with its daily nutritional requirements. Sometimes a horse's needs can be met with a simple ration (for instance, a mature, idle horse on good pasture, with free access to water and salt). In other cases, it may be necessary to mix several different kinds of feeds to provide a ration that is balanced, palatable, easy to digest, and meets the horse's nutritional requirements.

Feed companies and animal nutritionists formulate rations by computer; they can factor in fluctuating market prices and adjust feed components to provide specified levels of nutrients at the lowest cost. The average horse owner or stable manager does not need to analyze his horses' ration to this degree of complexity. However, it is important to know your horse's nutritional needs, to make sure that your feeding program meets them adequately without deficiencies or overfeeding, and to do so as economically as possible. Balancing a ration requires a little math (a calculator is helpful), nutritional charts, knowing your horse's weight, and feeding by weight, not volume. It's mostly common sense, not difficult calculations.

How to Balance a Ration

Before you can balance a ration for a horse, you must know its weight, age, how much and what kind of work it is doing, and if it has special nutritional needs such as growth, lactation, or pregnancy.

The first step is to find your horse's total daily ration—the total amount he is fed per day, including both hay and grain. This is usually about 1.5 to 3 percent of his weight, depending on work and other factors, or from 15 to 30 pounds per day for a 1,000-pound horse. (See Chart 11-6: Recommended Daily Amounts of Concentrates and Hay.)

Then, determine your horse's daily nutritional requirements (see Chart 11-1). You will need to multiply the nutritional values given on the chart by the amount of your horse's total daily ration (TDR) in order to calculate the amount of energy (Megacalories), protein (pounds), calcium (pounds), and phosphorous (pounds) he needs per day.

Chart 11-6 also gives recommended daily amounts of concentrates and hay for horses of various weights and classifications.

Next, determine what roughage (hay) you will feed and in what amount per day. (This varies with the horse's age, work, and other factors.) From this, you can calculate the amount of each nutrient supplied by hay, and whether they meet the horse's daily nutritional needs or not. It makes sense to start with hay because roughage should make up the greater part of any horse's diet, and also because hay must be

CHART 11-6: RECOMMENDED DAILY AMOUNTS OF CONCENTRATES AND HAY

Type of Horse	Hay (lbs per 100 lbs body weight)	Grain (lbs per 100 lbs body weight)	(Example)	Daily Hay Ration (lbs.)	Daily Grain Ration (lbs.)	Total Daily Ration (lbs.)
MATURE HORSE (EX.: 1000 LBS ÷ 100 = 10)						
Maintenance	1.5–2.0	—	×10 =	15–20	—	15–20
Light work	1.05–1.4	.45–0.6	×10 =	10.5–14	4.5–6	15–20
Moderate work	1.0–1.5	.75–1.0	×10 =	10–15	7.5–10	17.5–25
Intense work	.75–1.5	1.0–1.5	×10 =	7.5–15	10–15	17.5–30
Pregnant mare	1.0–1.5	.25–.75	×10 =	10–15	2.5–7.5	12.5–22.5
Lactating mare	1.0–1.5	1.0–2.0	×10 =	10–15	10–20	20–35
Aged horse	1.25–1.5	0.5–1.5	×10 =	12.5–15	5–15	17.5–30
MATURE PONY (EX.: 700 LBS ÷ 100 = 7)						
Maintenance	1.0–1.3	—	×7 =	7–9.1	—	7–9.1
Moderate work	.75–1.0	0.3–0.5	×7 =	5.25–7	2.1–3.5	7.35–10.5
WEANLING (EX.: 500 LBS ÷ 100 = 5)						
	.75–1.25	1.75–2.0	×5 =	3.75–6.25	8.75–10	12.50–16.25

Worksheet: Balancing a Ration

Horse_____ Age _____ Height _____ Weight _____

Condition: poor, thin, moderately thin, good, slightly fat, fat, obese.

Special needs: pregnancy (month_____), growth, getting fit, other:

_____

Work: idle, light, moderate, intense. _____ Hours/Day _____ Days/Week

Other Considerations (temperament, health, etc.):

_____

1. Daily Ration (see Chart 11-6), expressed in lbs, using **lbs per 100 lbs of body weight.**

Weight (_____lbs) ÷ 100 = _____ (100 lbs body weight)
_____(100s lbs) **x** _____ recommended lbs hay   = ____ lbs **Daily Hay Ration**
_____(100s lbs) **x** _____ recommended lbs grain = ____ lbs **Daily Grain Ration**
Add _____lbs daily hay and _____ lbs daily grain = _____ **Total Daily Ration(TDR)**

2. Daily Nutritional Requirements (see Chart 11-1), expressed in Mcals and lbs, using **total body weight.**

_____lbs TDR   **x** _____ Mcal = _____ Mcal/day (Energy)
                     x _____ %   = _____ lbs/day (Protein)
                     x _____ %   = _____ lbs/day (Calcium)
                     x _____ %   = _____ lbs/day (Phosphorus)

3. Calculate nutrients available in **Total Daily Hay Ration** (see Chart 11-6), considering type of hay (see Chart 11-3).

_____ lbs hay **x** _____ Mcal/lb (energy)   = _____ Mcal energy in hay
_____ lbs hay **x** _____ % (protein)   = _____ lbs protein in hay
_____ lbs hay **x** _____ % (calcium)   = _____ lbs calcium in hay
_____ lbs hay **x** _____ % (phosphorous)   = _____ lbs phosphorous/hay

4. Compare nutrients supplied in hay to daily nutrient requirements.

Daily energy req.   = _____ Mcal Hay supplies _____ Mcal _____Mcal needed
Daily protein req. = _____ lbs   Hay supplies _____ lbs _____lbs needed
Daily calcium req. = _____ lbs   Hay supplies _____ lbs _____lbs needed
Daily phos. req.   = _____ lbs   Hay supplies _____ lbs _____lbs needed

5. Determine type, amount, and nutrient value of concentrates (see Chart 11-5).

Grains fed in concentrate ration		*Energy* Mcals/lb	*Protein* %	*Calcium* %	*Phos.* %
(grain type) _____	_____ lbs	_____	_____	_____	_____
(grain type) _____	_____ lbs	_____	_____	_____	_____
(grain type) _____	_____ lbs	_____	_____	_____	_____
(grain type) _____	_____ lbs	_____	_____	_____	_____
Total Grain Ration:	_____ lbs				

6. For each grain, calculate energy, protein, calcium, and phosphorous supplied in amount fed; add totals of each nutrient and compare with Recommended Daily Grain Ration (step 1).

Total Energy supplied in **grain ration** = _____ Mcals
Total Protein supplied in **grain ration** = _____ lbs
Total Calcium supplied in **grain ration** = _____ lbs
Total Phosphorous in **grain ration** = _____ lbs

7. For each nutrient (energy, protein, calcium, phosphorous), add total amount supplied in hay to total supplied in grain.

Total nutrients supplied in Total Daily Ration (hay plus grain):

Energy from grain = _____ Mcal + _____ Mcal from hay = _____ Mcal total
Protein from grain = _____ lbs + _____ lbs from hay = _____ lbs total
Calcium from grain = _____ lbs + _____ lbs from hay = _____ lbs total
Phosphorous/grain = _____ lbs + _____ lbs from hay = _____ lbs total

8. Compare total amounts supplied in ration to daily nutritional requirements.
Daily Nutritional Requirements (from step 2):

Energy: _____ Mcal   Does ration meet nutritional needs of horse?
Protein: _____ lbs   _____ Yes _____ No
Calcium: _____ lbs   Ration is deficient in _____
Phosphorous: _____ lbs   Ration is too high in _____

Note: For calcium and phosphorous, it is not enough to meet daily requirements. These minerals must be supplied in proper balance, or neither can be used by the horse and nutritional deficiency disease may result. For mature horses, ratio of calcium to phosphorous should be from 1:1 to 3:1. Never feed more phosphorous than calcium, and always meet minimum daily requirement of each.

bought in bulk, and there are usually fewer options available than in selecting concentrates.

You will need to calculate the amounts of energy (Megacalories), protein, calcium, and phosphorous (pounds) contained in your horse's hay ration, using Chart 11-3 and the worksheet.

Compare the nutrient amounts supplied in hay with your horse's daily nutritional requirements. Are they adequate, below required levels, or do they exceed requirements? Is the calcium/phosphorous ratio correct, or is the phosphorous too high? This will tell you whether your horse needs additional nutrients supplied by grain and/or supplements, and how much.

Finally, you need to determine the kind and amount of concentrates necessary to provide any nutrients that are lacking, without overfeeding any nutrient. (See Chart 11-5: Types of Concentrates and Nutritional Values.)

Once you have balanced your horse's ration, you can make adjustments as necessary without going through all the calculations again. For instance, if your horse's work increases and hence his energy requirements increase, you can add grain with a higher energy percentage. When you do so, check the nutritional values of the grain you are adding or increasing to be sure that you have not seriously altered the protein, calcium or phosphorous levels. This helps you make intelligent decisions about which grain or supplement to use. (For example, if you added several pounds of bran to the ration, it would increase the energy but would also increase the phosphorous levels, possibly enough to throw the calcium/phosphorous ratio out of balance. Another grain, like barley or corn, might be a better choice.)

BUYING AND STORING FEED AND BEDDING

Buying Economically

Economy in purchasing feed and bedding requires planning, careful shopping, and room for storage.

Starting from the daily ration and amount of bedding used, you can estimate the amount of hay, grain, and bedding you use per week, and project total amounts needed each month. Take into account seasonal variations, such as feeding more hay during the winter months.

It pays to investigate all the feed stores and hay and bedding suppliers in your area, and compare their products, quality, and prices. Ask other horse owners and stable managers which suppliers they use and recommend. Feed prices fluctuate with the market, depending on availability, season, and demand; you should be aware of current feed prices and factors that may affect them.

If you buy in quantity, you get a lower price and save frequent delivery charges or the time and labor of pickup. Large stables should consider purchasing grain at bulk rates, or even having the basic feed ration custom-mixed at the feed mill. If you have storage space, you can buy hay most economically out of the field at harvest time. If hay or bedding must be shipped to your area, the cost per bale or bag is lower when you buy by the truckload. If your stable is too small to buy in such quantities, you may be able to find other horse owners who will share the cost.

Sweet feeds and feeds with a high fat content are somewhat perishable, especially in hot, humid climates. These should be purchased in small enough quantities to be used within a week or two. Use up the oldest feed before pouring new feed into the bin, and don't use any feed that has a rancid or fermented odor.

Storage of Feed, Hay, and Bedding

Feed and bedding storage should be:

Clean   Metal or heavy plastic containers with tight-fitting lids keep feed from contamination by dust, dirt, and rodents.

Dry   Prevent mold and spoilage by dampness, exposure to weather, or leaks. Hay and feed bags should be placed on pallets instead of directly on concrete or dirt floors.

Secure   Horses must be prevented from getting into feed stores, especially grain.

Efficient   Feed and bedding must be easily accessible during delivery and daily chores; you should have sufficient capacity for economical buying.

Safe   To reduce fire risk, hay and bedding should be stored in a building separate from the stable, if possible.

NUTRITION FOR HORSES AT GRASS

Feed Value of Pasture

The feed value of a pasture depends on many factors, including the variety of grasses and weeds, soil fertility and mineral content, weather, condition of the pasture, the point in the growing cycle, the number of horses and length of time the pasture has been grazed. Pastures are most nutritious in the spring, when the grass grows quickly and is new, tender, and high in protein and other nutrients. As the grasses mature, they become more coarse and more stemmy, and nutritional value drops. Pastures that are damaged by overgrazing, high traffic, drought, or flooding, or that are choked with weeds or covered with snow, may have almost no nutritional value. In these cases, supplementary hay and possibly concentrates must be fed. (See Chart 11-4: Pasture Grasses and Nutritional Values.)

Seasonal Variations in Care and Feeding of Horses at Grass

Seasonal changes in care and feeding depend on the climate and the part of the country in which you live. In some parts of the country, winter may be a growing season instead of cold weather, or summer may be a poor grazing season due to lack of rainfall. You must adjust your feeding according to the seasonal changes where you live.

Fall

In temperate and northern regions, nutritional value of pasture drops in the late summer and fall, as plants and grasses mature and go to seed. Supplementary feeding of hay will be necessary.

Check pastures for toxic plants. As pasture grasses deteriorate, horses are more likely to eat toxic plants if they are present.

Horses that live outdoors through the winter will do better if they carry a little extra fat in the fall. Horses that are underweight are more severely stressed by wet or cold weather, and are more vulnerable to disease.

Winter

When pasture grass is covered with snow and of low nutritional value, supplementary feeding of hay is essential. The process of digesting fiber generates heat and helps horses maintain their body temperature during cold weather.

Horses require more calories to handle the stress of extreme cold or wet weather, especially if they are aged, pregnant, very young, or debilitated. Reduce stress by providing shelter from wind, cold, and rain, and increase the energy content of the feed as well as feeding extra hay.

Make sure that horses have free access to water during cold weather. This may mean breaking ice twice a day or more often, insulating stock tanks, or using stock tank heaters. Insufficient water intake can result in impaction and colic, which can be fatal.

Make regular checks of the condition of horses kept on pasture during the winter. Long hair coats may hide the first signs of weight loss, and it can be hard to reverse the process if you do not notice it early.

Spring

In the spring, the grass grows quickly and has a high water content and high levels of protein. This lush grass can cause diarrhea and digestive upsets in horses that are not used to it. When horses are first turned out on grass, limit their grazing time to an hour a day at first, and increase it gradually over two to three weeks.

Obese horses, small ponies, and animals that have had previous attacks of laminitis may develop laminitis from overeating lush grass, especially in spring. These horses should have their grazing time limited; some may not be able to tolerate any amount of new grass.

As the nutritional value of the pasture increases, supplementary hay feeding can be cut back. Use hay consumption as a guideline; if horses are eating all the hay you give them, they still need it. When they begin to leave hay, it can safely be cut back.

Summer

Salt should be available free choice throughout the year, but it is especially important during hot weather, when horses lose salt as they sweat.

Keep track of the condition and nutritional value of the pasture. If it is damaged by drought or overgrazing, or if it becomes choked with weeds, supplementary hay feeding will be necessary.

Check water sources daily, to be sure they are not dried up.

Horses may be worked harder and more often during the summer. They may need additional concentrates to provide energy for work.

Horses must be dewormed regularly throughout the year, to prevent internal damage from parasites, to improve digestion and efficient use of feed, and to keep pastures from being contaminated with parasite eggs and larvae. (For more about parasite control, see Chapter 12, p. 340.)

CHAPTER 12

······················

Health Care, Diseases, and Veterinary Knowledge

This chapter covers veterinary information for horse owners, including dental care and aging by teeth, parasite control, ailments and disease processes, preventing the spread of disease, and drugs and medications. While you must not take on decisions and treatments that should be determined by a veterinarian, you should be informed about current medications and treatment, including sedation and other methods of restraint. As further research is done and we learn more about horse health, recommended treatments and medications may change. You should stay up to date on the best methods of horse health care through reading about current developments and consulting with your veterinarian.

The *USPC C Manual of Horsemanship (Book 2)* covers information basic to this chapter, and should also be reviewed.

TEETH AND DENTAL CARE

Basic anatomy of the mouth and teeth, and routine dental care are covered in the *USPC C Manual of Horsemanship (Book 2)*.

DETERMINING THE AGE OF A HORSE BY TEETH

The horse's teeth grow continuously over its lifetime; the **tables** (wearing surfaces) of the teeth wear down at the same rate as the teeth grow out. This causes changes in the appearance, shapes, and markings of the teeth (particularly the incisors), which appear at certain ages. By examining the incisor teeth, a horse's age can be determined quite accurately up to the age of nine or ten. After this age, the changes are less consistent and age can only be estimated.

Order of Eruption and Wear

The incisor teeth erupt in pairs, with the central incisors first, then the intermediates, and finally the corner incisors. Marks of wear appear and disappear in these pairs in the same order.

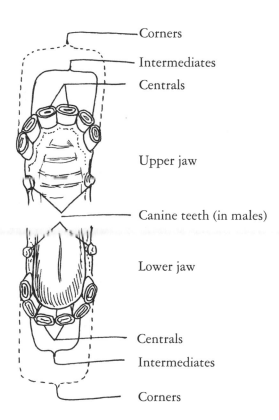

Corners
Intermediates
Centrals

Upper jaw

Canine teeth (in males)

Lower jaw

Centrals
Intermediates

Corners

Determining Age in Foals and Young Horses

A foal is born with both sets of teeth (temporary and permanent) present in the jaws. The temporary teeth (deciduous or milk teeth) are smaller and whiter, with shorter roots than permanent teeth. The incisors erupt through the gums in pairs in this order: first the central pairs, then the intermediates, and lastly the corners. Temporary molars are also present at birth.

ERUPTION OF TEETH: FOAL TO TWO AND A HALF YEARS

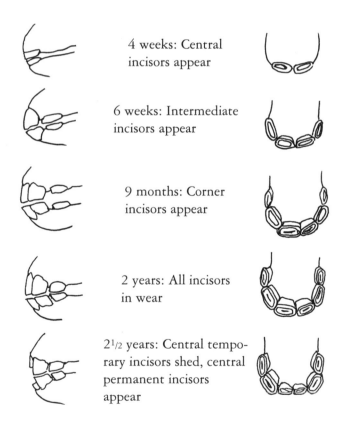

4 weeks: Central incisors appear

6 weeks: Intermediate incisors appear

9 months: Corner incisors appear

2 years: All incisors in wear

2¹/₂ years: Central temporary incisors shed, central permanent incisors appear

The permanent teeth are also growing, and starting at about two and a half years of age, they erupt through the gums and push the temporary teeth out. The remains of a temporary tooth is called a **cap**. Caps usually fall out as the permanent teeth grow near the gum line, but occasionally one may need to be removed to allow the permanent tooth to grow in.

Permanent teeth appear in pairs at fairly consistent intervals. The central incisors appear at two and a half years, intermediates at three and a half years, and corner incisors at four and a half years. Canine teeth appear in males between four and five years. When all permanent teeth are present (at approximately five years), the horse is said to have a **"full mouth."**

Molars and premolars also erupt during this period. The first premolars come in at five to six months, and the first molars between nine and twelve months. The second molars erupt at two years, and the second premolars at two and a half years. At three years, the third premolars are present; the fourth premolars appear between three and a half and four and a half years. At four, the third molars appear, completing the **dental arcade** (the rows of upper and lower back teeth).

Determining Age by Permanent Teeth (2½ to 10 years)

As each tooth grows long enough to meet its corresponding tooth, the "tables" or tooth surfaces come into wear. The shape of the tooth changes and marks appear at certain ages as the teeth wear down to a certain level. With experience, you can determine the horse's age by the appearance, shape, and marks of the teeth.

Cups   Cups (not "caps," or temporary teeth) appear as a hollow rectangle or oval on the tables of the permanent incisors. Cups are present in the permanent teeth when they emerge, and disappear at specific ages, as the teeth wear down. The cups are worn away in the lower central incisors at six years, the intermediates at seven, and the corner incisors at eight. The upper central cups are gone at nine, the intermediates at ten, and the corners by eleven. When all cups are worn away, the horse is called **"smooth mouthed."**

Dental Star (Pulp Mark)   As the tooth wears down enough to expose the central pulp cavity, the dental star or pulp mark appears. (Don't confuse dental stars with cups, which are found only in younger teeth.)

Dental stars begin to appear at six, beginning as a dark line in front of the cups in the lower central incisors. As the cup disappears, the dental star becomes larger, and its shape becomes oval and later, round. Dental stars are clearly visible in the central incisors at eight; at nine, in the intermediates, and in all incisors by ten to twelve years.

CUPS AND DENTAL STARS

5 years:    Cup; tooth coming into wear

7–8 years:    Dental star beginning to show above cup

12 years and older:    Dental star; cup has disappeared

Hook or Notch on Upper Corner Incisor   A hook or notch appears on the upper corner incisor at age seven, and disappears at eight. A similar hook or notch also appears at around thirteen years, and is gone at about fourteen.

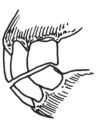

Hook or notch on upper corner incisor

CROSS-SECTION OF TOOTH

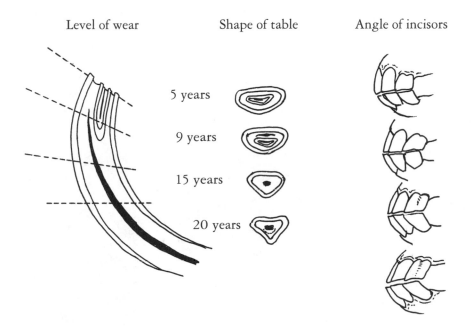

Level of wear	Shape of table	Angle of incisors
	5 years	
	9 years	
	15 years	
	20 years	

Estimating Age in Older Horses

In older horses (after age ten), the changes in the appearance of the teeth appear at a less predictable rate, and age cannot be determined as accurately as in younger horses. Factors such as the horse's dental care over his lifetime, the kind of feed he eats, cribbing, and mouth abnormalities can affect the rate of wear and appearance of his teeth. In the past, unscrupulous horse traders sometimes altered the teeth to make a horse appear younger, a practice called "bishoping."

Some clues to look for are:

Shape and Angle of Incisors The shape and angle of the incisors change as they wear down. The first portion of the tooth is oval in shape and is quite vertical. Between eight and thirteen, the tables become rounder in shape, and the teeth begin to slant forward. In old age, the shape of the tables becomes triangular, and the teeth slant forward at an acute angle.

APPEARANCE AND WEAR OF PERMANENT TEETH

3 years: Permanent
centrals in wear;
intermediates appear

7 years: Cups gone in
lower intermediates;
hook on upper corner

4 years: Permanent
intermediates in
wear; corners appear

8 years: Cups gone
in all lower incisors;
dental star appears

5 years: "Full mouth":
all permanent teeth in
wear

9 years: Cups gone in
upper centrals; dental
stars present

6 years: Cups gone
in lower central
incisors

10 years: Cups gone in
upper intermediates; Gal-
vayne's groove appears

11–12 years:
All cups gone;
"smooth mouth"

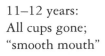

APPEARANCE OF TEETH IN OLDER HORSES

10 years: Galvayne's groove
appears on corner tooth

15 years: Galvayne's groove
halfway down tooth

20 years: Galvayne's groove
extends length of tooth

Teeth become more triangular and slanted with age

Galvayne's Groove   A vertical groove that appears on the upper corner incisor teeth, beginning at ten years of age. It reaches halfway down the tooth at fifteen, and extends the full length of the tooth at twenty. After twenty, Galvayne's groove begins to disappear, beginning at the top of the tooth, and is gone at thirty years.

Shape of the Lower Jaw   Young horses (under age five) have a thick lower jaw that may appear lumpy, because of the presence of the permanent teeth within the jaw. Very old horses' jaws may appear lean and shallow, as the roots of the permanent teeth disappear and bone erodes.

TOOTH AND MOUTH PROBLEMS

Some horses have abnormalities of the mouth, teeth, or jaws that can affect their dental health and ability to eat. Teeth problems should be suspected if a horse is eating slowly, quidding (discarding chewed masses of hay), or underweight. Horses with mouth abnormalities need their teeth checked and floated more often than other horses.

Parrot Mouth (Overshot Jaw) and Undershot Jaw

A parrot mouth is an abnormality in which the upper teeth project forward over the lower teeth. An undershot jaw occurs when the lower teeth project forward ahead of the upper teeth. Both are hereditary defects that make it difficult for the horse to graze normally.

Parrot mouth

Undershot jaw

Step Mouth, Wave Mouth

These are abnormalities of the dental arcade (the back rows of molars and premolars). A step mouth occurs when one or more teeth are longer than the rest, creating a sharp "step." This may be the result of a lost tooth; the opposing tooth continues to grow but is not worn down, because there is no tooth to grind against it. A wave mouth is a smoother but irregular surface. These conditions make it difficult for the horse to chew properly, and may require special dental treatment.

Abscessed Tooth

Horses do not get cavities as humans do, because their teeth are made of a harder substance. However, an abscess may develop at the root of a tooth. Signs of a tooth abscess are bad breath, and sometimes swelling in the jaw. Bad breath is not normal for horses, and usually indicates an abscess or infection in the mouth, guttural pouch, or nasal cavity; it should be investigated by a veterinarian.

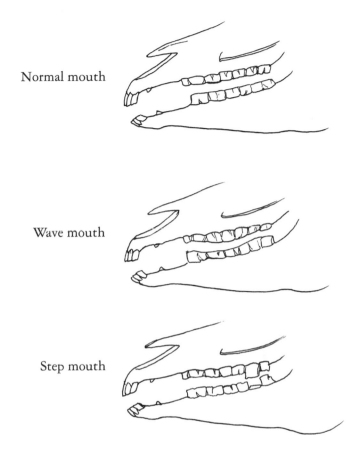

Normal mouth

Wave mouth

Step mouth

Cribbing

Cribbing causes the front surface of the incisor teeth to be worn down in a characteristic pattern, which makes it possible to detect the habit. Severe cribbing can also result in inflamed gums or even broken front teeth.

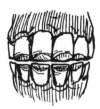

Wear pattern of cribber

INTERNAL PARASITES AND THEIR CONTROL

All horses are exposed to internal parasites to some degree. Internal parasites live in the stomach, intestines, blood vessels, and other internal organs. They damage their host by sucking blood and nutrients, causing tissue damage, obstruction of blood vessels and the digestive tract, and producing toxins. The heaviest damage is caused by larvae (especially large strongyles) migrating through the intestines, liver, and arteries. It is believed that more than 80 percent of fatal colics are caused by parasite damage to the intestinal tract and the blood vessels that supply it. Horses that are subject to frequent attacks of colic usually have extensive parasitic damage.

Very young horses, old horses, and those in poor condition are most vulnerable to parasite damage. Outward signs of parasite infestation include colic, weight loss, lethargy, poor appetite, pot belly, rough coat, poor growth in young horses, diarrhea, constipation, and tail rubbing. Larger parasites such as bots, ascarids, or pinworms may be visible in the manure. However, an infested horse may suffer extensive, irreparable internal damage before any visible signs appear. A fecal parasite count (microscopic examination of a fecal sample) is the best way to check for the kind and number of internal parasites present.

COMMON INTERNAL PARASITES AND THEIR LIFE CYCLES

Parasite control depends on a knowledge of the various internal parasites, and on breaking the cycle by which each parasite develops, matures, infests the horse, and reproduces.

Strongyles (Bloodworms)

Large Strongyles *(Strongylus vulgaris, S. edentatus, S. equinus)*
Large strongyles (especially *S. vulgaris*) cause the most serious damage of all parasites. Strongyle eggs are laid in the intestine and pass out in manure. They hatch into larvae, which mature into infective larvae. This takes less than a week in warm weather, or up to several weeks in cool weather. Infective larvae crawl up stems of grass and are eaten by the horse. On reaching the intestinal tract, the larvae penetrate the walls of the small intestine, cecum, and colon, and invade the arteries. They migrate through the layers of the arterial walls, where they may cause inflammation, blockage of an artery, or an aneurysm (a weakened

area of the arterial wall, which bulges like a balloon and may rupture). Some are carried to the heart, lungs, and liver. Blockage of the mesenteric artery (which supplies the intestine) by a buildup of larvae or cellular debris may lead to severe damage or death of a portion of the bowel, resulting in life-threatening colic; a similar blockage of the iliac artery, which supplies the hind legs, can cause lameness or paralysis. Mature strongyles return to the cecum and colon, where they suck blood and lay their eggs.

LIFE CYCLE OF LARGE STRONGYLES

Larvae migrate through blood vessels and organs

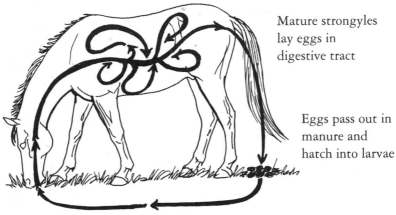

Mature strongyles
lay eggs in
digestive tract

Eggs pass out in
manure and
hatch into larvae

Horse swallows infective
larvae with contaminated
grass, feed, or water

Larvae mature and
become infective

Small Strongyles (Cyathostomiac) Small strongyles can also cause problems. Unlike large strongyles, they do not migrate out of the intestinal tract. Instead, the larvae burrow into the lining of the intestine and remain dormant until late winter and early spring, when they emerge and mature, laying their eggs in the intestines. Large numbers of small strongyles emerging at once can break down the intestinal lining, causing weight loss, loss of appetite, severe diarrhea, colic, and even death.

The life cycle of small strongyles is similar to that of large strongyles, except that they do not migrate out of the intestinal tract.

Ascarids (Parascaris Equorum or Roundworms)

Ascarids are large worms, up to 10 inches long. They are a common problem in foals, especially up to nine months of age, and to a lesser extent in yearlings, but are seldom a threat to mature horses. Ascarids cause damage to the intestines, liver, and lungs; large numbers of roundworms may block the intestine or even cause it to rupture. Signs of ascarid infestation include rough coat, pot belly, coughing, diarrhea, dullness, lack of appetite, and poor growth.

Ascarids have a rather complex life cycle. Eggs are laid in the intestines and pass out with manure. Ascarid eggs are very hardy; they may survive in the soil, on walls, or on stall floors for a year or longer. The eggs mature into infective larvae, which are ingested soon after birth as foals nibble grass or bedding. The tiny larvae migrate through the intestinal walls to the liver and lungs. They are coughed up and are swallowed, and develop into adults in the small intestine, where they lay their eggs.

LIFE CYCLE OF ASCARID

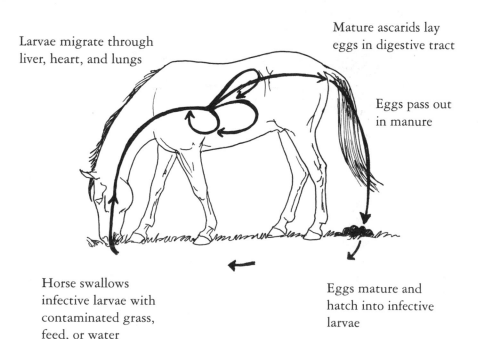

Larvae migrate through liver, heart, and lungs

Mature ascarids lay eggs in digestive tract

Eggs pass out in manure

Horse swallows infective larvae with contaminated grass, feed, or water

Eggs mature and hatch into infective larvae

Bots (Gastrophilus)

"Bots" are the larvae of the botfly. The female botfly (which resembles a bee) lays small yellow eggs on the hair of the horse's fetlocks, forelegs, shoulders, and mane. As the horse rubs its muzzle over the eggs, they are stimulated to hatch and the larvae enter its mouth, where they burrow into the tissues of the cheek and gums for a month before they are swallowed. Second- and third-stage larvae attach themselves to the lining of the stomach, where they live on blood and tissue and mature through the winter. They are passed out with manure and pupate in the soil for five to six weeks, then hatch into mature botflies in spring and early summer.

LIFE CYCLE OF BOTFLY

Larvae (bots) remain in stomach 8–10 months

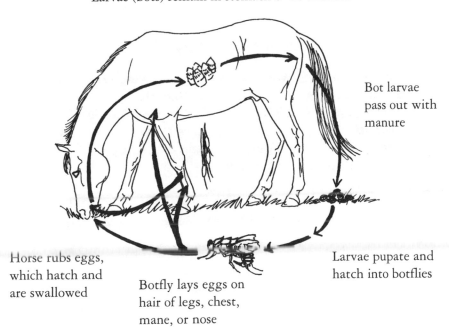

Bot larvae pass out with manure

Horse rubs eggs, which hatch and are swallowed

Botfly lays eggs on hair of legs, chest, mane, or nose

Larvae pupate and hatch into botflies

In addition to the common botfly (gastrophilus intestinalis), other species of bots may lay their eggs on the face or other parts of the body.

Bots cause less damage than most other internal parasites. Botflies annoy horses when laying eggs, and the migrating larvae may cause sores in the mouth. Large numbers of bots sometimes cause ulcers in the lining of the stomach, and sometimes interfere with passage of food through the pyloric valve into the intestines.

Pinworms

Pinworms live in the large intestine. They lay their eggs on the skin outside the anus, forming a gray or yellow mass. The eggs drop off onto the bedding or manger, and are ingested along with feed, reinfecting the horse. Pinworm eggs dehydrate and die fairly quickly outdoors, so pinworm infestations are usually seen in stabled horses.

Pinworms cause horses to rub their tails, and the gray or yellow eggs may be visible around the anus. Because dewormers that control strongyles are effective against pinworms, the presence of pinworms suggests that the overall deworming program is ineffective and should be reviewed.

Other Internal Parasites

Strongyloides (Threadworms)   Strongyloides are tiny worms found in the intestines of foals. They are passed from the mare to the foal as it nurses during the first few days of life. Strongyloides are believed to cause diarrhea in foals as young as ten days old. Treating the mare with ivermectin before foaling reduces the foal's exposure to this parasite, as does good hygiene and clean bedding.

Tapeworms   Tapeworms have only recently been recognized as a problem in horses. Most modern dewormers, including ivermectin, are ineffective against tapeworms, so it is possible for a horse to be dewormed regularly and still be infested. Tapeworms can cause weight loss, anemia, colic, and general unthriftiness. Detecting tapeworms can be difficult, as tapeworm segments are not always found in an ordinary fecal exam. Deworming products for tapeworms must be prescribed by a veterinarian.

Haebronema (Summer Sores)   Haebronema larvae are carried by house and stable flies, and may infect horses when flies feed on moisture from horses' lips and nostrils, or from wounds. When the larvae are swallowed, they mature in the stomach, laying eggs that pass out in the manure. Haebronema can cause large tumorlike growths in the stomach. When flies contaminate open wounds, haebronema larvae may cause lesions called summer sores, which are very irritating and difficult to heal. The dewormer ivermectin kills haebronema at all life stages.

Lungworms Lungworms are carried by donkeys, which are their natural host. Lungworm eggs pass out in manure and mature into larvae, which are swallowed with grass. The larvae migrate to the lungs (of donkey or horse), where they mature and lay eggs, which infect the mucus and are swallowed, then pass out in manure. Donkeys seldom show symptoms of lungworm infestation, but horses develop an intermittent cough which gets worse with exercise.

Donkeys and horses kept with them should be tested for lungworms, which can be effectively treated with ivermectin.

PARASITE CONTROL MEASURES FOR STABLES

Keeping horses as parasite-free as possible is essential for their health. The greater the number of horses, and the smaller the area in which they are concentrated, the greater the exposure factor. An effective parasite control program includes regular deworming, rotation of dewormers, testing, and measures to prevent infestation. Such a plan must be adapted to local conditions, climate, time of year, the ages and numbers of horses kept, and the needs of individual horses. Your veterinarian's advice is invaluable in creating and maintaining the best parasite control program for your horses and stable.

Deworming

Horses should be dewormed on a regular schedule, according to the recommendations of your veterinarian. Most veterinarians recommend deworming every six to eight weeks; sometimes more often. Another alternative is to use a deworming product (Strongid C™) designed to be fed in small doses daily.

The deworming product chosen must be safe for the age and type of horse (mature horses, young stock, pregnant or lactating mares, aged horses), and must be administered in the correct dosage. You must know which parasites the product is effective against, and at which stage of their life cycles. To determine the correct dosage, you must know the horse's weight.

CHART 12-1: CLASSIFICATION AND
EFFECTIVENESS OF VARIOUS DEWORMERS

Drug	Brand-Name Products	Form	Effective Against
Dichlorvos	Cutter Dichlorvos Horse Wormer	Pellets	Ascarids, bots, large & small strongyles

Comments: Not for foals. May cause diarrhea. Do not withold feed. Avoid muscle relaxants, general anesthetics and insecticide use for 2 weeks after use.

Drug	Brand-Name Products	Form	Effective Against
Febentel	Rintal, Combotel, Negabot-Plus	Paste, liquid	Ascarids, pinworms, large & small strongyles
Fenbendazole	Panacure	Granules, paste, liquid	Ascarids, pinworms, roundworms, large & small strongyles, tapeworms, threadworms

Comments: Effective against large strongyle larvae when given in double dose for 5 days. Double dose required for tapeworms, roundworms.

Drug	Brand-Name Products	Form	Effective Against
Telmin, Telmin B		Paste, powder, suspension	Ascarids, pinworms, large & small strongyles
Ivermectin	Equalvan, Equimectrin, Zimecterin	Paste, liquid	Ascarids, bots, onconchera, pinworms, large & small strongyles, threadworms

Comments: Effective against all internal parasites, including larvae, except tapeworms.

Drug	Brand-Name Products	Form	Effective Against
Piperazine	Piperazine 17% or 34%, Piperazine water wormer, Pipfuge, Pip-Pop 320	In water or on feed	Ascarids, pinworms, large & small strongyles

Comments: Treated horses may show colic symptoms or muscle tremors (especially in case of overdose).

Drug	Brand-Name Products	Form	Effective Against
Oxfendazole	Benzelmin, Benzelmin plus	Paste, powder, liquid	Ascarids, pinworms, large & small strongyles
Oxibendazole	Anthelcide Eq, Equipar R	Paste, suspension	Ascarids, pinworms, large & small strongyles, threadworms
Pyrantel Pamoate	Imathal, Strongid	Paste, suspension, on feed	Ascarids, pinworms, large & small strongyles
Pyrantel Tartrate	Banminth, Purina Horse & Colt Wormer	Feed additive, suspension	Ascarids, pinworms, large & small strongyles, threadworms
	Strongid C	Daily feed additive	
Thiabenzadole	Equizole, Equizole A		Ascarids, pinworms, large & small strongyles

(*Continues*)

Drug	Brand-Name Products	Form	Effective Against
Trichlorfon	Combot Liquid, Combot Paste, Negabot Paste, Telmin B, Benexelmin Plus, Combotel, Dyrex	Liquid, paste	Ascarids, bots, pinworms

Comments: May cause diarrhea & mild colic symptoms. Do not withold feed. Avoid stress, surgery, muscle relaxants & insecticide use for 2 weeks after use.

Dewormers must be administered in a way that is safe and ensures that the horse gets the full dose. Methods include:

Oral Paste   The most common method today, and usually the easiest for horse owners.

Rinse the horse's mouth clean first, as he can spit out the paste if he has a mouthful of hay or grass.

Stomach Tube   The advantage of this method is that you can be sure that the horse receives a full dose. Some dewormers can only be given by stomach tube, as they are too caustic to be given orally. Disadvantages are that tube worming must be done by a veterinarian, and some horses are difficult to tube.

Powder or Granules in Feed   This the least reliable method, as a horse may refuse to eat the dewormer or may only eat part of a dose.

Rotation of Dewormers

Deworming products kill most, but not all, internal parasites. If the same drug is used repeatedly, those parasites that survive may develop resistance to it. To prevent this, dewormers should be rotated periodically. It is important to know the active ingredients of the dewormers you use, and to use different classifications of drugs when rotating dewormers, not just a different brand-name product. Rotating dewormers should be done with a veterinarian's advice, in order to be sure that the products used are effective against all parasites.

Testing for Parasites

A fecal parasite count (microscopic examination of a fecal sample) shows the number and types of parasites present in a horse. However, fecal tests only show how many mature, egg-laying parasites are present; they do not reveal migrating larvae, which are much more damaging. An annual fecal parasite count can be done in late June or early July, when the adult parasite population is greatest, to check the effectiveness of the parasite control program. New horses should also be tested, especially if they show signs of parasite infestation.

Reducing Exposure to Internal Parasites

Although complete prevention of parasite infestation is nearly impossible, good management practices can keep exposure to very low levels. These center on good hygiene, preventing the contamination of pastures and feed by parasite eggs and larvae, and measures that break parasites' life cycles and reduce their numbers.

Some recommendations include the following:

- New horses should have a fecal test and should be dewormed forty-eight hours before being turned out in pastures or paddocks.
- Avoid overcrowding and overgrazing of pastures. The more horses (and manure) per acre, the greater the parasite load.
- Keep feed, hay, and water from becoming contaminated with manure. Avoid feeding from the ground; use feeders instead.
- Picking up manure from paddocks at least twice a week will significantly reduce exposure to parasites.
- Do not spread manure directly from stables onto pastures. The heat generated during composting will kill some eggs and larvae; however, large strongyle larvae can survive for several weeks and small strongyle larvae for up to eight months. Ideally, horse manure should not be spread on horse pastures at all.
- If possible, rest or rotate pastures periodically.

PREVENTIVE HEALTH CARE

Preventive health care emphasizes the prevention of diseases through inoculation, reducing exposure, and good management practices.

Inoculations

Inoculations are discussed in USPC D and C Manuals, Books 1 and 2, which should be reviewed. Some points to remember about inoculations, in connection with management of a stable, are:

- Consult your veterinarian about which diseases to inoculate against, considering the age and type of horses, risk of exposure, and incidence of disease in your area. Horses that travel or compete usually need different inoculation programs than those that remain at home.
- For each inoculation, know how long and how many inoculations it takes to establish initial immunity, how long immunity lasts, and when booster shots are required. (See chart below.)
- Keep records up to date for individual horses and for the stable. Note dates when boosters are due on the stable calendar.
- Horses may have a reaction, go off feed, or be sore for a day or two after inoculation. Schedule inoculations so horses can have a day or two off if necessary; not right before a competition.
- Vaccines must be stored at the correct temperature, prepared properly, and administered in the proper dosage, according to manufacturer's specifications. For this reason, they should be administered by a veterinarian.

CHART 12-2: INOCULATIONS AND IMMUNITY

Innoculations	Initial Dose	Length of Immunity
Tetanus		
(Toxoid)	1 dose	Up to several years
Booster Shots: Annually.		
(Antitoxin)	1 dose	2 weeks

Antitoxin provides short-term high-level immunity, given in case of wounds, surgery, newborn foals, in case of wounds when horse's immunization is unknown or not up to date.

Encephalomyletis		
Eastern (EEE), Western (WEE)	2 doses 2 t o 4 weeks apart	6 months

Booster Shots: Annually; if mosquitos are active year-round, every 6 months.

Innoculations	Initial Dose	Length of Immunity
Encephalomyletis		
Venezuelan (VEE)	1 dose	2 years
Booster Shots: Every other year.		
Influenza		
(A-1 and A-2 strains)	2 doses 6 to 12 weeks apart	2 to 3 months
Booster Shots: Every 2 to 3 months, especially young horses, competition horses, and broodmares. Inoculate before travel, competition, or breeding season. Broodmares should receive last dose 1 month before foaling.		
Rhinopneumonitis		
(EHV-1 and EHA-4 strains)	1 or 2 doses	2 to 3 months
Booster Shots: Every 2 to 3 months, as for influenza.		
Strangles	2 doses 3 to 4 weeks apart	1 year
Booster Shots: Annually. Inoculate before travel, competition, or breeding season.		
Rabies	1 dose	up to 3 or 4 years
Booster Shots: Annually.		
Potomac Horse Fever	2 doses 3 to 4 weeks apart	1 year
Booster Shots: Annually.		
Equine Viral Arteritis	1 dose	1 year
Booster Shots: Annually. Inoculate 3 weeks before breeding season.		
Botulism	3 doses 4 weeks apart	1 year
Booster Shots: Annually.		

Exposure to Strange Horses

Exposure to strange horses is a major source of contagious disease, and should be limited as much as practical. Whenever a new horse is brought into the stable, or a horse returns to the stable from a show, rally, or another farm, the risk of exposure increases. Maintaining a "closed herd" (no horses going in or out) greatly reduces the chances of contracting contagious diseases.

Precautions that reduce exposure to strange horses include:

- Isolate new horses for two weeks, taking temperature daily, before exposing them to resident horses. This is also a good precaution when a horse returns from a competition.
- Do not borrow or lend buckets, tack, or equipment unless it is thoroughly disinfected before and after use.
- Require visiting horses to be in good health and show a current Coggins test and proof of inoculations.
- If visiting horses are stabled on the property, keep them isolated from resident horses. Strip and disinfect stalls before arrival and after they depart; use their own feed and water buckets; avoid sharing paddocks or water troughs.

Travel

Stress affects a horse's immune system and lowers his resistance to disease. During travel, horses are exposed to strange horses and possibly to communicable diseases while their resistance is lowered by the stress of travel, new surroundings, and competition. In addition to following the guidelines for avoiding exposure to strange horses, here are some tips:

- Horses should receive inoculations or booster shots far enough in advance to provide immunity before traveling.
- Provide your own buckets, feed tubs, tack and equipment, and do not lend or borrow these items. Never let your horse drink from a watering trough used by other horses.
- Take along a supply of the horse's regular feed and hay, to avoid digestive upsets caused by a change of feed.
- Horses may become dehydrated during travel through sweating and drying, or failure to drink enough. Offer water frequently, and bring water along, as some horses may refuse to drink water that tastes different.
- Take every opportunity to reduce stress on your horse, including regular stops for rest, watering, and checking horses, being aware of temperature extremes and changes, and putting on or removing

clothing as needed. For more information on care during travel, see *USPC C Manual of Horsemanship,* Book 2, pages 262–263.

Preventing the Spread of Contagious Disease

When a horse suffers from a contagious disease, you must care for him while avoiding exposing other horses. Some precautions are:

- Stable the sick horse as far away from other horses as possible; in a separate building, if available. Do not turn him out in or adjacent to paddocks used by healthy horses.
- Set aside buckets, feed measures, stall cleaning equipment and other utensils for the sick horse; store them separately and keep them clean.
- When cleaning and caring for a sick horse, use disposable materials such as plastic or rubber gloves and paper towels instead of items like rags or sponges, which can carry infection.
- If possible, only one person should care for the sick horse. If you must care for other horses, do the healthy horses first, then the sick horse. Wash hands and change clothes and boots afterward, before going to other horses.
- Disinfect the stall, buckets, and feed tubs, and any equipment used on the sick horse after use. (Ask the veterinarian which disinfectant is effective against the particular disease.)
- During an outbreak of contagious disease, take temperatures of healthy horses morning and evening. An elevated temperature may be an early sign that a horse is coming down with the disease and should be isolated.
- Stop all travel of horses to and from the stable, and discourage visitors from other stables. Infectious organisms can be carried to other stables on people's shoes and clothing.
- Consult your veterinarian about whether other horses on the farm should receive inoculations, or any other necessary precautions.

DISEASE PROCESSES

Certain disease processes may be at work in various illnesses, injuries, or conditions. Horse owners and stable managers should recognize them and know how they work and how they should be treated, although in most cases, they will require treatment by a veterinarian.

Shock

Shock is the body's response to trauma. It is an acute and progressive failure of the peripheral circulation (blood circulation to outer body parts such as the legs and head), which takes place as the body tries to conserve its resources to deal with a serious injury.

Signs of shock include:

- Trembling, sweating, cool skin.
- Depression, apathetic attitude.
- Cold extremities (ears and legs), subnormal temperature.
- Rapid, weak pulse; low or falling blood pressure.
- Pale or bluish mucous membranes.
- Weakness; collapse.

Shock can be caused by massive bleeding, severe trauma, burns, major infections, intestinal obstructions, dehydration, heart failure, and anaphylactic shock (severe allergic reaction). Shock can progress until blood pressure falls dangerously low and death follows.

Shock must be treated promptly by a veterinarian, because it requires intravenous replacement of fluids to restore blood volume and blood pressure. First-aid measures include keeping the horse quiet and warm (but not raising the temperature, which worsens shock), controlling bleeding, and avoiding dehydration. It is important to call the veterinarian before shock progresses to a dangerous point. Never administer tranquilizers to a horse in shock, as this can lower the blood pressure further and endanger the horse.

Fever

Fever is an abnormal rise in body temperature that is not caused by exercise, diet, or environment. It may be the result of toxins that accompany an infection or tissue destruction. Fever is a byproduct of the process by which a horse's body fights infectious diseases or toxins, but high fevers can lead to weakness, dehydration, and tissue damage. One or more degrees above the horse's normal temperature (from 99.0 to 100.5 degrees Fahrenheit) indicates fever. Other signs of fever are chills, shivering, increased pulse rate, and sometimes sweating. Very high fevers (7 to 10 degrees above normal) can be life threatening.

Because fever is usually a sign of infection or disease, a veterinarian should be called to determine the cause and treat the horse. Antibacterial drugs may be used to control an infection, and the veterinarian may use special drugs to lower the fever if it is high enough to be dangerous.

Dehydration

Dehydration occurs when the body's water level becomes deficient. This can happen when the body loses too much water (as in heavy sweating), or fails to take in enough water (as in failure to drink enough). Dehydration is serious because sufficient water is essential for vital functions such as the circulation of the blood, digestion, cooling, and maintaining chemical balance in the cells of the body.

Dehydration can be caused by sweating heavily, which is usually obvious, or continuous sweating that dries rapidly, which is not so noticeable (this can occur during travel in hot weather). Failure to water horses often enough can lead to dehydration. This can easily happen during the winter, when water sources may freeze or horses may not drink enough because the water is cold. Dehydration can lead to hard, dry manure, slow digestion, impaction, and colic, which are more common in older horses.

A test for dehydration is the "pinch test." If you pinch a fold of skin on the horse's shoulder, it should snap back immediately when released. If the skin fold remains "tented" or subsides over a second or two, the horse is dehydrated.

Dehydration is treated by encouraging the horse to drink (a little at a time, not a large amount of cold water, especially if he is hot). In severe cases, a veterinarian may have to administer fluids intravenously.

Inflammation

Inflammation is the body's natural defensive response to injury or infection. When a part is injured or invaded by an infectious organism, the body responds by increasing circulation at the site, delivering defense cells (leukocytes and antibodies) and carrying away cellular debris. The defense cells attempt to destroy, dilute, or wall off the irritating agents, and the increased circulation helps to carry away the debris left by dead or damaged cells and foreign material. Material such as fluid, cells, and cellular debris is exuded, or escapes out of the capillaries into the surrounding tissues; this material (exudate) may include blood, serum, pus, fibrin, or mucous, depending on the location and type of inflammatory reaction. Eventually inflammation leads to healing and repair of the damaged tissues.

Inflammation may be caused by injuries, wounds, burns, disease-causing organisms (pathogens), and the toxins they produce, poisons, venoms, and antigens (substances against which the animal possesses antibodies).

Five signs of inflammation are:

- Heat (from increased blood supply to inflamed area).
- Pain (from swelling and nerve irritation).
- Swelling (from fluid portions of blood seeping into tissues).
- Redness (not always visible).
- Loss of function in the inflamed area (because of pain and swelling).

Inflammation is an essential part of the healing process. Normal inflammation should be adequate to heal the wound, defeat the infection, and repair damaged tissue, but excessive inflammation can result in damage to the body, proud flesh, excessive scar tissue, and loss of function. Wounds and other injuries need to be protected from excessive inflammation due to irritation from strong antiseptics, flies, or excessive movement. First aid for sprains, strains, and bruises includes the application of cold and immobilizing the part, which reduces the initial inflammatory reaction.

Sometimes the body's natural defenses are inadequate to defeat an infection, and help may be necessary in the form of antibiotics. These should be used only on the advice of a veterinarian, because improper use of antibiotics can be dangerous, and can lead to the development of antibiotic-resistant organisms.

Certain drugs (corticosteroids, and non-steroidal anti-inflammatory drugs like phenylbutazone) can reduce inflammation. These must be used with the advice and supervision of a veterinarian, as misuse of these drugs can suppress healing and leave the horse vulnerable to infection or further injury.

Edema

Edema is swelling, or the accumulation of excess fluid in the tissues. In non-inflammatory edema, the swelling is cool and painless. If pressed with a finger, a "pit" or imprint remains. Edema may show up along the midline of the abdomen and in the sheath. Lack of exercise may result in "stocking up" or edema in the hind legs, or all four legs.

Edema may be caused by certain illnesses, parasite infestation, inactivity, or by heart or kidney disorders that interfere with normal circulation of the blood and lymph. Edema is related to low pressure in the veins, and to an abnormal protein or salt content in the blood. To treat edema, the veterinarian must look for and treat the underlying cause.

Stocking up is common in horses confined to stalls, especially older horses. It does not cause lameness and usually disappears quickly with gentle exercise. Measures to prevent stocking up include use of stable bandages, access to a turnout paddock, and regular exercise.

Arthritis

Arthritis is inflammation of a joint. It may be acute (for example, a recent sprain) or chronic (a long-term condition), and may range from mild to severe. Symptoms of arthritis are heat and swelling in the joint, and pain on movement.

There are several types of arthritis:

Traumatic Arthritis   Caused by trauma to the joint, such as a sprain or blow; usually acute. First aid consists of cooling the injury (by cold-hosing, cold water bandages, or applying cold gel or ice packs for twenty minutes at a time), applying a pressure bandage (to limit movement and swelling), and rest.

Septic Arthritis   Occurs when a joint is invaded by infectious organisms, through a wound or puncture, or a systemic infection. It is extremely painful, and the joint swells badly. Septic arthritis requires prompt veterinary treatment, as infection can destroy the joint.

Degenerative Arthritis   A chronic condition that usually develops from trauma and long-term wear and tear, leading to inflammation over a long period of time. The surface of the cartilage lining the joint slowly erodes and the synovial fluid changes consistency, so that the joint surface is less smooth and not as well lubricated. Eventually, coral-like calcium deposits may form, or small pieces of bone may chip off. The joint becomes tender and painful, and loses its range of motion; eventually it may become "fused" or immovable.

Degenerative arthritis is usually seen in older horses, although trauma and the abuse of steroids may cause it to occur in young horses. The degree of lameness and whether the horse can be ridden or not depends on the joints affected and the severity of the arthritis. In mild cases, the horse may be stiff at first, and move better as he warms up. Anti-inflammatory drugs such as aspirin and phenylbutazone ("bute") may give some relief; careful warming up, the right shoeing, and therapies such as massage or whirlpool therapy may help. Arthritic horses usually do best when worked lightly but regularly, and should not be overstressed.

SPECIFIC DISEASES AND AILMENTS

CHART 12-3: DISEASES AND CONDITIONS OF VARIOUS SYSTEMS

Disease	Systems Affected	Cause/Transmission
Azoturia (tying up syndrome, equine exertional rhabdomyolysis, Monday morning disease)	Muscular	Non-contagious metabolic condition. Breakdown of muscle tissue by metabolic changes due to exertion. Associated with electrolyte imbalance at cellular level.

SYMPTOMS: Stiffness/shortened hind leg stride; unwillingness to track up, which may worsen until unable to move. Tense, quivering hindquarter muscles, sweating, restlessness, anxious expression. Often occurs in horses left idle for several days on full feed, when first put back to work. PREVENTION: By proper balance of feed and exercise; always cut grain ration on idle days. TREATMENT: Stop work at once. Requires prompt veterinary attention.

Disease	Systems Affected	Cause/Transmission
Botulism	Nervous	Toxin produced by Clostridium bacterium; found in hay (especially large round bales) when animal carcasses are baled in hay.

SYMPTOMS: 3 to 7 days after ingestion of toxin: paralysis of tongue and jaw, drooling, inability to swallow; weakness, shuffling gait, paralysis; death due to respiratory failure. Causes "shaker foal syndrome." PREVENTION: Vaccination. TREATMENT: Mild cases may survive if treated promptly.

Disease	Systems Affected	Cause/Transmission
Choking (obstruction of esophagus)	Digestive	Non-contagious condition caused by blockage of esophagus by a mass of feed or piece of apple, carrot, etc.

SYMPTOMS: Inability to swallow, with signs of anxiety, drooling, arching neck, return of food through nostrils. Sometimes a mass may be felt partway down the esophagus. Choking may result in narrowing of esophagus with scar tissue, making repeat episodes more likely. TREATMENT: Requires immediate veterinary attention. PREVENTION: Slow down greedy eaters; have water available at all times; cut treats into small slices.

Disease	*Systems Affected*	*Cause/Transmission*
Colic	Digestive	Abdominal pain; non-contagious condition. Many causes, including parasite damage to bowel & blood vessels, gas, spoiled or unsuitable food, change of diet, impaction, overeating, others.

SYMPTOMS: MILD COLIC—Restlessness, pawing, curling upper lip, lying down and getting up, increased pulse & respiration, sweating, stretching out as if to urinate, increased or absent gut sounds. SEVERE COLIC—Above, plus rolling, thrashing, red or blue mucous membrancs, slow capillary refill, shock, death. PREVENTION: Effective parasite control program, good feeding and management practices. TREATMENT: Requires prompt veterinary treatment; surgery may be necessary.

Equine Infectious Anemia (EIA, swamp fever)	Circulatory/ lymphatic	Virus carried in blood; transmitted by bloodsucking flies, mosquitos, contaminated needles.

SYMPTOMS: ACUTE FORM—Acute symptoms, including fever, edema of legs & midline, depression, loss of appetite, weight loss. Often fatal. SUBACUTE FORM—Symptoms similar to acute form but less severe; death seldom occurs. CHRONIC FORM—Unthrifty appearance, lack of stamina; periodic flareups of acute or subacute form of disease. INAPPARENT CARRIER—No apparent symptoms, but horse tests positive for EIA antibodies. PREVENTION: No vaccine available. Require negative Coggins test for prepurchase exams, entry to stables, shows & rallies, interstate shipping. Isolate horses testing positive for EIA from healthy horses.

Equine Encephalomyletis (sleeping sickness): Eastern (EEE), Western (WEE), Venezuelan (VEE)	Brain/nervous system	Virus carried in blood; transmitted from infected birds to horse or human by mosquito bite.

SYMPTOMS: High fever (up to 106°F), drowsiness, circling, pressing head against walls, paralysis, death. Survivors often have permanent brain damage. PREVENTION: Vaccination, before mosquito season.

(Continues)

Disease	Systems Affected	Cause/Transmission
Equine viral arteritis (EVA, pinkeye)	Respiratory, reproductive	Herpes virus. Transmitted by inhaling droplets and in breeding.

SYMPTOMS: Fever (102° to 106°F), nasal discharge, increased respiratory rate, edema of limbs. Causes abortion. Stallions may become "shedders" that show no symptoms but pass virus in semen. PREVENTION: Vaccination, testing, and restricting use & importation of affected stallions.

Disease	Systems Affected	Cause/Transmission
Equine Viral Rhinopneumonitis (EVR)	Respiratory, reproductive (rarely, nervous system)	Herpes viruses: EHV 1, 2, or 3. Transmitted by inhaling droplets, contact with infected horses, contaminated feed or water.

SYMPTOMS: Fever (up to 106°F), cough, nasal discharge. Secondary bacterial infections may occur. Causes abortion or weak foals that die soon after birth. Rare form affects the nervous system, causing paralysis. PREVENTION: Vaccination. TREATMENT: Good nursing care; isolate from other horses. Antibiotics are not effective against virus but may be used in case of secondary bacterial infection.

Disease	Systems Affected	Cause/Transmission
Heaves (chronic obstructive pulmonary disease)	Respiratory	Non-contagious condition; may be caused by allergy or degeneration of lung tissues. Seldom seen in pastured horses.

SYMPTOMS: Cough or wheeze, more obvious during exercise. Extra lift of abominal muscles during expiration causes "heave line" (ridge along edge of ribs). Mild cases can do light work, but stamina is affected and fast work is impossible. PREVENTION: No cure. Treatment aims at controlling symptoms. Avoid exposure to dust; dampen feed; use hay substitute.

Disease	Systems Affected	Cause/Transmission
Influenza	Respiratory	Myxoviruses: Influenza A/Equi 1 and A/Equi 2. Transmitted by inhaling droplets, exposure to infected horses, contaminated feed and water.

SYMPTOMS: Fever, depressed appetite, nasal discharge, cough. Secondary bacterial infections or pneumonia may occur, especially in foals. PREVENTION: Vaccination. TREATMENT: Good nursing care; isolate from healthy horses. Antibiotics are not effective against virus but may be used in case of secondary bacterial infection.

Disease	Systems Affected	Cause/Transmission
Laminitis	Circulatory/ Digestive	Non-contagious disorder; inflammation of laminae in feet, due to endotoxemia, carbohydrate overload, excessive concussion, general toxemia, or retained placenta after foaling. Obesity, overeating grain and grazing lush pastures are common causes.

SYMPTOMS: ACUTE—Usually both front feet or all four feet; feet are hot, painful, with strong digital pulse. Horse stands with hind legs drawn up under him, is extremely reluctant to move. Coffin bone may rotate or sink through sole of foot. CHRONIC (founder)—Dropped sole, irregular rings on wall of hoof, separation at white line (seedy toe), toes may grow excessively long and curl up. Feet tender, may be lame. PREVENTION: Good management practices, including maintaining healthy weight, limiting access to lush pasture, avoid carbohydrate overload (especially getting into grain). TREATMENT: Requires immediate veterinary treatment (especially if horse gets into grain but has not yet developed symptoms). Chronic founder may be managed with corrective shoeing, depending on severity.

Disease	Systems Affected	Cause/Transmission
Periodic Opthalmia (recurrent uveitis, moon blindness)	Eye (usually one eye, but may occur in both eyes)	Non-contagious condition, but multiple cases may occur in same stable. Cause is not defined, but leptospirosis and Onchocerca infection have been implicated.

SYMPTOMS: Acute pain with closed eye, unwillingness to expose eye to light, tears and discharge from eye. Cornea is cloudy and pupil contracted. Symptoms ease, but may return in weeks or months. Each attack causes additional damage, eventually resulting in blindness. PREVENTION: Some veterinarians recommend vaccination for leptospirosis. TREATMENT: Requires prompt veterinary treatment. Keep horse in dark stall.

Disease	Systems Affected	Cause/Transmission
Potomac Horse Fever	Digestive	Rickettsia ehrlichia, believed to be carried by bloodsucking ticks.

SYMPTOMS: Depression, loss of appetite, decrease in gut sounds, profuse watery diarrhea, distended abdomen, severe colic, sometimes laminitis. May be fatal. PREVENTION: Vaccination. TREATMENT: Requires prompt veterinary treatment. *(Continues)*

Disease	Systems Affected	Cause/Transmission
Rabies	Brain/nervous system	Rhabdovirus. Transmitted by bite of rabid animal, especially skunks, foxes, raccoons, bats, dogs, or cats.

SYMPTOMS: All warm-blooded animals, including man, are susceptible. Signs vary, including facial paralysis, lameness, colic, faulty vision, and personality change. Incubation period may be up to several months after bite of rabid animal. Always fatal. PREVENTION: Vaccination of horses, pets, barn cats. No cure.

Roaring (laryngeal hemiplegia)	Respiratory	Non-contagious condition, more common in very large horses.

SYMPTOMS: Damage to laryngeal nerve causes paralysis of one side of muscles controlling vocal cords. One cord hangs in airway, causing "roaring" sound during inspiration, especially during exercise. Affects stamina in racing or fast work. TREATMENT: Can be corrected by surgery.

Strangles (distemper)	Respiratory/ lymphatic	Bacterium (*streptococcus equi*). Transmitted in mucus, contaminated feed/water. Horses are infective for 4 to 6 weeks; organism can live in environment for a month or longer.

SYMPTOMS: Lack of appetite, fever (103° to 105°F), nasal discharge which becomes purulent. Upper respiratory tract is inflamed and lymph nodes swell, abcess, break open, and drain pus. Complications include abcesses in internal organs (called "bastard strangles"). PREVENTION: Vaccination. TREATMENT: Antibiotics given before abcesses form. Good nursing care. Isolate infected horses. NOTE: Highly contagious; take precautions to prevent spreading disease from stable to stable.

DRUGS AND MEDICATIONS

Horse owners and stable managers often keep certain drugs and medications on hand for use in emergencies, or to treat minor ailments or chronic conditions. However, any medication strong enough to have potential benefits also has the potential to do harm if misused. Drugs and prescription medications should be given only on orders from the veterinarian. It is dangerous to assume that because a certain medication was used successfully in one case, that it can safely be given in another.

In some cases, the veterinarian may prescribe certain drugs or medications for you to administer, or may leave a supply of a drug to be used under certain circumstances. Here are some guidelines for using medications safely:

- Keep on hand only those drugs and medications that your veterinarian agrees you should have. They should be given only with the advice and approval of your veterinarian. He or she should give you instructions regarding any medications he approves for you to use on your own.
- When a drug is prescribed, get (and write down) complete information on how to administer it, how often, for how long, and any symptoms or side effects to watch out for. Be sure the veterinarian knows about any other drugs or medications the horse has been given recently, including dewormers.
- Have your veterinarian teach you how to administer medications by mouth and by intramuscular injection, including necessary precautions.
- Store drugs and medications in a clean place, at a temperature recommended by the manufacturer. Many drugs must be refrigerated to remain effective.
- Check the date stamped on the vial or box, and throw away medications that are beyond the effective date.
- The possession of needles, syringes, and certain drugs is regulated by law; regulations vary from state to state. You should have a prescription for any controlled items, and they must be kept under lock and key and disposed of properly after use.

Types of Drugs and Medications

There are many more types and classifications of drugs than can be covered here. Some of the drugs more commonly used by horse owners and managers are tranquilizers, pain relievers, anti-inflammatory drugs, and antibiotics.

Tranquilizers

Tranquilizers—or sedatives—are drugs that produce a calming effect by working on the brain or the central nervous system. They are used to calm and restrain horses during veterinary treatment and for clipping, shipping, and other procedures. Most tranquilizers raise the horse's pain threshold, but they do not block pain. A tranquilized horse can still feel pain and may kick, jump, or react violently to a startling or painful stimulus.

Tranquilizers work best when administered while the horse is calm. The horse should be allowed to remain undisturbed for 5 to 15 minutes, until the drug takes effect. Individual horses' sensitivity to tranquilizers can vary greatly.

A tranquilized horse may be unsteady on his feet and may fall more easily than usual. This should be kept in mind when holding a horse for veterinary work or other procedures. If a horse must be tranquilized for shipping, the dose must be carefully calculated to avoid putting him at risk for falling during loading, travel, and unloading. Heavily sedated horses may have difficulty in swallowing. They should not be allowed to eat or drink until they have returned to normal alertness, or choking may result.

Tranquilizing horses for training purposes is not recommended, because tranquilizers block conditioned responses and learned behavior. In addition, a tranquilized horse's reflexes and balance are impaired, so it is more likely to stumble or fall, and its reactions are unpredictable. *Never ride a tranquilized horse; this is dangerous for both horse and rider!*

Tranquilizers are forbidden substances under American Horse Shows Association and other competition rules, and a positive drug test may result in severe penalties.

Commonly used tranquilizers include the following:

Acepromazine (PromAce™, Promazine Granules™)   A tranquilizer that depresses the central nervous system, causing sedation, relaxation, and reduction of involuntary movements (such as flinching). It does not provide relief from pain, and will not prevent a horse from moving or kicking if it is startled or feels pain. It may be administered intramuscularly, intravenously, or as granules added to feed.

Dangers: Acepromazine causes a drop in blood pressure, and *must not* be given to horses that are in shock, dehydrated, septic (severe infections), in poor condition (malnutrition), or suffering from colic. Do not use acepromazine in horses recently dewormed with phenothiazine or piperazine. Accidental injection into an artery (especially the carotid artery) can produce signs ranging from excitement and disorientation to seizures and death.

Xylazine (Rompun™)   A sedative that affects the brain, with some pain relief and muscle-relaxing effects. It slows the heartbeat and rate of breathing, producing a condition similar to sleep. Tranquilizing with Rompun™ causes the horse to hold his head very low, which makes it the best drug for dental procedures, work on the head or eyes, or in cases of choke. CAUTION: Horses tranquilized with xylazine may appear to be relaxed and sleepy, but can kick or jump if startled.

Dormosedan™   A sedative with some analgesic (pain-relieving) properties, used to sedate horses and control pain during veterinary procedures.

Non-Steroidal, Non-Narcotic Analgesics (Pain Relieving Drugs)

Analgesics are drugs that relieve pain by blocking the sensation of pain, but not other sensations. The painful area does not become numb, as it would with an anesthetic, but the pain is decreased or relieved.

Narcotics are powerful pain relieving drugs that act on the central nervous system. They may cause serious drug reactions or side effects. Narcotics must be used *only* by veterinarians, and their possession is regulated by law in all states.

Non-narcotic and non-steroidal anti-inflammatory drugs (called "NSAIDs") are drugs that relieve pain by reducing inflammation. Some may be prescribed by a veterinarian for the horse owner to administer.

Analgesics that include narcotics, non-narcotics, and NSAIDs are regulated or forbidden substances under AHSA and other competition rules, and penalties may result if a horse shows a positive drug test.

Some commonly used non-narcotic, non-steriodal anti-inflammatory drugs include the following:

Banamine™(Flunixin Meglumine)   Anti-inflammatory drug that acts directly on inflamed tissues; used for relief of colic pain, muscle, bone and joint diseases; also reduces fever and relieves pain.

Banamine™ may be administered in oral paste form, granules added to feed, intramuscularly, or intravenously. It is not intended for long-term use and must not be given for more than 5 days. High oral doses over a prolonged period may produce gastrointestinal ulcers.

Dipyrone   An analgesic (pain reliever) and antipyretic (fever-reducing) drug commonly used to control fevers (for instance, in viral illnesses) and to relieve colic pain. It may be given intravenously or intramuscularly.

Dipyrone must not be given with phenylbutazone, chlorpromazine, or barbiturates. Overdose can cause seizures, especially in old or debilitated horses, or those with heart disease.

Torbugesic   A non-narcotic analgesic (pain-relieving) drug, particularly effective for relief of colic pain.

Non-Steroidal Anti-Inflammatory Drugs (NSAIDs)

Non-steroidal anti-inflammatory drugs reduce pain by controlling inflammation. They are used to treat a variety of musculo-skeletal problems, including sprains, strains, overuse of muscles, joint injuries, and arthritis. They are also anti-pyretics (anti-fever), and may be used to reduce fever when a horse suffers from a bacterial or viral infection.

NSAIDs do not cure musculo-skeletal problems, nor do they block pain in the same way that an anesthetic does. They may be given to make it more comfortable for the horse to move, which helps to keep the affected area from "scarring down" and losing its range of motion during healing. However, pain control and exercise must be carefully balanced, under veterinary supervision, to avoid overstressing the area, re-injuring it, and worsening the original injury.

NSAIDs (especially phenylbutazone or "bute") are often used to help older, arthritic horses continue to work more comfortably. However, NSAIDs can be abused if used to suppress symptoms for hard work or competition, without regard to the horse's long-term soundness. For this reason, NSAIDs should only be used with the advice of a veterinarian who is familiar with the horse's history, and the level of work must be appropriate for the horse.

NSAIDs tend to be hard on the gastrointestinal tract, and overdosage or prolonged usage can result in ulcers, especially in foals. Ulcers or soreness in the mouth can be an early sign that the dosage may be producing gastrointestinal ulcers.

Commonly used NSAIDs include the following:

Phenylbutazone ("Bute", Pro-Bute™, Others)   Acts directly on inflamed tissues. It is widely used for relief of musculo-skeletal disorders, including strains, sprains, muscle overuse, tendonitis, acute joint injuries, and arthritic conditions. It is also used to control pain from injuries, infections, laminitis, and other painful conditions, and to control fever associated with bacterial or viral infections. Phenylbutazone is not especially effective against colic pain.

Phenylbutazone can be given as oral gel or paste, in tablets or powder, or intravenously. It is very irritating to tissues and can cause severe tissue damage if injected outside a vein, or if repeated injections are made into the same vein.

Overdoses of phenylbutazone can cause mouth and tongue lesions, gastrointestinal ulcers, and kidney damage. It must not be used in conjunction with blood thinners (such as warfarin or Coumadin) sometimes used to treat navicular disease, or with other NSAIDs.

Specified levels of phenylbutazone are permitted under AHSA and some other competition rules, but exceeding permitted levels is a drug rule violation.

Aspirin   Aspirin is a common fever-reducing and anti-inflammatory drug. It is more often used for reducing fever than for controlling pain. Aspirin reduces fevers resulting from bacterial infections, but is ineffective against other types of fever, such as that due to heat stroke.

Aspirin is usually given orally, in tablets or powder. It is quite irritating to the stomach lining, and should not be used for long periods of time.

Ketoprofen (Ketofen™)   Similar to the human drug ibuprofen. It is used to control inflammation and relieve pain in musculo-skeletal disorders, including strains, sprains, muscular overuse, tendonitis, joint injuries, and arthritis.

Dexamethazone (Azium™) and Other Corticosteroids

Corticosteroids are among the most powerful anti-inflammatory drugs. The body produces natural corticosteroids when the adrenal gland is stimulated by adrenocorticotrophic hormone (ACTH). When administered as drugs, corticosteroids are used to control inflammation. They may be given orally, intramuscularly, or intravenously, and are sometimes injected directly into a joint.

While reducing inflammation, corticosteroids suppress immune responses, both locally and throughout the body. This makes the horse more vulnerable to infections of all kinds. Other possible side effects are suppression of the body's ability to produce natural corticosteroids, depressed calcium and potassium levels, weakness, loss of muscle mass, and laminitis. Corticosteroids are sometimes injected into inflamed joints, but this is risky, as organisms introduced into the joint can cause a crippling joint infection, and repeated injections may cause deterioration of the joint and permanent damage.

Dexamethazone (Azium™) is one of the most powerful of the corticosteroids. Because of its potential for harmful side effects, it should never be given except on a veterinarian's orders. Horse owners should realize that dexamethazone and other corticosteroids will reduce pain, heat, and swelling and can make an injury *appear* better very quickly, but it is not healed and is extremely vulnerable to further damage if the horse is worked inappropriately. Abuse of corticosteroids can cause permanent damage.

Antibiotics

Antibiotics are drugs that kill bacteria. They are only effective against bacterial infections, *not* against viral infections. Specific antibiotics are only effective against certain types of bacteria. A culture may have to be grown in the laboratory to determine which antibiotics work best against a particular organism.

Antibiotics are often misused by horse owners, which can lead to problems. Giving antibiotics unnecessarily (for instance, for viral infections), in too small doses, or for too short a period to be effective can cause bacteria to become resistant to certain antibiotics. In addition, some antibiotics may produce serious side effects.

Antibiotics should be used only on the advice of a veterinarian. It is important to follow the recommended schedule and to continue giving the medication for as long as it was prescribed.

Some antibiotics are forbidden substances under AHSA and other competition rules, especially if they contain procaine. Consult the AHSA Drugs and Medications pamphlet, or current competition drug rules.

Some examples of antibiotics are penicillin, streptomycin, sulfonamides, ampicillin, and tetracycline.

RESTRAINING HORSES

Sometimes horses must be restrained in order to perform veterinary treatment or diagnostic procedures, to medicate minor wounds, or for clipping or other purposes. In using restraints, the following principles are most important:

- Any restraint must be safe for the handler, and for the veterinarian or person working on the horse.
- The restraint must be safe for the horse, and applied humanely.
- Minimize stress on the horse by using the least severe restraint that will work safely under the circumstances, and for no longer than necessary.
- Plan ahead. Teach horses to accept routine handling procedures; have suitable restraint equipment and experienced help; work in a safe and suitable area.
- Restraints must be used with good judgement, taking into account the situation, the individual horse, and the experience of the handler. Apply them kindly but firmly, and *never* lose your temper!

TYPES OF RESTRAINT

Distracting the Horse

In many cases, holding a horse safely while distracting him from the procedure is sufficient. Some ways to distract a horse's attention are:

- Patting or scratching him on the neck, between the jawbones, or around the base of the ears.
- Cupping one hand over an eye (to prevent the horse from seeing a needle, etc.).
- Holding the upper lip and/or the ear with the fingers. (Do not twist the ear or interfere with the breathing.)
- Gripping the loose skin at the shoulder.

Chain End Lead Shank

A chain end lead shank is one of the simplest and most effective forms of restraint. It should be used with a sturdy, properly fitted halter. The handler should stand at the horse's shoulder (never directly in front of a horse), out of the way of the head and front feet, on the same side as the veterinarian or person working on the horse. For safety, hold the shank, not the chain.

When held quietly, a chain shank does not bother the horse. A short tug or two will get his attention; never hang on a shank with continuous hard pressure. Severe jerking on a chain shank is abusive and dangerous; it can cause a horse to run backwards, rear, or resist violently.

Some ways of using a chain end lead shank are:

Chain under Chin   Tends to make horse raise his head.

Chain over Nose   Adjust so that the opposite side of the halter is not drawn into the horse's eye. Severe use can cause damage to the nose.

Chain in Mouth   More severe method that can injure the mouth if misused. However, some horses respect this restraint more than any other.

Chain across Gum, under Upper Lip   Severe method sometimes used when a horse cannot be twitched or tranquilized. It may cause bleeding if the horse fights it, but is almost as effective as a twitch. A slight pressure should be kept on the chain, so that it does not slacken and drop off the gum.

Holding Up a Foreleg

Holding up a foreleg is a simple restraint that works well to keep a horse from fidgeting or picking up his legs. Hold up the foreleg on the same side the veterinarian or other person is working on, using a toe hold (see diagram). Don't rely on this restraint to stop a horse from violently kicking or struggling.

Twitches

A twitch is used to apply pressure to the upper lip. It was once thought that the pain inflicted by a twitch distracted the horse from the procedure. Recent research has shown that pressure of the twitch on the nerves of the upper lip causes the horse to release natural painkilling substances called endorphins into the bloodstream, which alleviate pain and help to calm the horse. Some horses will fight when a twitch is applied; the calming effect only begins to work after the horse submits to the twitch.

A twitch must never be applied to any place but the upper lip, and should not be left on longer than 15 to 20 minutes. The horse should be held with a lead shank, never by a twitch alone.

There are several types of twitches, including short and long wood-handled twitches, and tongs or clamp twitches which can be fastened to the halter.

USE OF CHAIN END LEAD SHANK FOR RESTRAINT

Chain over nose

Chain under chin

Chain in mouth

Chain across gum, under upper lip

Chain snapped to bottom of
upper ring on opposite side

Holding up a foreleg with toe hold

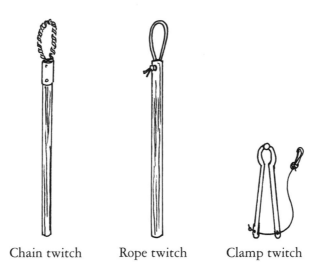

Chain twitch   Rope twitch   Clamp twitch

Restraining a Foal

A small foal can be restrained by encircling it with one arm around the chest and the other around the hindquarters. The handler can also use his body to place the foal against a wall.

Another method is to hold it with one arm around the neck and chest. The other hand grasps the dock firmly at the base of the tail.

When handling a foal that has not yet been halter-broken or taught to lead, restraints that work on the halter or head are ineffective and can be dangerous to the foal.

RESTRAINING HORSE WITH A TWITCH

Applying a twitch:
Place loop over thumb
and three fingers

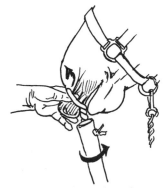

Grasp upper lip, slip
twitch over lip and
twist toward horse

Tighten enough for safe
and effective restraint

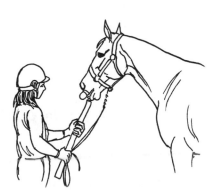

Hold twitch with both hands; stand
to one side; always hold horse with
halter shank as well as twitch

CHAPTER 13

Stable Management

Managing a stable requires more than horse care and routine chores. As a stable manager, you are responsible for the horses, the facility, and the economical operation of the stable. You must organize a program of horse care and facility maintenance, budget your time and money, and be aware of the overall picture as well as the details of getting the work done.

EFFICIENCY AND ORGANIZATION

Efficiency and good organization are the hallmarks of a well-run stable or program. Efficiency means making the most intelligent use of available resources (including time) and to do the job without wasting time, effort, or money. Organization means planning and putting together different elements into a smoothly working whole. Disorganization and inefficiency make you work harder to accomplish less, often leading to slipshod and substandard horse care, and to becoming harried, frustrated, and overworked to the point of burnout.

Here are some tips for organizing stable management:

- Define your job. What are your most important goals and responsibilities? Which are of secondary importance?
- List the work that must be done: daily chores, weekly and occasional jobs.

- What does each job require (in skills, equipment, time)? Is there a more efficient way to do it?
- Consider how to make the best use of the resources you have, including yourself and other workers. Trying to do everything yourself is less efficient and more stressful than delegating some responsibilities when appropriate.
- Budget your time. Set up a schedule that allows you to do your essential work at the best time for you to accomplish it. Try to identify "time stealers"—activities or people that frequently waste your productive time—and change your schedule to avoid them.
- Communicate with those you work with; have regular meetings to discuss plans, keep everyone informed, and get important input. Post schedules, notes, tasks, and assignments.
- Don't rely on memory. Make it a habit to carry a notebook and write down everything you need to take care of, and check it off as you complete it.
- Set aside a time for keeping up records, paying bills, making phone calls, and other office duties.

STABLE MANAGEMENT RECORDS

Good records are essential for the business and financial aspects of stable management, and for keeping track of horse information, health and farrier care, and other management activities. For records to be useful, they must be complete and accurate. It's important to keep records in a form that is easy to use and in a convenient place, and to keep them up to date.

Horse management records might include:

Individual Horse Records   A file for each horse, containing:

- Name, description, and identification information.
- Registration papers.
- Health record (inoculations, deworming, vet notes, etc.).
- Vital signs (resting pulse, temperature, and respiration rates).
- Shoeing record (dates; notes on type of shoes or special needs).
- Breeding record.
- Insurance documents.

Stable Log Book for daily notes, including work done, medications and treatments, training notes, vet or farrier visits, etc.

Planning Calendar Shows when inoculations, worming, shoeing, and other periodic maintenance are due, and the time of competitions and other events.

Shoeing Chart Lists all horses with individual shoeing notes, dates of farrier visits, and what was done for various horses.

Vehicle and Machinery Records Registrations, warranties, and service records for farm vehicles and equipment.

Business and financial records may include (depending on nature of business):

- Bookkeeping system for recording expenses and income, essential for paying bills promptly and for tax purposes. If clients are billed for stable services, these must be posted and bills sent out on time. File paid bills and receipts in an orderly manner so they are available for accounting and tax purposes.
- Loan, lease, or mortgage and tax records.
- Insurance policies, plus inventory of tack, equipment, and machinery, including value and registration numbers. (Keep a separate copy in a safe deposit box.)
- Contracts and release forms: boarding, training, or lesson contracts; liability release forms (as recommended by your attorney and insurance agent).
- Client records: name, address, phone number, and pertinent information for boarders, students, and so on.
- Vendors and suppliers: list of suppliers from whom you obtain feed, bedding, supplies; repairmen and service facilities; professionals (veterinarians, farriers) with whom you do business.

SAFE AND EFFICIENT HORSE FACILITIES

The first impression you get on entering a stable or horse facility is often a true one. The way it is set up and kept says a lot about the competence and horsemanship of the people in charge. A horse facility need not be elaborate to be excellent; a simple, workmanlike facility that is well organized and intelligently managed provides a better working environment than a fancy facility that is poorly planned or operated.

General Considerations

A horse facility must be designed with *horses* in mind—taking into account the size, behavior, and nature of horses, and the safety of people and horses. It must be designed for durability, efficiency, simplicity, and neatness.

Location, Zoning, and Planning

Before starting, buying, or expanding a horse facility, check with your local building department and zoning board to find out whether local ordinances, zoning restrictions, or homeowner covenants might affect your plans or even prohibit such a facility. Land values, property taxes, utilities, and the cost of complying with local requirements (such as manure disposal and environmental laws) will affect operating costs.

It is important to consider your neighbors, especially in suburban or semirural areas. If your acreage is small or your facility is close to the property line, neighbors may be annoyed by noise, flies, dust, odors, traffic, straying horses, or the appearance of your property. If you are close to a residential area, trespassing children may pose a problem. These factors can lead to legal disputes, liability problems, and increased costs in insurance and security measures. Secure fencing, good sanitation, maintaining a clean and attractive facility, and consideration and good public relations are essential in keeping a good relationship with your neighbors.

Land

The topography of the land (flat, rolling, or steep) and the type of soil (clay, adobe, loam, gravel, or sandy) affect the drainage, the grass and hay grown, footing, and usefulness for a horse facility. Stables, riding areas, paddocks and pastures must be located on well drained soil. Wet or swampy ground and areas prone to poor drainage, runoff or flooding are unhealthy for horses, subject to damage and deterioration, and extremely difficult to maintain. They also breed flies and mosquitoes.

Stables and outside pens must be built on a well-drained site, ideally on top of a knoll or hill. If located below a hill or on poorly drained soil, more site preparation, grading, or filling may be required.

Access

A horse facility needs a hard-surfaced road or driveway capable of handling trucks, farm machinery, and trailers. Parking and traffic patterns (including vehicles, trailers, pedestrians, riders, and led horses) should be taken into account in planning the layout.

Security

Two security concerns are keeping horses safely confined and keeping control of who can enter your facility. A perimeter fence with a gate barring access to the highway is a safety factor. A security light, mounted on the barn or in the yard, makes it easier to check on the horses and discourages intruders at night; a dog can also be a security measure. The stable itself should never be locked, because of the danger of fire, but tack rooms, feed rooms, garages, and storage areas should be secure.

Ventilation

Stabled horses require a constant supply of fresh air for health and comfort, but should not be exposed to drafts, which can cause chills and illness. Good ventilation provides fresh air and carries away excess moisture, ammonia fumes, and odors, and prevents condensation of moisture in cold weather. Horses are healthier and more comfortable in a cold but airy stable (even if blanketing is required) than in a warm barn that is closed up tightly. Consider the following:

- Manure, urine, and soiled bedding produce ammonia fumes, which pollute the air and damage the eyes and respiratory system.
- A horse gives off up to two gallons of moisture daily into the air as he breathes. In cold weather, this moisture condenses and may freeze or drip. The resulting dampness favors the growth of fungus and bacteria, aggravates arthritis and stiffness, and contributes to respiratory ailments.
- Constant exposure to dust, especially when hay is stored in an overhead loft or when the stalls face an indoor arena, can cause or aggravate chronic respiratory problems such as heaves.

A stabled horse needs a minimum of 1,600 square feet of air space. High ceilings, open stall partitions, and windows and doors placed for cross-ventilation help to achieve this. In hot climates, stall partitions are usually made of open gridwork as much as possible, and stall gates may be used instead of solid doors, to promote the free flow of air.

Means of providing ventilation include:

Windows   Placed high, opening at the top or louvered, to direct air upward instead of creating a direct draft on the horse. Windows should be unbreakable (plexiglass or safety glass) and protected by a grid.

VENTILATION METHODS FOR STABLES

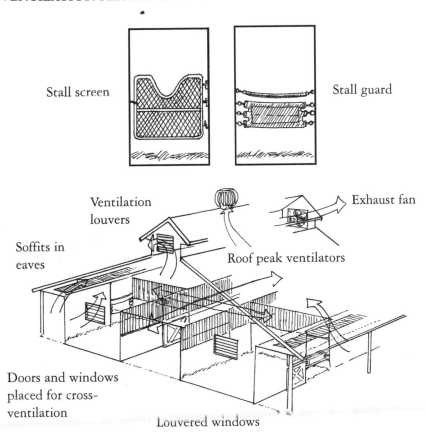

Roof Peak Ventilation   Openings along the ridge of the roof that allow stale air to escape.

Louvers   Overlapping boards, set at an angle with an air passage in between. They may be installed in the upper wall, in the soffits (eaves), or in the gables. They direct fresh air upward and stale air outward.

Exhaust Fan   Power-driven fan in the roof peak, removes stale air.

Stall Fans   In very hot, humid conditions, stalls may be equipped with individual box fans, installed high, out of reach of the horse.

Drainage

Good drainage is essential for a horse facility. Poor drainage results in constant dampness, mud, and possible flooding; such conditions are unhealthy, inefficient, and can lead to damage that is difficult and costly to repair. Solving drainage problems can be expensive, especially if construction is necessary. Expert advice during planning and site preparation and when solving drainage problems can save time, money, and inconvenience.

Drainage depends on location, soil, terrain, rainfall and snow load, and on the design, engineering, and maintenance of the facility. Important factors in regard to drainage include:

- Stables and manure piles must be located on well-drained ground, but not where runoff can contaminate groundwater or streams.
- Areas under eaves and gutters need good drainage and eaveshoots that divert rainwater away from the foundation of the building.
- Stall floors need good drainage for cleanliness, the health of the horse, and to minimize odors and fly population. Methods of providing drainage in stall floors include:
  - Dig floor down and fill with a 24-inch layer of rocks (approximately 1½ to 2 inches in diameter), then a 12-inch layer of ¾ inch crushed stone. Top with a 6-inch layer of clay, leveled and well tamped down.
  - Fill and level stall floor with a 6-inch layer of "blue stone," decomposed limestone, or road base.
  - Sand, limestone or dirt floors can be kept level by installing a stall floor grid, which prevents horses from digging holes.
  - Hard-surfaced floors (concrete, brick, or asphalt) may be sloped slightly toward a concrete gutter at the front or rear, or toward a center drain. These surfaces are better for aisles and wash stalls than for stall floors.
- Drainage problems in large areas such as riding arenas and paddocks may require drainage ditches or a French drain (a ditch filled with crushed rock).

STALL FLOORING AND SUBSOIL

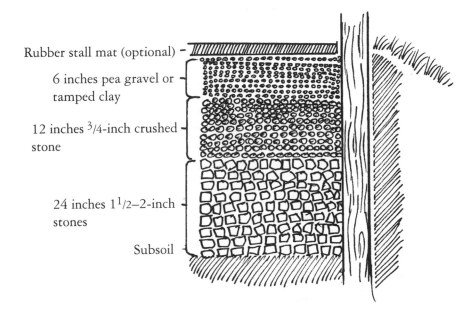

Rubber stall mat (optional)

6 inches pea gravel or
tamped clay

12 inches ³/4-inch crushed
stone

24 inches 1¹/2–2-inch
stones

Subsoil

Utilities

Water   A reliable supply of clean water is essential. In cold climates, pipes must be buried below the frost line, and frost-free hydrants should be installed.

Electricity   Electric service must meet local fire codes. Wiring must be properly grounded and protected from chewing by horses or rodents. Explosion-proof light fixtures (protected by a glass cover and metal cage) should be used.

Stalls

Most modern stables employ box stalls, which allow horses freedom to move and lie down. Straight or standing stalls are sometimes used for day stalls in riding school stables where horses and ponies are kept in pasture.

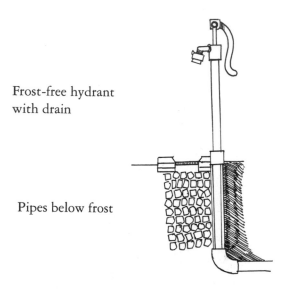

Frost-free hydrant
with drain

Pipes below frost

Stall fittings must be designed and installed so as to prevent a horse from getting caught on them. There must be no gaps in which a horse could catch a leg. (See USPC C manual, pp. 156–158.)

CHART 13-1: STALL SIZE

Type of Stall	Small Pony	Small Horse	Large Horse	Foaling Stall
Box	9' × 9'	10' × 10'	12' × 12'	16' × 16'
Standing	4' × 8'	5' × 10'	6' × 12'	

Aisles, Gates, and Doors

Aisles should be wide enough for safe handling of horses, and to accommodate a tractor and manure spreader (8 feet minimum; 10 to 12 feet is better). They must be kept clear of obstructions.

Gates and doors must be wide enough for a horse and handler (minimum 4 feet wide; $4^1/2$ feet is better), without projecting hardware which can injure a horse or catch on tack or blankets. Swinging doors and gates should open outward (except for metal stall gates designed to hang on the inside of the door). Sliding doors must have a guard to prevent them from being pushed outward at the bottom, creating a dangerous gap.

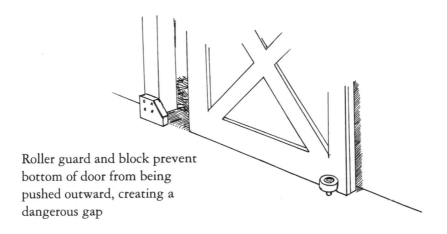

Roller guard and block prevent
bottom of door from being
pushed outward, creating a
dangerous gap

Floors

Floors may be made of several materials; each has good points and
drawbacks. Durability, drainage, comfort, maintenance, and cost of
installation and upkeep are important factors.

CHART 13-2: FLOOR MATERIALS

Material	Suitable For	Drainage
Concrete	Aisles, tack rooms, feed rooms, wash stalls	Needs slope or drain

Notes: Too hard for stall floors. Use texturized concrete for nonslip surface.

Asphalt	Aisles	Needs slope or drain

Notes: Easy to sweep but can be slippery.

Dirt	Stalls, pens	May be muddy

Notes: Horses create holes and uneven surface; needs frequent maintenance; odors linger. Hard to disinfect.

Clay	Stalls	Slow to dry

Notes: Same as dirt.

(Continues)

Material	Suitable For	Drainage
Sand	Pens, outdoor aisles	Good

Notes: Horses may ingest sand along with hay and feed, resulting in sand colic. Heavy; difficult to clean when wet.

Material	Suitable For	Drainage
Wood	Tack room, office	Needs spaces between boards to drain

Notes: Not suitable for aisles and stalls because it is hard and slippery, rots and breaks up, and harbors pests.

Material	Suitable For	Drainage
Bricks	Aisles, tack room	Needs drain or slope

Notes: Expensive to install but durable and attractive. Hard to sweep.

Material	Suitable For	Drainage
Gravel (pea gravel)	Stall base, outdoor aisles	Excellent

Notes: Good traction; hard to keep clean. Stalls require mats over gravel.

Material	Suitable For	Drainage
Road base (limestone/ gravel/dirt mix)	Stalls, aisles	Good

Notes: Can be dusty. May develop holes or uneven surface.

Material	Suitable For	Drainage
Rubber mats	Stalls, aisles, wash stalls	Depends on base underneath

Notes: Good over concrete, gravel, or dirt in aisles; over dirt, sand, gravel, or other base in stalls. Prevents holes, but requires bedding to absorb urine.

Material	Suitable For	Drainage
Stall floor grid	Stalls	Plastic grid to retain stall floor material and keep flooring level

Notes: Use with dirt, gravel, road base, or limestone.

Hay and Bedding Storage

Because of the danger of fire, hay should be stored in a barn, shed, or stack separate from the stable. Storing hay over stalls also increases exposure to dust and spores, which may aggravate respiratory ailments.

Hay should be stacked on pallets, not directly on the ground or on a concrete floor, to prevent moisture damage to the bottom layer. Loose hay is a fire hazard and a breeding place for flies; keep it swept up!

Bedding may be stored in a shed or in the hay barn. Green sawdust can generate heat, so it should not be piled against a wooden building. A two-wheeled garden cart may be used to transport hay and/or bedding to stalls.

Feed Storage

Feed storage must keep feed clean, dry, and safe from rodents, and prevent horses from getting into the feed. There should be clean, rodent-proof storage bins with tight-fitting lids for various types of grain and supplements, scales, measuring cans, and a feed cart.

Large stables may use bulk feed bins equipped with feed chutes or dispensers. Spilled feed should be cleaned up immediately, as it is a breeding ground for flies.

Manure Disposal

A horse produces approximately 35 to 50 pounds of manure per day (up to 10 tons per year); if stabled, wet and soiled bedding may equal the volume of manure. Manure, urine, and soiled bedding must be removed daily, as they harbor bacteria, draw flies, and are destructive to horses' feet and health. Urine releases ammonia gas, which is detrimental to the lungs and eyes of both horses and humans, and also causes tack, paint, and wood to deteriorate.

Horse manure makes excellent fertilizer for farm and garden use, especially when broken down by composting for up to 3 months.

Manure can be managed by:

- Having it hauled away (by a farmer, nursery, or mushroom grower).
- Spreading it on cropland or pastures not grazed by horses. (Spreading fresh manure on horse pastures contaminates the pasture with parasite eggs and larvae.)
- Composting (to be spread or sold later).

To avoid flies and odors, a manure pile must be kept at a distance from the stable, downwind from the stable and house, and away from neighbors' residences. It should be placed on well-drained ground (or better, on a concrete base with 4-foot walls). Because the process of decomposition creates heat, a manure pile should not be placed against a wooden building. It works best to have three manure piles: a "finished" pile ready for use as fertilizer or spreading, one in the process of breaking down, and a "working" pile to which new manure is added daily. Another alternative is to keep adding fresh manure to the end of a pile about 6 feet high and 6 feet wide.

Fly Control

Fly control measures include:

- Sanitation: daily stall cleaning, trash removal, keeping stable area swept clean.
- Keeping manure pile covered and at a distance from the stable.
- Insecticides (fly strips, fogging, periodic automatic sprayers, residual fly sprays, fly bait). Because insecticides are poisonous and can pollute the environment, it is essential to read directions, take all recommended precautions, and obey environmental laws when using and disposing of them. Organophosphate pesticides (found in chemical fly strips) are cumulative; using them in conjunction with certain dewormers can lead to an overdose.
- Fly traps, strips, and flypaper.
- Feed-through fly control products (substances treated to pass through the horse and release insecticide in the manure).
- Fly predators: beneficial insects that destroy fly eggs and larvae in the manure pile. They can be purchased from biological fly control companies.
- Fly repellents and fly masks may be used during turnout and work. Horses may be turned out at night and kept in during the day. Shade or a dark area like a stall or barn provides relief from flies.

Tack Room and Equipment Storage

Tack must be stored in a dry environment, away from direct heat (which cracks leather) and excessive humidity, which causes mildew, and protected from dirt, dust, and rodents. Racks should be designed to allow saddle pads and blankets to air and dry, and saddles and bridles to keep their shape. In winter, heating the tack room to 55 or 60 degrees Fahrenheit helps keep tack in better condition and provides a better working environment. If used, heaters must be safely designed and installed, because of the danger of fire.

A tack room needs cabinets and shelves for storage of supplies, a locked cupboard for medications, and counter space for a work area. A small refrigerator is useful for medications. If the tack room also serves as an office, a desk, chair, and file cabinet will be needed.

To prevent theft, tack rooms must be secure, with solid wood or metal doors, security locks, and windows inaccessible from outside. The tack room should be locked when staff are not present.

A utility room, containing a deep sink with hot and cold water, washing machine, and additional storage space is very helpful, as is a space for storing trunks, blankets, and other large items. Tools, wheelbarrows, muck baskets, and similar equipment must be kept neat, accessible, but out of the way.

Vehicles and Machinery

A horse facility may have some or all of the following maintenance vehicles and machinery:

Tractor   Preferably mid-sized tractor (25 to 27 horsepower) or farm tractor (40 to 70 horsepower), ideally equipped with a power takeoff (PTO) and hydraulically operated three-point hitch for farm machinery. Attachments such as a bucket loader and blade make a tractor more versatile.

Manure Spreader   Ground-driven (powered by turning of the wheels when towed) or powered by the tractor's PTO.

Mower (Rotary, Sickle Bar, or Bush Hog)   For mowing, clearing, and maintaining pastures.

Discs, Harrow, or Chain Drag   For arena surfaces and pasture maintenance.

Utility Trailer, Flatbed Trailer, Wagon, or Dump Cart   For hauling and dumping feed, hay, dirt, stones, and other chores. A flatbed trailer or wagon can be used for hauling hay and transporting jumps.

Post-Hole Digger   For building and repairing fences.

Hay Elevator   For loading bales in mow or high stacks.

Caution: Tractors and farm machinery can be dangerous! Operators must be trained in proper operation and safety practices, and must be aware of hazards to themselves and others. Never remove safety guards or operate machinery in a way for which it was not designed. Machinery and vehicles must be serviced regularly, kept in safe operating condition, and stored in a safe location. Machinery workshops, sheds, and garages should be separate from the stable.

Arenas and Riding Areas

Riding areas may include outdoor rings and jumping fields, trails, and indoor arenas. They must be designed for safety, kept neat, and properly maintained. Important factors include:

Size   Suitable for purpose and number of riders.

- All-purpose outdoor ring: 100 × 200 feet or larger.
- Small dressage arena (also suitable for beginner or small group lessons): 66 × 132 feet (20 × 40 meters).
- Large dressage arena: 66 × 198 feet (20 × 60 meters).
- Jumping field: 150 × 300 feet or larger.
- Longeing ring: 60 feet in diameter.

Footing   Level, well drained, without holes, rocks, wet places, or obstructions. Footing should be secure and provide traction, to prevent slipping. Too hard footing causes soreness and concussion and may be very slippery; too soft or deep footing causes strain on tendons and ligaments.
   Types of footing:

- Natural turf: ideal, but is quickly cut up by overuse or use in wet weather; requires careful maintenance.
- Dirt: dusty; muddy when wet; packs down hard; may be rocky or uneven.
- Sand: dusty; nonslip even when wet, but can cause fatigue, muscle soreness, and tendon strains if too deep.
- Wood surfaces (fiber, shavings, sawdust, tanbark): more resilient than sand but somewhat more slippery; less suitable for jumping. Wood eventually becomes dusty as material breaks down into small particles.
- Rubber particles: resilient and nonslip; often mixed with sand or installed over a sand base.

- Mixed footings: sand mixed with wood, rubber, fibers, or other particles to provide more stability than lighter materials, more resilience than sand alone.
- New footing materials are constantly being developed, both for indoor and outdoor applications.

Dust Control   Dust may be controlled by watering (by hand, lawn sprinklers, or automatic watering system). Some footings (dirt, sawdust, sandy loam) may be oiled to keep down dust.

Maintenance   Arenas should be dragged with a harrow, chain drag, or leveler, as often as necessary to prevent the footing from becoming hard-packed or uneven, especially along the track, in the corners, and around jumps. Turf arenas and jumping fields are easily damaged by overuse, especially in wet weather; they need mowing, rolling, fertilizing, and rotation of jumps, to prevent wearing out the turf.

FACILITY MAINTENANCE

Maintenance is one of the most important aspects of stable management. Horses and people are hard on equipment and their environment. Major and minor breakages occur, and daily wear and tear takes its toll. Without constant maintenance, a facility quickly deteriorates and becomes unsafe. Neglecting small repairs or maintenance jobs can result in breakdowns, accidents, or losses requiring a costly major overhaul.

In order to maintain the facility, property, and equipment, someone must be responsible for carrying out routine maintenance and repairs. This person needs to have the necessary skills and knowledge, the proper tools, and time. A horse facility needs a workshop area and tools for maintenance and repairs.

Routine Maintenance

Daily maintenance chores depend on the size and complexity of the facility and the season. Every facility needs a workshop, tools, and maintenance supplies so that repairs and maintenance can be done as needed. Routine maintenance jobs in many stables might include the following:

- Check stalls, aisles, fences, and working areas daily during chores; fix minor items (pulling out a nail or fixing a faulty latch) immediately.
- Check pastures and paddocks (fences, water supply, operation of electric fencer, etc.), and make any necessary repairs.
- Cleaning, sweeping, dusting, removing cobwebs, removing trash.
- Drag/level arena footing.
- Cleaning of public and office areas, bathrooms, etc.
- Landscaping maintenance chores (mowing, snow plowing, and maintaining drives, walkways, and parking lot).
- Check and service vehicles and machinery.
- Repairs, rebuilding, and improvements to facility.
- Seasonal maintenance (winterizing, etc.) of buildings, pastures, vehicles, and machinery.
- Periodic cleaning and organization of feed rooms, tack rooms, storage areas, and so on.

CHAPTER 14

Bandaging

This chapter covers bandaging materials and techniques for special purposes, including tail wraps, exercise bandages, and various types of treatment bandages. An introduction to bandaging, including shipping and stable bandages, is found in the *USPC C Manual of Horsemanship, Book 2*.

BANDAGING MATERIALS

In addition to the bandage materials discussed in the USPC C Manual (Book 2), the following materials may be used for special-purpose bandages:

Bandages (Wraps)

Elastic Crepe Bandage (VetRap™, Other Brands) Self-adhering elastic bandage sold in tack shops. Excellent for bandaging hard-to-reach areas such as heel grabs, hoof wraps, and pressure bandages. Reusable once or twice.

Ace Bandage Elastic bandage sold in drugstores and tack shops. Because it is very stretchy, care must be taken not to pull it tightly enough to cut off circulation. The 6-inch width works well with an ice pack, as it will contract as the ice melts.

Elastic Adhesive Bandage (Elastoplast™, Elastikon™)   Strong elastic adhesive bandage, used mainly for bandaging wounds. It can be used to wrap around a foot that has thrown a shoe to prevent the wall from chipping. Available in several widths from veterinarians, drugstores, and tack shops.

Conforming Gauze   Gauze rolls of various widths, with some ability to stretch. It conforms gently to the contours of even hard-to-bandage areas, and is used mostly to hold wound dressings in place.

Super K Vet Wrap™   4-inch-wide roll of synthetic cotton, nylon reinforced for added durability. Because it conforms to the contours of a leg, it is useful for holding wound dressings in place. However, it is not sturdy enough for an outside wrap.

Padding and Dressing Materials

Kendall Cottons™   Sheets of synthetic cotton, about 1/8 inch thick, nylon reinforced for durability. They are conforming, can be cut to size, and can be rinsed carefully. They can be used to cover dressings and as leg pads for exercise bandages, but be careful to use enough padding and to avoid wrinkles.

Nonstick Sterile Gauze Dressings   Available in roll form or in square pads; 4 × 4 inches is most useful. Applied to a wound after cleaning and medication, they keep the healing wound from adhering to the bandage.

Quilts   Durable quilted cotton pads, available ready-made, or can be made from quilted mattress covers. Two problems are that the ready-made quilts are often too short for shipping bandages, and the sewn seams or binding may cause ripples that prevent the pad from conforming to the leg, creating pressure points.

Packaged Paddings   Ready-made packaged paddings are sold in tack stores. They come in a variety of materials, including polyester, cotton sheets covered with cheesecloth, synthetic felt, and combinations, including a layer of foam rubber. Most are machine washable.

Other dressing materials:

U.S. Army Sterile Compress and Bandage Large sterile wound dressing made of cotton between a layer of paper and muslin, available from surplus stores and some tack shops. It is inexpensive, large, and thick enough to serve for a shipping bandage, but cannot be washed or reused.

Disposable Diapers Large-size square type (without elastic edges) can be used for a variety of padding purposes. The plastic backing can be used to make a sweat bandage, but must be removed for other bandages.

Terrycloth Towels Effective padding for wet applications, such as cold-water bandages or ice packs.

Sanitary Napkins Thick, clean, and absorbent, they make an effective first-aid pad to stop bleeding.

Special Purpose Bandages

Polo Wraps (Sandown Bandages) Washable synthetic fleece bandages, with some stretch. Used in polo to protect against accidental mallet blows, they are popular for protection during work, longeing, and turnout.

Properly applied exercise bandages are preferred over polo wraps for Pony Club use. The drawbacks of polo wraps are that they are used without padding underneath, which can result in "cording" or tendon damage if improperly applied. In addition, they are more likely to slip or come unfastened than a correctly applied exercise bandage.

Foam-Padded Elastic Bandage Specialized bandage with foam rubber adhered to the inside of the elastic, used for exercise bandages.

Gel Packs and Cooling Wraps Made of a special gel that retains cold, these items can be cooled in a freezer and applied in place of an ice pack.

TAIL WRAPS

Tail wraps are used to protect the hair of the dock during shipping. They are also used to confine the tail hairs out of the way during breeding, foaling, and body clipping, and to shape the hair of the dock or to protect a braided tail before a show.

Tail wraps may be cotton or synthetic stockinette knitted bandages, or synthetic crepe (Vetrap™, etc.). Ace bandages are sometimes used, but must never be applied too tightly or for too long, which can cut off circulation and cause damage to the dock. Tail wraps should be fastened with Velcro, pins, or tape, not string ties, which may cause a ring of pressure around the dock.

Tail Wrap (To Shape Top of Tail/Protect Braided Tail)

MATERIALS NEEDED:
1. Stretchy bandage such as a cotton or polyester knitted track bandage, elastic crepe bandage, or Ace bandage.
   Caution: An Ace bandage should not be left on for more than half an hour.
2. Fasteners: Velcro closure or strips of masking tape.

PROCEDURE:
1. Dampen the tail hair slightly. *Caution: Do not wet the bandage, as it may shrink.*
2. Start the bandage close to the top of the tail. Wrap around once to secure the end of the bandage, then wrap up to the very top of the tail.
3. Wrap downward to the end of the dock, then upward to the end of the bandage.
4. Fasten with strips of tape or Velcro closure, but not tightly enough to cause an indentation, and not in a continuous ring.
5. To remove the bandage from an unbraided tail, grasp the bandage firmly with the fingers hooked over the top of the bandage and pull straight down. For a braided tail, unwrap the bandage.

Tail Wrap (To Contain Tail Hairs for Foaling, Breeding, or Body Clipping)

MATERIALS NEEDED:
As above; elastic crepe bandage (Vetrap™) works best.

Tail Bandage (to lay hair of dock)

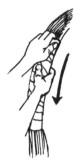

Removing tail bandage

PROCEDURE:
1. Braid the skirt of the tail into a long single braid and fold it up over the dock.
2. Proceed as above, wrapping over the dock and braided skirt.

Tail Wrap (To Protect Tail during Shipping)

MATERIALS NEEDED:
As above; cotton or polyester stockinette bandage preferred.

PROCEDURE:
1. Start as above and wrap downward for 8 to 10 inches.
2. To prevent the bandage from slipping off, separate a few hairs from the side of the tail and hold them upward while taking one wrap over them. Then fold the hairs downward and wrap over them again. Repeat this once or twice more.

3. To keep the skirt clean and tangle-free during shipping:
   - Slip a nylon stocking over the skirt; fasten it to the tail bandage with safety pins.
   - Bandage over the skirt of the tail. A second bandage may be used if the first is not long enough.

Caution: Tail wraps must not be left on for extended periods, or they can cause loss of hair, tissue damage, sores, and in extreme cases, gangrene, requiring amputation of the tail. Do not use tail wraps for long trips; for this purpose, a tail guard (made of padded leather or synthetic material) is safer.

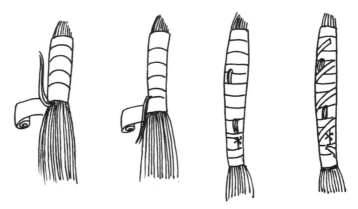

Nonslip Tail Bandage (for shipping)

Tail Bandage (to cover skirt of tail)

EXERCISE BANDAGES

Exercise bandages protect the lower legs, especially the flexor tendons and suspensory ligaments, during work. They are used when horses are more likely to strike themselves or require extra protection, especially during longeing, lateral work, galloping, and jumping, and on young horses or horses recovering from a leg injury. It was previously thought that exercise bandages supported the flexor tendons and suspensory ligaments, but most experts now believe that they offer protection rather than significant support. Exercise bandages are always applied in pairs (i.e., both front legs or both hind legs).

Exercise wraps extend from just below the knee or hock joint to the fetlock joint. Care must be taken not to restrict the movement of the fetlock joint.

Caution: Exercise bandages **must** *be applied correctly or they may do great harm.* They are applied over parts of the leg that are vulnerable to injury, and are used during demanding athletic work. An improperly applied bandage can restrict movement of the fetlock joint and can damage or even bow a tendon. A too loose or incorrectly fastened bandage can slip down or come undone and cause a serious stumble.

To learn to apply exercise bandages, you must have hands-on instruction from an expert. If your horse requires lower leg protection and you are not experienced enough to put exercise bandages on correctly, it is safer to use protective boots such as galloping boots.

Exercise Bandages

MATERIALS NEEDED:

1. Elastic crepe bandage (VetRap™ or other brand) is preferred. Saratoga™ bandages are preferable for use in wet conditions because they do not absorb water. Cotton or polyester stockinette "track" bandages are less satisfactory, as they have less stretch and tend to become heavy and loosen when wet.
2. Leg padding: Sheet cottons folded or cut to fit, or Kendall™ cottons. Leg padding is thinner than that used in stable bandages, but must be thick enough to compress and to distribute the pressure of the wraps. Padding must be wrinkle free, as wrinkles cause areas of uneven pressure.
3. Fasteners: Safety pins; for sewn fastening, needle and carpet thread.

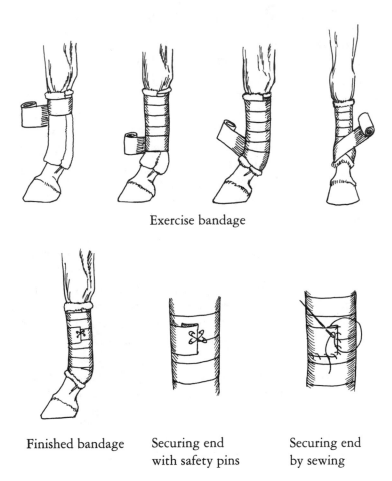

Exercise bandage

Finished bandage   Securing end   Securing end
                     with safety pins   by sewing

PROCEDURE:

1. Start ¹/2 inch from the top, on the outside of the leg, with the end of the wrap tucked inside the edge of the leg pad. Wrap from front to back and outside to inside.
2. Wrap down the leg, keeping each wrap horizontal and parallel to the last wrap, and overlapping each wrap by about ¹/2 the width of the bandage. When wrapping, pull backward against the shin, not forward against the tendon, and keep the tension even.
3. At the fetlock joint, drop one half width of wrap down under the back of the joint, bringing it up to the top of the fetlock joint in front to form an upside down **V**. This protects the fetlock joint and

the suspensory ligament, while still allowing free movement of the joint.

4. Wrap back up the leg, taking care not to wrap too tightly. Finish the bandage on the outside of the leg, at the middle of the cannon bone. If necessary, fold any excess bandage underneath itself.

5. Fasten the bandage securely. For fast work, the end of the bandage should be sewn down. Safety pins may be used for ordinary work.
   - Two safety pins, applied horizontally through several layers of bandage and padding.
   - Sewn fastening: using a large needle and carpet thread, sew the end of the bandage to the wraps underneath. (A curved needle is easiest to use.)
   - Do not use tape on exercise bandages, especially in a continuous ring around the leg.

Polo Wraps

Polo wraps are often used in place of exercise bandages for longeing, schooling, turnout, and ring work. They are not recommended for jumping or cross-country work because they are not as secure or as protective as correctly applied exercise bandages or galloping boots. Polo wraps are not permitted in USPC competition.

How to Apply Polo Wraps

MATERIALS NEEDED:
   Fleece polo or sandown bandages (usually used on all four legs).

PROCEDURE:
1. Unroll 8 to 10 inches of bandage. Starting at the back of the knee or hock, hold the bandage end diagonally across the outside of the knee or hock, with the end toward the front of the horse.
2. Take one turn around the leg, over the base of the diagonal bandage end.
3. Fold the bandage end downward, over the first wrap and down the back of the flexor tendons. This cushions the tendons and keeps the bandage from slipping.
4. Wrap downward, over the bandage end, keeping each wrap parallel to the last, overlapping half the width of the bandage and keeping the tension even.

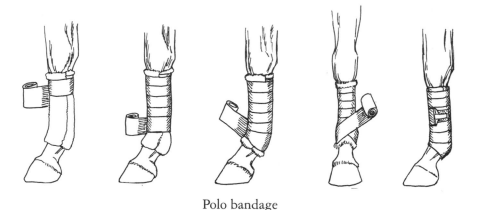

Polo bandage

5. At the fetlock joint, drop half the width of the bandage down underneath the joint, bringing it up in front to form an upside-down **V**. It should not be loose, but must not be tight enough to restrict movement of the fetlock joint.
6. Wrap upward and finish the bandage on the outside of the cannon bone (not on the tendon, shin, or fetlock joint). Most polo wraps have Velcro closures. These should be reinforced with pins or spiraled tape.

TREATMENT BANDAGES

Treatment bandages are used to treat and protect wounds, sprains, strains, and other injuries, or to prevent swelling caused by a recent injury.

When bandaging a wound, the wound should be cleaned and treated and a dressing applied. The padding and bandage should be applied in the direction that best supports closure of the wound.

Treatment bandages may be left in place for varying periods, depending on their purpose. Wound dressings are usually not removed more often than once a day, to avoid disturbing the healing surface too often. Ice packs and cold water bandages are usually used for relatively short periods (twenty minutes to several hours), while a sweat or a poultice may be left on for twelve hours or so.

Follow the veterinarian's instructions on how often to change treatment bandages.

Caution: The following are special-purpose bandages that must be applied by an experienced person, along with the proper course of treatment.

Pressure Bandage

A pressure bandage may be used to stop bleeding, to prevent swelling caused by a recent injury, or to inhibit the formation of proud flesh. It is applied snugly, with sufficient padding to create a uniform counter-pressure that prevents swelling or stops hemorrhage.

MATERIALS:

Depending on the kind of wound and the purpose of the pressure bandage, any of the following materials may be used:

1. Dressing or pressure pad (sterile nonstick gauze pads are preferable); sanitary napkins are good for stopping bleeding.
2. Leg padding: sheet cotton or equivalent, folded to fit.
3. Wraps: Elastic adhesive tape (Elastikon™, Elastoplast™), Vetrap™ (preferred for bandaging heel grabs), Ace bandage, or knit stockinette "track" bandage.
4. Fasteners: Safety pins and/or strips of masking tape.
5. Duct tape: used to protect the bottom of a bandage used on the hoof.

PROCEDURE:

1. To hold the edges of a cut together or to inhibit the growth of proud flesh, use a sterile gauze dressing covered by a few layers of padding, then two pieces of sheet cotton. Wrap with elastic adhesive tape or Vetrap™, using firm, even pressure. The leg pad and bandage should be applied in the direction that best supports closure of the wound.
2. To stop bleeding, a pressure bandage must be applied quickly and proficiently. The wound should usually be cleaned first, but if bleeding is serious, skip this step and apply pressure at once. Place a clean pad (sterile gauze pad or sanitary napkin, if available) over the wound and apply elastic adhesive tape or VetRap™ directly over the pad. If blood soaks through the pad and bandage, do not remove the first pad, but add more over it. Removing

PRESSURE BANDAGE TO CONTROL BLEEDING

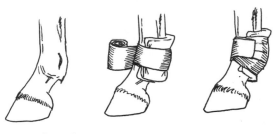

Place dressing   Secure with firm,
pad over wound   even wraps

PRESSURE BANDAGE FOR HEEL GRAB (OVERREACH INJURY)

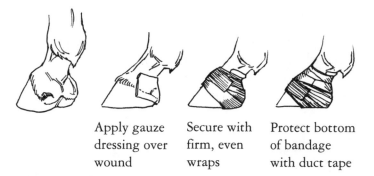

Apply gauze   Secure with   Protect bottom
dressing over   firm, even   of bandage
wound   wraps   with duct tape

the pad may cause bleeding to start again; this should be left to the veterinarian. This type of pressure bandage should not be left in place for more than a few hours, and must not cut off circulation.

3. To treat a heel grab (overreach injury), clean the wound and apply Nitrafurazone or another mild topical ointment. Cover with a sterile gauze dressing, then wrap the heel, coronary band and foot with elastic adhesive tape or VetRap™. Wrap tightly enough to hold the edges of the wound together so it can heal. The bottom part of the wrap can be protected with duct tape, but do not use duct tape above the coronary band.

Poultice

A poultice is a "drawing" medication that draws infection or inflammation from wounds such as puncture wounds, or reduces the inflammation, (pain, heat, and swelling) that accompany a sprain or bruise. Poultices are sometimes used on tendons as a precautionary measure, to prevent swelling or "filling," after especially hard work. A hot poultice is used to increase circulation; a cold one is used to decrease heat and inflammation.

MATERIALS:
1. Bandage and leg padding (of a type suitable for the area to be poulticed).
2. 4 × 4-inch gauze pad (unfolded), or gauze material.
3. Brown paper bag or newspaper.
4. Plastic food wrap.
5. One leg cut from a pair of pantyhose.
6. Poultice material such as Antiphlogistine™ or poultice powder.

APPLYING A POULTICE

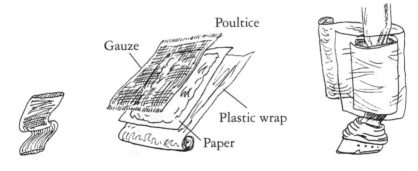

Cut piece of pantyhose

Prepare poultice

Gauze
Poultice
Plastic wrap
Paper

Place poultice on leg, paper side out; cover with plastic wrap

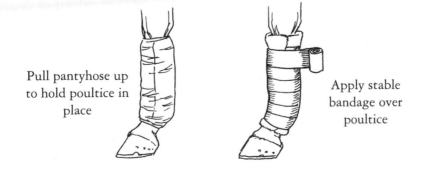

Pull pantyhose up to hold poultice in place

Apply stable bandage over poultice

PROCEDURE:

1. Prepare the poultice according to manufacturer's directions. For a hot poultice, mix poultice powder with warm water, heat in a double boiler, or place poultice on brown paper and heat in a microwave oven. The poultice must be warm, not hot, as it will hold heat for a considerable length of time and can burn the leg if it is too hot.
2. Cut paper to the size of the padding. Apply the poultice to the paper and form it to the size and shape of the area to be covered, 1/4 inch thick. To make removal easier, cover the poultice with gauze material.
3. Clean the horse's leg, and place pantyhose over the foot. Then apply the entire pack (gauze side next to the horse) to the area to be poulticed. Cover with plastic wrap to keep in the moisture and heat. Pull up the pantyhose, which will help keep the poultice in place as you bandage.
4. Place padding over the wrap and bandage.
5. Leave on for twelve to twenty-four hours. When the poultice is removed, any remaining poultice material should be washed off the leg with soap and water.

Sweat Bandage

A sweat bandage is used to reduce swelling by increasing blood circulation through heat application. Sweats are usually used for swellings that are more than forty-eight hours old; a fresh injury usually benefits more from cold applications. A sweat is left on for eight hours and then removed. It can be repeated if necessary.

Sweat bandages should not be applied over liniments, blistering agents, or leg paints, or they may cause blistering of the skin.

MATERIALS:

1. Sweat medication: Nitrafurazone ointment, or other sweat medication approved by your veterinarian.
2. Plastic wrap, brown paper bag, or newspaper; or disposable diaper with the plastic liner left intact.
3. Bandage and leg padding suitable for area to be sweated.

PROCEDURE:
1. Wash the leg and allow it to dry.
2. Apply Nitrafurazone ointment or sweat medication, rubbing it in as directed.
3. Cover the area lightly with plastic wrap, newspaper or brown paper; do not pull it tight.
4. Place padding over the leg and bandage.

Ice Packs

An ice pack is used to reduce pain, heat, and swelling due to a recent injury, especially sprains, strains, and bruises. For best effect, ice packs should be applied to the injury as soon as possible and left on for twenty to thirty minutes at a time, repeating as often as necessary. Cold applications are most effective immediately after an injury and for the first forty-eight hours.

MATERIALS:
1. Two Ace bandages, 6 inches wide.
2. Padding: terrycloth towels are most effective.
3. Two plastic bags (food storage size) with zipper closures or freezer tape.
4. Ice or gel cooling packs. A bag of frozen peas or corn works well as an ice pack, as it conforms easily to the shape of the leg.
5. Fasteners: Safety pins work best.

PROCEDURE:
1. If using ice, double-bag the plastic bags; fill with chopped ice and tape them shut. Gel cooling packs must be placed in the freezer to cool them before use.
2. Apply the cold pack to the injured area, and wrap with several layers of terrycloth towel for insulation as well as padding.
3. Wrap an Ace bandage firmly over the ice and towels, and fasten with safety pins.
4. When the ice begins to melt, apply the second Ace bandage over the first to keep the whole application from sagging away from the injury site.

5. Remove the entire wrap as soon as the ice is melted, or it will become a sweat wrap, producing heat instead of cold. Apply fresh ice packs as often as necessary.

Cold Water Bandages

Cold-water bandages are used to apply cold and pressure to a hot, strained leg. They are most effective when applied after cold-hosing (see USPC C Manual, Book 2, p. 232).

Cold-water bandages must be kept wet. If allowed to dry, they may shrink and cause excessive or uneven pressure, compounding the injury. For this reason, they cannot be left on overnight.

MATERIALS:
1. Knit stockinette "track" wrap.
2. Padding that is durable when wet (preferably terrycloth towels).
3. Fasteners other than tape (safety pins are best).
4. Bucket of ice water.
5. Petroleum jelly (Vaseline™).

PROCEDURE:
1. Apply petroleum jelly to the skin of the heels and pastern, to protect against chapping.
2. Soak the padding in ice water until it is thoroughly wet and cold.
3. Without wringing it out, apply the padding to the leg. Bandage snugly, as pressure is part of the purpose of this wrap.
4. Frequently run cold water over the entire wrap, especially between the leg and the padding. Keep the entire bandage wet.

BANDAGING THE KNEE AND HOCK

Bandaging joints such as the knee and hock presents special problems. It is more difficult to achieve uniform pressure, and a bandage must not bind or apply excessive pressure to bony prominences like the back of the knee or the point of the hock. In some cases, the purpose of the bandage is to restrict or prevent movement of the joint; in others, the bandage must remain in place without slipping even though there will be some movement.

Immobilizing Bandage

An immobilizing bandage is used to prevent movement of a joint. It should be used only on the advice of a veterinarian, or as a temporary emergency measure to stabilize the leg if a fracture is suspected.

MATERIALS:
1. Many layers of padding, depending on the application. Large terrycloth towels or large bed pillows work well.
2. Several track or flannel bandages, Ace bandages, or a spider bandage (see below).
3. Splints (suitable lengths of PVC pipe, cut in half): These should be applied only by a veterinarian, because of the dangers of cutting off circulation, or puncturing the joint if the splint should break.
4. Fasteners: safety pins.

PROCEDURE:
1. Apply a stable bandage to the leg below the immobilizing bandage.
2. Wrap the padding around the joint. If it is unwieldy, it can be held in place by an Ace bandage. Bandage with very firm pressure, to compress the padding evenly; end the bandage on the outside of the leg.

Spider (Many-Tailed) Bandage

A spider bandage is used to protect thick wraps covering a joint or, over large, bulky padding, as an immobilizing bandage.

MATERIALS:
1. Spider or many-tailed bandage, made from a large piece of fabric such as bandage flannel, a T-shirt, or blanket material. It should measure 24 × 30 inches. The two ends are cut into 10-inch strips roughly $1^1/2$ inches wide, leaving a 10- to 12-inch section in the middle.
2. Sufficient padding to protect bony prominences on the knee or hock; terrycloth towels or sheet cottons work well.
3. Wound dressings and medications, if needed.
4. Leg pad and wrap for stable bandage, to be applied below the spider bandage.

SPIDER (MANY-TAILED) BANDAGE FOR KNEE OR HOCK

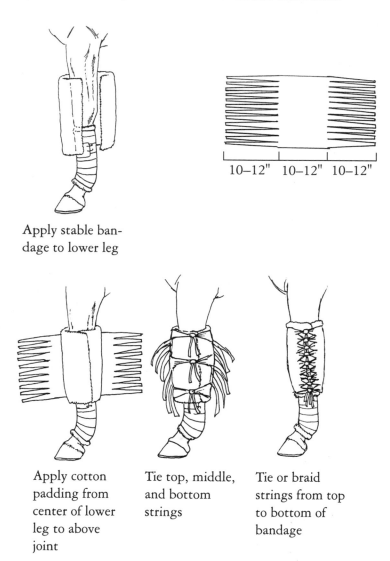

Apply stable bandage to lower leg

10–12" 10–12" 10–12"

Apply cotton padding from center of lower leg to above joint

Tie top, middle, and bottom strings

Tie or braid strings from top to bottom of bandage

PROCEDURES:

1. Apply a stable bandage to the leg below the knee or hock to be bandaged. This keeps the spider bandage in place and helps to prevent swelling of the leg below the joint.
2. Apply dressing and medication as needed, then cover the joint with padding (terrycloth towels or sheet cotton) that extends from mid-cannon to mid-forearm or mid-gaskin. There must be

sufficient padding to prevent pressure damage to the Achilles tendon above the hock, the point of the hock, or the bony prominence at the back of the knee.

3. Place the spider bandage over the joint with the middle of the bandage over the front of the knee, or over the back of the hock. The "tails" or strips will be tied on the outside of the joint.

4. Start by tying at the middle, to hold the bandage in place. Then begin at the top, tying each set of ties in a square knot. Tuck the ends of the previous knot under the next one, to eliminate loose ends.

5. Another method is to braid the ties, using a French braid as in braiding a tail. This method conforms better to the leg as it moves, and is less likely to cause pressure points than knots.

Figure-8 Bandage

A figure-8 bandage is used to wrap joints such as the knee or hock. It allows some mobility in the joint, so it is not suitable for an immobilizing bandage.

MATERIALS:
1. Wrap and padding for a stable bandage, to be applied below the figure-8 bandage.
2. Sufficient padding for the joint; terrycloth towels or sheet cottons.
3. Several long bandages (knit stockinette "track" bandages work best).
4. Dressing and/or medication, as needed.
5. Fasteners (safety pins).

PROCEDURES:
1. Apply a stable bandage to the leg below the joint, to prevent swelling of the lower leg, and to keep the figure-8 bandage from slipping down.
2. Apply wound dressing and/or medication, as indicated.
3. Place padding around the joint, from mid-cannon to mid-forearm or mid-gaskin.
4. Begin wrapping at the bottom of the padding. Make several turns to secure it, working upward and overlapping each wrap by half the width of the bandage.
5. For the hock: Pass bandage diagonally upward, across the front of the hock. Take one complete wrap around the gaskin. Then pass

FIGURE-EIGHT BANDAGE (KNEE)

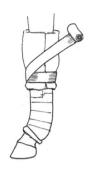
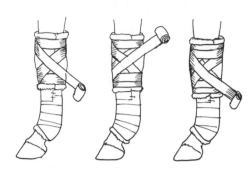

Apply stable bandage to lower leg

Apply cotton pading from center of lower leg to above joint

Anchor bandage and apply in cross-over pattern

Fasten bandage on outside of leg; crossover point should be opposite to site of injury

the bandage diagonally downward, across the front of the hock, and take a complete wrap around the base of the hock. This forms a figure 8, with the crossover point on the front of the hock, allowing the joint to remain mobile. Repeat this process (diagonally upward, complete wrap, diagonally downward, and complete wrap) until reaching the end of the bandage. Try to finish the bandage at the bottom of the wrap, making one or two wraps to complete the bandage.

6. For the knee: When bandaging a knee, the same method is used. The crossover point may be either on the front of the knee or on the back of the knee. Normally, the crossover point is opposite the site of the injury.

CHAPTER 15

•••••••••••••••

Travel Safety

This chapter includes trailer and tow vehicle maintenance checklists, training horses to load, and tips for transporting horses that are difficult travelers. More information on travel preparation, long-distance trips, and safe loading and unloading can be found in the travel safety chapters of the USPC D and C Manuals, Books 1 and 2.

TRAILER CARE AND MAINTENANCE

If you have your own trailer, you should learn how to check the trailer and tow vehicle before a trip. Even if you are not yet old enough to drive or trailer horses yourself, you can be responsible for (or at least help with) regular trailer maintenance chores like:

- Cleaning out the trailer after every trip. (Leaving manure and urine in the trailer will rot the floorboards.)
- Checking air pressure in the tires, and checking the tires for cuts, bulges, or uneven wear (once a week, and before a trip).
- Pulling out the floor mats, cleaning the mats and the floor underneath, and inspecting the floor. (If you can push a penknife blade into the floorboards, there may be a rotten spot. You should check the floor before using the trailer, because a rotten board might give way under a horse.)

411

- Checking and lubricating the trailer nose wheel, jack, hitch coupler, and tailgate or trailer doors (especially if the trailer is stored outside).
- Checking and lubricating the hitch receiver and electrical receptacle on the tow vehicle, and keeping them free from rust and corrosion.
- Washing and waxing the trailer, and cleaning the interior with soap and water (once a month).

TOW VEHICLE AND TRAILER HITCH

A vehicle used to tow a horse trailer must be in excellent running condition, and must be capable of the task. Subcompacts or "mini" vehicles are not suitable for this purpose, especially in hilly terrain. A full-sized or 3/4-ton vehicle, with a heavy-duty tow package, is the best choice. Too light a vehicle may lack the braking capacity to handle a heavy trailer, and the engine, drive train, and transmission will quickly wear out if overloaded.

The tow vehicle must be equipped with a Class III heavy-duty hitch, and the trailer must be balanced so that it is level when it is hitched. When pulling a tow-behind trailer, a weight-distributing hitch, equipped with torsion bars, distributes the tongue weight over all four vehicle wheels instead of placing it mainly over the rear wheels. This results in less wear and tear on the tow vehicle and better control of the trailer, with less tendency to sway. Gooseneck trailers require a special hitch installed in the bed of a pickup truck. All trailer hitches must be designed for the tow vehicle (requirements of different years and models vary) and the weight of the trailer, and installed by an expert.

The trailer hitch should be adjusted so that the trailer, hitch, and tow vehicle are level when loaded. If the trailer is high in front, it increases the wear on the tow vehicle and forces the horses to ride on a sloping surface, which is tiring. A trailer that is low in front is even worse, as this increases the likelihood of sway and may result in loss of control in an emergency.

The tow vehicle and trailer should be checked and serviced regularly, especially before a long trip. Towing puts more strain on the engine, cooling system, transmission, and tires than ordinary driving, so these points are especially important. A breakdown is a problem at any time, but when towing horses, it can become a much larger problem. Be sure to carry the necessary equipment (see the trailer equipment checklist) to handle any problems that might occur while on the road.

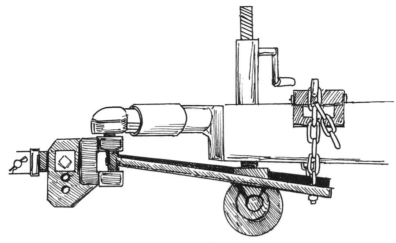

Weight-distributing hitch with torsion bars

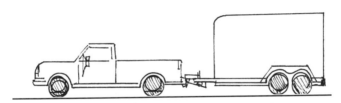

Right: trailer and tow vehicle level

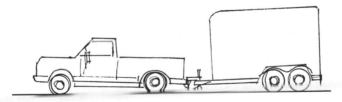

Wrong: trailer low in front (unsafe)

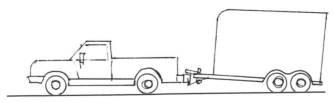

Wrong: trailer high in front

YEARLY MAINTENANCE PROGRAM
FOR A TRAILER OR HORSE VAN

Horse vans, trailers, and tow vehicles must be well maintained for the safety of people and horses. You probably don't tow your trailer or drive the van as frequently as you drive your car, and when you do, you may be concentrating on the horses, or the event you are going to, instead of the vehicle. If the trailer or van is forgotten until you are going somewhere, it is a perfect setup for neglected maintenance and a costly and potentially dangerous breakdown. Maintenance must be done on a regular schedule, even if the trailer or van is used irregularly.

Some vans and trailers are used heavily during the competition or hunting season, and out of service for the winter. Your yearly maintenance schedule should take into account seasonal changes in storage, use, climate, and road conditions.

Here are some points to remember about year-round van and trailer maintenance:

- Use the safety checklist for your van or trailer and tow vehicle before *every* trip, no matter how short.
- Clean and check the trailer or van after each trip, and attend to any minor repairs or maintenance chores promptly.
- Set up a yearly maintenance plan with a mechanic who knows your vehicle, including the following points:
  - Annual inspection, including brakes, lights, signals, and hitch safety devices, as required by your state vehicle code.
  - Annual safety inspection, scheduled before using the trailer (usually in spring), including:
    - Check floor, supports, and braces.
    - Check interior for loose welds, rust, sharp edges, exposed wiring.
    - Check partitions, doors, latches, butt bars, and tailgate for soundness, security, and proper operation.
    - Check axles, spindles, and suspension or springs; lubricate as needed.
    - Check brake system and its operation, including emergency breakaway braking system.
    - Check coupler for proper operation, correct size ball, safety chains, locking pins; lubricate as needed.
    - Check electrical plug, receptacle, and wiring. Use WD-40 or protective spray to protect contacts against corrosion.

- Check balance of trailer and hitch when hitched to tow vehicle; have height of hitch and torsion bars adjusted so that hitch and trailer are level. Riding uphill puts more strain on the tow vehicle; riding downhill causes poor balance of trailer and can be dangerous.
  - Check tires for wear, balance, and proper inflation (including spare).
- Trailer wheel bearings should be cleaned and repacked once a year.
- A horse van is essentially a large truck. It should be maintained and serviced regularly by a truck mechanic, who can help you set up a regular maintenance program, with special attention to the engine, transmission, tires, suspension, and chassis.
- If possible, park a van or trailer under cover, on a hard, dry surface. Exposure to weather (especially strong sunlight) causes tires and exterior finish to deteriorate. Wash and wax it regularly (frequency depends on use, climate, and exposure to mud and road salt).

TRAILER SAFETY CHECKLIST

The following items should be checked on the trailer and tow vehicle *every time* you tow a trailer, even for short trips. (You may want to copy this list and keep it in the tow vehicle.)

On the tow vehicle, check:

- Fluid levels: oil, transmission fluid, brake fluid, and radiator. Check engine belts and hoses. Fill up fuel.
- Tire pressure: examine tires for cracks, bulges or signs of excessive wear. (For trucks with dual tires: strike the inside tire with a hammer. If the air pressure is okay, the hammer will bounce back.)
- Hitch and receiver (no rust, loose bolts, or cracked welds, ball is correct size for trailer and is tight).
- Electrical connectors and wiring on both vehicles (no loose connectors or broken wires).
- With the trailer hitched, test the brakes and trailer brake controller, and adjust trailer brakes for the load. Check running lights, turn indicators, and brake lights.

On the trailer, check:

- Hitch and coupling (be sure coupler fastens securely over ball).

- The battery and cable of the trailer's breakaway system. Check safety chains, hooks, and points where they connect.
- Tire pressure and condition of all tires.
- Signal and brake lights, running lights, and emergency flashers.
- Trailer floor for soundness (no signs of rot); mats in place.
- Interior for wasp or hornet nests. (These can appear within a day!)

Be sure you have:

- Spare tires and tire-changing equipment for tow vehicle and trailer.
- Registration for both tow vehicle and trailer, with current inspection stamp; insurance card.
- Maps, directions, and phone numbers if needed.
- Coggins tests, health papers, and any other transport papers required for horses.
- Tool kit and first aid kits (horse and human).
- Auto club membership, towing insurance, or other arrangements for emergency road service that covers trailer and tow vehicle. A credit card may be necessary for major repairs on the road. A cellular phone or CB radio is helpful in case of emergency.

TRAILER EQUIPMENT LIST

The following items should always be carried in the trailer:

- Spare tire and jack for trailer and tow vehicle.
- Jumper cables, tow chain.
- Road flares or warning signal in case of breakdown.
- Blocks (two) to put behind front and back tires when parked (the type of block that can serve as a ramp for changing a tire is especially useful).
- Longe line, extra lead rope and halter, sheet or blanket, extra cotton and leg wraps, pins, masking tape.
- Large container of water (can be used for drinking water, first aid, or some vehicle problems).
- Small pail with sponge or cloth.
- Water and feed buckets, hay net (fastened so it won't swing or drop too low), with fresh hay for every trip.
- Broom, shovel, rake, fork, muck basket, manure disposal bags. (Leave parking areas clean!)

- First-aid kits (horse and human).
- Tool kit, containing:
  - Flashlight and extra batteries.
  - Screwdrivers, pliers, hammer, wrenches, and so on.
  - Extra bulbs for trailer lights and extra 20-amp fuses.
  - Electrical tape.
  - Extra quart of oil for tow vehicle.
  - Crowbar (essential in case you need to remove center divider quickly).
  - Sturdy knife (to cut tie ropes in an emergency).
  - WD-40, grease, or lubricating oil.
  - Can of bee/wasp/hornet stun spray.
  - Work gloves and waterless hand cleaner.

SAFE LOADING CHECKLIST

Before a trip, make sure that your horse (and any other horses you are hauling) is used to loading, traveling, and unloading quietly. Pack the trailer and tow vehicle and check off all items before loading the horses.

Review safe loading and unloading procedures (USPC D Manual, p. 224).

When hauling only one horse in a two-horse trailer, load him on the driver's side. This makes the trailer tow better, and is more comfortable for the horse.

When hauling two horses, put the larger one on the driver's side. Use a barrier or hay net to keep their heads apart so they cannot nip each other, but don't tie them so tightly that they cannot ride comfortably.

Load and unload with the trailer parked on level ground, on good footing, and in a clear area away from traffic. If it is necessary to unload at a rest stop or beside a road, put a longe line on the horse first. If he should pull back, he is less likely to get loose.

Be quiet, patient, and confident when loading and handling horses. Get the horse's attention by practicing proper leading, walking, halting, and backing before asking him to load.

Never enter an enclosed trailer stall (without an escape door) with a horse.

When loading, *always* fasten the rear chain or bar before tying the horse's head. When unloading, *always* untie the horse's head before unfastening the rear chain or bar, or opening the trailer door or tailgate.

Keep fingers clear of the trailer door, hinges, latches, and tailgate. Wear gloves; never wear rings when loading or unloading horses.

Keep the rear door or tailgate closed when the horse is standing in the trailer (for instance, between classes at a show, or at a rest stop).

TRAINING HORSES TO LOAD AND UNLOAD

Entering a trailer, traveling, and unloading quietly are skills that must be taught. It goes against a horse's natural instincts to step up into an enclosed box with a floor that may sound hollow or move slightly under his feet. Proper preparation, good training, unhurried practice, and calm, patient handling produce a horse that is obedient, confident, and relaxed during loading, travel, and unloading. The worst possible approach is to attempt to force a green horse to load when you are in a hurry to get somewhere.

Safety Precautions when Loading Green or Difficult Horses

Always wear gloves and remove rings when loading horses.

Work in a quiet, secure area (not on a road) away from crowds and distractions. Any helpers must be competent and experienced horse handlers who will follow your instructions.

Park the trailer on level ground with good footing, hitched to a tow vehicle with the brake on for stability. A step-in trailer should be placed so that the step is as low as possible. A ramp should be firmly supported, not wobbly.

The trailer should be made as light and inviting as possible:

- Open escape doors and windows; turn on interior lights.
- Swing the partition to one side for maximum room.
- Cover the floor with several inches of shavings.
- Place a flake of hay and a small feed of grain in the manger or front of the trailer.

Parking the trailer beside a wall or fence can prevent the horse from escaping sideways. Don't create a dangerous gap between fence and ramp.

Assemble any equipment and have it in place before you begin loading.

If available, a quiet, familiar horse that loads easily may give the green horse confidence.

The horse should wear shipping boots or bandages, a poll guard, and a strong, well-fitting halter.

Use equipment that permits safe control. A chain end lead shank can help to keep the horse's attention. A longe line attached to the halter makes it less likely for a horse to get loose if he should pull back unexpectedly.

Work quietly, calmly, and patiently, and use good judgment to prevent accidents to yourself, your helpers, and the horse. Never wrap a rope around your hand or any part of your body; keep fingers clear of hinges and trailer posts, and never enter an enclosed trailer stall with a horse. If the horse becomes upset or resists violently, stop and think before the situation gets worse!

Steps in Trailer Training

Work in Hand Before trailer training can begin, the horse must be taught to lead properly without crowding, hanging back, or pulling; to move forward, stop, turn, and back up on command, and to pay attention to his handler. This is essential for safe handling and control during trailer training.

Teaching the horse to walk over a large piece of plywood on the ground is good practice for trailer training.

Familiarization with Trailer and Equipment The horse should be accustomed to travel equipment (particularly shipping boots or bandages) before trailer training. Let him investigate the trailer; feed him a little grain from the tailgate or trailer floor. Loading a quiet, familiar horse first may give him confidence.

Loading Lead the horse straight toward the trailer entrance, moving forward briskly and with confidence. Keep him straight; don't let him turn his head or veer away. If he hesitates, halt and wait. Don't allow him to back up or turn away from the trailer, but don't try to force him forward. Instead, wait until he is relaxed, then ask him to move forward.

The horse should be asked to move forward with a familiar signal: a voice command or cluck, with the handler in the leading position. A 48-inch training whip (used to touch or tap, not for punishment) can be helpful. A longe line placed around the hindquarters can be used to keep the horse straight, encourage forward movement, and discourage backing up (see diagram on following page). Any such aids must be used to signal and encourage the horse to move forward, not to force him into the trailer. Forceful methods are dangerous for horses and handlers, and can create long-term loading and trailering problems.

When asking the horse to step onto the ramp or into the trailer, it may help to have an assistant pick up the horse's foot and place it on the ramp or trailer floor. When the horse puts his head inside the trailer, allow time for his eyes to adjust to the darker interior.

If the horse backs away from the trailer at any time, *do not* try to restrain him forcibly by pulling on his head. This scares a horse and can cause him to resist harder. Instead, go with him, stop him, then lead him forward again; try to return to the place from which he backed up.

When the horse first goes into the trailer, reward him and let him stand for a few minutes before unloading him. Do not close him in immediately, and *never* tie him unless the back chain or bar has been fastened and the door or tailgate is closed.

Teaching a Horse to Unload Quietly   Unloading, like loading, should be taught in small steps. Ask the horse to put one foot in the trailer (or on the ramp), stand for 30 seconds or so, and then to back out quietly. Practice this several times, then have him put both front feet in the trailer, wait, then back out. With patience and practice in loading and unloading one step at a time, he will learn to back out one step at a time.

Loading Difficult Horses

Loading a difficult horse requires patience, experience, tact, and confidence. The approach chosen must fit the individual; methods that might work on a calm but stubborn horse could be all wrong for a fearful horse. The handler must never get impatient or let his temper get the better of him.

For the safety of all, it is essential to stay cool and calm, and always to work below the horse's panic level. Using force can provoke violent resistance, endangering handlers and horse, or cause the horse to enter the trailer in such a state of tension that he "blows up" once inside. If the horse (or handler) begins to get excited, stop and let him calm down.

Some techniques for difficult loaders are:

Linking Arms   If the horse is gentle and not too big, two helpers can link arms behind his hindquarters and "boost" him into the trailer. This often works well with foals.

Caution: Never attempt this with a "kicky" animal!

Single Longe Line   A longe line or cotton rope is attached to one side of the trailer and passed behind the horse's hindquarters. It can be used to discourage the horse from moving sideways or backing up. Brief tugs on the longe line can be used to encourage forward movement.

Caution: If the horse rushes backward, the longe line must be released, or it may cause him to fall over backward.

USING LONGE LINE IN TRAILER LOADING

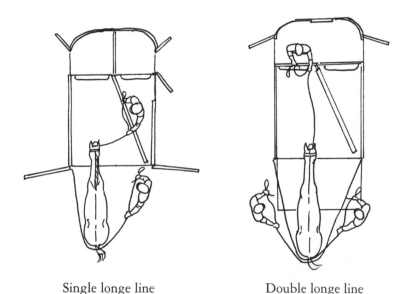

Single longe line   Double longe line

Double Longe Lines   Two longe lines are attached to the sides of the trailer to form a chute, in order to keep the horse from moving sideways. Each longe line is handled by an assistant. They cross behind the horse to keep him straight and discourage backward movement. As with a single longe line, both lines must be released if the horse should rush backward.

Some horses that are extremely difficult to load in a two-horse trailer will load in a stock trailer. This is also useful for horses that ride poorly in a regular trailer stall.

Poor Travelers

Horses that travel badly may sweat up, kick the trailer, lean on the divider, or scramble, especially on turns. This behavior is due to fear and tension, which may be caused by bad driving (especially taking turns too fast), or a previous bad experience in the trailer. However, the most common cause is inability to balance securely because of lack of foot room.

Try moving the partition over, using a half partition (one that does not reach to the floor) or removing it entirely, giving the horse the entire width of the trailer. Some poor travelers ride better in a slant load trailer or in a stock trailer, or facing backward.

Poor travelers should be especially well protected with shipping boots or bandages, a head bumper, and tail wrap or tail guard. Bell boots may offer better protection to the heels than ordinary shipping bandages.

Transporting a Mare with a Foal

Special measures are necessary when transporting a mare with a foal. A young foal cannot be tied by the halter like an older horse, and it may lie down. The foal must be prevented from getting underneath the mare, or it may be stepped on and injured. Foals may try to climb out of a trailer stall, so the trailer must be completely enclosed. Be sure to provide adequate ventilation, especially in hot weather.

A small foal can be hauled in the front of a trailer with breast bars, with the front area partitioned off with plywood to form a box stall. This lets the mare see, smell, and touch her foal, and the foal can lie down safely.

A foal can also be hauled loose in a trailer stall with a full partition, or in a stock trailer.

On long trips, rest stops should be planned in order to allow the foal to nurse.

CHAPTER 16

•••••••••••••••••

Bitting, Tack, and Presentation

This chapter covers bits and bitting; tack and miscellaneous equipment; and care, storage, and temporary adjustment of tack. More information about tack (types of tack, tack care, condition and safety, fitting to horse and rider, and selection) is found in the USPC D Manual.

B, HA, and A Pony Clubbers are expected to be able to prepare and present themselves, their tack, and their horses correctly for formal and informal occasions. The details of formal and informal attire and turnout inspection are covered in the USPC D and C Manuals. HAs must also be able to present a horse as if for sale, evaluate its suitability for various purposes, and show it in hand to its best advantage.

BITS AND BITTING

Modern humane bits are designed to influence and control horses by pressure, not pain. However, any bit can cause pain and damage the horse's training if it is used or fitted incorrectly, especially in the hands of a rider trying to ride a horse in activities beyond his level. There is a great variety of bits designed for different purposes, ranging from mild to severe in their effects.

Pressure Points

Bits and control devices (such as hackamores) work on specific pressure points on the horse's head; some work on more than one pressure point. Pressure on different points has specific effects:

Pressure Point	Characteristic Effects
Tongue	Encourages flexion and yielding of the jaw, chewing, and activation of salivary glands, producing foam. The tongue cushions the effect of the bit on the bars. Some horses have extremely thick, sensitive, or scarred tongues and cannot tolerate excessive tongue pressure.
Bars (bones of lower jaw, in the interdental space)	Encourages flexion and yielding of the jaw and flexion at the poll. The bars may be wide and flat (less sensitive) or sharp and thin (more sensitive). The bars become thinner and sharper lower in the mouth.

PRESSURE POINTS

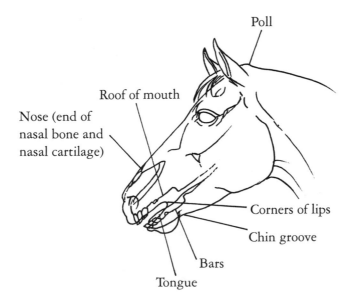

Pressure Point	Characteristic Effects
Corners of the lips	The skin is flexible and less sensitive than the tongue and bars. Pressure here encourages the horse to extend his head and neck, and sometimes raise his head.
Roof of the mouth (palate)	Less sensitive than the bars. Pressure here tends to encourage the horse to open his mouth. When the port of a curb bit touches the roof of the mouth, it acts as a fulcrum, causing the cannons of the bit to press more strongly against the bars.
Curb groove (under the chin)	Pressure on this spot alone tends to cause the horse to raise his head. When applied by a curb chain in conjunction with a curb bit, it acts as a fulcrum, creating more pressure on the bars.
Sides of jaws	Lateral pressure here exerts a guiding effect, encouraging the horse to turn his head to the left or right. Pressure against the cheek teeth can be painful, especially in young horses that are cutting teeth.
Bridge of nose	Pressure encourages horse to flex at the poll. The point where the nasal bone and cartilage meet is especially sensitive to pressure.
Poll	Pressure encourages horse to lower his head.

Severity of Bits

The severity of a bit depends on the following factors:

Direct pressure or leverage	Direct pressure bits apply the same degree of pressure in the mouth as that applied to the reins. Leverage bits multiply the pressure. Length of shank, tightness of curb chain, and ratio of upper shank to lower shank affect leverage and hence severity.
Shape of mouthpiece	Smooth, flexible mouthpieces that conform to the shape of the mouth are milder than rigid, angular mouthpieces or those shaped to concentrate pressure on a particular portion of the mouth.
Thickness of mouthpiece	Thicker mouthpieces distribute pressure over a wider area; thin mouthpieces concentrate it.

Surface of mouthpiece	Smooth or soft mouthpieces are milder; twisted, serrated, or sharp-edged mouthpieces are more severe.
Pinching effect	Jointed bits (especially those with long cannons) have a pinching effect on the mouth.
Auxiliary devices	Dropped, crossed, or flash nosebands and control devices (such as martingales) make the effect of the bit more severe by limiting the horse's options (such as opening his mouth or raising his head). Some (such as draw reins and running martingales) act directly on the bit and change its effect.

The U.S. Pony Club prohibits the use of any bit considered inhumane, excessively severe, or detrimental to good horsemanship. It is important to remember that *any* bit can be severe if used severely or fitted improperly.

Mouthpiece Materials

Mouthpieces may be made of or covered in metal, rubber, hard rubber, leather, or synthetic materials. Softer materials are milder in effect, but some horses prefer or dislike certain materials, especially rubber. Stainless steel is longer lasting, smoother, and easier to keep clean than other metals.

Copper is believed to stimulate the flow of saliva. (However, acceptance of the bit and correct flexion at the poll are better ways to stimulate the flow of saliva.)

Bits for Various Disciplines

Most bits for dressage, jumping, and combined training are intended to be used with continuous light contact. Some bits (especially those for polo, western riding, and certain other disciplines) are designed to be used with a loose rein and a "check and release" method. Some bits facilitate turning by lateral rein aids (especially opening rein); others are more effective when used with a direct rein or neck rein.

Dressage Bits   Dressage bits include snaffles (required for training through Third Level competition) and simple double bridles (required for Fourth Level through FEI Levels). Bits must be smooth and solid, and may be of metal, synthetic materials, or covered with rubber or leather. The mouthpiece must be entirely of one metal, without insets or parts made of any other metal.

Snaffles may be single-jointed, double-jointed, French mouth, unjointed (half moon or Mullen mouth), or Dr. Bristol. (Please note that Dr. Bristol snaffles are *not* permitted in the dressage phase of combined training events.) Twisted, wire, or roller bits are prohibited. Most types of rings and cheeks are permitted, including loose ring, dee-ring, egg butt, full and half cheek, hanging cheek (Baucher), and Fulmer. When a full cheek bit is used, keepers are permitted; these are required as a safety measure in Pony Club activities.

When a double bridle is used, the lever arm of the curb may not exceed 10 centimeters (4 inches) and must be straight. Curb bits may be Mullen mouth, low, medium or high port, and may be fixed or sliding. A lip strap is optional. The ring of a bradoon may not exceed 8 centimeters ($3^1/8$ inches) in diameter.

Cross-Country Riding and Jumping Bits All types of bits are permitted in the cross-country phase of combined training events, but snaffles are usually preferred, with or without a running martingale. Many horses require a stronger bit for control when galloping and jumping in the open, which might include stronger snaffles such as the slow twist or Dr. Bristol, a short shanked pelham, or (rarely, and only in the hands of an expert) a gag bit or double bridle. Similar bits are used for foxhunting, along with a martingale if needed.

Show Jumping Bits Typical bits used in show jumping include snaffles, kimberwickes, pelhams, and more rarely, double bridles, gag bits, and hackamores. Snaffles are usually preferred because they are less likely to inhibit a horse's balancing gestures during jumping than are leverage bits. Full cheek and dee-ring snaffles are often used because they have a lateral guiding effect for turns on course or over a jump. Running martingales are optional.

Selecting a Bit

When selecting a bit, the following should be considered:

- The horse's age, experience, and level of training.
- The rider's skills and experience.
- The discipline and activity, and the level at which the horse is competing or being ridden in that activity.

- The horse's mouth conformation, including size and shape of lips, tongue and bars, and any injuries or peculiarities of the mouth. A horse with sharp bars and thin skin usually needs a softer bit than one with wide, flat bars and thick skin. Thick mouthpieces may be uncomfortable for horses with small, shallow mouths. A horse with a thick, scarred, or sensitive tongue may need a mouthpiece that relieves the tongue from excessive pressure.
- The size and proper fit of the bit. A bit should have 1/8 to 1/4 inch of space outside the lips. A too narrow bit may pinch the lips and cause abrasions. Snaffles that are too wide have a severe nutcracker action, and the center joint may hit the roof of the mouth. Curbs that are too wide tend to rock and bear unevenly on the bars, which may cause the horse to tilt his head. (For correct fitting of bits, see USPC D Manual, p. 268.)
- The horse's temperament and response to the bit, including any problems (getting behind the bit, above the bit, etc.), and his preference for a particular bit or mouthpiece material.

In addition, keep in mind any factors that may require stronger bitting for safe control, such as fast work, riding outside in a group, cross-country jumping, or foxhunting. When bitting a strong horse or a puller, remember that horses tend to pull against or run away from pain. Often a milder bit (sometimes in conjunction with a martingale or some variety of dropped noseband) gets better results than a more severe bit.

TYPES OF BITS

Direct Pressure, Non-Leverage Bits (Snaffles)

A non-leverage bit is one that applies the same amount of pressure to the mouth as is applied to the reins. A direct pressure bit has the reins fastened directly to the mouthpiece or noseband, making it easy to use the bit in a lateral direction without tilting it or distorting its effect.

A snaffle bit is a direct pressure, non-leverage bit that consists of two rings connected by a mouthpiece. (*Note: A snaffle bit may or may not have a jointed mouthpiece, and a bit with a jointed mouthpiece is not necessarily a snaffle.*)

SNAFFLE BIT RINGS

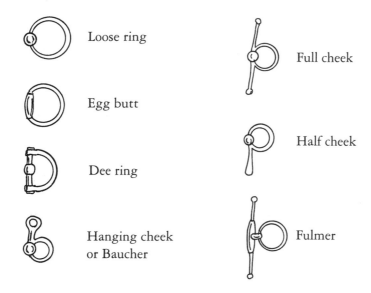

Loose ring

Full cheek

Egg butt

Half cheek

Dee ring

Hanging cheek
or Baucher

Fulmer

Types of snaffle rings include:

Loose Ring Allows the mouthpiece to slip around the ring and rotate freely, encouraging the horse to relax his jaw, chew the bit, and make foamy saliva. If the holes are large, loose rings may pinch the corners of the lips.

Egg Butt (Barrel Head) Extended joint prevents pinching of the lips. Bit is more stable in the mouth and rotates less freely than loose ring.

Dee-Ring (Racing) Joint extended to upper ends of the "dee." Non-pinching, but tends to fix the bit in the mouth. The sides of the dee have a lateral guiding effect when used for turns.

Full Cheek Cheeks extend up and down from mouthpiece, preventing the bit from slipping sideways through the mouth and exerting lateral control for turns. For safety, "keepers" should be used, which make it less easy for the horse to catch the upper cheek on an obstruction. These fix the bit in the mouth and tend to concentrate pressure on the bars and tongue.

Half Cheek Has upper or lower cheeks only. Effect is similar to that of full cheeks; lower cheek bits are used in driving and racing bridles to prevent cheeks from becoming caught on harness or starting gate. Upper cheek bits (with or without keepers) are permitted in dressage.

Hanging Cheek (Baucher)   Snaffle ring with upper cheek and bridle ring. Tends to fix the bit in the mouth, concentrating pressure on the bars. Sometimes used as preparation for a curb.

Fulmer   Full cheek with loose ring. Permits more free play than conventional full cheek, but has lateral guiding effect.

Snaffle Mouthpieces

Single Jointed, Standard Weight   The most common type; acts on tongue, lips, and bars with "nutcracker" action. Mild to moderate; permitted in dressage competition.

SNAFFLE MOUTHPIECES

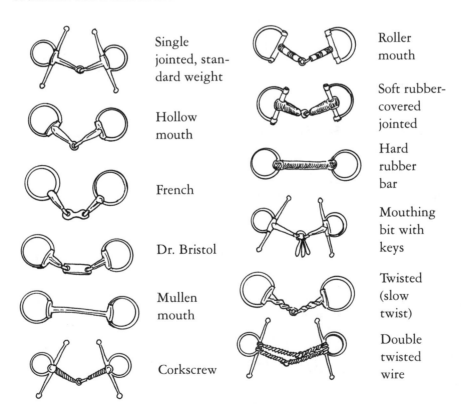

Single jointed, standard weight

Hollow mouth

French

Dr. Bristol

Mullen mouth

Corkscrew

Roller mouth

Soft rubber-covered jointed

Hard rubber bar

Mouthing bit with keys

Twisted (slow twist)

Double twisted wire

Thick (Hollow Mouth, German)   Usually single-jointed; spreads pressure over a wider surface. Some horses have small mouths that cannot accommodate an extra-thick bit. Mild; permitted for dressage.

Double Jointed (French Mouth)   Has smooth "bone-shaped" center link. Lies flat on tongue; reduces pinching effect; flexibility makes it milder and encourages chewing and jaw relaxation. Mild; permitted for dressage.

Dr. Bristol   Double-jointed like French snaffle, but having a flat rectangular plate instead of a rounded center link. The bit should be placed so that the plate lies flat on the tongue; if put in backward, the edge of the plate lies against the tongue, creating severe pressure. Effect is similar to that of French snaffle, but with more tongue pressure. Not permitted for dressage phase of combined training events.

Mullen Mouth (Half Moon, Bar Snaffle)   Unjointed, solid mouthpiece with slight curve. Places pressure on tongue and bars, across width of bit. Some horses tend to lean against a solid mouthpiece. Mild; permitted for dressage.

Roller (Roller Mouth, Single Roller, Cherry Roller, Magenis)   Rollers encourage chewing, activation of tongue, and relaxation of jaw, especially in horses inclined to stiffen the jaw. Sometimes used to pacify a nervous horse. Not permitted for dressage.

Mouthing Bit (Key Bit)   Has keys that dangle from a center link. The keys lie on the tongue, encouraging the horse to mouth and play with the bit and relax his jaw. Used to introduce young horses to the bit; not for dressage.

Twisted (Slow Twist)   Edges create clearly defined pressure for a stronger effect. Severe; not permitted for dressage.

Corkscrew (Serrated)   Many sharply twisted edges create serrated mouthpiece that acts strongly on bars, tongue, and corners of lips. Severe; not permitted for dressage.

Twisted Wire (Single or Double)   Thin mouthpiece and edges of twisted wire concentrate the pressure for a severe, abrasive effect. A double twisted wire mouthpiece has offset angles that act severely on tongue, bars, and corners of mouth. Severe; not permitted for dressage.

Double Mouth ("W" or "Y" Mouth)   Double mouthpiece with off-set joints creates sharp angles, which act strongly on bars, tongue, and corners of mouth. Severe; not permitted for dressage.

There are many other special types of bits and mouthpieces designed for special purposes or specific mouth problems. The use of twisted, corkscrew, twisted wire, and other severe bits by Pony Clubbers of any level is prohibited in dressage and strongly discouraged, even if a particular horse sport allows them.

Leverage Bits (Curbs)

Leverage bits multiply the pressure applied to the mouth (i.e., 1 or 2 ounces of pressure on the reins creates several ounces of pressure in the mouth). A curb bit applies leverage to the mouthpiece by means of shanks and a curb chain. Because leverage bits increase the pressure the horse feels, they must be used with light contact and sensitive, independent hands.

The parts of a curb bit and their functions are:

Shanks   Side pieces that form the lever arm of the curb, having a ring for the bridle at the top and for the rein at the bottom. The leverage (and severity) increases with the length of shank and ratio of upper shank to lower shank. A longer lower shank in relation to upper shank increases the leverage and the pressure on the curb groove and bars. A longer upper shank has less leverage and mouth pressure, but increases the pressure on the poll.

PARTS OF CURB BIT

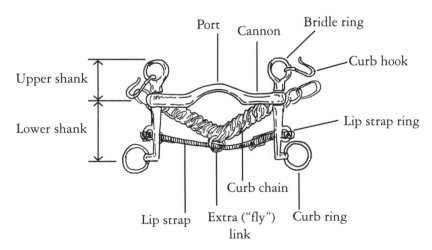

The length of shank varies from very short shanks ("Tom Thumb") of 2 inches or so to long shanks (5 inches or longer). Most shanks are 4 inches or less.

Mouthpiece Applies most pressure to the bars of the mouth through the cannons. Some include a port (a raised center portion). Curb bits may have a solid, swivel, or sliding mouthpiece. Swivel shanks and sliding mouthpieces provide more looseness and flexibility and may encourage some horses to chew the bit and relax their jaws.

Curb mouthpieces include:

- Mullen mouth (half moon): Distributes pressure evenly across tongue and bars.

CURB, PELHAM, AND KIMBERWICKE MOUTHPIECES

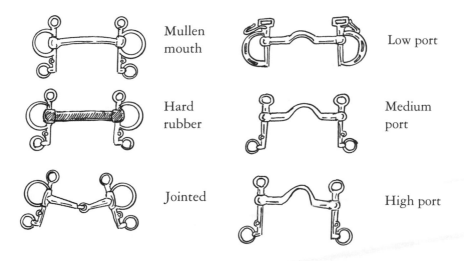

Mullen mouth

Hard rubber

Jointed

Low port

Medium port

High port

- Low to medium port: Puts most pressure on bars; port provides some tongue relief.
- High port: Port provides tongue relief; concentrates pressure on bars. High ports may touch the roof of the mouth, acting as a fulcrum that increases the pressure on the lower bars.
- Jointed: Breaks at center joint with strong "nutcracker" effect, squeezing sideways on bars. (Not to be confused with snaffle bits, which do not have leverage).

Curb Chain (or Curb Strap)   Attached to the upper shanks (usually by curb hooks), passes under the curb groove at the back of the chin. Acts as a fulcrum for the lever arm of the curb bit. The curb chain must be smooth, flat, and correctly adjusted for the bit to work properly.

Lip Strap   A small strap attached to the lower shanks, passing through the extra link of the curb chain. It prevents the horse from reaching back with his lip to grab the shank of the bit, and keeps the curb chain from being lost when it is unfastened.

Adjustment of Curbs and Pelhams

Curb bits (including pelhams and related bits) must be adjusted correctly in order to work as they are designed to do. They should rest in or near the corners of the mouth, without a wrinkle. The bars are thinner and sharper lower down, so placing a curb lower in the mouth makes its effect more severe.

ADJUSTMENT OF CURB AND PELHAM BITS

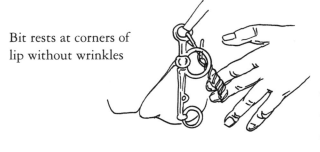

Bit rests at corners of lip without wrinkles

Two fingers between curb chain and curb groove

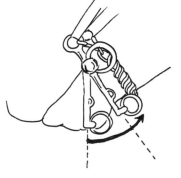

Bit rotates 45 degrees to tighten curb chain

The curb chain must lie flat against the curb groove, and should be adjusted so that the bit rotates 45 degrees to tighten it against the jaw. If adjusted tighter, the curb "grabs" and acts too severely with very little pressure. If too loose, the bit "falls through" with insufficient pressure and the curb chain may pinch the corners of the lips. On a pelham bit, the curb chain is sometimes run through the snaffle ring before being hooked to the curb hook. This prevents it from pinching the corners of the lips, but it somewhat inhibits the ability of the snaffle ring to swivel laterally.

A lip strap is buckled through the extra link ("fly" link) of the curb chain, snugly enough to prevent the horse from reaching back with his lip to grab the shank of the bit.

In a double bridle, the bradoon is placed high against the corners of the lips, creating one or two wrinkles. The curb bit and curb chain are placed below it. The bradoon must not drop low enough to become caught under the mouthpiece of the curb, which would be extremely uncomfortable.

Double Bridle (Weymouth)

A curb bit is almost never used alone. It is combined with a small snaffle bit (called a bradoon) to make a double (or Weymouth) bridle. The bradoon has smaller rings than a regular snaffle (a maximum of 8 centimeters in diameter) and is placed above the curb bit and curb chain. Snaffle reins are wider than curb reins, which makes it easier to identify the reins by feel.

Combination Bits (Pelhams and Kimberwickes)

Combination bits combine some of the effects of a curb and a snaffle. They include pelhams and kimberwickes (or kimblewickes). A pelham has curb shanks equipped with upper (snaffle) rings at the mouthpiece and double reins. As in a double bridle, the snaffle rein is slightly wider than the curb rein.

Pelhams and kimberwickes come in a variety of mouthpieces; the most common include half-moon (Mullen mouth); low, medium, and high ports; and jointed mouthpieces. The length of shank varies from very short shanks ("Tom Thumb") of 2 inches or so to 5 inches or longer.

When riding with a pelham, the snaffle rein is normally carried on the outside and underneath the fourth finger; the curb rein is carried inside the snaffle and lies between the ring finger and the fourth finger.

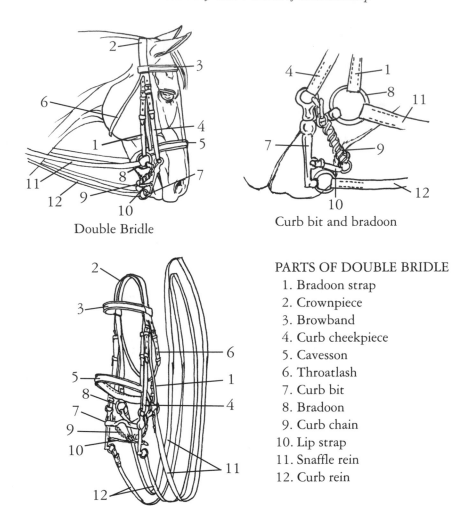

Double Bridle

Curb bit and bradoon

PARTS OF DOUBLE BRIDLE
1. Bradoon strap
2. Crownpiece
3. Browband
4. Curb cheekpiece
5. Cavesson
6. Throatlash
7. Curb bit
8. Bradoon
9. Curb chain
10. Lip strap
11. Snaffle rein
12. Curb rein

The snaffle rein should be slightly shorter, while the curb rein maintains a lighter contact. This allows the snaffle to act first and protects the horse from accidental overuse of the curb. If equal pressure is applied to both reins (snaffle and curb) at once, each prevents the other from acting with a clear curb or snaffle effect, resulting in an indistinct general pressure.

When a pelham is used with a single rein and bit converters (short, rounded leather straps connecting the curb and snaffle rings on each side, to which a rein is attached), the effect is neither clearly curb nor snaffle. This is acceptable for relatively simple activities, but not for control or schooling beyond a very basic level. Riders above the beginner level who need to use a pelham should learn to use double reins correctly.

A kimberwicke (kimblewicke) has dee-shaped rings without a shank and a single rein. The Uxeter kimberwicke has slots in the rings that fix the rein in position, creating a stronger curb effect than when the rein slides freely around the ring. When the rein slides freely around the ring, the curb effect is minimal and the bit acts more like a snaffle.

Pelhams and kimberwickes and their adjustment are described in the USPC D Manual, p. 269.

Gag Bits

Gag bits are related to snaffles, but employ leverage for increased severity. They concentrate pressure simultaneously on the corners of the lips and the poll, raising the horse's head to avoid the pressure. They tend to produce a high, stiff head carriage.

Most gag bits can (and should) be equipped with double reins: a snaffle rein, which allows the bit to be used as an ordinary snaffle, and a gag rein, which is only brought into play when necessary.

Gag bits are severe; they are most often used to retrain spoiled horses or to manage strong pullers in speed events such as polo, cross-country jumping, or show jumping. They should only be used by experts!

Types of gag bits:

Gag Snaffle Resembles a snaffle bit with rings inserted in the top and bottom of each snaffle ring. Special cheekpieces made of rounded leather or rope pass through these rings, terminating in a ring for the reins. When pressure is applied, the bit rotates and slides upward, causing strong pressure simultaneously on the corners of the mouth and the poll.

Elevator Bit A variety of gag bit, with a snaffle mouthpiece and cheeks or shanks with bridle rings at the top of the upper shank and rein rings at the bottom of the lower shank. The bit rotates, putting pressure on the lips and poll simultaneously, encouraging the horse to raise his head.

Dutch Gag Resembles the elevator bit, but has three or more rings in place of cheeks. Severity may be adjusted by placing the gag rein on a higher or lower ring.

GAG BITS

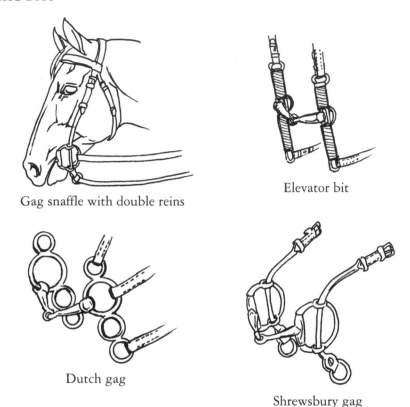

Gag snaffle with double reins

Elevator bit

Dutch gag

Shrewsbury gag

Hackamores and Bitless Bridles

Hackamores and bitless bridles work on the horse's nose, chin, and muzzle instead of the mouth. Although they are not commonly used for English riding and are not permitted in most types of competition (except for endurance competitions, show jumping, and the cross-country and show jumping phases of combined training events), they are sometimes useful for lesson horses, therapeutic riding, training young horses, retraining spoiled horses, and for horses whose mouths have been injured.

A hackamore should be adjusted so that the noseband rests on or slightly above the point where the nasal bone ends and the cartilage begins. If placed lower, it cannot cut off the horse's breathing, but it may interfere with the expansion of the nostrils, irritate his muzzle, and lead to head tossing. The chin strap should be adjusted so that the shanks rotate 45 degrees to tighten it, or for non-leverage hackamores,

Non-leverage jumping hackamore

Leverage (mechanical) hackamore

so that two adult-sized fingers can be slipped between the jaw and the chin strap.

The two basic types of hackamores are leverage and non-leverage.

Leverage Hackamores (Mechanical Hackamores)   These employ a noseband, curb strap or chain, and shanks. Their action is similar to that of a curb bit, except that pressure is applied to the nose and curb groove instead of the mouth. They range from moderate to severe, depending on the construction of the noseband and length of shank. Like curb bits, they encourage flexion at the poll but are not as effective for turning as direct pressure devices, as a lateral pull tends to tilt the shank and dig the upper shank into the side of the horse's face.

Non-Leverage Hackamores   These consist of a noseband and chin strap with rings placed on the sides of the noseband. Pressure causes the noseband to rotate and tightens the chin strap, but there is little or no leverage. Because the rings are on the side of the nose, they are more effective for turning, especially when using an opening rein. Non-leverage hackamores include leather-covered jumping hackamores, side-pull hackamores, and western bosals.

MISCELLANEOUS EQUIPMENT

Protective Boots

Boots may be used to protect horses' legs during longeing, work, competition, turnout, and shipping. Like bandages, they must be applied and used correctly in order to be safe and effective. Most boots are made in pairs for the left and right legs; it's important to put the boot on the proper leg.

To put on a leg boot, place it high on the leg, fasten it snugly but not tightly, then slide it down into place, keeping the hair smooth. Then recheck the tightness, making sure that the fastenings exert even pressure. Boots must be tight enough to be secure, but you should be able to slip a finger underneath at the top and bottom. Always check the security and adjustment of boots after warming up for ten minutes and before jumping; the horse's legs may go down, causing the boots to loosen.

Boots must be fitted properly in order to be secure and to protect the legs. Boots that are too large will slip down and may come loose or be stepped on, which can cause a fall; if too small, they do not protect the area adequately and may pinch, rub, or bind.

Sand, dirt, and debris under boots can cause abrasions or skin irritation, especially when aggravated by sweating. The inner lining must be kept clean, and the horse's legs should be clean and dry before they are put on. Using baby powder or a thin sheet of cotton under boots may help prevent irritation, especially when working in sand.

Types of protective boots include:

Bell (Overreach) Boots   Rubber or plastic bell boots are used to protect the heels from "grabs" or overreaching, especially in jumping, when working in mud, or during turnout. Open-style boots are fastened with Velcro or other closures; closed bell boots, which slip over the foot, are the most secure.

To put on closed bell boots, turn them inside out and stretch them over the hoof, toe first. They go on more easily if they are warmed by placing them in hot water.

Splint or Tendon Boots   These protect the inside of the cannon and splint bones and fetlock joint, and may have extra protection over the flexor tendons. They are used for horses that interfere, for longeing, on young horses, and for activities in which a horse is more likely to strike himself, such as lateral work or polo.

PROTECTIVE BOOTS

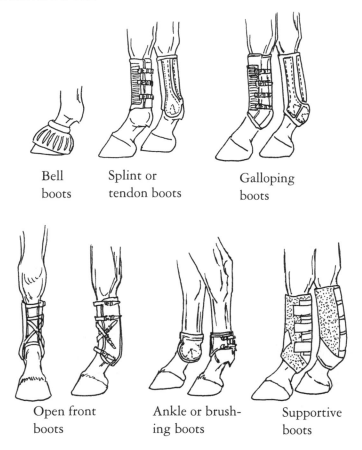

Bell boots Splint or tendon boots Galloping boots

Open front boots Ankle or brushing boots Supportive boots

Galloping Boots, Polo Boots   Galloping boots offer more protection than splint or tendon boots. They cover the cannon and splint bones, tendons, and fetlock joint, from the base of the knee or hock to the bottom of the fetlock joint. Some galloping boots have extra reinforcement over the flexor tendons, to guard against high overreach injuries. They are used for fast work, jumping, polo, and other strenuous activities.

Open Front Boots   Open front boots serve the same purpose as tendon boots or galloping boots, but the front is left unpadded so that a jumper will feel it if he knocks a pole with his shins.

Ankle (Fetlock or Brushing) Boots   Ankle boots protect the inside of the fetlock joint from interference injuries caused by the opposite foot. They may be of leather, synthetic materials, or folded felt. They are usually used on the hind feet.

Supportive Boots   Supportive boots are a recent innovation. Styled like galloping boots, they are equipped with Velcro closures and an elastic support band that passes underneath the back of the fetlock joint. The support strap is intended to keep the fetlock joint from "running down" (sinking so low that it hits the ground) under the stress of galloping and jumping, or to protect the back of the fetlock joint if this should occur. Studies seem to indicate that some concussion is absorbed by the boot instead of being transmitted to the foot and leg.

Breastplates and Breast Collars

Breastplates and breast collars are used to prevent the saddle from sliding back. They are often necessary on horses with large shoulders and flat, narrow ribs. Breast collars are used for extra security when carrying a weight pad (in show jumping or three-day events), which may make the saddle more prone to slipping than in ordinary riding.

Because breastplates and breast collars are potential sources of irritation and sores, and can restrict the movement of the shoulders, they should be used only when necessary, and must be correctly adjusted.

Types of breastplates and breast collars (and adjustment):

Hunting Breastplate (Also Used in Endurance Riding)   Consists of a yoke (neck straps and wither strap), adjustable breast strap (which passes between the front legs and encircles the girth), and two adjustable straps, which buckle to the dee rings of the saddle. A martingale attachment (standing or running) may be attached to the center ring of the yoke. The breast strap and/or neck straps are sometimes covered with fleece to prevent chafing.

The best type of breastplate has adjustable buckles on each side of the neck straps. The breast strap and the two connecting straps that attach to the saddle dees are also adjustable.

A breastplate must keep the saddle from sliding back, but must not bind or restrict at the chest, shoulders, or between the forelegs. When correctly adjusted, you should be able to fit a fist between the chest and the center ring of the yoke, or one hand (sideways) between the wither strap and the withers. The breast strap must be slightly slack, and the buckle must not rub the horse's sensitive skin between the front legs.

BREASTPLATES AND BREAST COLLARS

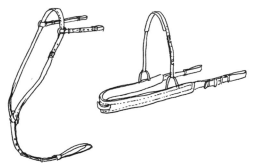

Hunting
breastplate

Breast collar

Breast girth attaches
to saddle dee rings
and slip-on dee ring
attachments

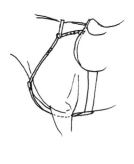

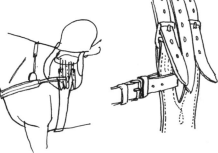

Hunting breastplate attaches to saddle dee
rings and girth

Breast collar
attaches to split
girth and first billet

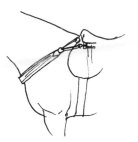

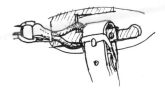

Elastic breast girth

Slip-on dee rings attach-
ments slip over stirrup bar
in front of stirrup leather

Caution: Consider the fit of the saddle when using a breastplate that attaches to the saddle dees. If the saddle does not fit correctly or slips back too far, or if the breastplate is too tight, the breastplate may pull the front of the saddle down, digging the tree points into the muscles and causing severe discomfort.

Breast Collar (Eventing, Polo, or Racing Style)   Consists of a chest strap of leather, webbing, or strong elastic, buckled around the first billet of the girth. A wither strap adjusts the height and keeps the breast collar from slipping down. Some have a slot at the front to accommodate a martingale. The breast strap may be covered with fleece to prevent chafing.

Breast collars hold the saddle more securely than hunting breastplates, so they are preferred for events in which a weight pad is carried, and for polo.

A breast collar should run horizontally from the chest to the girth, not angled upward. It must not be placed so low as to interfere with the points of the shoulders, nor so high as to press against the bottom of the windpipe. You should be able to slip a fist between the chest and the front of the breast strap, and between the wither strap and the withers. A split-end girth, which is divided for the first 10 inches to accommodate the breast collar straps, is best for placing the connecting straps securely.

Elastic Breast Girth   A breast girth is similar to a breast collar, but it attaches instead to the dee rings of the saddle, or to a special loop that is attached to the stirrup bars. The breast strap is made of heavy elastic, and there is no wither strap. Breast girths are used mostly in show jumping, as they restrict the freedom of the shoulders less than other types of breast collars.

An elastic breast girth can be adjusted more snugly than a breast collar, and it is placed at the base of the neck. It should not restrict the horse's breathing by pressing on the base of the windpipe.

Overgirths

An overgirth is a narrow elastic girth that is placed over the saddle and run through keepers on the outside of the girth. It keeps the flaps from shifting and increases security of the saddle, especially for cross-country jumping, show jumping, racing, and steeplechasing. An overgirth should always be used (along with a breast collar) when a weight pad is carried.

An overgirth requires a Fitzwilliam girth (a girth equipped with keepers that hold the overgirth in place).

Overgirth and
Fitzwilliam girth
with keepers

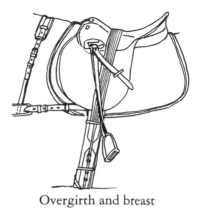

Overgirth and breast
collar in place

Caution: Place overgirth so stirrup
leather can slide freely off safety bar.

To put on an overgirth, adjust the saddle and main girth first, tightening the main girth to the correct tension for work. Place the overgirth over the seat of the saddle with the billet pointing downward and run it through the three keepers on the girth. The overgirth should be snug but not tighter than the main girth. It should be removed immediately after riding.

Caution: An overgirth must never be placed so that it could prevent the stirrup leathers from running off the safety bars in case of a fall. Always check both the main girth and the overgirth before jumping, galloping, or going cross-country.

Crupper

A crupper is a strap attached to a saddle, harness pad, or surcingle, connected to a padded strap that passes under the horse's tail, used to prevent the saddle or surcingle from slipping forward. Cruppers are most often used on small, round-backed ponies and on mules.

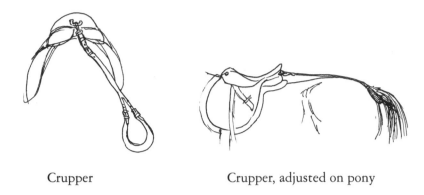

Crupper   Crupper, adjusted on pony

To put on a crupper, double up the skirt of the tail and slip the tail-piece over the tail. All hairs must be freed from underneath the tail-piece before attaching the crupper to the saddle.

A crupper should fit snugly enough to keep the saddle from slipping forward, but not tightly enough to irritate the horse or abrade the skin of the dock. It must be kept clean and soft. A stiff, dirty crupper, hair caught underneath the dock, or too tight a crupper may make the dock tender, cause sores, and lead to kicking.

TEMPORARY ADJUSTMENT OF ILL-FITTING TACK

When teaching or assisting with Pony Club activities, it is sometimes necessary to make a temporary adjustment in ill-fitting tack so that it can be used safely. Any such adjustments must be made so that the tack is safe for the rider and comfortable for the pony, and should be strictly temporary. Don't send a child home with a temporary tack adjustment; be sure that he knows that this is only temporary, and that he and his parents understand what needs to be done to make the tack fit correctly.

Tool Kit

A simple tool kit makes temporary "fixes" and emergency repairs to tack much easier. It helps to carry the following items whenever you teach or assist at Pony Club activities:

- Leather punch with assorted size tubes.
- Sharp knife (a utility knife with an awl is especially useful).
- Sharp scissors, heavy-duty type.
- Duct tape.
- Self-sticking padded tape (such as Vetrap or Sealtex latex tape).
- Bath towel.
- Pieces of foam rubber (2 inches thick, size of a saddle pad).
- Several pieces of neoprene or hiker's sleeping pad material (1/4 inch thick, 6 × 12 inches).
- Girth extender.
- Rubber bit guards.

Saddle Fit

Padding a saddle is never as satisfactory as having the saddle sized and stuffed to fit the horse correctly. Any temporary extra padding should be placed over the saddle pad, not next to the horse's skin. Sometimes a thick, noncrushable western saddle pad will make a saddle useable (temporarily) when nothing else works.

Saddle Resting on Withers
Caution: This condition will quickly cause a severe wither sore, which can lead to fistula (a deep sore draining down into the space between the spinous processes of the withers) if not corrected. A horse must *never* be ridden with the saddle resting on the withers.

Problem: Tree too wide or panels flat in front. (*Note:* check for broken tree; do not use saddle if tree is broken.)

To fix: Pad both sides of the back, leaving a clear channel over the withers and spine. If available, a back protector pad may help. Padding must stay in place and keep saddle clear of withers and spine when rider is mounted. Do not stuff padding between the arch of the saddle and the withers, as this increases the pressure. The saddle should be restuffed to fit, or exchanged for a saddle with a tree that fits.

Too Low in Cantle
Problem: Rear panels flat or tree too narrow; places dip of seat too far back. (*Note:* If tree is too narrow, saddle cannot be used. Raising the back of the saddle will drive the tree points into the pony's shoulders and back muscles, causing soreness.)

TEMPORARY SADDLE ADJUSTMENTS

Saddle too wide

Padding on sides
of back, leaving
channel over spine

Saddle low in cantle due
to flat rear panels

Lift-back pad
levels saddle

Wrapping stirrup leather

Girth extender

To fix: Use a lift-back pad or folded towel to raise the cantle until the dip of the seat is in the center. Make sure saddle does not pinch the shoulder blades and that padding is smooth, even, and effective when rider is mounted.

Leathers Too Long

Problem: Not enough holes to adjust stirrups for rider.

To fix: Unbuckle stirrup leather and wrap buckle end around top of iron once, then rebuckle. One wrap usually equals about $1^1/2$ holes. Leathers should have holes measured and punched at correct length.

Girth Too Short

To fix: Use girth extender, buckled to billets.

Saddle Slides Forward

Problem: Tree too wide, front panels flat, and/or conformation of pony's back (especially roach back or built downhill). Tree points jab pony in shoulders; rider may sit tilted forward, with hollow back.

To fix: Place saddle at "lock-in" point (hollow behind shoulder blades). Use neoprene pads, back protector pad or folded towels to fill in space at sides of back so that saddle sits level, with dip in center. If available, a crupper may be used (but pony must be accustomed to crupper before riding).

Bridle

Too Large

Problem: Cheekpieces and/or crownpiece too long; no more holes to adjust height of bit.

To fix: Tie a knot in each cheekpiece, then buckle to crownpiece. Cheekpieces (or bridle) of proper size should be obtained.

Bit Too Wide

Problem: Bit slips from side to side; if jointed, it acts with severe pinching effect, and center joint may strike the roof of the mouth. If unjointed, bit acts with uneven pressure and may cause pony to tilt his head.

To fix: If only slightly too wide, rubber bit guards may take up some room. If bit is excessively wide, do not use.

Bit Rubs Sores at Corners of Mouth

Problem: Loose ring snaffle with large hole, or bit too narrow; pinches or rubs corners of mouth, causing sore lips. Curb chain adjusted too long, catches a fold of lip as bit rotates.

TEMPORARY BRIDLE ADJUSTMENTS

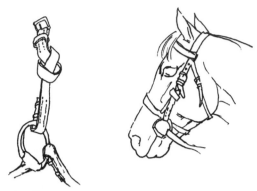

Shortening too-large bridle with knot in cheekpiece

Shortening reins with knot in each rein

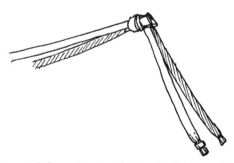

Shortening reins with knot in doubled end of rein; unbuckle rein to prevent loop that could catch rider's foot

To fix: For loose ring bits, use rubber bit guards. If bit is too narrow, do not use. If curb chain pinches, adjust chain correctly. Curb chain may be run through snaffle ring (on pelhams and kimberwickes) to keep it away from corners of mouth.

Caution: A horse must not be ridden with a bit touching an open sore. Try using a hackamore while sores are allowed to heal.

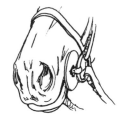

Bit guard prevents
bit pinching lips

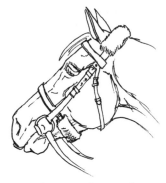

Fleece or foam tubes
for padding bridle

Wrap items with latex or
crepe tape for padding

Rubs or Sores from Bridle

Problem: Improperly adjusted tack, rough leather or sharp edges abrade the skin.

To fix: Readjust the tack so that pressure is removed from sore spot. Rough or sharp edges can be padded by wrapping with crepe or rubber tape.

Reins Too Long

Problem: Extra rein forms dangerous loop in which rider may get caught, or pony's feet may be entangled in the excess, in case of a stumble or fall.

To fix: Tie reins in a knot (as shown), taking up extra rein. If reins are tied, they may be unbuckled to prevent a dangerous loop. For children with small hands, unbuckle the reins and tie a knot in each rein, to avoid a large knot at the withers.

STORING TACK

Tack and equipment are expensive and must be stored properly to prevent damage from excessive heat, dryness, dampness, or rodents.

Leather loses a little of its fat content each day because of the effects of the atmosphere, especially as it dries. It is better for leather to be used daily and properly cared for (cleaned, conditioned, and sealed) than for it to sit unused for long periods.

Tack must be stored in a well-ventilated room, protected from dust, dampness, dryness, and excessive heat, and secure from rodents. Tack should be stored on racks that allow it to keep its proper shape. Creases cause leather to crack and weaken, and may develop dry rot.

When leather tack must be stored, it should be dismantled and thoroughly cleaned and conditioned, and any repairs taken care of. Apply a preservative (such as Kocholine dressing or glycerin saddle soap) and wrap the leather in newspaper, which (unlike plastic) allows the necessary circulation of air. Metal parts may be coated with petroleum jelly to prevent rust or corrosion.

Saddle pads, blankets, bandages, and washable girths should be cleaned or laundered before storage. Dirty items are prone to mildew, rot, and moth damage, and are more attractive to rodents. Woolen items should be placed in plastic bags with moth repellent and stored in trunks or closets.

RECLAIMING NEGLECTED TACK

Tack that has been neglected or that has come out of long-term storage may need special treatment to reclaim it.

First, inspect the tack for condition and repair, and decide whether it can be safely reconditioned, or if certain parts must be replaced. If it is cracked, weakened, or shows signs of dry rot, it may not be reclaimable. Pay special attention to billets, reins, bit fastenings, stitching, holes, and any point where the leather is folded.

Next, clean and dampen the leather. While it is damp, condition the leather by applying warm neatsfoot oil or another conditioner to the unfinished side of the leather. Work the conditioner in a little at a time, bending the leather back and forth so that it absorbs the conditioner and becomes supple. Don't apply so much oil or conditioner that the leather becomes saturated, which can damage it. Finish by applying glycerine saddle soap to seal the pores of the leather.

It is better to repeat this process several times, or to use the tack and clean and condition it daily until it becomes soft and supple, than to overcondition it.

TURNOUT AND PRESENTATION

B- and A-Level Pony Clubbers are expected to present themselves and their mounts in a neat, clean, correct, and workmanlike manner for all events, no matter how formal or informal. The horse should be in proper condition and should show evidence of good ongoing management, including thorough daily grooming and proper shoeing and foot care. Tack must be safe, correctly adjusted, in good repair, and thoroughly clean, with metal parts polished. The Pony Clubber should know the correct name of each item of equipment he uses, and be able to explain its purpose, how it works, why it is used on his horse, and its proper adjustment.

Both B- and A-Level Pony Clubbers must know requirements for formal and informal attire, and must appear correctly turned out according to the requirements of the occasion. Clothing must be neat and clean, and should fit properly. (For details on formal and informal attire, see USPC D Manual, pp. 289–92.)

In addition, HA-Level Pony Clubbers must evaluate, prepare, and present a strange horse as if for sale. To do this, you must be able to:

- Recognize the horse's breed and/or type, age, and condition.
- Evaluate the horse's conformation, way of going, faults and strong points, and temperament, and discuss its potential uses and limitations.
- Groom and prepare the horse as if for sale (taking into account how this breed or type of horse should be presented)
- Present the horse in hand, showing it to best advantage (showing off its good points and minimizing its faults).
- Present yourself in an appropriate and horsemanlike manner (dressed as if ready to ride, neatly and correctly turned out).

Preparation

A horse presented for sale should be in good condition, ideally carrying a little extra condition or "bloom." His feet should be in good condition, recently trimmed or shod. Other preparation tips include:

Upper-level Pony Clubbers should present themselves and their mounts spotlessly turned out. Here a Pony Club team member accepts an award at a national Pony Club rally. *Photo: U.S. Pony Clubs, Inc.*

- The horse should be spotlessly clean, with a healthy, shiny coat that reflects good daily nutrition and grooming, not coat polish. The mane, tail, and white markings should be shampooed.
- The head, ears, bridle path, and legs should be trimmed, and the mane and tail pulled and/or trimmed according to the breed or type of horse. Hunters, sport horses, and hunter ponies' manes may be braided to show off the head and neck. (See USPC C Manual, pp. 178–79.)
- The hooves should be clean and polished with hoof oil or a non-sticky hoof dressing. If not braided, the mane should be dampened and brushed to lay it on the correct side, and a tail bandage may be used to shape the hair of the dock.

- The horse should be presented in properly fitted tack, with leather clean and supple and metal parts polished.
- Even though it is the horse that is being presented, a neat, clean, and attractive stable area and an appropriately turned-out handler make a good impression. The handler should wear clean, informal riding attire, with helmet, gloves, stick, and spurs at hand.

Presenting a Horse in Hand (Showing to Best Advantage)

When presenting a horse in hand, you should show him to his best advantage. This means showing off his best points and minimizing faults or less attractive points. To do this, you must first evaluate his conformation and way of moving. You will also need to practice leading and setting him up (posing) properly.

- Lead the horse briskly at walk (or trot, as requested), moving straight away from the viewer. Give a preparatory half-halt before stopping, so that he halts squarely with his hocks under him. Turn him away from you, using half-halts to make him turn on the haunches. Give a half-halt to balance him before leading him back to the viewer at a walk or trot (as requested).
- When moving at the walk or trot, stay on a straight line. (Pick an object at a distance and aim for it.) Stay beside the horse's head and neck, and do not look back at him.
- To "set up," halt and turn to face the horse. Switch the rein or lead shank to your left hand. Back the horse with short steps until his hind legs are squarely under him with cannon bones vertical (one hind leg may be slightly behind the vertical). Then move the forelegs until they are standing squarely, with both cannon bones vertical. Step back (still facing the horse) and encourage him to look alertly forward. (This takes practice!)
- Avoid emphasizing conformation defects (or creating them where they do not exist!) by allowing the horse to stand incorrectly. Don't let him stand base narrow, with front or hind legs too far under him or camped out in front or behind. Holding the head too high or too low makes the neck appear unattractive and may make the shoulder look straighter than it is.
- Know the breed or type of the horse you are presenting, and how it is properly presented. (For instance, Morgans and certain other breeds are posed "parked out," with hind legs stretched backward; Quarter Horses and stock horse breeds are posed "square," and

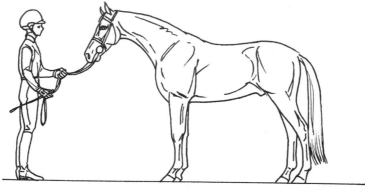

Showing a horse in hand

hunters, sport horses, and Arabians are posed with forelegs vertical and parallel, with one hind leg slightly behind the other.)

- Take advantage of terrain. If possible, pose a horse on slightly rising ground. Never set him up with hind legs on higher ground than the front legs; this will make him appear hollow backed and sickle hocked.
- Step back and allow the viewer to see the whole horse, including the head. Encourage the horse to look alert, but do not nag at him.

Evaluating a Horse for Sale

When evaluating a horse for sale, it is important to get a complete picture of the individual horse, and to assess his good points, faults, and overall usefulness.

Points to remember:

- Observe the horse in his stall, noting his stable manners and any signs of stable vices.
- Have the horse stood up in hand, and evaluate his conformation. Look at his overall outline, balance, and proportions from a distance, then view him from each side, front, and rear. Compare the two sides for symmetry and even muscle development. Make notes on his strong points, conformation faults, blemishes, and unsoundnesses. (See Chapter 8, "Conformation, Soundness, and Movement.")

- Examine the horse closely, including the mouth and teeth, legs, and feet. Note the condition of his feet and type of shoes. Corrective or therapeutic shoeing may indicate soundness or movement problems.
- Watch the horse move at a walk and trot straight away from you, toward you, and from a side view. Note soundness and evenness of stride, freedom of movement, engagement, type of movement, and straightness of movement. Note any movement faults (plaiting, winging in, forging, etc.).
- Observe the horse's attitude, temperament, and stable manners as he is groomed, tacked up, and otherwise handled.
- Watch the horse ridden on the flat and over fences (to his level of training). Evaluate his performance, manners, and way of going under saddle, taking into account the level and experience of the rider.
- Ride the horse yourself, to evaluate his level of training, gaits, and rideability. Try the horse under the circumstances in which you plan to use him (with other horses, hacking out, hunting, etc.). (For details on evaluation ride, see USPC C Manual, p. 119.) If he is to be ridden by someone else, have that person ride him and handle him.
- Ask for all pertinent information, including any warranties. *Always* have a prepurchase veterinary examination performed by your own veterinarian.

USPC Standards of Proficiency—
B, HA, and A Ratings
(Current as of 1996)

B, HA, and A ratings are scheduled on a national basis and require a greater depth of knowledge and proficiency than the earlier ratings. Successful candidates are competent, all-around horsepersons, active and contributing members of USPC, who participate in a variety of Pony Club activities. They are also thoughtful leaders and set an example for all levels.

In addition to its instructional programs, USPC offers a variety of activities at Club, Regional, Inter-Regional and National Levels for team and individual participation. These activities include Combined Training, Dressage, Foxhunting, Know-Down, Mounted Games, Show Jumping, Tetrathlon, and Vaulting.

Achieving a rating does not necessarily qualify the Pony Clubber for competition in any horse sport. To be a team member for a particular activity, further study and preparation may be necessary.

THE B RATING

The B rating is for the active horseperson and Pony Club member who is interested in acquiring further knowledge and proficiency in all phases of riding and horse care. The B is able to ride experienced horses with confidence and control on the flat, over fences, and in the open, and should be able to ride and care for another person's experienced horse, maintaining proper mental and physical condition without undoing any of the horse's education. The B understands and is able to explain the reasons for what he or she is doing, and to contribute to the education of younger Pony Club members.

B Riding Expectations

Candidates should demonstrate an independent seat and effective, tactful use of the aids on the flat and over fences. Candidates should ride a horse forward while establishing and maintaining a regular pace with the horse accepting the aids; should be confident in coping with disobediences; should be able to explain the application and reasons for aids; and should be able to discuss the basic principles of dressage.

Riding on the Flat
- Demonstrate warmup for work on the flat.
- Discuss the reasons for warmup, the amount of time required for the horse being ridden, and why.
- Be prepared to ride the following movements, demonstrating accurate and smooth transitions and correct use of the aids:
  - Serpentine, three loops, sitting and/or posting trot
  - Change of rein across diagonal
  - 10-meter half-circle, walk and/or trot
  - 20-meter circle, sitting trot, and/or canter
  - Canter change of lead through walk and/or trot
  - Lengthening of stride at trot and/or canter
  - Leg-yielding at walk and/or trot
  - Rein-back
- Evaluate and discuss performance with examiner, including strong and weak points of the horse being ridden.
- Ride on the flat without stirrups at all gaits.
- Demonstrate ability to ride different horses with confidence and tact at all gaits, while performing basic schooling figures.
- Discuss performance, including whether or not the horses were balanced, supple, and moving forward with rhythm and impulsion.

Riding Over Fences
- Discuss the benefits of cavaletti/trotting poles, and know how to adjust distances for own horse.
- Demonstrate warmup for jumping, including work over cavaletti.
- Demonstrate ability to ride over fences (height not to exceed 3'7"). Course to include combination fences.
- Critique performance in relation to the effectiveness of the riding plan.
- Ride without stirrups over a grid, showing a secure and independent seat.
- Ride without stirrups over two or three fences.

- Demonstrate ability to ride different horses over fences, showing tact and confidence.
- Critique performance, showing understanding of causes of any disobediences.

Riding in the Open

- Demonstrate a knowledge of pace, and galloping position when appropriate, for an estimated pace of 240 meters per minute, developing to 350 m/m and to 400 m/m.
- Ride own horse over a variety of cross-country obstacles, at height not to exceed 3'7".
- Candidates may be asked to demonstrate ability on a different horse over several natural fences.
- Critique performance, showing understanding of causes of any disobediences.
- Time allowing and terrain suitable, ride safely in a group at a controlled trot and canter, to include several natural fences.

HORSE MANAGEMENT

Candidates must demonstrate sound judgment and maturity in the care of horses and equipment, and an understanding of the reasons for what they are doing. They must show, through discussion, knowledge of veterinary care, longeing, and teaching principles.

Presentation of Horse and Rider

- Correct formal or informal attire.
- Candidate to be dismounted, standing in front of and facing the horse, holding one rein with each hand, close to the bit. Thumbs should not be hooked into bit rings. Spurs are optional.
- Horse to be clean, showing the results of effective daily grooming.
- Tack to be safe and clean, indicating consistent care.
- Discuss the purpose and correct fit of horse's equipment, as well as different types of bits, bridles, nosebands, saddles, pads, girths, martingales, breastplates, cruppers, and boots.

Nutrition

- Relate feeding principles to their effect on the horse's digestive system.
- Discuss the six classes of nutrients and why they are needed.
- Discuss the nutritive value of own horse's feed and supplements.
- Discuss seasonal variations in planning a horse's ration.
- Evaluate hay, grain, and bedding as to suitability and safety.

Stable Management

Discuss the life cycle of parasites and preventive measures for strongyles, bots, ascarids, large stomach worms, and pinworms.

Conformation and Lameness

- Discuss anatomy of front and hind leg from shoulder and hip down, to include principle bones, tendons, and ligaments.
- Discuss conformation, both good and not so good, of horse being presented.
- Have knowledge of what makes good conformation desirable.
- Discuss conformation of the horse as it relates to interfering, overreaching, and forging.
- Discuss the following common causes of lameness, giving location and inner structures involved: navicular disease, sidebone, ringbone, splints, osselets, bog spavin, bone spavin, curb, bowed tendon, bucked shins, cracks, corns, and suspensory problems.

Travel Safety

Discuss trailer care and travel preparation.

Record Book

Record book (health, maintenance, immunizations) must be kept up to date and brought to test.

Health Care and Veterinary Knowledge

- Determine and discuss age by teeth on presented horse; discuss special problems such as: overshot mouth, undershot mouth, cribbing, and reasons for floating periodically.
- Discuss colic, laminitis/founder, azoturia/tying up, common diseases, and respiratory ailments.
- Discuss signs of horse in distress (including vital signs) and care needed.

Teaching

- Discuss the care of D and C Pony Clubbers to keep them safe, interested, and happy during a lesson situation.
- Discuss and compare courses suitable to be ridden by a D, C, or B Pony Clubber.

Longeing

- Discuss proper fit and use of equipment.
- Discuss how to teach a horse to longe.
- Discuss benefits and dangers of longeing the horse.
- Discuss benefits and dangers of longeing the rider.

Longeing should be a regular part of test preparation from C2 onward. B level discussion should reflect regular instruction in longeing skills.

Foot and Shoeing

- Discuss the structure and function of the hoof.
- Discuss shoes, different types for specific reasons, fit to the hoof, and removal.

Bandaging

Demonstrate shipping, stable, and tail bandages; discuss materials used, reasons for wrapping, and potential dangers.

THE A RATING

The A, the highest rating, is divided into two parts: the HA, which covers horse management, teaching, and training, and the A, which tests the riding phase. The HA has the knowledge, experience, and maturity to evaluate and care for a horse's needs efficiently and in a variety of circumstances, and to teach riding and horse care to others. The A is able to ride horses at various levels of schooling with judgment, tact, and effectiveness, to train young horses, and to retrain spoiled horses.

HA STANDARD HORSE MANAGEMENT

Candidates must demonstrate a sound knowledge of horses, their care, equipment, and training requirements. They must be able to teach stable management and conduct mounted lessons, showing an understanding of safety practices and teaching techniques appropriate to different age levels. They must demonstrate the ability to make informed decisions about all aspects of running a barn, including daily routine and emergency procedures.

HA PART 1: STABLE AND PASTURE MANAGEMENT

Presentation

- Show a horse in hand as if for sale. Show horse to its best advantage, according to its suitability for the breed. The horse should be shown in a correctly fitted bridle and the candidate should show control of the horse while at the halt, walk, and trot. The candidate should dress appropriately, that is, in riding attire, including gloves and a whip, as if prepared to show how the horse performs under saddle.
- Discuss general condition of the horse, giving an evaluation of age, breeding, and shoeing. Discuss the horse's conformation, way of going, and disposition related to the suitability for a specific activity and performance level.
- When aging by horse's teeth, be familiar with the foal's mouth, the maturing and aging of incisors, tooth angles, wolf teeth, Galvayne's groove, and molar wear.
- When identifying horse's shoeing, be familiar with: keg, feathered edge shoe, polo, fullered, egg bar, heart bar, rocking toe, aluminum wide web, aluminum race plates, clips, caulks, studs (tapped shoes).
- Discuss suitability and fit of tack used on the presented horse.

Tack

- Describe inspection of saddlery for safety and fit, to determine need for adjustment, repairs, and/or padding.
- Describe procedures for reclaiming neglected tack, and for storing tack.
- Know how to make temporary adjustments in ill-fitting tack, such as: saddle on withers, cantle too low, leathers too long, bridle too large, reins too long, bit too large or small, broken tree.
- Recognize types of bits and saddles, their fit, actions, and applications for various horses. Indicate which discipline and/or rider the equipment is appropriate for. Bits: English snaffle, double bridle, curb, pelham, gag, elevator, and hackamores. Saddles: all-purpose, dressage, jumping, close contact, etc.
- Discuss correct fitting, uses, and misuses of different types of bits, saddles, girths, martingales, overgirths, draw reins, side reins, boots, cruppers, and breastplates.

Record Book

Purpose: to supply an accurate and detailed record of candidate's (or borrowed) horse's health care, feed and schedule, hoof care, conditioning, and competitive schedule, so, in case candidate were laid up or called away for a prolonged period, the horse could be properly maintained. Candidate must present a written outline supplying the above information; may use the USPC Pony Health & Maintenance Record, or *preferably*, his or her own record system.

Stable Management

- Outline a complete parasite control program for a stable; give reasons for this program, including deworming drug classifications relative to parasite cycles.
- Discuss a program for yearly inoculation and for tooth care.
- Describe ways to prevent the spread of contagious diseases throughout a stable.
- Describe routine morning inspections of a stable and horses to determine if problems have arisen during the night.
- Describe an inspection procedure to ensure the safety of stable and horses in pasture for the night.
- Describe ways to aid a horse that is cast in its stall.
- Describe a horse in poor condition and suggest several possible causes.

Stable Construction / Pasture Management

- Discuss good stable construction for safety and health, with attention to ventilation, drafts, light, drainage, protection of pipes in freezing weather, manure management, refuse disposal, rodent and insect control, and storage of feed, bedding, stable equipment, and tack.
- Discuss proper grazing and paddock management, including watering systems, fencing, mowing, shelter, and poisonous plants in your area.
- Discuss importance of soil testing, fertilizers, and seeding for proper soil management.

Nutrition

- Demonstrate ability to purchase feed responsibly, by discussing the characteristics, advantages, and disadvantages of different types of oats, pellets, sweet and mixed feeds, bran, and extruded feeds.
- Discuss common sources of protein, fat, and carbohydrates in typical equine rations.
- Discuss interpretation of the nutritional value of feed available from label information, and know resources to expand this information. Discuss minerals, vitamins, and electrolyte sources and possible dangers involved in misuse.
- Discuss appropriate rations, including percentage of protein, for aged, growing, working, idle, and breeding horses.
- Discuss cost of and safe storage methods for different varieties and quantities of feed used.
- Discuss criteria used to determine whether or not feed supplements are needed, benefits and dangers of use.

• Discuss differences in care, as related to seasonal weather changes, for horses at grass.

HA PART 2: VETERINARY KNOWLEDGE

Health, Symptoms, and Diseases

• Identify major anatomical parts and describe basic functions of the following systems: respiratory, urinary, circulatory/lymphatic, nervous, digestive, reproductive, and musculo-skeletal.
• Locate and discuss the following disorders/diseases according to the anatomical system involved, causative agent, signs, and treatment: colic, choking, heaves, laminitis, azoturia, periodic opthalmia, rhinopneumonitis, influenza, encephalomyletis, tetanus, strangles, equine infectious anemia, rabies, Potomac horse fever, equine venereal (viral) arteritis, and botulism.
• Discuss predisposing factors, symptoms and treatment of the following: fever, inflammation, edema, arthritis, shock, and dehydration.
• Discuss diseases associated with travel and exposure to strange horses.

Bandaging

• Discuss and demonstrate proper application of shipping, exercise, and stable bandages.
• Demonstrate application and know how to maintain any of the following bandages: sweat, poultice, pressure, spider, figure 8, knee, hock, cold water, and ice. Discuss values and potential dangers when any of them are prescribed.

Special Care

• Discuss common tranquilizers, sedatives, and analgesics, using "trade" names, specifically: Ace (Prom-Ace), Rompum (Xylazine), Banamine, Arium, Duvuulldon, Iurbugeslc, Ketoprofen, Dormosedan, and Dipyrone, plus aspirin. Know why above listed drugs are used and possible hazards involved.
• Discuss specific precautions when shipping, feeding, and restraining a sedated horse.
• Discuss both benefits and dangers of using twitches.
• Describe other methods of physical restraint, from mild to aggressive.

Travel Safety

• Discuss techniques for loading and unloading difficult horses.
• Discuss possible causes for loading problems.

- Discuss a year's overall maintenance program for keeping a trailer or van operationally safe.
- Discuss ways to transport mares and foals.

Conformation and Lameness

- Discuss lameness that might be associated with conformation faults, to include: base wide, base narrow, straight upright pasterns, over at the knee, calf knees, standing under, camped out in front, bench knees, knock knees, long sloping pasterns, toe in, cow hocks, sickle hocks, bowed hocks, straight stifle, contracted heels.
- Observe a horse in action, and assess his athletic ability as it may be affected by any of the conformation faults listed above and below: straight shoulder, various slopes of croup, long back, slab sided, too long or too short neck, ewe neck, mutton withers, high withers, parrot mouth, overshot jaw, shortness of stride.
- Observe a horse's motion and identify front and hind leg soundness and unsoundness.
- Discuss the anatomy of the leg, including appendicular skeleton, principle tendons, and ligaments from the shoulder and hip down.
- From a selection of horses, choose the best horse for a specific purpose.

HA PART 3: TEACHING AND TRAINING

Teaching Techniques

- Know techniques included in Instructor's Handbook, and be able to demonstrate knowledge of these skills as acquired through teaching experience.
- Discuss ways to handle the following lesson situations:
  - Mixed age or skill group
  - Disobedient mount
  - Effective use of assistant
  - Fall of rider
  - Interfering coach or parent
  - Arguing student
  - Unsuitable mount
  - Uninterested student
  - Runaway mount
  - Fearful student
- Discuss techniques to discover if students have:
  - Physical handicaps
  - Problems beyond teacher's ability or training to solve
  - Visual handicaps

- Learning disabilities
- Hearing handicaps
- Discuss skills that would be covered in teaching a C Pony Clubber to longe a horse safely and effectively.
- Demonstrate knowledge of D, C, and B Standards requirements.
- Discuss first-aid equipment and emergency preparedness suitable for a teaching situation.

Candidates should have regular instruction in teaching and longeing from C3 onward, in preparation for the HA test.

Teaching a Class

- Demonstrate teaching a safe fifteen- to twenty-minute lesson to a group of three to five riders (D1 to C3 or adult volunteers) on the flat and/or over fences.
- Evaluate the lesson plan used. Was teaching objective achieved? How could the lesson be improved?
- Discuss a student's riding positions and suggest three exercises to help solve any problem, including exercises on the longe.
- Discuss safety considerations when setting up a jumping lesson, including use and spacing of cavaletti/trotting poles.

Training/Longeing

- Discuss and demonstrate proper fit and use of equipment, including side reins.
- Discuss and demonstrate safe, confident, effective longeing techniques.
- Demonstrate techniques for longeing appropriate to the horse's level for exercise, training, and/or warmup, to include free forward movement and to establish regular rhythm.
- Discuss additional safety precautions to be considered when longeing with a rider.
- Evaluate performance and level of horse before, during, and after longeing session.

A-STANDARD RIDING

Candidate must be able to ride different horses at various stages of training, displaying a confident, consistent, and effective performance on each. Candidate must demonstrate competence and tact on a schooled, green, or spoiled horse, discuss and/or demonstrate schooling techniques required for each horse, and display a knowledge of the proper use of natural and artificial aids.

Candidates are expected to assess each horse's level of schooling and to ride with tact and sympathy for its capabilities. After each performance, the candidate will evaluate and discuss the stage of schooling, strengths, and weaknesses of each horse.

Riding on the Flat

- Demonstrate efficient warmup appropriate for level of the horse. Perform exercises to improve each horse's relaxation, free forward movement, impulsion, rhythm, lightness, engagement, and ride the horse "on the bit."
- Ride the following school figures and movements, maintaining rhythm and impulsion, as well as correct bend, carriage, and balance, to the horse's ability:
  - Leg-yielding
  - Canter from walk
  - Shoulder-in
  - Change of lead through the walk
  - 10-meter canter circle
  - Turn on the haunches at walk
  - Working and lengthened stride at all three gaits
- Ride on the flat without stirrups.

Riding over Fences

- Set up and ride effectively over cavaletti, gymnastic fences, and stadium fences at height and distances appropriate for level of horse (height not to exceed 3'9").
- Ride over fences without stirrups.

Riding in the Open

Ride at the gallop up to 520 meters per minute, demonstrating effective galloping position, pace, and adaptation to varied terrain, over fences not to exceed 3'7", to include ditches, banks, drops, water, and combinations, when appropriate.

Training

- Ride one or more assigned horses on the flat and over fences, demonstrating schooling techniques.
- Evaluate the performance of each horse, with comments on the level of schooling, strong and weak points, resistances.
- Handle difficult or refusing horse effectively and with understanding.
- Discuss problems that were not apparent until candidate rode the horse, and offer a long-term plan to improve schooling of the horse.
- Discuss and/or demonstrate effectiveness of cavaletti, gymnastic exercises, shape of fences, and distances as training aids.
- Demonstrate longeing techniques to improve the horse's way of going.

Index

Numbers in *italics* refer to illustrations and photographs